ENCYCLOPAEDIA OF INDIAN
EVENTS & DATES

ENCYCLOPAEDIA OF INDIAN EVENTS & DATES

(Fifth Revised Edition)

S. B. BHATTACHERJE

NEW DAWN PRESS, INC.
USA• UK• INDIA

NEW DAWN PRESS GROUP
Published by New Dawn Press Group
New Dawn Press, Inc., 244 South Randall Rd # 90, Elgin, IL 60123
e-mail: sales@newdawnpress.com

New Dawn Press, 2 Tintern Close, Slough, Berkshire, SL1-2TB, UK
e-mail: sterlingdis@yahoo.co.uk

New Dawn Press (An Imprint of Sterling Publishers (P) Ltd.)
A-59, Okhla Industrial Area, Phase-II, New Delhi-110020
e-mail: info@sterlingpublishers.com
www.sterlingpublishers.com

Encyclopaedia of Indian Events & Dates
© 2006, S. B. Bhattacherje
ISBN 1 932705 49 X
Fifth Revised Edition 2006

PRINTED IN INDIA

Dedicated

to

my grandchildren

Priyanka & Ritankar,

the torch-bearers of tomorrow,
who will in this book get
glimpses of some of our yesterdays.

Preface to the Fifth Revised Edition

When in 1986 this encyclopaedia saw the light of the day, perhaps it was the first ever such venture by an Indian. Its acceptability encouraged to bring out this fifth revised edition.

Inclusion of hundreds of more events further enriched this edition. To assist readers plenty of cross references of years are given within bracket.

The exhaustive index has more than 11,000 entries to pinpoint any specific information. The index ends with two compilations:

(a) First Time in India (General)

(b) First Time in India (Women)

These compilations are my tribute to those shining stars whose radiance inspired others to march forward.

2B Ratnabali,   **S. B. Bhattacherje**
7A Judges Court Road,   1st February, 2006
Kolkata 700 027.

Preface to the First Edition

At one time I was asked to develop a weekly commercial programme for All India Radio based on national events. I acutely felt the absence of any source having a chronological list of events. The idea of compiling such an encyclopaedia thus germinated in my mind.

My professional career necessitated frequent travels all over India. I started picking up threads from here and there to weave them into a texture of national panorama embedded with the events of history, politics, social reform, art, science, literature, cinema, theatre, sports, etc. These are interspersed with anecdotes to make it more interesting reading. This is a single-handed effort of many years without any financial patronage from any quarter.

The name India in the title has been used in the historical sense till the march of events divided the country into India and Pakistan in 1947. I hope this book will have a universal appeal where India's past and present progress are studied and discussed. The Indians who live abroad and are separated from the mainstream are likely to find it quite handy. It will also help the upcoming generation to keep themselves abreast with the country's evolutionary process.

It will be an injustice if I do not mention of my wife Kalpana and daughter Urmi, who sacrificed much of their social life on endless evenings while I was at my desk working on this encyclopaedia.

1986   **S. B. Bhattacherje**

Contents

Contents

PART A
EVENTS BY YEARS

Part A
Events by Years

It is believed that 365-day calendar-year was adopted as early as in 4241 B.C. Some historians consider it as the oldest known date in history.

BATTLE OF KURUKSHETRA
(MAHABHARATA BATTLE)

The Battle of Kurukshetra, as described in the epic *Mahabharata,* is an incident of the greatest singular importance in the panorama of Indian history. It occurred long before the Christian era. Views of historians and other authorities vary widely on the year of its occurrence. Some of the probable dates indicated by various authors are given below:

B.C.

3201 D. R. Mankad: Puranic Chronology.

3137 M. M. Krishnamachari: *History of Classical Sanskrit Literature.*

3127 A. N. Chandra: *The Date of Kurukshetra War.*

3110 As per the age of Manu Vaivaswata.

3102 Brahmagupta.

C.V. Vaidya: *History of Sanskrit Literature* (Vedic period).

3101 As per Aihole inscriptions of Raja Pulakesin II (609 A.D. – 655 A.D.) of Chalukya dynasty of Maharashtra, based on astronomical calculations of Aryabhatta I.

3067 By application of modern astronomical methods based on the data available in *Mahabharata.* The battle is supposed to have been fought in November-December.

3016 V. B. Athvale.

2449 Probodh Chandra Sen Gupta: *Indian Chronology.*

2448 Varahamihir: *Brihat Samhita.*

Kalhana: *Rajatarangini.*

B.C.

1450   Meghnad Saha.

1432   Tarakeswar Bhattacharya.

1424   Alexander Cunningham: *Archaeological Survey First Report,* 1864.

       Vol. 1, page 131.

       K. P. Jaiswal.

       **Most of the historians accept this year as the most probable
       one. In this book also, this year is taken as the base.**

1416   Girindra Shekhar Basu: *Purana Pravesha.*

1400   Bankim Chandra Chattopadhyay: *Krishna Charitra.*

       Bal Gangadhar Tilak: *Gita Rahasya.*

       Swami Vivekananda.

       A. D. Pusalkar: *History and Culture of Indian People.*

       H. C. Deb: *First All India Oriental Conference.*

       Jogesh Chandra Vidyanidhi.

1267   B. B. Ketkar: *Oriental Conference.*

1197   K. L. Daptary: *Astronomical Chronology of Ancient India.*

       K. G. Shankar: *Annals of Bhandarkar Institute.*

1191   Sri Aurobindo: *Vyasa and Valmiki.*

1151   Sitanath Pradhan: *Chronology of Ancient India.*

1000   L. D. Burnett.

 950   F. E. Pargiter: *Ancient Indian Historical Tradition.*

 900   Hem Chandra Roy Chowdhuri: *Political History of Ancient India.*

DIFFERENT PERIODS

Based on 1424 B.C. as the year of the Battle of Kurukshetra

A. Pre-Vedic Period (Before 3102 B.C.)

B.C.

6100-5500   Aditi Rishi era.

5500-4400   Daksha Rishi era.

4400-3102   Birabhadra era

B.C.

B. Vedic Period (1st Phase 3102 B.C. – 2550 B.C.)

3102-3100 There was a devastating flood which is the most important landmark of the world's history. It has reference in the Indian, Hebrew and Babylonian scripts. *Satapatha Brahmana* mentions that Manu Vaivaswatta was the saviour of mankind. This may also be the reason for considering this time as the beginning of Kali Yuga era on February 18, 3102 B.C.

3101 According to Aryabhatta I, the Battle of Kurukshetra took place in this year which ushered in the Kali Yuga era on February 18, in the next year.

3100-2750 Yayati era.
Nabanedistha Rishi era.
Sharbani Atri Rishi era.

2750-2550 Mandhata era.

C. Vedic Period (2nd Phase 2550 B.C. – 1950 B.C.)

2550-2350 Viswamitra I, contemporary of King Harishchandra.
Viswamitra II, originator of 'Nakshatra System' (celestial study) and contemporary of Bharata, son of King Dushyanta. The Era of Kartyavirya Arjuna, Jamadagni and Parasuram.

2350-1950 Ramchandra and Sita of Ramayana.
Garga I and his son Gargya, the great astronomers.
Viswamitra III.
Aryans started coming to India.

D. Vedic Period (3rd Phase 1950 B.C. – 1400 B.C.)

1895 Vamdeva.

1630 Vagambhrini.

1466 Birth of Krishna (of *Mahabharata*) at Mathura. (d.1388 B.C.).

1439 The Crystal Hall was constructed by the Pandavas at Indraprastha for Yudhisthir's coronation and the 'Rajsuya Yajna'.

1424 Battle of Kurukshetra (Mahabharata battle) took place during November-December.

B.C.

1423 Bhishma Pitamaha died. He initiated 'Pitamaha Siddhanta' method of celestial study, which became the basis of Vedanga Jyotish.

Also the era of Parashara and Garga II, who made reasonably accurate observations of celestial study.

Parikshit was born.

1421 The first edition of the *Mahabharata* was composed by Vyasa Deva, perhaps at Kurukshetra, and was titled 'Jaya'. (See 1364 B.C. and 1316 B.C.)

1410 In a philosophical conference Yajnavalkya, the author of *Brihadaranyak Upanishad*, was acknowledged as the supreme authority on philosophy.

1409 Dhritarashtra, Gandhari and Kunti renounced materialistic world to lead hermit's life in a forest.

1406 Dhritarashtra, Gandhari and Kunti immolated themselves in a forest fire near Haridwar.

E. Vedanga Jyotish Period (1400 B.C. – 1200 B.C.)

1388 Krishna (of *Mahabharata*) died at Dwarka in Gujarat. (b. 1466 B.C.).

After Krishna's demise the Pandavas lost interest in life. Yudhishtir abdicated in favour of his grandson Parikshit. The five Pandava brothers and their consort Draupadi left for the Himalayas and beyond to face the ultimate nemesis.

1364 Parikshit was killed by Takshaka. His son Janamejaya became the ruler of Indraprastha. He avenged his father's death by defeating Takshaka Nagas and performing 'Sarpayajna' at Taxila. During the recess period of the 'Yajna', the second edition of the *Mahabharata* was composed and recited by Vaishampayan to Janamejaya. It was titled as 'Bharata Samhita'. (See 1421 B.C. and 1316 B.C.)

1316 The sages held a conference in Naimisaranya, under the presidentship of Saunaka. In this conference the third edition of the *Mahabharata* was composed and recited by Ugrashrava Shauti to Saunaka, and was titled 'Mahabharata'. Additions and alterations continued till about 300 B.C. (See 1421 B.C. and 1364 B.C.)

1300 Ashwalayana and Patanjali I noticed the Pole Star (Dhruva Tara). Hastinapur was abandoned by the Kauravas.

B.C.

1270 End of the Upanishad period. The original *Upanishads* related to four Vedas numbered only twelve. But in course of time these kept on increasing by the sages and great thinkers. Presently there are more than one hundred and ten *Upanishads.* (See 1657.)

1250 Dark age of India's protohistory began. Perhaps a new horde of unknown people invaded and completely devastated the north-western part of India. The unaccounted for gap continued till 642 B.C., i.e., until Sisunaga dynasty was established in Magadha.

877 Traditional date of the birth of Parswanath. (d. 770 B.C.)

770 Parswanath expired. (b. 877 B.C.)

642 Sisunaga started to rule Magadha with Rajgir as his capital. He was the founder of Sisunaga dynasty, the earliest dynasty which has a historical base.

618 The oldest Indian sculptures were made, whose dates could be determined with some certainty. These are Parkham statue now in Mathura museum and Yakshi statue in Calcutta museum.

600 Mahavira Vardhamana Jnataputra, founder of Jainism, was born as a prince at Vaisali. (d. 525 B.C.)

587 Jews of Cochin claim to have arrived. (See 68, 774 and 1567.)

569 Mahavira renounced his worldly possessions to seek spiritual bliss.

544 Gautam Buddha, the founder of Buddhism, was born in a noble family in Lumbini Garden, now in Nepal. (d. 461 B.C.)

525 Jain Saint Mahavira died on April 24 at Pawa Puri in Bihar. (b. 600 B.C.)

520 Darius, king of Persia, crossed the Indus with a large army and brought Gandhar, Kamboj and the Indus region under his control.

519 Skylax, a Greek general of Persian emperor Darius, sailed down the Indus on a peaceful mission on his way back to Persia across the Persian Gulf.

Bimbisara sat on the Magadha throne and established the real imperial power. He built the new Rajgir. Exploration of this site began in 1905.

494 Bimbisara, the Buddhist ruler of Magadha, was put to death by starvation by his son Ajatasatru, for restoration of Hindu religion. Ajatasatru became the Magadha ruler. (See 490 B.C.).

B.C.

490   Ajatasatru converted himself to Buddhism. (See 494 B.C.)

461   Buddha died at Kushinara. (b. 544 B.C.)

459   Ajatasatru expired and was succeeded by Darsaka.

434   Udaya succeeded Darsaka on Magadha throne. He built the city Kusumpura on the Ganga near Pataliputra.

414   There was a formation of Tamil confederacy, which was unique at that time, for the purpose of defence. (See 174 B.C.)

377   A Buddhist council was held at Vaisali.

369   King Gopaditya built the original temple of Jyestheswara on the top of Gopadri hill in Srinagar, Kashmir. The hill is also known as Shivji hill or Sankaracharya hill. For some time Sankaracharya meditated on this hill. His statue was put up there only in 1962.

361   Mahapadmananda, said to be the son of the last Magadha ruler Mahanandin and born out of a woman belonging to a lower caste, usurped the Magadha throne. He was hostile to Brahmins and Kshatriyas and established Nanda dynasty which lasted till 321 B.C.

350   Panini, the great Sanskrit grammarian, was born.

327   Alexander the Great arrived at the banks of the Indus around the end of June at the age of only 33. He defeated Porus (Purusattam) and captured Punjab. (See 317 B.C.)

      Chandragupta Maurya met Alexander and joined his army perhaps to seek his assistance to capture Magadha.

325   Alexander left Karachi in October for Persia. He died in Babylon on June 10, 323 B.C.

324   Chandragupta attacked Macedonian garrison and captured Punjab.

321   With the support of Chanakya (Kautilya), Chandragupta captured Magadha. His Maurya dynasty lasted till 184 B.C.

317   Eudemos, the Greek governor of Punjab, treacherously murdered Porus (Purusattam) and took possession of his empire which was earlier returned to Porus by Alexander. (See 327 B.C.)

305   Seleucus Nikator, king of Syria and a general of Alexander, crossed the Indus and fought an indecisive battle with Chandragupta, who forced Seleucus to surrender Kabul, Kandahar, Herat and Baluchistan.

B.C.

302 Megasthenes, a Greek emissary, visited India. His writing *Indika* gives a valuable picture of life and customs of India in those days.

297 On Chandragupta's death Bindusara Amitraghata, father of Ashoka, started to rule Magadha and continued till 272 B.C.

272 Ashokavardhana or Ashokapriyadarshin, commonly known as Emperor Ashoka, ascended the throne of Magadha after his father Bindusara's death and ruled till 232 B.C. That was a golden period in India's history.

269 Ashoka's coronation took place. The coronation was delayed since his accession was perhaps contested by an elder brother Susima. (See 272 B.C.)

267 Ashoka captured Kalinga (Orissa) after a sanguinary battle at Dhauli hills near Bhubaneswar. The great devastation and miserable suffering of the people after the bitter fight brought profound remorse in Ashoka's mind. Since then he took refuge in the laws of duty and piety.

259 Ashoka abolished royal hunting of animals, it being contrary to the Buddhist teaching, not to take the life of a man or an animal.

257 Ashoka embraced Buddhism at Sanchi.

251 On the initiative of King Dewanampiya Tissa of Ceylon, Ashoka sent a mission of Buddhism to Ceylon, led by his son Arahat Mahendra and daughter Sanghamitra.

250 The third Buddhist council was held in Pataliputra.

249 Ashoka made a pilgrimage to Lumbini, the birth place of Buddha, alongwith his preceptor Upagupta and daughter Charumati and erected a 11 metre high monolithic pillar to mark the birth place. His journey was marked by five monolithic pillars on the way.

242 Ashoka made seven pillar edicts laying down the code of regulations.

240 Emperor Ashoka became a monk and started wearing a yellow robe.

232 Ashoka died after a long reign of sixty years in the history of India.

220 Simuka established Satavahana (Satakarni) dynasty in Andhra, which ruled till 236 A.D. After a few years he became very wicked. He was dethroned and killed.

B.C.

209 Kharavela, the king of Kalinga (Orissa), was born. (d. 172 B.C.)

206 Antiochus the Great of Syria invaded north-western India.

204 Ashoka's son Arahat Mahendra died in Ceylon.

203 Ashoka's daughter Sanghamitra died in Ceylon.

185 Coronation of Kharavela took place as the King of Kalinga. (See 209 B.C.)

184 Pushyamitra Sunga usurped the Magadha throne and started Sunga dynasty which ruled Magadha till 72 B.C. Pushyamitra was the commander-in-chief of the Maurya King Brihadratha, whom he killed while reviewing the army. Pushyamitra was perhaps an Iranian, but with Brahmin orthodoxy. Patanjali II, the celebrated grammarian, was possibly Pushyamitra's contemporary and witnessed the 'Ashwamedh Yajna' performed by Pushyamitra.

180 Indo-Greek empire was founded by Dometrius. (See 165 B.C.)

174 Kharavela annihilated Pithunda and broke the Tamil confederacy. (See 414 B.C.)

173 Kharavela invaded Magadha.

172 Kharavela convened a council of Jain monks, which met on Mt. Kumari of Udaygiri hill in Orissa, and was attended by nearly 3,500 monks. Kharavela died. (b. 209 B.C.)

165 Nagarjuna, venerated Buddhist philosopher, was born. He was also renowned as an alchemist. His book *Rasa Ratnakar* is considered as the beginning of proper chemistry in India.

Menandar, a Greek king, invaded north-western India and became the Indo-Greek ruler there till 160 B.C.

140 Antialkidas, a Greek, became the king of Taxila and ruled till 130 B.C.

80 Malles became the first Shaka king of western India.

Karla caves near Lonavala of Maharashtra was dedicated by Hinayan Buddhist monks, the same sect that carved Kanheri caves.

72 Devabhuti, the last Sunga king was killed in an intrigue of his Brahmin minister Vasudeva, who founded a short-lived Kanya dynasty of Magadha. (Ended 27 B.C.)

65 The teachers sent to India by the Chinese Emperor Ming-ti went back to China and Buddhism was introduced there.

B.C.

57 Vikramaditya, the famous king of Ujjain, ascended the throne by repelling the Shaka invaders who earlier overthrew Vikramaditya's father Gardhabhilla. Vikram era started from that date. He built the famous Mahakala temple in Ujjain which was destroyed by Altamas (Iltutmis) in 1234. (See 400.)

27 Susarman, the Kanya king of Magadha, was probably killed by Sata Satkarni belonging to Satavahana dynasty. This ended the Kanya dynasty of Magadha.

21 The joint Indian mission from the mighty kingdoms of Pandya, Chola and Chera, which sailed from Broach in 25 B.C., was presented to Emperor Augustus in Rome on terms of equality. (See 138.)

6 Metal coins were introduced for the first time. Those were flat silver and bronze pieces of irregular shape but fairly accurate in weight.

DIVISION OF MAIN PERIODS AFTER CHRIST
(The dates are A.D. unless mentioned B.C.)

462 B.C.	
-236 A.D.	Magadha sovereignty and Satavahana imperialism.
320-750	Gupta empire and Harshavardhana.
750-1000	Gurjara-Pratihara, Rastrakuta, Pala empire of Bengal and Cholas of Tanjore.
800-1000	Paramer empire of Malwa.
1000-1026	Raids of Mahmud of Ghazni.
1026-1300	Chalukyas of South: Raids of Md. Ghori.
1300-1525	Turkish power and Sultanate of Delhi.
1526-1707	Mughal supremacy.
1707-1818	Maratha supremacy.
1818-1947	British supremacy.
1947-onward:	Independent India after partition.

A.D.

10 Huemo Kadphises I, the Kushana chief, invaded India and established his authority in north-western India.

B.C.

20   Gondophernes became the Indo-Parthian king of Taxila.

45   At the death of Kadphises I at the age of eighty, his son Wima Kadphises or Kadphises II succeeded him.

52   Apostle St. Thomas's mission (Thomas Dadymus) arrived in India by the north-western route. He was the first person to preach Christianity in India. He established a small church at Mylapore in Madras known as St. Thomas's Church, where he was buried. (See 73 and 1510.)

67   Kashyapa Matanga is the recorded first Indian scholar to visit China. He settled down at Lo Yang by the Lo river.

68   Ten thousand Jewish refugees with their families emigrated from Jerusalem to the Malabar coast, after the destruction of the second temple of Jerusalem. (See 774 and 1567.)

69   Hala, the seventeenth Satavahana king, ascended the throne. Prakrit literature flourished under his patronage.

73   St. Thomas, according to Marco Polo, was accidentally killed by a peacock hunter while he was in meditation at Mylapore.

78   Kanishka ascended Kushana throne, who extended his authority to Punjab and Uttar Pradesh. He introduced Shaka era probably to commemorate his coronation. His relationship to the previous monarchs Kadphises I or II is not known. (See 1957.)

100   Kanishka with his religious preceptor Parswa, summoned a Buddhist Council in Kashmir like the one at Pataliputra in 250 B.C.

111   Kushana King Kanishka was suffocated to death with his quilt at the instance of his minister Mathara and other chiefs, since Kanishka was considered too ambitious and greedy to rule the world. Hubiska succeeded Kanishka as the Kushana ruler. (See 78 and 180.)

119   Nahapana established Shaka rule of Gujarat and western Rajasthan. As many as twenty-seven rulers ruled during a span of hardly 290 years.

126   Vilivayakura II Gautamiputra, the Satavahana ruler, expelled the Shaka invaders from north-western Deccan.

138   An Indian embassy was sent to Roman Emperor Antonius Pius. (See 21 B.C.)

A.D.

145 Rudradaman, the Shaka king, attacked his son-in-law Pulumayi II of Satavahana dynasty and grabbed a large portion of his territory.

155 Pandya army of south India invaded Ceylon and captured the capital Anuradhapura.

180 Kushana ruler Hubiska died and was succeeded by Vasudeva during whose regime the Kushana empire started to break up. (See 226.)

200 Chinese monk Chang Yang Sung visited Nicobar Island, which supposedly got its name from the monk's writings *Lo Jen Quo* or Land of Naked, and *Nalo Chen Quo* or Land of Coconut. He visited Andaman Island in 209.

226 Kushana ruler Vasudeva died and Kushana power collapsed. (See 180.)

236 Satavahana dynasty virtually extinguished; although a branch line, the Chutus continued to rule around Vanavasi, a city in south Maharashtra. Abhiras (foreigners) succeeded Satavahanas and ruled for 67 years. Isvarasena was perhaps the founder of this new dynasty.

275 Pallava dynasty of Kanchipuram was established by Simhavarman I.

305 Ghatotkacha, father of Chandragupta I, established himself as a feudal ruler in Pataliputra. (See 320.)

320 Chandragupta I succeeded his father Ghatotkacha in Pataliputra on February 26 and established Gupta dynasty. The epoch-making Gupta era began. (See 305.)

345 Thomas Cana, a merchant from Syria, came to Travancore and founded a Christian colony there.

Kadambas established themselves in south-west Deccan under Mayurasarman.

353 Pope Julius I declared that December 25 was to be observed as the date of birth of Jesus Christ and is so observed in India as well. Earlier different countries fixed different dates such as January 6, February 2, March 25, April 19, May 20 and November 17. None seems to know the correct date of birth of Jesus.

360 Meghavarna, king of Ceylon, who earlier concluded a treaty of alliance in 352, sent an embassy to Samudragupta's court in Pataliputra, for the permission to erect a monastery in Bodh Gaya

A.D.

where people could live in comfort. The embassy included one of the brothers of Meghavarna.

375 Reign of Chandragupta II began. (See 400.)

386 Amarnath cave of Siva in Kashmir was discovered. The impressive temple is in a fissure in the great barren range, 3,980 metres high.

399 Fa-Hian of China visited India by land route to collect Buddhist manuscripts, texts, etc. He left India in 414 by sea route and died in the same year.

400 Chandragupta II Vikramaditya of Gupta dynasty shifted his capital from Pataliputra to Ujjain after he defeated the Shakas. (See 57 B.C.)

401 Buddhist inscriptions of Udyagiri hill were made.

412 Buddhist inscriptions of Sanchi were made.

431 Gunavarman, the crown prince of Kashmir who converted the Javanese to Buddhism, died in Nanking in China.

432 Buddhist inscriptions of Mathura were made.

455 Skandagupta was the last renowned Gupta ruler of Pataliputra. After his death in 480 Gupta empire declined, but lasted for about a century thereafter.

The first white-Hun attack under Chu-Khan (Konkha) on Gupta empire was repulsed.

465 The Huns under Toramana entered India. (See 500.)

470 Nayan Pal conquered Kanauj slaying its monarch Ajaipal. The race was since then named as Kanauj Rathore. Jaichand was the last monarch of Kanauj. (See 1193.)

473 Kesari family obtained the throne of Orissa and held it till 1131.

476 Aryabhatta I, the astronomer and mathematician, was born. He is supposed to be the inventor of Algebra and the author of *Aryashtaka* and *Dasagitika*. (See 1975.)

495 Pallabhi dynasty was established in Gujarat by Senapati Bhatarka, who defeated a foreign tribe called Maitraka, probably of Iranian origin.

500 The Hun leader Toramana established himself in central India as a maharaja. (See 465.)

505 Varahamihir, the astronomer and mathematician, was born. (d.587).

A.D.

510 The Hun leader Toramana was defeated and perhaps died in the battle with Bhanugupta of Gupta dynasty of Pataliputra. Toromana was succeeded by his son Mihirkula, who made Sialkot of Punjab his capital. Mihirkula was branded as a bloodthirsty tyrant. (See 528 and 542.)

515 A ruler named Bhagadatta of some unidentified region sent his ambassador Aditya to China.

522 Bhaskara I, the great Indian mathematician, was born.

524 Nasirban, the king of Persia, attacked Gujarat. The Rajput king lost and fled. His queen gave birth to a child in a cave. He was named Guhil (Grahaditya or Goho), who was the ancestor of the Ranas of Udaipur. (See 713, 735, and Surya Race.)

525 Gwalior fort, one of the oldest in India, was built. As the legend goes, a local leader named Suraj Sena was suffering from leprosy. A Hindu saint named Gwalipa cured him and in gratitude Suraj Sena built the fort and named it after him. The present fort contains a mosque on the site of the shrine of saint Gwalipa.

528 The combined forces of Isvara Varman, Maukhari king of Gaya and Bhanugupta, the king of Pataliputra, defeated the Hun leader Mihirkula, who retired to Kashmir and captured the throne there. Huns thereafter never seriously threatened India. (See 510 and 542.)

542 The Hun chief Mihirkula died in Kashmir. (See 510 and 528.)

568 Guhil (Grahaditya or Goho) founded the state of Mewar of Rajasthan. Most likely his ancestors came from Kashmir. (See 524.)

587 Astronomer Varahamihir died. (b. 505).

598 Brahmagupta, the great mathematician, was born. He developed the usage of *shunya* or zero. He was the author of *Brahmasphuta-Siddhanta,* when only 30 years old. (d. 648).

600 Mahendravarman I of Pallava dyanasty of Kanchipuram ascended the throne.

605 After the death of Prabhakarvardhana, the king of Thaneswar, his son Rajyavardhana II became the king. But he was treacherously killed the next year by Sasanka, the king of Gaur (Bengal).

Grahavarman, Maukhari king of Kanauj and husband of Harshavardhana's sister Rajyashree, was defeated and killed by the king of Malwa. (See 606.)

A.D.

606   Prabhakarvadhana's younger son Harshavardhana took the thrones of Thaneswar and Kanauj at the age of about seventeen years as prince Siladitya. His formal coronation was delayed till 612. (d. 647. See 605.)

609   Chalukya (Badami) Prince Pulakesin II came of age. But his uncle Mangalesha, the Regent for the young prince, refused to hand over the power. Pulakesin II by his own prowess waged war on Mangalesha, killed him in battle and declared himself the king. He was the ablest monarch of the dynasty. Aihole inscriptions were made during the rule of King Pulakesin II.

610   Sasanka of Bengal captured Orissa.

612   Harshavardhana's formal coronation took place in October and he took the title 'Rajputra'. (See 606.)

620   Bana wrote *Harsha Charita*.

622   The Muslim year 'Hijri' began and is now followed by the Muslims everywhere. (See 1556.)

624   Kubja Vishnuvardhan I, brother of King Pulakesin II of Maharashtra, established Chalukya dynasty of Eastern Vengi in Andhra Pradesh.

625   Pulakesin II sent an embassy to Persian court of Khusru II.

629   Hiuen Tsang (b. 600) came to India alone by land route. The traveller-pilgrim sojourned in different parts of India and left India in 644 and died in China in the same year..

        Cheramon mosque, the first mosque in India, was built in Cranganore in Kerala. Unlike other mosques it faces East and not Mecca; and is constructed in traditional style of Hindu temples. It has no minaret, dome or arch.

635   Fireworks were first brought to India from China by the Buddhist monks.

636   The first recorded Arab expedition in India took place by a naval enterprise under Uthman-ath-Thakafi, the governor of Bahrain. It plundered the west coast of India during the rule of Caliph Omar bin Khattab, perhaps without his knowledge.

637   King Sasanka of Gaur (Bengal) died. It ushered in a political turmoil in Bengal. Anarchy continued until Gopala was made the king of Bengal in 750 by the people themselves.

A.D.

641 Harshavardhana despatched a Brahmin envoy to *Tai Tsung,* the second Tang emperor of China. (See 647.)

642 Chalukya king Pulakesin II of Chalukya (Badami) was utterly defeated by Narasimhavarman I, the Pallava king of Kanchipuram, perhaps with the assistance of king of Ceylon.

643 Harshavardhana launched a campaign against Ganjam, which was his last military campaign.

644 Harshavardhana organised 'Kumbh Mela' at Prayag near Allahabad which was perhaps the sixth one.

645 Hiuen Tsang left India. (See 629.)

647 Harshavardhana died. (See 606.)

Tai Tsung sent an envoy named Wang Hiuen Tse to Harshavardhana's court. Harshavardhana died before his arrival. Arjuna, an ex-minister of Harshavardhana, usurped his throne. He attacked Tse who escaped to Tibet. (See 648 and 657.)

648 King Strong-Tsan Gampo of Tibet sent an army with Wang Hiuen Tse, which attacked and captured Trihut of Bihar. Arjuna was caught and taken to Tibet. Trihut was under Tibet's rule till 703. (See 647.)

Brahmagupta expired. (b. 598).

649 While the first Somnath temple was built sometime in the first century, the second temple was consecrated by Pallabhi ruler Dharmasena IV of Gujarat. (See 1951.)

651 Sanskrit poet Bhartihari died. (See 1650.)

657 Wang Hiuen Tse again came to India through Nepal and visited sacred spots like Vaisali, Bodh Gaya etc. He returned home through Afghanistan and Pamir. (See 647 and 648.)

662 Munjala, the astronomer, wrote *Laghumanasa Ganakatarangini.*

672 Chinese pilgrim I-Tsing reached India. He took up his residence in Nalanda monastery in 675 and returned to China in 695. Exploration of this site began in 1915. (See 750.)

680 Jaya Varma started to rule in Orissa. He was the first powerful ruler of Ganga dynasty.

688 Raja Kanak Pal belonging to the Dharangare family founded Garhwal dynasty of Tehri-Garhwal state. Its ruling family was Paramar Rajputs of Agnikula (Fire) race. They ruled for 61 direct male descendants until the state merged with the Indian Union after independence in 1947.

694 Malla kings established a small but powerful kingdom in Bishnupur area of Bengal. Surprisingly they enjoyed full independence of Mallabhum for over eleven hundred years, after which it was annexed by the British in 1806. (See 1587 and 1694.)

710 A small Arab trading vessel from Basra arrived at the mouth of the Indus and was promptly seized by the local Hindu authorities. (See 712.)

712 Arabs attacked and captured Sind under the command of Muhammad Bin Quasim. Debal fell in April. Muhammad defeated and killed Dahir, the Hindu king, at Rawar on June 20. He then took the capital Alor in the same month. The widow queen and other women burnt themselves to death to escape dishonour. All males of the age of 17 years and above who refused to embrace Islam were killed. But the Arabs lost control in 779. Thereafter Sind continued as a small independent Muslim state. (See 710.)

713 Bappa of Guhila (Sisodia) dynasty of Mewar was born. He belonged to the Surya (Solar) race and theoretically was the 148th descendant starting from Brahma. (See 735 and 764.)

Arabs captured Multan.

724 Lalitaditya I Muktapida of Naga or Karataka dynasty, the most famous of all Kashmir rulers and the builder of renowned Martanda temple, succeeded to the throne of Kashmir.

731 King Yashovarmana of Kanauj sent an embassy to the emperor of China for his assistance against Yashovarmana's enemies. (See 740.)

735 Bappa's son Guhila Khuman I was born who later captured Chittorgarh throne from Manmori belonging to Paramar dynasty. He established the Guhila dynasty of Mewar. (See 713 and 764.)

736 Dhillika, the first city of Delhi, was founded by Anangapal Tuar, the Tomara prince. Tomaras (Tuars) ruled in the Haryana region and they belonged to one of the 36 celebrated Rajput tribes. Tomara rule of Delhi ended in 1151 when Visala Deva, one of the Chauhans of Ajmer, captured Delhi. Since then capital Delhi was constructed at eight different sites including New Delhi in 1931. (See 1060 and 1206.)

A.D.

740 King Yashovarmana of Kanauj was defeated and slain by Lalitaditya I Maktapida of Kashmir. (See 731.)

745 Parsees for the first time landed at Sanjam in Gujarat.

746 Vanaraja, prince of Deo, laid the foundation of Anhilwara Patan of Rajasthan.

750 After a prolonged anarchy in Bengal since the death of Sasanka in 637, people of Bengal selected Gopala as their king. Gopala ruled till 770 and founded the Pala dynasty in eastern India, which lasted for about 400 years. Gopala revived Nalanda University.

760 Krishna I succeeded to the throne of Rastrakutas. His reign is famous for the rock-cut Kailasha temple of Ellora, the most extensive and sumptuous of the rock-cut shrines in India. The size is 84 mt x 47 mt and the height is 32.8 mt. It was carved out from the top of a hillock and over 2,00,000 tonnes of rock were removed. Accuracy was essential as once the rock was cut, it could not be replaced. The complex has in all 34 caves. The 12 southern caves are Buddhist (600 to 800 A.D.), 5 northern caves are Jain (800 to 1000 A.D.) and the 17 middle ones are Brahmin (around 900 A.D.). Between 1920 and 1922 two Italian art experts conducted a meticulous restoration work.

764 Bappa was defeated by the 21st Caliph Al Mansoor. Bappa, after the defeat, departed for Persia (Iran) and perhaps never returned to India. (See 713 and 735.)

770 Dharmapala succeeded Gopala in Bengal. He raised the Pala kingdom to imperial power and virtually became the emperor of northern India. He founded Vikramsila University near Bhagalpur. (See 1203.)

774 A Jewish colony settled down in Cochin. (See 587 B.C.)

779 After Lalitaditya's death in 760, four weak kings ruled Kashmir. Then Jayapida Vinayaditya ascended the throne of Kashmir. Jayapida revived the glory of Naga (Karataka) dynasty.

Caliph Mutahid appointed Yaqub Ibn Lails Saffari as the governor of Sind. From that date Sind became virtually independent of Khilafat. (See 712.)

784 Jinasena completed *Harivansa Purana* of the Digambar Jains.

A.D.

788 Adi Sankaracharya was born at Kaladi in Kerala. He founded four 'Maths' in four corners of India at Sringeri, Puri, Dwarka, and Joshi (Badrinath), for the resurrection of Hindu religion. He attained 'samadhi' at Badrinath in 820.

794 Govinda III, son of Dhruva, became the Rastrakuta king and was the most remarkable ruler of his dynasty. He expanded his territory over a vast area. He shifted his capital from Nasik to Manyakheta and ruled till 814.

795 Mahashivagupta Yayati II came to the throne of a part of Orissa and with him began a brilliant epoch of the rule of Kesari dynasty. He revived the imperial tradition of Orissa under Kharavela. A great champion of Brahminism, Yayati II is said to have settled 10,000 learned Brahmins of Kanauj in his territory.

809 Manikya, the Indian physician, was called to the court of Harun-ur-Rashid of Arabia to attend to his illness.

810 Devapala became the king of Bengal. During his reign he deposed the reigning king of Kanauj and put his own nominee on Kanauj throne. Devapala had 50,000 elephants in his army. (See 816.)

814 Amoghavarsha I, son of Govinda III, became the Rastrakuta king. He was a devout Jain. But he did not hesitate to cut off one of his fingers and to offer it to Goddess Mahalakshmi to propitiate her to remove the epidemic which was ravaging his kingdom.

816 Nagabhata II, a descendant of Nagabhata I of Gurjara-Pratihara dynasty, captured Kanauj from the nominee of Devapala. Nagabhata's descendants ruled Kanauj till 1017 when Sultan Mahmud of Ghazni captured it.

820 Adi Sankaracharya attained 'samadhi' at Badrinath (See 788.)

825 Paramar rule of Malwa commenced under Krishna Upendra.

831 The Chandellas of Bundelkhand or Jejekabhukti first came into notice, when Nanika Chandella overthrew a Parihar chief and became the Lord of Bundelkhand.

840 Mihira Pratihara, commonly known as Raja Bhoj, became the king of Gurjara-Pratihara empire. He was a great patron of magic. During his rule, Gurjaras rose to a great height. His rule continued till 885. (See 1010.)

A.D.

846 Vijayalaya established the Chola dynasty of Tanjore (Thanjavur).

855 Avantivarman of Utpala dynasty started his reign in Kashmir. He was notable for his enlightened patronage of literature, and beneficient work like drainage and irrigation schemes.

883 After Avantivarman, Sankaravarman was the next king of Kashmir. He was obsessed by his love for fiscal oppression and plunder of temple treasures.

885 Mahendrapala I, son of Raja Bhoj, succeeded to the Gurjara-Pratihara throne. During his regime Gurjara-Pratihara empire reached its zenith. He drove the Palas of Bengal out of Magadha. (See 840.)

894 The idol of Sriranganathaswamy of Srirangapatnam was installed. (See 1120.)

916 Mahipala I, the Gurjara-Pratihara king, suffered a severe set back when Indra III, the Rastrakuta king of Deccan captured Kanauj and plundered Pratihara territory upto Prayag near Allahabad.

942 Mularaja became the king of Gujarat and founded Solanki dynasty of Anhilwara.

949 The war between the Cholas and the Rastrakutas was remarkable for the death of Chola king Rajaditya I on the battlefield. Much bitterness developed between Jainism and orthodox Hinduism.

950 Kshemagupta of Pravagupta dynasty became the king of Kashmir and married Didda, daughter of King Simharaja of Laharu. These two are the most notorious couple in Indian history. After Kshemagupta's death in 958 Didda virtually ruled Kashmir. She had no mercy, no scruple, indulged in sex with royal officers and murdered her two grandsons—Tribhuvana and Bhimagupta—to sit on Kashmir throne in 981. (See 1003.)

Aryabhatta II of Kusumapura wrote a treatise on astronomy called *Arya Siddhanta* or *Maha Siddhanta*.

955 Dhanga, the most powerful Chandella king, sat on the throne. Some of the grandest of the original 85 Khajuraho temples were built during his regime. He joined Jaipal to resist Subuktigin in 977. (See 1029.)

967 Dhola Rai, the expelled son of Sova Singh of Gwalior, laid the foundation of the state of Dhandoor, later Amber and now Jaipur.

A.D.

973   Nurmadi Taila II established Chalukya dynasty in Kalyani of South India. Much of his time was spent in fighting Munja, the Paramar Raja of Dhar, who claimed sixteen victories. On the seventeenth encounter in 995 Munja was caught, forced to beg from door to door and ultimately beheaded.

      Al Biruni or Abu Ar Rayhan Muhammad Bin Ahmed was born in Birun of Uzbekistan. His famous history of India *Tarikh Al Hind* gives a comprehensive survey of India of the 11th century. He also excelled in philosophy, astronomy, physics, chemistry, medicine and Sanskrit. (d.1048).

977   Chandella King Dhanga of Khajuraho fame and King Jaipal of Lahore jointly and successfully opposed Subuktigin. (See 979.)

979   King Jaipal of Lahore encountered Subuktigin at Luckman. A treaty was agreed upon. (See 977.)

981   The seventeen metre high world's third tallest monolith statue of Gomateshwara, was erected by King Virapandiya on Vindhya (Indragiri) hill at Sravanabelagola for Bahubal, son of Vrishava, the first Tirthankar. The sculptor is believed to be Aristonemi.

982   Atisa (Dipankar Srignana), the Buddhist sage of Magadha, was born. He went to Tibet in 1038 and died near Lhasa in 1053.

997   After Nurmadi Taila's death the Chalukya crown was conferred to his son Satyashraya. During his reign Chalukya kingdom suffered heavily from the invasion by the Chola King Rajaraja I.

1000   Sultan Mahmud of Ghazni, a Turk, hovered on India's border and captured some frontier posts.

1001   Sultan Mahmud of Ghazni made his first real expedition to India and began his crusade against the Hindus. He defeated King Jaipal at Peshawar on November 27. The proud king, unable to withstand the humiliation of defeat, burnt himself to death. His son Anandapal succeeded him. Mahmud's fourteenth and last expedition was in 1026.

      The Muslim scholar Al Biruni accompanied Sultan Mahmud of Ghazni to India.

1003   Queen Didda of Kashmir died. (See 950.)

1006   Mahmud had his second expedition to India against Raja Bhira Rao and captured the fortress of Bhatia in Bikaner desert.

A.D.

The same year Mahmud made his third expedition against his subordinate Wali of Multan.

1007 Mahmud was on his fourth expedition to India against Sukpal, a Hindu converted to Muslim, whom he made the governor of some of his conquered territories.

1009 Mahmud's fifth expedition was against Anandapal, son of Jaipal, and captured Nagarkote near Lahore. He carried away 7 tonnes of pure gold, 7 tonnes of jewels and 25 tonnes of gold and silver utensils from the temples in Nagarkote.

In Mahmud's sixth expedition he captured Narain, capital of Matsya.

1010 Mahmud's seventh expedition to India was against Abul Fath Lodi, his own governor of some of the conquered territories.

Raja Bhoj, the renowned king of Paramar dynasty, ascended the throne of Malwa. In 1060 he was defeated by the allied armies of Gujarat and Chedi. This Raja Bhoj is different from that of Gurjara dynasty. (See 840.)

Chola King Rajaraja I consecrated the magnificent Siva temple Brihadeeswara at Thanjavur. This was the first temple in South India in which the height of the sanctum sanctorum exceeded that of its 'gopuram.'

1012 Rajaraja I and his son Rajendra I jointly ruled the Cholas for two years. Rajendra I completed the conquest of Ceylon which his father began.

1013 Mahmud was on his eighth expedition for plunder of India.

1014 Mahmud's ninth expedition was aimed at Thaneswar. He sacked the town and took two lakh Hindu captives from Thaneswar to Ghazni.

1015 In his tenth expedition Mahmud tried to penetrate into Kashmir, but could advance no further than Lohkot (presently Lahore).

Gangeyadeva ascended Kalchuri throne. Perhaps he was the first ruler to issue gold coins.

1016 An embassy of Cholas reached China. (See 1033.)

1017 Mahmud, in his eleventh expedition, captured Kanauj from the ruler of Gurjara-Pratihara origin, as well as took Mathura. (See 816.)

A.D.

Acharya Ramanuja, the Vaishnav philosopher, was born in Sriperumbudur in Chinglepet district.

1021 Mahmud advanced into India for the twelfth time to help the king of Kanauj, who was attacked by Nanda, the king of Kalanjara. Trilochanapala of Lahore opposed and lost his life in the battle. Mahmud annexed Lahore to Ghazni and thus laid the foundation of future Muhammedan empire in India.

1023 Mahmud invaded India for the thirteenth time. He besieged Gwalior and brought Nanda, the Chandella Raja of Kalanjara, to terms. (See 1021.)

The Chola King Rajendra I of Tanjore launched a campaign in north India and attacked Mahipala I of Bengal. Rajendra I made himself proud on having advanced as far as the banks of the Ganga. Soon after, most of western and southern Bengal came under the rule of a new dynasty from the south known as Sena.

1026 Mahmud's fourteenth and last expedition in India was mainly aimed at Somnath temple – the third one, rebuilt sometime in the ninth century by some Chalukya ruler under subjudication of Gurjara-Pratihara dynastic rule. He plundered and completely destroyed the temple on January 8. In a desperate bid to save their deity, in three days 50,000 defenders sacrificed their lives. The idol was broken into pieces. Some of these pieces were taken to Ghazni where they were placed under the steps of a mosque. Mahmud took away the sandalwood gates of the city as well. In 1842 Lord Ellenborough, the Governor General of India, brought the gates back from Ghazni to India. (See 1001, 1395, 1783, 1842 and 1951.)

1027 The Sun temple of Modhera in Gujarat was reconstructed. It is one of the best Sun temples from the point of view of stone sculpture and architectural design. The chief image of Sun is now missing. It was ruined by Mahmud of Ghazni.

Nrikampa of the famous Hoysala dynasty started his rule in Dorasamudra (Karnataka).

1029 Khajuraho's most famous and the largest temple Kandariya Mahadeva was completed. The construction started in 1017. (See 995.)

1030 Sultan Mahmud of Ghazni died in his capital on April 30, much to the relief of the people of North India. (See 1034.)

A.D.

1032 Vrishavadeva Jain temple of Dilwara in Mt. Abu was built by Vimal Shah, a Jain merchant of Anhilwara. Later in 1231 Tejpal temple was built and dedicated to Neminath in the same complex by Tejpal and Vastupal, both of whom, like Vimal, were co-ministers of Gujarat. There are three other temples of lesser significance. (See 1439.)

1033 Another embassy of Chola kings reached China. (See 1016.)

1034 Masud, son of Sultan Mahmud of Ghazni, attacked and captured Kashmir. (See 1030.)

1036 Dhola Rai's son Kakil Deo laid the foundation of Kachhwa rule of Amber.

1038 The mission of Atisa was sent to Tibet during the reign of Mahipala I in Bengal. (See 982 and 1053.)

1053 Atisa died near Lhasa in Tibet. (See 982 and 1038.)

1054 Somesvara I, the Chalukya king, fought Rajadhiraja, the Chola king, at Koppam in Mysore. Rajadhiraja lost his life in the battle. Somesvara also defeated Raja Karna, the valiant king of Chedi. Somesvara later contacted some incurable disease. To end his suffering Somesvara drowned himself in the Tungabhadra river in 1068.

1060 Ambernath temple of Thane (Maharashtra) was constructed.
Anangapal II built Lalkot, which formed the inner citadel of Rai Pithora fort in Delhi. (See 736.)

1063 Nabadwip town of Nadia district was founded by one of the Sena kings of Bengal, who shifted his capital from Gaur in north Bengal to Nabadwip. (See 1203 and 1560.)

1070 Karnavati was founded by Karnadeva of Gujarat on the present site of Ahmedabad, which got the new name in 1411. (See 1407.)
Katha Sarit Sagar a compilation of folk tales in 21,700 slokas, was written by Somdeva Bhatta.

1076 Vikramaditya VI sat on the Chalukya throne of Kalyani. He was the most remarkable ruler of his dynasty.

1077 Chalukya (Eastern) King Koluttunga Chodadeva I sent an embassy of 72 merchants to China.

1089 Utkarsha succeeded his father Kalasadeva of Kashmir, but he committed suicide in the same year. His younger brother

A.D.

Harshadeva became the king of Kashmir. Because of his cruelty, Harshadeva is branded as the Nero of Kashmir. Utpala dynasty of Kashmir ended with him in 1111.

1090   The famous Lingaraj temple of Bhubaneswar in its present form is dated from this year, though parts of it were more than 1400 years old.

1097   Vijaya Sena succeeded Hemanta Sena, who was a local chief in Burdwan Division. Vijaya Sena captured the whole of Bengal and put to an end of Pala rule of Bengal by defeating Madanapala. He had two capitals, one at Vijaypuri, currently in West Bengal, another at Vikrampura, now in Bangladesh

1098   Nayanadeva of Mithila (Trihut) conquered Nepal.

Raja-Rani temple of Bhubaneswar temple was completed.

1100   Chauhan king Ajaydeva founded Ajmer.

Mitakshara, the famous Hindu legal work, was completed by Vijaneswara under the Chalukya ruler Vikramaditya VI of Kalyani.

1114   Bhaskaracharya II, the great mathematician cum astronomer, was born. He wrote three books on astronomy, algebra and arithmetic. His famous book on arithmetic is known as *Lilavati,* perhaps named after his daughter. (See 1150, d. 1185.)

1117   Channa Kesava (Vishnu) temple of Halebid was consecrated on March 27 by Hoysala king Tribhuvanamalla Vishnuvardhana. The temple took 103 years to be completed and is still unique for its exquisite stone carvings. (See 1311.)

1120   Udayadya, brother of Vishnuvardhana of the Hoysala dynasty, built the township of Srirangapatnam. (See 894.)

Belur temple of Mysore – a prime example of Chalukyan architecture, was completed.

1129   Construction of the famous temple of Neminath, the 22nd Jain Tirthankar on Mt. Girnar near Junagarh started. The construction continued till about 1500. The 10,000 stone steps to the summit were constructed between 1889 and 1908.

1131   Chodagangadeva of Ganga dynasty of Orissa came to power. The famous Jagannath temple of Puri was constructed by him. It was rebuilt in its present form in 1198. (See 1697.)

A.D.

1143 Kumarapala, the most important personality of Solanki or Chalukya dynasty of Saurashtra, sat on the throne, succeeding uncle Jayasimha Siddharaja. He was an earnest Jain and a patron of the great Jain doctor Hemachandra. (See 1169.)

1150 Bhaskaracharya II wrote his great work *Siddhantasiromoni,* of which *Lilavati* is one of the four parts. (See 1114.)

Rajatarangini – the river of history of kings of Kashmir – was completed by Kashmiri poet Kalhana.

1151 Visala Deva, a Chauhan chief of Ajmer, became the king of Delhi. (See 736.)

1156 The state of Jaisalmer was founded by Jaisal of Bhati tribe, a branch of Jadu race. (See 1570.)

1159 Ballala Sena, the most famous of Sena kings of Bengal, came to power.

1167 The mystic, religious and social reformer Basaveswara passed away. His date of birth is not known. He was born in Bijapur district of Karnataka. At one time he was the chief minister of king Bijjala's court, but that did not deter him from spiritual pursuit.

1169 Poet Jayadeva of Kendubilla village in Bengal wrote *Gita Govinda.*

The fifth Somnath temple was rebuilt by Kumarapala Chalukya, king of Gujarat, at the request of the head priest Pasupat Acharya Bhava Brihaspati. It is believed that the fourth one was built sometime between 1024 and 1042 by Raja Bhoj of Paramar dynasty. (See 1026, 1297 and 1951.)

1173 Ghiasuddin sat on Ghazni throne and jointly ruled with his brother Muizuddin. Ghiasuddin was later known as Muhammad Ghori. Muhammad was the real founder of Muhammedan power in India. (See 1175 and 1192.)

1175 Muhammad Ghori made his first expedition to India and captured Multan. (See 1173.)

Prithviraj II or Rai Pithora abducted Sanyukta, daughter of Jaichand, and married her against Jaichand's wish. (See 1177.)

1177 Prithviraj Chauhan II succeeded his father Someswara Chauhan as the ruler of Ajmer and Delhi. (See 1175.)

1178 Muhammad Ghori tried to invade Gujarat but was defeated by Bhimadeva, the king of Gujarat.

A.D.

The last actual ruler of Sena dynasty of Bengal, namely Lakshmana Sena, sat on the throne of Bengal.

1182 Chandel Raja Paramardideva of Khajuraho was defeated by Prithviraj Chauhan II who captured Mahoba and Kalanjara.

1185 Bhaskaracharya II, the great mathematician and astronomer, died. (b.1114).

1187 The invincible Devagiri fort near Aurangabad, later known as Daulatabad fort, was built by Daloma, the Hindu king of Devagiri.

1190 Hoysala king of Mysore obtained full independence from the Chalukyas of Kalyani, which came to an end in 1200.

1191 In the first battle of Tarain, Muhammad Ghori was defeated and severely wounded by the combined Hindu forces under the leadership of Prithviraj Chauhan II.

1192 In the second battle of Tarain, Muhammad Ghori assisted by Qutub-ud-din Aibek, a slave, defeated Prithviraj Chauhan II who was captured and executed. His city of Ajmer was sacked and its inhabitants massacred. (See 1195.)

Prithviraj's son was appointed governor of Ajmer. Muhammad proceeded toward Delhi, but its ruler submitted and Muhammad left Delhi unmolested.

Muhammad left his slave Qutub-ud-din Aibek behind to look after his conquests. Qutub-ud-din captured Meerut and Delhi.

1193 Muhammad Ghori along with Qutub-ud-din attacked Jaichand, father-in-law of Prithviraj II, at Kanauj. Jaichand was defeated and in an attempt to escape he was drowned in the Ganga. (See 470.)

Delhi was made the seat of Muhammedan power in India by Qutub-ud-din Aibek. He constructed the first five storeys (29.5 metres) of Qutub Minar as a tower of victory over the Hindu king of Delhi. Iltutmis added another five and Feroz Shah Tughlak III raised it to its present height of 71.24 mt, which narrows down to 2.75 mt at the top. (See 1206, 1231 and 1351.)

1194 Qutub-ud-din ransacked Ayodhya which since then remained under Muhammedan domination until the British captured it in 1856 and Qutub-ud-din's general Muhammad Khilji, son of Bakhtiar Khilji, captured Bihar.

A.D.

1195 Qutub-ud-din quelled a rising in Ajmer headed by Bhiraj (or Hamir), a brother of Prithviraj II. (See 1192.)

Muhammad Ghori captured Varanasi and destroyed hundreds of temples.

1196 Parihar Raja surrendered Gwalior to the Khiljis. Qutub-ud-din appointed his son-in-law Samsuddin Altamas or IItutmis, also a slave, as its governor.

1197 Anhilwara, the capital of Gujarat, was plundered by Qutub-ud-din.

1198 Qutub-ud-din Aibek established his headquarter in Delhi.

1202 Qutub-ud-din defeated Chandel Raja Paramardideva. The strong Chandel fort of Kalanjara in Bundelkhand was surrendered. This was virtually the end of Chandella glory. 50,000 captives were taken away as slaves and temples were converted into mosques.

1203 The famous Vikramsila University, established near Bhagalpur by Raja Dharampala of Bengal in the 8th century, was destroyed by Bakhtiar Khilji. (See 770.)

Bakhtiar Khilji attacked Lakshmana Sena I, 80 year old king of Bengal, the last Sena king, who was at that time in Nabadwip. Lakshmana Sena fled to East Bengal. Bakhtiar later shifted his headquarters from Nabadwip to Lakshmanavati or Gaur in Malda district, the historic capital of Bengal. (See 1063 and 1560.)

1205 Bakhtiar Khilji, on his way back from his Tibet expedition, suffered a miserable defeat in Assam at the hands of Assam rulers.

1206 Qutub-ud-din Aibek was crowned at Lahore on June 24 and sat on Delhi throne as Sultan. He was in effect the first Muslim ruler of India. He himself being originally a slave, initiated the first Muslim dynasty, namely Slave dynasty. He also built the Kwat-ul-Islam mosque by destroying the old Lalkot fort of the Tomaras. The mosque was built with the wealth plundered from at least 27 Hindu temples. The remnants of the mosque could be seen near Qutub Minar in Delhi. The first Delhi capital was built around the Minar. (See 736.)

Bakhtiar Khilji, the governor of Bengal, was assassinated by Ali Mardan who escaped after arrest and took refuge in Delhi under Qutub-ud-din Aibek.

Khwaja Moinuddin Chisti arrived in Delhi. (d. 1036).

A.D.

1210 After an accident on polo ground Qutub-ud-din Aibek died at Lahore early in November and was succeeded by his son Aram Shah. (See 1211.)

1211 Aram was deposed in June by Samsuddin Altamas or IItutmis, who himself was a slave and son-in-law of Qutub-ud-din. (See 1210.)

Cuttack was founded by Ananga Bhimadeva II, ruler of Orissa.

1212 Shivaji (not of Maharashtra) established the Rathor (Rao) rule of Jodhpur. (See 1459.)

1216 IItutmis defeated Tajuddin Yilduz in the battle of Tarain. Tajuddin earlier claimed suzerainty of India. He was captured in the battle, sent to Budaun, and put to death.

1217 IItutmis recaptured Lahore from Nasiruddin Qubacha who under Tajuddin Yilduz established himself in Multan.

1221 Chenghiz Khan, original name Temuchin, the great Mongol, made the first Mongol appearance in the north-western frontier of India in search of a political refugee named Jalaluddin Mangbarni, a prince of Khwarizm.

1222 Chenghiz Khan left India through the Hindu Kush mountains for his own territory. IItutmis avoided all actions which might offend Chenghiz Khan.

1225 IItutmis led an army against Ghiasuddin I'waz who declared himself as the independent Sultan of Bengal. Ghiasuddin submitted without resistance but reasserted his independence after IItutmis returned to Delhi. (See 1227.)

1227 IItutmis sent his son Nasiruddin to Bengal who captured Lakshmanavati, the capital of Bengal, and killed Ghiasuddin, the ruler of Bengal. (See 1225.)

1228 Ahoms of Mao Shan tribe came to Assam from Thailand. They ultimately ousted the Bodos of Tibet-Mongoloid stock, who once ruled a large part of north-east India. Kachari kingdom of the Bodos ultimately disintegrated in 1854.

1230 Ahoms captured Assam. Chu Kapha was the first Ahom Raja of Assam.

1231 IItutmis raised the height of Qutub Minar by five storeys in honour of the famous saint Khwaja Qutubuddin Bakhtiyar al-Kaki. (See 1193 and 1235.)

A.D.

1232 Gwalior was captured by Iltutmis on December 13 from its Hindu king Mangal Deva.

1234 Iltutmis plundered Ujjain and destroyed the famous Mahakala temple built by Vikramaditya nearly 1,300 years earlier. (See 57 B.C.)

1235 The famous saint Khwaja Qutubuddin Bakhtiyar al-Kaki expired in Delhi. (See 1231.)

1236 Iltutmis died on April 29 in Delhi. His second son Ruknuddin Feroz Shah sat on Delhi throne. But he was thrown out by the court nobles within six months because of his vices. He and his mother Shah Turkan were tried and Rukmuddin was executed on November 9. He was replaced by his sister Raziya who happens to be the only lady to sit on the Delhi throne as Sultan.

The saint Nizamuddin Aulia was born in Budaun and died in Delhi in 1327. The poet Amir Khusru was one of his disciples. (See 1253.)

Khwaja Moinuddin Chisti died in Ajmer. (See 1206.)

Construction of Iltutmis's tomb started near Qutub Minar. It is one of the earliest Muslim tombs in India.

1238 Narasimhadeva I of Ganga dynasty became the king of Orissa. During his reign the famous Sun temple of Konarak in Orissa was built. Kona means angular and Arka means the sun. (See 1255.)

1240 Turkish nobles rebelled against Sultan Raziya because of her favouritism to an Abyssinian slave Jalaluddin Yakut, on whom she bestowed the highest dignity. Sultan Raziya fought the nobles. But she was defeated on October 13 at Kaithal near Karnal alongwith her twelve days old husband Ikhtyaruddin Altuniya. Both were executed on the next day. After Raziya, Muizuddin Behram Shah, the third son of IItutmis, became the sultan only for a short period. (See 1242.)

1241 The Mongols under their leader Bahadur Tair, a lieutenant of Hulagu Khan, captured Lahore on December 22 and destroyed it.

1242 The royal house of Bundi was founded by Rao Devsinghi by killing the tribal chief Jeta Mina who ruled that region. It was the capital of Kota. (See 1572.)

Delhi Sultan Muizuddin Behram Shah's army revolted, seized his fort, and put the Sultan to death on May 15. The victorious army

A.D.

put Alauddin Masud Shah, a very young son of Ruknuddin Feroz Shah, on the throne.

1246   After a short reign of six years by Muizuddin Behram Shah and Alauddin Masud Shah, Nasiruddin Muhammad Shah I sat on Delhi throne on June 10 and ruled for 20 years. Nasiruddin was a very noble man.

1250   Construction of Hoysaleswar temple in Halebid began, but it could not be completed because of Muhammedan conquest.

1254   Vira Narasimha III became the Hoysala ruler. During his regime, the famous Prasanna Channa Kesava temple was built under the supervision of Somanatha, the king's military commander. (See 1268.)

1255   The famous Konarak Sun temple was consecrated by King Narasimhadeva I. The temple depicts the mythical Sun chariot speeding through the heaven on 24 gorgeously sculptured wheels, representing 24 fortnights in a year of the Hindu almanac, and drawn by seven magnificent horses. A renowned mason Bishu Maharana designed and worked on the temple. In fact, the construction of the temple was never completed and was abandoned because of subsidence. (See 1238.)

1256   From Hulagu Khan, the grandson of Chenghiz Khan an embassy arrived in Nasiruddin's court. Nasiruddin's chief minister and son-in-law Ghiasuddin Balban received the embassy in great respect.

1257   Mughisuddin Yuzbak, the governor of Bengal, led an expedition to Kamrup (Assam) where he was defeated and killed. After his death the authority of Delhi was restored in Bengal.

1261   Thohar Chand established the Chand dynasty of Kumaon, which ruled for more than 500 years.

1266   Nasiruddin Muhammad Shah I died on February 18 without a son. His son-in-law Ghiasuddin Balban (Ulugh Khan), a Turkish slave, succeeded Nasiruddin in Delhi. Balban was a ruthless ruler and never smiled. He stopped promotion and new appointment of Hindus in government services. (d. 1287).

Kota town was established. (See 1242 and 1572.)

1268   Prasanna Channa Kesava (Vishnu) temple of Srirangapatnam was constructed within the fort area by Somanatha, the commander-in-chief of Hoysala king. (See 1254.)

A.D.

1270 Sant Namdeo, the Maharashtrian poet savant, was born at Narasi Bamani on November 9. This saintly man was a householder and spent most of his days at Pandharpur singing and spreading the message of God. (d. 1338).

1275 Balban's son Muhammad utterly routed the Mongol raiders who were disturbing northern India. (See 1285.)

1281 Balban, accompanied by his second son Bughra Khan, came to Bengal with a large army and attacked Mughisuddin Tughril Khan, ruler of Bengal, who was captured and beheaded.

1285 Balban's able and beloved son Muhammad was killed on March 9 by the Mongol raiders in Punjab. (See 1275.)

1286 After Muhammad's death in the previous year, Balban descended from the throne with a broken heart and put Muhammad's son Kai Khusru on Delhi throne.

1287 Immediately after Balban's death Kai Khusru was ousted by his cousin brother Muizuddin Kaikobad, another grandson of Balban. (d. 1290).

1288 The Italian merchant and traveller Marco Polo visited Kayal, a port on the east coast under Pandya kingdom with Madurai as its capital. He visited many places on the west coast from Cape Comorin to Somnath. (See 1293.)

1290 Muizuddin Kaikobad proved to be an inefficient ruler. Confusion broke out all around. He was killed in his bed on April 11. (See 1287.)

Khilji chief Feroz Shah captured the throne of Delhi on June 13 and called himself Sultan Jalaluddin Khilji. He killed Kayumars, the infant son of Muizuddin Kaikobad and thus ended the Slave dynasty of Delhi.

1292 Mongols, at least 1,00,000 strong, invaded India under the command of Abdullah, a grandson of Hulagu Khan. Sultan Jalaluddin purchased a humiliating peace from him and Ulgu Khan, a grandson of Chenghiz Khan, was permitted to settle down in Delhi with his 3,000 followers. They embraced Muhammedan faith and were known as New Musalmans.

Sohanpal established Bundela kingdom. (See 1531.)

A.D.

1293   Marco Polo visited the south-eastern Indian port Kayal for the second time. (See 1288.)

1294   Jalaluddin's nephew and son-in-law Alauddin crossed the Narmada river. That was the first Muhammedan threat to the Deccan area in south India.

       Muslim invaders conquered Jaisalmer. The women as well as the soldiers performed *Jauhar*. (See 1303.)

       John of Monte Corrins was the first priest to visit India. He baptised a number of people of Malabar into Catholic faith.

1296   While Jalaluddin embraced Alauddin at Kara in Allahabad district on his victorious return from the Deccan, Jalaluddin was killed on July 20 by assassins Muhammad Salim and Ikhtiyaruddin, who were appointed by Alauddin. He then hastened to Delhi, deposed Jalaluddin's son Ruknuddin Ibrahim Shah I, and proclaimed himself as the Sultan of Delhi. His coronation took place on October 21 and he took the title Muhammad Shah I.

       Jnanadev, the great poet-saint of Maharashtra, expired at Alandi. He helped in loosening the social and religious barriers and thereby bringing the Maratha people closer.

       Alauddin Khilji for the first time introduced regular mail delivery system by mail-runners.

1297   Alauddin conquered Gujarat where Raja Karna II Vaghela had earlier declared himself independent, the last independent king of Gujarat. The magnificent marble city Patan was demolished. Raja Karna fled with his daughters Devala Devi and her elder sister, who died later as a fugitive. But the exquisitely pretty queen Kamala Devi was captured and was sent to Alauddin's harem. Alauddin married Kamala Devi – the first marriage on record between a Muhammedan ruler and a Hindu princess. (See 1306.)

       Alaf Khan, commander of Alauddin Khilji's army, destroyed the fifth Somnath temple. (See 1169 and 1951.)

1298   The Mongol Chief Qutlugh Khan, a descendant of Chenghiz Khan, crossed the Indus and advanced towards Delhi with two hundred thousand horsemen, the largest invading army in India so far, with a view to conquer India. Alauddin's army routed them in 1299.

A.D.

1300 The great Adina mosque of Gujarat, containing about a thousand richly ornamented pillars of Hindu temples, was constructed.

1301 Hamir became the ruler of Mewar. He later captured Chittorgarh and was virtually the only Hindu prince with real power in India.

Alauddin Khilji declared prohibition on the sale and use of wine and intoxicating drugs in Delhi.

1303 Alauddin captured Chittorgarh on August 26. Padmini, the pretty wife of Rana Bhim Singh, along with several hundred ladies, sacrificed their lives in fire (*Jauhar Brata*). Chittorgarh was sacked for the first time. (See 1534 and 1568.)

Mongol raiders under Targhi approached up to the gates of Delhi and after two months retired on their own. They came back again in 1306.

Alauddin Khilji laid the foundation of Siri fort, around which the second Delhi capital was built. (See 1206 and 1320.)

1305 Mahalak Deva, Raja of Malwa, died in a battle with Alauddin's army under Ainul Malik. Ujjain, Mandu, Dhar and Chanderi were annexed. Ainul Malik was made the governor of Malwa.

1306 A Mongol army under Kabak crossed the Indus. Alauddin sent Gazi Malik to repulse them. The Mongols were defeated. Enraged Alauddin ordered about 3,000 male prisoners to be trampled to death by elephants. A pillar was erected with their skulls as a warning to the future Mongol raiders. (See 1307.)

Alauddin sent a large army to South India under Malik Kafur, a converted Hindu slave. Malik Kafur captured Devala Devi, the pretty daughter of Kamala Devi, near Ellora caves by sheer luck. Her elder sister meanwhile died. Devala Devi was married to Alauddin's son Khizr Khan. (See 1297.)

1307 A Mongol chief named Iqbalmand crossed the Indus. He was defeated and killed by Alauddin. No further Mongol intrusion took place in the remaining years of Alauddin's reign. (See 1306.)

Alauddin sent Malik Kafur to capture Devagiri fort (Daulatabad), which was considered impregnable. Through treachery the fort was entered by the enemy on March 24. Raja Ramdeva was taken prisoner and sent to Delhi, where Alauddin received him favourably and reinstated him as a tributary to Delhi until Ramdeva's death in 1312. (See 1187 and 1318.)

A.D.

1308   The sixth Somnath temple was built by King Chandrasama Mahipal of Junagarh. (See 1297, 1395 and 1951.)

1311   Starting from Daulatabad, Malik Kafur attacked Dorasamudra (Halebid), the Hoysala capital of Raja Vira Ballala III, in February. Halebid was finally destroyed by the Muslim forces in 1327. The name Halebid had its origin from the word Halebeedu, meaning the old capital. (See 1117.)

Malik Kafur proceeded further south and the Muhammedans for the first time reached Cape Comorin. He returned to Delhi in October. Possibly Kohinoor diamond was amongst the jewels he brought from Deccan.

1312   Ramdeva, the Yadava ruler of Devagiri, died. Malik Kafur was sent by Alauddin to drive out Ramdeva's rebellious son Sankara which was accomplished. Devagiri was annexed by Alauddin and thus the whole of Marathawada came under Delhi rule. (Also see 1307 and 1318.)

1315   Jayasimha became the king of Trigarta (Kangra), which maintained its independence until it was subdued by the British in the nineteenth century.

1316   Alauddin fell sick. Malik Kafur was reported to be instrumental in bringing it to a fatal culmination on January 6. Malik Kafur virtually captured the throne which lasted only for 35 days. Alauddin's third son Qutubuddin murdered Kafur and blinded his minor brother Sahib-ud-din and in April ascended the throne as the Sultan of Delhi. The Khilji dynasty ultimately disintegrated from internal strifes in September 1320.

1318   Harapala, the son-in-law of Ramdeva of Devagiri, revolted against the Muslim rulers. He was caught and flayed alive. That was the end of the Yadavas in Devagiri. (See 1307 and 1312.)

1320   Qutub-ud-din Mubarak Khilji was murdered by his own favourite employee Khusru, who was a converted Hindu. Khusru ascended the Delhi throne with the title Nasiruddin Khusru Shah. Gazi Malik, governor of Punjab and a Turki slave of Balban, took upon the task of punishing the traitor. Khusru was defeated on August 22, captured and beheaded. On September 8 Gazi Malik was hailed as Sultan by the court nobles and he came to be known as Ghiasuddin Tughlak Shah I. He built the third Delhi city about eight kilometres east of Qutub Minar and named it Tughlakabad. (See 1325.)

A.D.

Zulju, a Mongol chief, invaded Kashmir. The ruler Suha Deva (since 1301) fled. In the confusion that followed Rinkana, a Ladakhi prince usurped the throne. Probably he embraced Islam.

1321   The Christian missionaries Peter, James Thomas and Dometrius were killed by the Muhammedans at Thane, Maharashtra.

1323   Ghiasuddin Tughlak Shah's son Juna Khan captured Warangal, capital of Telengana and finally the two and a half century of Kakatiya rule ended there.

1325   Juna Khan schemingly entertained his father Ghiasuddin Tughlak Shah I in a cleverly built structure near Tughalakabad, which was crushed by the elephants as per plan. The Sultan was killed in February along with his favourite younger son Mahmud. Juna Khan sat on the throne with the title Muhammad Tughlak Shah II, also styled as Ulugh Khan. He established the fourth capital city Jahanpana. (See 1320 and 1351.)

Amir Khursru, the Urdu poet, died. (b. 1253).

1327   With a view to keep away the Mongol invaders, Muhammad Tughlak Shah II ordered shifting of his capital from Delhi to Devagiri and renamed it as Daulatabad. The court officials, army, tradesmen, servants and even cripples were forced to shift from Delhi. Soon he realised the mistake and the capital was reshifted to Jahanpana (Delhi).

1329   The Chaghtai chief Tarmashirin Khan of Transoxiana invaded India. He ravaged the plains of Punjab and reached the outskirts of Delhi.

Muhammad Tughlak Shah II returned to his original capital Jahanpana (Delhi) from Daulatabad

1330   Muhammad Tughlak Shah II introduced token copper and brass coins of the same value of silver and gold coins. There were large scale frauds. After three years of experimentation the token coins were withdrawn.

1331   Saint Burhanuddin Gharib, a celebrated saint of Deccan and a disciple of Nizamuddin Aulia, died.

1333   Ibn Batuta, a north African Arab, reached Sind and later came to the court of Muhammad Tughlak Shah II. For some time he was a judge of the Sultan. (See 1370.)

A.D.

1335 The Muslim governor of Madurai in the South revolted against Delhi rule and the independent Muslim kingdom of Madurai came into existence. (See 1378.)

1336 A new Hindu kingdom was established in the south with Vijayanagar as its capital by Sangama Bukka, Harihara (Hukka) and their three other brothers Kampana, Murappa and Madappa guided by the sage Vidyaranya of Sringeri Math. Within ten years it became an important power. The dynasty is known as Sangama as well as Taluva dynasty. It appears that Bukka and Harihara were first in the service of Prataparudra Deva II, the Kakatiya ruler. When his kingdom was conquered by the Muslims in 1323, they switched over to Kampili. When the same fate fell to Kampili too, they were taken to Delhi as prisoners and were forced to embrace Islam. However, they were subsequently released and they re-converted themselves into Hindus. (See 1565.)

1337 Bengal and many other territories revolted against Muhammad Tughlak Shah II. Bengal remained virtually independent until Akbar's rule. (See 1576.)

1338 Sams Shah Mirza, a Muslim adventurer from Swat, who was then the minister of Udayanadeva, the Hindu Raja of Kashmir, seized Kashmir throne under the title Samsuddin Shah, and married the late Raja's widow Kota Devi.

Saint Namdeo attained samadhi. (b.1270).

1341 Toghan Timur, the Mongol emperor of China, sent an embassy to Muhammad Tughlak Shah II's court. (See 1342.)

1342 Ibn Batuta was sent to China by Muhammad Tughlak Shah II. Ibn returned to India four years later. (See 1341.)

Krittivasa Ojha Mukhuti, the translator of Sanskrit *Ramayana* into Bengali, was born in Fulia in Nadia district of West Bengal. The translation was completed in 1418.

Hoysala kingdom was conquered by Vijayanagar.

Shamsuddin Elias Shah, who made himself the Sultan of western Bengal the previous year, overran Trihut. (See 1352.)

1347 Zafar Khan alias Alauddin Hasan Gangu, an Afghan or a Turk soldier, revolted against Delhi and established the Muslim kingdom of Bahmani dynasty on August 11 in the south, as Sultan Alauddin.

A.D.

He made Gulbarga his capital and renamed it as Hasanabad. He ruled till 1358. Eighteen kings ruled during 1347 and 1538, of whom four were murdered and two were deposed and blinded. All the sultans were cruel and bloodthirsty. Bahmani kingdom ultimately did spilt up into five separate sultanates.

Kadamba territories were annexed by Vijayanagar.

1350   Samsuddin Elias Shah of Bengal entered Nepal and advanced as far as Kathmandu. He destroyed the temple of Sambhunath. It was more of a raid than an invasion.

1351   Sultan Muhammad Tughlak Shah II died in Sind on March 20. The chiefs enthroned his nephew Feroz Tughlak Shah III on March 23. He entered Delhi on August 25. He was an efficient and benevolent ruler. He repaired and raised the Qutub Minar to its present height of 71.24 metres with 379 steps. He shifted the site of the capital towards the north-east on the Jamuna and named it Ferozabad which happens to be the fifth Delhi city. (See 1325, 1533 and 1540.)

1352   Samsuddin Elias Shah was the first independent Muslim Sultan of the whole of Bengal. (See 1346.)

1354   Feroz Shah Kotla was built by Emperor Feroz Tughlak Shah III. Here stands the famous Ashoka pillar weighing 27 tonnes.

1359   Sultan Feroz Tughlak Shah III set out to invade Bengal. (See 1351.)

1360   Sultan Feroz Tughlak Shah III led an expedition to Orissa. The Hindu king of Orissa fled. Feroz captured Puri and desecrated the Jagannath temple. He founded Jaunpur.

1367   Bukka I of Vijayanagar was severely defeated by Muhammad Shah I of Bahmani kingdom in the great battle of Kanthal. A large number of Hindus were massacred within Bukka's territory. The diamond mines on the south of the Tungabhadra river in Vijayanagar territory explains the chronic warfare so characteristic of relations between the two states.

1368   The famous Adina mosque of Pandua in North Bengal was built by Sultan Sikandar Shah I. The pillars were taken from the Hindu temples and palaces. The mosque has about 400 small domes and is one of the most remarkable old buildings of West Bengal.

1370   Ibn Batuta returned to Africa. (See 1333.)

A.D.

1374   Bukka I of Vijayanagar sent an embassy to China.

1377   Sant Ravidas, the spiritual leader of the depressed class people, was born. He propagated the necessity of removal of caste barrier in the country.

        Sultan Mujahid Shah became the third Bahmani ruler. He indulged too much in drinking and was murdered in 1378 by his uncle Daud Shah, who became the Sultan.

1378   Daud Shah assassinated Mujahid Shah on April 15 to become the fourth Bahmani Sultan, but himself was murdered by a slave on May 20. Daud's brother Muhammad Shah II became the fifth Sultan.

        The independent Muslim kingdom of Madurai fell to the rising power of Vijayanagar. (See 1335.)

1387   Feroz Tughlak Shah III abdicated in favour of his son Muhammad Tughlak Shah III, who proved inefficient. Feroz took back the imperial power of Delhi.

1388   Feroz Tughlak Shah III died on September 20 at the age of 83. His sceptre was transferred to his grandson Ghiasuddin Tughlak Shah II who was killed on February 19, 1389. Within ten years Hindustan was thrown into a complete state of anarchy.

1389   Sikandar Shah, the sixth Sultan of Kashmir, sat on the throne. He was very cruel and was responsible for converting a large number of Hindus into Muslim by free use of the sword.

1394   During the reign of Nasiruddin Mahmud Tughlak Shah II in Delhi, the eunuch slave Malik Sarwar declared independence of Jaunpur.

1395   Muzzaffar Khan, governor of Gujarat, son of a Rajput convert destroyed the reconstructed sixth Somnath temple. (See 1026, 1783 and 1950.)

        Nasrat Shah, one of the grandsons of Feroz Tughak III, deposed Delhi Sultan Nasiruddin Mahmud Tughluk Shah II. (See 1399.)

1396   Muzaffar Khan, governor of Gujarat, proclaimed Gujarat's independence and later took the title of Sultan Muzaffur Shah I.

1397   Bahmani dynasty was plagued with intrigues. Ghiasuddin, son of Muhammad Shah II, became the sixth Sultan. He was blinded and deposed by Lalchin, a Turkish slave, who made Samsuddin the seventh Sultan. He was also deposed, imprisoned and blinded. Tajuddin Feroz Shah became the eighth Sultan.

A.D.

1398 Amir Timur or Taimur Lang, a Central Asian Turk, reached the banks of the Indus on September 12 with 92 squadrons of horses. He crossed the river near Attock on September 20, where Alexander crossed it seventeen centuries earlier. The Delhi Sultan Nusrat Shah resisted, lost and fled to Gujarat. Timur captured Delhi on December 18. He sacked Delhi, Meerut and Hardwar, followed by a massive destruction of northern India.

1399 Timur left Delhi on January 1, recrossed the Indus on March 11 and took the title 'Emperor of India'.

Mahmud Tughlok Shah II, ex-Sultan of Delhi who was deposed in 1395, was reinstated on Delhi throne after Timur's departure. There was hardly a government in north India.

Harihara II, the ruler of Vijayanagar, attacked Bahmani kingdom, lost the battle as well as his son. (See 1406.)

Mysore Raj dynasty came into being when the two brothers Vijaya Raja and Krishna Raja came to Mysore and established their rule with a few villages. The name Mysore originated from the word 'Mahishasuranagar' from the demon Mahishasura, who was killed by Goddess Chamundi on the hill-top.

1400 The seventh Somnath temple was built by public finance. (See 1395 and 1951.)

1401 Dilwar Khan Ghori, the Afghan governor of Malwa and a descendant of the great Sultan Sahabuddin Ghori, declared himself the independent ruler of Malwa under the style Sultan Sahabuddin Ghori. This Ghori dynasty had a short spell of only 35 years.

1405 Calicut's Zamorin sent an embassy to the court of Chinese Emperor Yongle at Nanking.

Grand Admiral Cheng Ho led a naval expedition in Malabar and Coromondal coasts. Up to 1433 he made seven expeditions, when he died in Calicut. (See 1421.)

1406 Hushang Shah (Alp Khan) killed his father Dilwar Khan Ghori and became the second Sultan of Ghori dynasty of independent Malwa. (See 1401.)

Sultan Tajuddin Feroz Shah of the Bahmani kingdom defeated the Hindus of Vijayanagar, securing a Vijayanagar princess for his harem. The city of Bunkapur was given as a dowry. (See 1399.)

A.D.

1407 Sultan Muzaffur Shah I of Gujarat was succeeded by his grandson Sultan Nasiruddin Ahmed Shah, who was the real founder of a prosperous independent Gujarat state. He built the beautiful city of Ahmedabad in 1411. (See 1070.)

1413 Nasiruddin Mahmud Tughlok Shah II died at Kaithal in February. Daulat Khan Lodi was raised to the Delhi throne. But he did not assume royalty.

1414 Khizr Khan Sayyid, governor of Lahore, replaced Daulat Khan Lodi on May 28 (see 1413), which brought an end to the Tughlak dynasty in Delhi. There was a short spell of Sayyid dynasty ruling Delhi.

1415 Raja Ganesh, actually a zamindar (landlord) of Dinajpur seized the throne of Bengal and took the title Danujabarmandev. (See 1419.)

1419 Jadu, son of Raja Ganesh of Bengal (see 1415), embraced Islam and ruled Bengal as Jalaluddin Muhammad Shah. He was murdered in 1442.

1420 Zain-ul-Abedin sat on the Kashmir throne. He was very liberal like Akbar about religion. Under his patronage the *Ramayana* and the *Mahabharata* were translated from Sanskrit into Persian. He introduced 'papier mache' in Kashmir through Iranian craftsmen. In Iran it was known as 'kari kamdari'

Tajuddin Feroz Shah of Bahmani kingdom suffered a severe defeat in Pangal. Being dejected, he left the affairs of the state in the hands of his two Turki slaves. (See 1422.)

1421 Khizr Khan died in May 20 and Muizuddin Mubarak Shah II became the second Sayyid Sultan of Delhi.

The Ming emperor of China sent his envoy Cheng Ho to Bengal. He again came in 1431. (See 1405.)

1422 Ahmad Shah I, brother of Tajuddin Feroz Shah of Bahmani kingdom, being disgusted with the administration of Turki slaves, murdered Tajuddin along with his son and ascended the throne. He shifted his capital to Bidar. (See 1420.)

1424 An Italian traveller named Nicholo Conti, the first European, visited Vijayanagar court.

Possibly the earliest use of the term Hindu in context of religion is in copper plate inscription of King Devaraya II of Vijayanagar

A.D.

found in Satyamangalam. Therein he has been described as 'Hindurayo Suratrano' which means the best amongst the Hindu rulers.

1433 Delhi Sultan Mubarak Shah II was killed by his wazir. Two more Sultans of Sayyid dynasty followed – Muhammad Shah IV and Alauddin Alam Shah. (See 1451.)

1435 Kapilendra, minister of Bhimdeva III, usurped the throne of Orissa. He adopted the title Gajapati and claimed to be descendant of the sun. Hence he started Suryavamshi Gajapati dynasty of Orissa.

1435 Sultan Mahmud Shah succeeded in Malwa throne after Hushang Shah. He was the third and the last ruler of the Ghori dynasty in Malwa. (See 1436.)

1436 Sultan Mahmud Shah of Malwa was poisoned by his cousin and minister Mahmud Khan, a Khilji Turk. The Ghori dynasty of Malwa ended. Mahmud Khan seized the throne and founded Khilji dynasty there which lasted for about a century. (See 1440.)

1439 One of the most important and big Jain temples, the extremely beautiful Ranakpur complex, dedicated to Adinath, was completed in Aravalli valley 98 km. from Udaipur. It has 29 halls and 1,444 pillars, no two of which are alike. (See 1032.)

1440 Rana Kumbha of Mewar defeated and caught Mahmud Khilji, sovereign ruler of Malwa, and kept him in Chittorgarh for sometime as a captive. Later Kumbha released him with due honour and gifts. In 1441 as a mark of that victory Rana Kumbha laid the foundation of the victory pillar of Chittorgarh which was completed in 1448. (See 1436.)

Saint Kabir was born. (d. 1518. Also see 1496.)

The 17.4 mt high image of the first Jain pontiff Adinath with a foot measuring about 2.75 mt was carved out of rock walls of Gwalior fort.

1443 Persia sent Abdur Razzak as its ambassador to the court of Vijayanagar.

1448 Vidyapati, the greatest and most famous of the Maithili poets, died. His date of birth is unknown. He became a court poet of Maithili king of North Bihar. His 'Padavali' poems are unique and unrivalled in their lyrical and artistic quality.

A.D.

1450   Basudeva Sarbabhauma, founder of the famous 'Nyaya' school of
Nadia, was born. (d.1525).

The Jhulta Minar of Sidi Bashir mosque of Ahmedabad was
completed by Malik Serang Shah. If someone shakes the wall of
one standing inside the minaret, it shakes and simultaneously the
other one shakes on its own. The bang on one produces an echo in
the other. It is a great feat of constructional engineering. Like Sidi
Basir mosque, Raj Bibi mosque had also two shaking minarets,
one of which was dismantled by an inquisitive Englishman in an
unsuccessful attempt to find out how it worked.

1451   Buhlul Khan, an Afghan of Lodi tribe, marched down upon Delhi.
He displaced the Sayyid dynasty on April 19 and started the rule
of Lodi dynasty from April 24, which had a short spell up to 1526.

The great Kankariya tank of Ahmedabad in form of a polygon
with 34 sides was completed.

1459   Sultan Mahmud Begara, a grandson of Ahmad Shah, ascended the
throne of Gujarat at the age of thirteen. He proved to be the most
eminent of all the sovereigns of his dynasty.

Jodhpur city was founded on May 12 by the the Rathor chief Jodha
Rao. (See 1561.)

1461   Bahmani ruler Alauddin Humayun Shah was assassinated by his
servants. His minor son Nizam Shah of 8 years became the twelfth
Bahmani ruler. But he suddenly died after two years.

1465   Virupaksha II became Vijayanagar ruler and the decay of the empire
started. On December 23 he was defeated in the battle of Tellikota
by the combined Muslim forces of Ahmadnagar, Bidar, Bijapur
and Golconda.

Sirohi town was founded by the descendants of Prithviraj Chauhan
of Delhi.

1468   Rana Kumbha of Mewar was murdered by his son Uday. (See
1473.)

1469   Guru Nanak, founder of the Sikh sect, was born on April 15
(traditionally observed on the first full-moon night in November)
in a Khatri family in Talwandi Rae Bhoe, now known as Nankana
Sahib in Pakistan, 65 km from Lahore. (d. 1539. Also see 1496.)

A.D.

Mahmud Khan Khilji of Malwa was succeeded by his eldest son Muhammad Shah under the title Ghiasuddin. He was a patron of arts and constructed the 'Jahaz Mahal' palace in Mandu for his harem.

Sultan Mahmud Begara of Gujarat destroyed the seventh Somnath temple and converted the temple into a mosque, which was never used as such due to some superstition. (See 1400 and 1951.)

1470   A Russian merchant Athanasius Niktin visited Bidar, capital of Bahmani kingdom.

1473   The nobles of Chittorgarh proclaimed Raimal, younger brother of Uday, as the king of Mewar. (See 1468.)

1479   The kingdom of Jaunpur was overpowered and absorbed in Delhi monarchy.

The Vaishnav saint and philosopher Vallabhacharya was born. The deity Srinathji of Nathdwara (see 1669), the manifestation of Lord Krishna, is the highest deity of Vallabha sect. Vallabhacharya propagated 'pustimarga' or religion of grace. (d.1531).

The third Sikh Guru Amar Das was born on May 5 in Basarki village of Amritsar district. He introduced the 'langar' or community kitchen and fought for the abolition of 'purdah' and 'sati'. Emperor Akbar paid homage to Guru Amar Das at Goindwal in Punjab. (d.1574).

1483   The first Mughal Emperor Zahiruddin Muhammad Babar, son of Umar Sheikh Mirza, chieftain of a small state Ferghana in Turkmenistan, was born on February 24. (d. 1530).

1484   Blind religious singer Surdas was born in Sihi village near Delhi on December 9. (See 1545.)

Purandaradasa was born at Purandaragada near Pune. He was originally a trader and amassed a big fortune. He renounced all his riches and sought spiritual guidance. Tradition credits him with having composed 4,75,000 devotional songs. (d. 1534).

1485   Imad Shahi dynasty was established in Bidar by Fateh Ullah Imad-ul-Mulk. He was a Hindu convert who defected from Bahmani kingdom. Bidar was absorbed by Ahmadnagar in 1574.

A.D.

Sangama dynasty of Vijayanagar ended with the murder of Virupaksha III by one of his own sons. Another son of Virupaksharandha Devaraya ascended the throne and was at once murdered. Immadi Narasimha, ruler of Chandragiri, usurped the throne. (See 1503.)

1486   Chaitanya Dev was born at Nabadwip in Bengal on February 18. He became an ascetic in 1509. He idolised the love of Krishna and Radha in Bengal school of Vaishnavism. (d. 1533).

1487   Joao Peres de Cavilhao mostly travelled overland and ultimately reached Cannanore in an Arab vessel. He was the first Portuguese to set foot on Indian soil. (See 1498 and 1500.)

1488   Bikaji, son of Jodha Singh of Mewar, founded his own capital Bikaner 30 years after his departure from his paternal home.

1489   On July 12 Buhlul Khan Lodi of Delhi died. On July 17 the nobles of the court chose his third son Nizam Khan Lodi as the successor who took the title Sikandar Shah II Lodi. (d.1517).

1490   Yusuf Adil Shah, the governor of Bijapur, established Adil Shahi dynasty of Bijapur, independent of Bahmani kingdom. The kingdom was annexed by Aurangzeb in 1686.

Ahmad Ibn Nizam Shah, the governor of Junnar of Bahmani kingdom, established an independent Nizam Shahi dynasty of Ahmadnagar, which city he founded himself in 1495 and gave the same name to his kingdom. (See 1600.)

In the first war between the Kacharis and Ahoms of Assam, the latter were defeated on the bank of the Dako River. (See 1531.)

1493   Alauddin Husain Shah fought and defeated Muzaffur Shah Habsi at Gaur. He was then selected to be the king of Bengal. He was a Sayyid of Arab descent, and was the best and the most famous of Muslim kings of Bengal. His reign (1493-1518) was noted for public works and promotion of Bengal literature. Shri Chaitanya Dev, the famous Hindu reformer, enjoyed the ruler's patronage.

Pope Alexander VI, under the Bull of May 1493, assigned India to Portugal in his division of the non-Christian world between Portugal and Spain. (See 1498.)

1494   Sikandar II Lodi, Sultan of Delhi, laid the foundation of Agra. He shifted the capital there from Delhi in 1505.

A.D.

1495 Ahmad Ibn Nizam Shah founded the city of Ahmadnagar. (See 1490.)

1496 Guru Nanak and Saint Kabir met for the first time.

1497 Prataprudra Deva became the last Suryavamshi king of Orissa.

1498 Vasco da Gama of Portugal cast anchor at Kapad near Calicut on May 17 in the territory of Zamorin whom he met on May 22. He left Lisbon with 170 men and four ships for India on July 1, 1497. (See 1493 and 1524.)

1499 Nanak had his first mystic experience at Sultanpur and he declared that division of people according to religion is arbitrary.

1500 The first European factory in India was established at Calicut by the Portuguese under Pedro Alvarez Cabral, who left Portugal on March 9 and reached Calicut on September 13. (See 1487.)

1502 Vasco da Gama came to India for the second time and erected a factory at Cochin. But Zamorin remained hostile. (See 1498.)

Varthema of Bologna, Italy visited Bijapur.

1503 Alphonso de Albuquerque erected the first Portuguese fortress in India at Cochin. (See 1515.)

Hita Harivansa, founder of Radha-Vallabhi sect, was born. The sect assigns a superior place to Radha than to Krishna. (d. 1553).

Immadi Narasimha of Vijayanagar was assassinated. Vira Narasimha became the Regent and de facto ruler, and he started Taluva dynasty.

1504 The second Sikh Guru Angad, original name Lehna, was born on April 23. He devised Gurumukhi script. (d.1552).

1505 Dom Francis de Almeida of Portugal arrived at Cochin on October 24 with the title Viceroy of India.

Sikandar II Lodi shifted to his new capital at Agra. (See 1494.)

1507 The Portuguese arrived at Madras. The city finally got its name from their leader Madra. (See 1640.)

1508 Zamorin of Calicut, Sultan Mahmud Begara of Gujarat and Sultan of Egypt combined their naval strengths and Portuguese navy was defeated at Chaul. (See 1509.)

Emperor Humayun, son of Babar, was born on March 6 in Kabul. (d. 1556).

A.D.

1509   The combined Muslim navy was annihilated by the Portuguese navy in the battle of Diu. Sultan Mahmud Begara allowed the Portuguese to set up a factory at Diu. (See 1508.)

Rana Sangram Singh I of Mewar succeeded his father Raimal. During his regime Chittorgarh reached the summit of her prosperity.

On November 4 Don Francis de Almeida was succeeded by Alfonso de Albuquerque as the Viceroy of Portuguese India. Albuquerque had first come to India in 1503 as a naval commander.

1510   The first church, for Europeans only, was constructed by Franciscan Friars in Cochin, who were brought by Alphonso de Albuquerque. The church was dedicated to St. Anthony but is presently known as Church of St. Francis.

Sikandar II Lodi of Delhi acknowledged independence of Gujarat.

Albuquerque of Portugal seized and occupied Goa, the principal port of the Sultan of Bijapur. It was the first territory to be occupied by any European nation since the time of Alexander the Great. Albuquerque either killed or expelled all the Muslim male folks and forced the women to marry his troops. He brought about marriages of his men with Hindu women too. The present Goanese Christians are mostly their progeny.

Nasiruddin Khilji, the ruler of Malwa, died. He was succeeded by his son Mahmud Khan II, the last of the Khilji rulers of Malwa.

The Portuguese attacked and captured Surat.

1511   The Portuguese established a factory at Calicut.

1512   Quli Qutab-ul-Mulk, a Turki officer, declared independence of Golconda region from Bahmani kingdom and took the title Quli Qutub Shah in 1518. Thus started the Qutub Shahi dynasty of Golconda which was finally annexed by Aurangzeb in 1687.

1513   A Portuguese factory was set up at Diu.

1515   Alphonso de Albuquerque, Portuguese Viceroy of India, died near Goa on December 16. (See 1503.)

1516   The Portuguese established a factory at Chaul.

1517   Sikandar Shah II Lodi of Delhi died on November 21 and was succeeded by his son Ibrahim II Lodi. During his regime Lodi dynasty came to an end after the first battle of Panipat with Babar in 1526.

A.D.

Eight Franciscan friars started a convent in Goa.

1518   Saint Kabir died. (b. 1440).

Sikh Guru Nanak and the Vaishnav ascetic Sri Chaitanya Dev met at Puri and discussed about removal of untouchability, casteism, as well as the protection of Hindu temples from Muslim destruction. Nanak's followers were far ahead of Chaitanya's disciples in this respect on an all India basis.

1519   Babar, a Turko-Mongol, the fifth descendant of Timur on the father's side and the fourteenth descendant of Chenghiz Khan on the mother's side, followed the steps of Alexander the Great and entered India for the first time. (See 1525.)

1520   Babar took Bijaur in Punjab, which had fallen to the Greeks eighteen hundred years earlier. (See 1524.)

Nanak founded village Kartarpur (now Dera Baba Nanak)on the bank of the Ravi river and settled down there.

1522   The Portuguese traveller Domingos Paes visited Vijayanagar.

1523   Babar fought with forces of Delhi sultan at Lahore. He won and burnt the city. (See 1524.)

1524   Babar again overran Punjab and burnt Lahore again before returning to Kabul. In between he came to India twice. (See 1523.)

Vasco da Gama came to India on September 25 as the Portuguese viceroy of India, but died in Cochin on December 24. He was buried in the St. Francis Church. Eight years later his remains were removed to Portugal, but the original tablet still remains in Cochin. (See 1498.)

1525   Babar entered India on November 17 for the fifth time by way of Sind with a bid to conquer India, which he did. (See 1519 and 1526.)

Basudeva Sarbavauma of Nadia died. (b. 1450).

1526   In the battle of Panipat on April 21, Babar defeated Delhi Sultan Ibrahim II Lodi, who was slain. Babar's army was equipped with matchlock rifles and field cannon. Thus the sultanate rule ended in India. The Mughal dynasty was established which took the title Badshah on April 27. On May 10 Babar entered Agra, then capital of India. Ibrahim Lodi's mother made an unsuccessful attempt on Babar's life in December by poisoning him through a royal servant.

A.D.

Incidentally Babar's mother Qulik Nigar Khanum who was popularly known as 'The Mughal', the Persian word for Mongol, and the dynasty acquired its name from her. (See 1517.)

1527   Rana Sangram Singh I of Mewar fought Babar in Khanua near Agra on March 17 and lost. The Rana promised not to enter Chittorgarh without a victory, but died disappointed on January 30, 1530.

Bareilly town was founded by Bas Deo and Barek Deo and took its name from the latter. (See 1657.)

Mandi state of Himachal Pradesh was founded.

1528   Babar captured Chanderi on January 29 from Medini Rai, one of the most distinguished lieutenants of Rana Sangram Singh I. (See 1527.)

Nunho da Cunha was appointed the governor of Portuguese India.

1529   Nasrat Shah, Afghan Sultan of Bengal, opposed Babar on the banks of the Gogra river on May 6. Nasrat Shah was defeated and accepted peace terms. Babar returned to Agra on June 25.

Burhan Nizam Shah of Ahmadnagar appointed a Maratha Brahmin Kanwar Sain as his prime minister and bestowed on him the title 'Peshwa'. Henceforth Hindus acquired a great influence in the Nizam Shahi government.

The Portuguese capital of India was shifted from Cochin to Goa.

The Portuguese captured Mangalore port.

1530   Rana Sangram Singh I of Mewar died a broken-hearted man on January 30. His son Ratna Singh became the Rana. (See 1527.)

Babar captured Oudh and south Bihar. His son Humayun was seriously ill at Dholpur. Babar prayed by his bedside that God should spare his son and he should be taken instead. Strangely Humayun started recovering and Babar died at Dholpur near Agra on December 26 (b. 1483). Humayun succeeded him on December 29.

The Portuguese established a mint in Cochin.

1531   Bahadur Shah of Gujarat defeated and executed Mahmud II of Malwa alongwith his seven sons. He annexed Malwa and the Khilji dynasty ended there. (See 1436.)

A.D.

Rudra Pratap, ninth in line from Sohanpal of Bundelkhand, founded Orchha as its capital. (See 1292.)

Ahoms renewed their hostilities against Cacharis and captured their capital Dimapur.

Vaishnava saint Vallabhacharya passed away. (b. 1479).

1532 Tulsidas, the great Hindu poet of *Ramayana* fame, was born. His original name was Rambola and he was abandoned by his parents. The name Tulsidas was given by his preceptor Naraharidas. (d. 1623).

Rana Ratna Singh died in an encounter with the prince of Bundi. Ratna Singh's brother Vikramaditya became the Rana of Mewar.

1533 Humayun built the city of Dinpanah in January on the site of 'Purana Quila' or Old Fort (Delhi) where stood the pre-historic city of Indraprastha. The fifth city Dinpanah stood only for six years and was razed to the ground by Sher Shah in 1539.

Shri Chaitanya Dev left his mortal remains at Puri on July 9. (b. 1486).

The oldest Durga Puja on record was performed by Prince Nara Narayan of Cooch Bihar and is continuing there ever since. (See 1583.)

1534 The fourth Sikh Guru Ram Das, son-in-law of Guru Amar Das, was born on November 2. (d. 1581).

As a defensive measure against the impending attack on Chittorgarh by Bahadur Shah of Gujarat and Malwa, Rani Karnawati, the widow of Sangram Singh I, acclaimed Humayun as her brother by sending him a *rakhi*. Humayun responded graciously. But before his arrival Bahadur Shah entered Chittorgarh on March 8 which was sacked for the second time. Rani Karnawati with 13,000 women shut themselves in a vault filled with gunpowder, which was set alight, and they passed into eternity. Humayun though too late to save his *rakhi* sister, reinstated Vikramaditya Singh as the ruler of Mewar. Humayun avenged Karnawati's self-immolation by capturing Mandu from Bahadur Shah in 1535. (See 1303, 1532 and 1568.)

The Portuguese captured Bassein of Maharashtra and Diu of Gujarat from Sultan Bahadur Shah who negotiated peace after offering Bombay including Elephanta Island. The original name of the island was Gharapuri.

A.D.

Humayunama, the last work of Khondamir, was written.

1535 Rana Vikramaditya of Mewar died. Following an anarchy his bastard brother Banbir usurped authority till 1537. (See 1534.)

Bahadur Shah of Gujarat and Mandu was defeated by Humayun. (See 1534.)

The Portuguese built a Fort at Diu.

1536 Nunho da Cunha built a Portuguese fort at Bassein.

1537 Bahadur Shah of Gujarat and Malwa was invited by the Portuguese at Diu for negotiation and they treacherously tried to detain him. On February 14 Bahadur Shah in an attempt to escape jumped into the water. He was hit on his head by a Portuguese sailor and Bahadur Shah died.

Uday Singh II, son of Sangram Singh I, ascended the throne of Mewar in succession to the usurper Banbir. (See 1535.)

Bangalore was established by a local chief Kempa Gowda of Mangdi. The city's name originated from 'benda kallarur' meaning boiled wild seeds, which satisfied Gowda's hunger during one hunting session. He built a mud fort there and demarcated the city area with four pillars. But the present city far exceeds those limits.

Goa was made an 'Episcopal See' by Pope Paul III. The first Bishop was Dom Francisco de Melo. (See 1557.)

1538 Sher Shah Suri, an Afghan noble, overthrew Ghiasuddin Mahmud Shah, the reigning Sultan of Bengal and became its ruler. Mahmud Shah fled to the Mughal camp at Chunar. Sher Shah Suri celebrated his coronation in the city of Gaur (Bengal) and declared his determination to drive out the Mughals from India. He was also a great road builder. The longest road built by him was Grand Trunk Road, now National Highway No. 2. (See 1839.)

A Turkish expedition arrived in India in September to exterminate the Portuguese from India and bombarded Diu for twenty days. With the arrival of a new Portuguese fleet, the Turkish armada retired on November 25.

1539 Humayun was defeated by Sher Shah Suri at Chausa near Buxar on June 7. Sher Shah took the name Abul Muzaffur Sher Shah. He became the independent ruler of eastern India. (See 1540.)

A.D.

Guru Nanak died at Dera Baba Nanak i.e. Kartarpur on September 22 (b. 1469). Angad became the Guru.

1540 Rana Pratap Singh of Mewar, the brightest star of Rajputana, was born on May 9. His very name personifies chivalry, complete dedication to the cause of liberty and the highest principles of nobility and self-sacrifice. (d. 1597).

Sher Shah defeated Humayun on May 17 for the second time at Hardoi in U.P., known as the battle of Kanauj. While fleeing across the Indus, Humayun sought the blessings of Guru Angad at Khadur Shahib in Punjab. Sher Shah established the sixth Delhi capital Shergarh. The fort therein is known as the 'Old Fort'. (See 1351, 1533, 1556.)

Brindavana Das wrote *Chaitanya Bhagavata* (*Chaitanya Mangala*).

Hyder Mirza Doghlat, a relative and general of Humayun, captured Srinagar in November and became an independent king of Kashmir.

1542 Akbar, son of Humayun, was born at Amarkot in Sind on October 13. Humayun at that ime had taken refuge with Rana Virsal there.

Saint Francisco Xavier, a Spanish national, landed at Goa as the first Jesuit missionary. He established the first Christian colony in Goa. The Christianisation of Indians began. (See 1552 and 1622.)

'Rupee' (Rupiya) was first minted in India during the reign of Sher Shah. It was a pure silver coin weighing 179 grains (see 1676) and was based on a ratio of 40 copper paisa per rupee.

Rama Raya, minister of Vijayanagar ruler Sadasivaraya, but defacto ruler established Aravidu dynasty which ended in 1649.

1543 Sher Shah captured Raisen fort. After promising safe conduct to Puranmal that the Hindu garrison could march out with arms and property, Sher Shah attacked and slaughtered them all when they came out of the fort.

1544 Sher Shah captured Ajmer, Chittorgarh and Nagore of Rajasthan.

1545 Humayun captured Afghanistan.

The Purana Quila (the Old Fort) of Delhi was completed by Sher Shah. (See 1533.)

Sher Shah was fatally wounded in an explosion in his own magazine on May 22 while preparing for an attack on Kalanjara fort. He suffered the agony till evening. When fall of Kalanjara was announced Sher Shah breathed his last with the words 'Thanks to Almighty God'. Jalal Khan supplanted his father and took the title Islam Shah.

Joa de Castro was the first Portuguese Viceroy of the East.

Surdas completed his *Sur-Saravali,* a compilation of songs. (See 1484.)

1549 Rumi Khan constructed the great Bijapur gun of 70 cm calibre weighing 40 tonnes. It was cast in bronze in Ahmadnagar.

D'Parsia de Orta purchased Bombay for a sum of Rs 537.

1551 Abul Fazl, the Indo-Persian writer, was born. His noted works are *Aain-e-Akbari* and *Akbarnama.* (d. 1602).

1552 Guru Angad expired on March 27 (b. 1504). The third Sikh Guru Amar Das was installed who compiled the *Adi Granth Sahib.* It included 907 hymns, not only composed by Sikh Gurus, but also by Hindu and Muslim saints and compiled by Gurus. (See 1604.)

Saint Francisco Xavier expired on December 2 near Macao. According to his wish, his body was enshrined in Basilica of Bom Jesus in Goa after 2 years. The body never decomposed and stayed that way. The exposition of the body takes place at regular intervals, the latest one being in 1984-85 for 54 days ending on January 13, 1985. (See 1542.)

1553 Hita Harivansa of Radha-Vallabhi sect expired. (b. 1503).

1555 Humayun crossed the Indus and captured Lahore in February. He fought and won the decisive battle of Sirhind on June 22 and ousted Sikandar Suri, the usurper of Delhi throne. On the same day Akbar was announced as heir – apparent of Humayun, who entered Delhi on July 23 and resumed the imperial dignity.

Mian Bayazid, better known as Baz Bahadur (of Rupmati fame), Governor of Malwa, crowned himself as Sultan and declared independence of Malwa. (See 1561.)

1556 Humayun slipped on the staircase of the library of the 'Old Fort' on January 24 and died two days later (b. 1508). Akbar's formal enthronement took place on February 14 at the age of 13 years 4 months, in a garden at Kalanaur in Gurdaspur district of Punjab.

A.D.

Fasli, year of northern India, and Saal, year of Bengal, were introduced by Emperor Akbar in April with the commencement of Hijri year 963. As an Indian year consists of 365 days as against 354 days of a Hijri year, at the completion of each Hijri year, the Indian year receded by 11 days. At the beginning of 1994 while both Fasli and Saal were 1400, Hijri year itself was 1414. Incidentally in 1994, as per the Indian National Calendar, 'Shaka' year 1916 commenced on March 21.

The second battle of Panipat took place on November 5 when Hemu, the Hindu general and prime minister of the last Afghan ruler Sikandar Suri, was defeated by Akbar's army led by Bairam Khan. Hemu was struck in the eye by an arrow which pierced through his brain, rendering him unconscious. Bairam and Akbar mutilated the body with their swords and Akbar severed his head from the body at the instance of Bairam. Sovereignty of Delhi finally went in favour of the Mughals.

1557   Pope Paul V made Goa a 'Metropolitan See', promoting the second Bishop Juan de Albuquerque to be the first Archbishop of India, and at the same time set up the Inquisition at Goa. (See 1537.)

The first printed book came out in Goa, printed by a Jesuit Christian missionary Joao de Bustamanti, including *Catechism of Xavier* in 1557 and a work on Bonaventure in 1578 – both in Roman script. The printing machine was supposed to go to Ethiopia (Abyssinia) but it was somehow unloaded at Goa in 1556 and stayed there. (See 1713.)

1559   The first stones of the city of Udaipur were laid by Udai Singh I and he named the city after himself.

1560   Gaur, the capital of Bengal except for a short spell in Nabadwip, was abandoned for unknown reasons after 2,000 years of its existence. The capital was shifted first to Tondah and then to Rajmahal, both in Bihar now. (See 1063, 1203 and 1639.)

Akbar, tired of Bairam Khan's tyranny, relieved him of all his duties. Bairam revolted and was defeated but was pardoned by Akbar. Bairam was asked to accept any of the three alternatives suggested by Akbar. Bairam preferred to go to Mecca on pilgrimage. (See 1561.)

Almora was founded by Raja Kalyan Chand. It was captured by the British in 1815.

The famous Meenakshi temple of Madurai, having 997 carved pillars, was consecrated. It was designed by Viswanath Nayak and took 100 years to be completed in 1660.

1561   Bairam Khan on his way to Mecca was assassinated on January 31 at Patan while visiting a celebrated Hindu temple, by an Afghan assassin Mubarak Khan Lohani, whose father was slain by Bairam Khan in the battle of Machiwara. (See 1560.)

Akbar invaded Mewar, then ruled by Uday Singh II. Akbar captured important castles of Nagore and Malkote. He gave these two forts and some lands to Rai Singh, prince of Bikaner, who then established a new independent state of Jodhpur. (See 1459.)

Beharimal of Amber (later Jaipur) became a vassal of Akbar. His son Bhagwan Das and grandson Man Singh played important roles in Akbar's Court. (See 1562.)

Daman of Maharashtra was captured by the Portuguese.

Akbar conquered Malwa from Baz Bahadur of Rupmati fame. When Baz Bahadur realised that he was losing the battle at Sarangpur, he fled leaving Rupmati to poison herself. Baz Bahadur however did not submit until November 1570. (See 1555.)

1562   Habib Shah of Shah Mirza dynasty of Kashmir was overthrown by Hussain Ghazi Shah of Chakk dynasty. (See 1338.)

Akbar who was on a pilgrimage to Moinuddin Chisti at Ajmer, married the daughter of Beharimal, Raja of Amber. Thus he united the house of Ramchandra (of Ramayana) with those of Taimur and Chenghiz Khan as the first step of reconciliation and peace between the Hindus and the Muslims. (See 1519 and 1561.)

Mian Tansen joined Akbar's court. The country's most renowned singer of all times expired on May 6, 1589.

1563   The fifth Sikh Guru Arjun Dev was born on April 14. (d. 1606).

1564   Akbar removed 'Jeziya' or toll-tax on his non-Muslim subjects on March 15, which was originally instituted by Qutubuddin Aibek of the Slave dynasty. (See 1679.)

The Muslim convert Kalapahar of Bengal destroyed Kamakshya temple near Guwahati. (See 1568.)

A.D.

Purandaradasa expired at Pandharpur. (b. 1484).

Rani Durgawati, the noble queen of Gondwana, fought Akbar's army led by Asaf Jah. She lost the battle and committed suicide.

1565   The Hindu kingdom Vijayanagar was virtually extinguished on January 23 after the great battle of Tellikota against the combined forces of five Muslim kingdoms of north Deccan – Ahmadanagar, Berar, Bidar, Bijapur and Golconda. Rama Raya, the haughty ruler of Vijayanagar, was captured and decapitated by the Ahmadnagar ruler with his own hands. (See 1336.)

The Nayaks established an independent kingdom in Thanjavur/ Madurai.

Construction of Agra fort was started by Akbar and this construction continued until the rule of his grandson Shahjahan.

1566   Akbar's cousin Khan Zaman revolted against Akbar with the support of Uzbeg chiefs. Akbar captured Khan Zaman and executed him.

The great Agra mosque was built.

1567   When the Portuguese came on the scene, the Jews of Kerala sought refuge in Cochin, whose Hindu ruler granted them a site for habitation. There they built a Jew town and the synagogue the next year. (See 774.)

Mira Bai, a woman saint, singer and a great devotee of Lord Krishna was born. She was married to Bhojaraj, a prince of Chittorgarh, who expired shortly after marriage. (d. 1614).

1568   Chittorgarh was sacked for the third time (see 1303 and 1534) when Akbar attacked the fort on October 20, 1567 and ultimately captured it on February 28, 1568 from Rana Uday Singh II, who survived the loss for four years. Gold ornaments collected from the dead Rajput warriors in the battlefield weighed 74 ½ maunds, the number which was later considered as an unlucky number. Jaimal and Putta became immortal for their bravery. Nine queens, five princesses and eight thousand Rajput women immolated themselves in the 'Jauhar' holocaust. Akbar ordered massacre of 30,000 non-combatants in Chittorgarh.

Kalapahar of Bengal, originally a Hindu, Raju by name, who accepted Muslim religion, attacked and captured Orissa. King

A.D.

Mukund Dev died in the battle. Kalapahar was notoriously famous for destroying Hindu temples and idols. He extensively damaged the Jagannath temple of Puri as well as the Konarak temple. According to the *Akbarnama,* Kalapahar was born as an Afghan Muslim. (See 1564.)

The Cochin synagogue was built by the local Jews. It is the oldest synagogue in the Commonwealth of Nations. (See 1567.)

Akbar's son Sultan Salim Mirza (Jahangir) was born of Amber's Jodha Bai on August 30 at Fatehpur Sikri.

1569 Chandrasen of Jodhpur tried to preserve his valiant spirit and honour untarnished. But he had to submit and acknowledge supremacy of Akbar.

Akbar decided to shift his capital from Delhi to Agra (Fatehpur-Sikri) and it continued there only till 1585. (See 1503 and 1571.)

Humayun's tomb in Delhi was completed.

1570 The powerful minister Tirumala (Aravidu dynasty) deposed the puppet King Sadasivaraya of Vijayanagar and usurped the throne. (See 1542.)

The combined forces of Bijapur, Ahmadnagar and Calicut attacked the Portuguese settlements including Goa.

Kalyana Singh, ruler of Bikaner and Rawal Har Rai of Jaisalmer accepted Mughal suzerainty. So the entire Rajputana with the partial exception of certain tracts of Mewar passed under Mughal supremacy.

1571 Construction of palace city Sikri near Agra began in honour of famous Sufi Saint Khwaja Moinuddin Chisti (1143-1236). It was completed in seven years. After Akbar's conquest of Gujarat in 1573, he renamed the new city as Fatehpur Sikri, the 'Victory Town'. (See 1569.)

1572 Rana Pratap Singh ascended Mewar throne on May 28 and established himself at Kamalmir, from where he started his memorable struggle against the Mughals.

The states of Bundi and Kota were separated. (See 1242 and 1266.)

1573 Surat capitulated to Akbar in February.

Akbar attacked Gujarat which had earlier revolted against Mughal rule.

A.D.

Etimad Khan, orginally a Hindu slave, challenged Akbar, who won the decisive battle near Ahmedabad on September 2.

1574 Guru Ram Das, son-in-law of Sikh Guru Amar Das, took over as Guru after the death of Guru Amar Das on October 1. (b. 1479).

Tulsidas began writing his famous *Ramcharita Manas* based on the story of *Ramayana.*

1575 Construction of Buland Darwaza, the world's largest portal, started. Its width is 40 mt and the height, including the steps is 53.5 mt.

1576 The great battle of Haldighati or Gogunda took place on June 18, when Rana Pratap lost and took refuge in a remote fortress. Haldighati is considered as the Thermopylee of Mewar. It is interesting to note that a Muslim general Hakim Khan Soor led the Rajput army, who himself was killed in the battle while trying to save Rana Pratap. On the other hand the forces of Emperor Akbar was under the command of a Hindu Rajput general Raja Man Singh.

In July, Akbar captured Bengal from the Afghan ruler Daud Khan Karrani after the battle near Rajmahal. Daud Khan was taken prisoner and executed. 238 years' rule of Bengal's independent Sultans virtually came to an end. (See 1337 and 1612.)

The great mosque of Fatehpur Sikri was completed.

1577 Amritsar city was founded by the fourth Sikh Guru Ram Das at a site granted by Akbar. It was then known as Ramdaspur. The name Amritsar was given by the fifth Sikh Guru Arjun Dev from the *Amrit sarovar* (pool of nectar) dug by Guru Ram Das. The foundation day is taken as October 24. (See 1588.)

1578 The Portuguese viceroy of Goa sent Antony Cabral as an ambassador to Akbar's court.

1579 The English Jesuit Father and the first Englishman S. J. Thomas Stephens arrived at Goa on October 24 in a Portuguese ship. He ultimately settled down in India and died at Goa in 1619.

The first Jesuit mission set out for Akbar's court from Goa on November 17. It was led by Rudolf Acquavia, a saintly scholar of noble birth and not yet thirty. (See 1580.)

The Portuguese settled down in Hooghly, the place which became the first international riverine port in India.

1580 The first Jesuit mission comprising of priests Aquavia and Monserrate arrived at Fatehpur Sikri on February 28. Emperor Akbar immediately received the mission with extraordinary warmth and affection in his own apartments. (See 1579.)

In October, Akbar announced his policy of Sulh-e-Kul or universal toleration of religion.

Bandel in Bengal was founded by a Portuguese Captain Pedro Teverse. It derived its name from the Persian word 'bunder' meaning port. (See 1599.)

The sovereignty of Spain was extended over Portugal and the Portuguese rights over Indian territory passed on to the Spanish crown.

1581 Ram Das, the fourth Sikh Guru, died on September 19 (b. 1534). The *Guruship* since then became hereditary. His son Arjun Dev succeeded him and changed the offerings to the Guru into a regular tax. Arjun Dev collected the materials of the *Granth,* the sacred code of the Sikhs. (See 1604.)

1582 Emperor Akbar proclaimed that he was not a Muslim but a follower of his newly promulgated religion Din-Ilahi or Divine Faith. It is basically the practice of sun and fire worship, as he saw in them the effulgence of God. Akbar was its Prophet from 1582 to 1605. Erection of new mosques and repair of old ones at government expense were prohibited. (See 1598.)

1583 The first large scale Durga Puja in the present form was performed by Raja Kangsanarayan of Taherpur in Rajsahi district in Bangladesh, under the direction of Ramesh Shastri, as a substitute of 'Aswamedh Yajna'. Durga Puja of Roy Chowdhury family of Behala commenced in 1610. Raja Raghab Roy of Nadia started Durga Puja at Diknagar in 1606 which was shifted to Krishnagar in 1662 by Raja Rudra Roy. (See 1533.)

Ralph Fitch with two other English merchants, William Leedes and James Storey reached India from London by the land route via Aleppo and Baghdad. They were thrown into prison by the jealous Portuguese, but all the three escaped. Leedes vanished. Storey entered Emperor Akbar's service. Ralph Fitch returned to London after a visit to Agra and assisted in forming the East India Company, at first incorporated as John Company. (See 1599 and 1833.)

A.D.

1584   Akbar changed the prehistoric name of Prayag to Allahabad.

Salim (Jahangir), son of Akbar married Man Bai, daughter of Bhagwan Das of Amber and sister of Man Singh.

Allahabad fort was built by Akbar.

1585   Akbar reshifted his capital from Fatehpur Sikri to Lahore because of acute water shortage there. (See 1569.)

The temple of Radha Vallabha was constructed at Brindavan.

Raja Todarmal built a grand edifice for Viswanath temple at Varanasi, which was later destroyed by Aurangzeb.

1586   Raja Birbal, real name Mahesh Das, Akbar's most intimate friend, a ready wit and physician, was killed on February 25 in a battle near Peshawar with the Yusufzai tribe.

On October 7 the Mughal army entered Srinagar. The last Kashmir ruler Yusuf Shah Chakk of Chakk dynasty submitted to Akbar and Kashmir's independence was lost. (See 1562.)

1587   The unique 'Ras Mancha' temple of Bishnupur of Bengal, resembling a stepped pyramid with beautiful terracotta work, was built by Bir Hambira, the great Vaishnava Raja of Mallabhum, the ancient name of Bishnupur. (See 694 and 1694.)

1588   Harimandir Sahib in the Golden Temple complex of Amritsar was built by the fifth Sikh Guru Arjun Dev. It then became the seat of the spiritual authority of the Sikhs. Arjun Dev invited the Muslim divine Mian Mir of Lahore to lay foundation of Har (Hari) mandir, the temple of God. (See 1577, 1609 and 1805.)

1589   Mian Tansen, the glorious singer of Akbar's court, expired on May 6.

Raja Todarmal, the great financial adviser of Akbar, passed away.

Raja Bhagwan Das, the valiant commander of Akbar, died. (See 1584.)

1590   Muhammad, the fifth Quli Qutub Shah of Golconda, established the new city Bhagnagar after the name of his pretty Hindu wife Bhagmati. When Bhagmati embraced Islam and was given the name Hyder Mahal, the city's name was changed to Hyderabad.

Raja Man Singh of Amber built Govind Dev temple in Brindavan which now contains nearly 4,000 temples.

A.D.

1591   Ali Rai of little Tibet sent presents and gave his daughter in marriage to Salim (Jahangir)

The famous 54.5 mt high Char Minar of Hyderabad was built by the ruler Muhammad Quli Qutub Shah as a mark of victory against the plague epidemic which was ravaging the state.

1592   Emperor Shahjahan was born on January 5 at Lahore. (d. 1666).

Orissa was annexed by Akbar.

The Amber palace in Rajasthan was built by Raja Man Singh. It is one of the finest examples of Rajput architecture.

After 15 years of revolt of Mughal officers in Bengal, Akbar got full control of Bengal after the expedition of Man Singh.

The Levant Company, founded in 1581 for trading with Turkey, got the charter from Queen Elizabeth I of England, to trade with India via the overland route. (See 1599.)

1593   Sind was conquered by Akbar.

1594   Vijayanagar fell to the Adil Shahi ruler of Bijapur.

1595   Faizi, the poet laureate of Akbar's court, died.

1596   The sixth Sikh Guru Har Govind was born on June 6 (d. 1645). He fashioned a military role for the Sikhs. The last Sikh Guru Govind Singh completed the Sikhs' transformation into a martial community. (See 1699.)

Princess Chand Bibi of Ahmadnagar ceded Berar to Akbar to save the rest of her kingdom. (See 1600.)

Aain-e-Akbari was completed by Abul Fazl.

1597   Rana Pratap Singh of Mewar died on January 19. He virtually recaptured most of Mewar except Chittorgarh, Ajmer and Mandalgarh. His son Amar Singh succeeded him. (b. 1540).

An indecisive battle took place at Sonepat between the Mughals and the combined forces of Ahmadnagar, Bijapur and Golconda.

1598   Sheikh Mubarak, the architect of Din-Ilahi passed away. (See 1582.)

1599   On September 22 twenty-four merchants gathered in London Founder's Hall under the auspices of Lord Mayor, to start a new company for business in India, with a share capital of £30, 133. It is generally referred to as Company or the East India Company, which name actually came as late as in 1833. Its first title was 'The

A.D.

Governor and Company of Merchants of London Trading into the East Indies'. The Company obtained Queen's (Elizabeth I) consent on December 31 for trade with India by sea route. (See 1592.)

Bandel Church in Bengal was constructed by the Portuguese. (See 1580.)

St. Peter's church and St. Paul's church were built in Cochin by the Portuguese.

1600 Ahmadnagar was seized for four months by Mughal army. Chand Bibi of Ahmadnagar (widow of Adil Shah of Bijapur) resisted heroically but ultimately was killed by her own people inflamed by Mughal enemies. Ahmadnagar was captured on August 19. Bahadur Nizam Shah and his royal family were sent to Gwalior fort as state prisoners. (See 1596.)

Hector (500 tonnes), the first ship of the East India Company, touched Surat on August 24. Capt. Lancaster was in command of the ship.

Isa Khan, the rebel Afghan ruler of Bengal, defeated Delhi army at Bhadrak. (See 1612.)

Hindu almanacs are presently prepared on the astronomical calculations made by Raghabananda Chakraborty in his two books *Siddhanta Rahasya* and *Dina Chandrika.*

1601 After eight months' siege, on January 17 Akbar entered Asirgarh fort, one of the strongest forts of India, through perfidy and bribery.

Dindayal, the great preacher of universal love to all, was born in Allahabad.

First attempt was made to enter into India's cloth market by two Dutch ships in Surat, where they were welcomed.

1602 United East Indies Company of the Netherlands was formed on March 20.

Abul Fazl, Akbar's devoted minister, was murdered by 500 Bundelas led by Bir Singh Bundela on August 12, at the instigation of Akbar's son Salim. Just before his death, the head was severed from the body and sent to Salim. Prince Salim set up independent Allahabad and sent an envoy to Akbar to negotiate peace. (See 1604.)

1604 Prince Salim's rebellion collapsed and a penitent Salim made his submission to the Emperor on January 4. (See 1602.)

Adi Granth Sahib of the Sikhs was brought from Ramsar Gurdwara and installed in the Golden Temple of Amritsar on August 27 at the dictates of their fifth Guru Arjun Dev with Bhai Buddha as the head granthi. It was written in verse in Gurumukhi script, now having 5,894 holy hymns (including 541 of Kabir), collected from the saintly teachers of various religions and sects. (See 1581.)

The Dutch made alliance with the Zamorin of Calicut for expulsion of the Portuguese from India, with a view to capture total pepper trade. Tobacco, unknown in India, was brought by the Portuguese and was introduced in Akbar's court.

1605 Emperor Akbar expired on October 17. Amongst the representatives of different creeds who congregated at Akbar's graveside, stood conspicuous in his simplicity, Jesuit priest Father Xavier (not St. Xavier), who always remained his devoted friend. Prince Salim sat on the throne on October 24 and took the title 'Jahangir'. (See 1542 and 1579.)

Inayatullah completed *Takmil - e-Akbari,* which was a continuation of Abul Fazl's *Akbarnama.*

1606 Prince Khusru rebelled against his father Jahangir and fled from Agra on April 6. He was pursued and captured on April 27. On May 1, handcuffed like an ordinary prisoner, he was brought to Lahore. By the Emperor's order hundreds of his followers were impaled alive in his presence.

Followers of Guru Nanak were massacred by Jahangir. Guru Arjun Dev, the fifth Sikh Guru, died on May 30 (b. 1563) after 5 days of torture by Jahangir, for having sympathy for prince Khusru. Guru Arjun's son Har Govind became the sixth Guru, who was the first to arm the Sikhs and to take revenge on the Muhammedans for his father's death.

1608 King James I of England sent William Hawkins, captain of the British ship Hector, to Jahangir. He reached Surat in August and met Jahangir an April 16, 1609 to obtain concessions for British trade in India. Hawkins was initially successful. Jahangir even forced him to marry an Armenian Christian girl out of his palace. But he had to leave Agra in November 1611 by the intrigue of the Portuguese. Hawkins died on his journey back to England.

A.D.

Tukaram, the Maratha ascetic, was born in Dehu village near Pune. Born of a lower caste as a businessman, he turned to a spiritual life. He enriched Marathi literature. (d. 1649).

1609 The Akal Takht (God's throne), a meeting place of the community, was erected in Amritsar by the sixth Sikh Guru Har Govind. The temple Harmandir Sahib was later named Golden Temple by the British. (See 1588 and 1805.)

1610 King of Chandragiri allowed the Dutch to have a settlement in Pulicat, which later became a chief slave trading centre.

1611 Jahangir married Meherunnisa, widow of Sher Afghan, on May 25. She received the title 'Noor Jahan', light of the world.

English settlements were established in Musalipatnam and Petapuli for the first time. (See 1626.)

The Portuguese established mints at Bassein and Daman. The mints were closed in 1739. (See 1643.)

United French East India Company, the second one, was formed.

Attar of roses is said to have been invented by Noor Jahan on the occasion of her marriage to Emperor Jahangir.

1612 Usman Khan Lohani, son of Isa Khan, was defeated in the battle of Nekujyal on March 12. He died of wounds and was the last of the independent rulers of Bengal. (See 1576 and 1600.)

Prince Khurram (later Shahjahan) was married on April 18 to Arjumand Banu Begum (later Mumtaz), daughter of Asaf Khan, the brother of Noor Jahan.

The East India Company's Marine, under the British, was formed on September 5 when the East India Company despatched a fleet of 4 small fighting ships – *Dragon, James, Osiander and Solomon* under the command of Capt. Thomas Best. The vessels arrived at Swally, the roadstead of Surat. (See 1686.)

The Portuguese attacked Pulicat and expelled the Dutch. By a convention in 1616 Pulicat went back to the Dutch.

The East India Company became a joint stock company. (See 1599 and 1617.)

Capt. Thomas Best with only two ships decisively defeated the Portuguese in a naval battle near Surat. Thereafter the Mughal governor of Surat and some of his officers spent an evening on the vessel of Capt. Thomas Best. He was thus the first Indian chief to partake English hospitality.

Danish East India Company was formed at Copenhagen. (See 1670.)

Coins bearing the name of Noor Jahan on the reverse, acknowledging her joint authority, were issued by Jahangir.

1613 Jahangir granted imperial firman to the East India Company to establish factories in Surat on January 11 and the first British factory was established there under Thomas Aldworth. (See 1687.)

Bir Singh Bundela of Orchha built Jhansi fort.

Jahangir was the only Muslim ruler to have his image on coins.

Akbar's tomb at Sikandra was completed. The construction was started by the emperor himself.

1614 In July Raja Man Singh of Amber died in Bidar in the Deccan. Sixty of his women were reported to have committed 'sati' in the funeral pyre.

Jahangir captured Mewar from Rana Amar Singh on February 18. A treaty was signed. The Rana and his son were treated with exceptional courtesies in the Mughal court on July 26.

Mira Bai expired. (b. 1567).

King of Spain ordered Portuguese viceroy of Goa to drive the English out of India by force.

1615 Thomas Roe, ambassador of James I of Britain, landed at Surat on September 18 and presented himself at Jahangir's court at Ajmer on January 10, 1616. He left India on February 17, 1618.

1616 The Dutch established a factory in Surat.

1617 The second Joint Stock Company of the East India Company was formed at London. (See 1612.)

Jahangir prohibited smoking tobacco. In spite of the order, people in Deccan, Gujarat and north India took a fancy for it.

1618 Thomas Roe, the British ambassador to Emperor Jahangir, left India on February 17 on his way back to England.

Mughal Emperor Aurangzeb was born at Dohad in Gujarat on October 24. (d. 1707).

A.D.

1620   Begum Rezabeebeh Sookeas, an Armenian, is the recorded first foreign lady to come to Calcutta. She expired on July 11, 1630.

Jahangir fell seriously ill and Noor Jahan took active charge of day-to-day administration of the empire.

Jahangir ordered to make the terraced garden Shalimar Bagh on the egde of Dal Lake. He was responsible for other magnificent gardens like Achabal, Verinag and Nishat Bag.

A Jat named Churu founded the town Churu in Bikaner.

1621   The ninth Sikh Guru Tegh Bahadur was born on April 12. (d. 1675).

The strong Kangra fort which resisted the onslaught of Akbar, surrendered to Jahangir on November 15 after an assault by Rai Rayan Vikramjit.

Prince Khusru was blinded by Jahangir.

1622   Prince Khusru died. He was perhaps murdered by Shahjahan.

1623   In April 1621 prince Shahryar got married to Noor Jahan's daughter Ladili by her first husband Sher Afghan. Prince Khurram (Shahjahan) was upset and he rebelled against Emperor Jahangir to prevent prince Shahryar getting the throne through Noorjahan's influence. Ultimately Shahjahan was defeated in the battle of Billochpur in March.

The great poet Tulsidas died at Varanasi on October 23. (b. 1532).

1625   The Dutch had their first settlement in Bengal at Chinsura.

1626   General Mahabat Khan feared his own downfall and took Jahangir and Noor Jahan as prisoners in March by a surprise move. Noor Jahan, after being in captivity with her husband for about six months, skilfully got the release of both in September.

The East India Company made a settlement in Aramgaon, which was their first fortified area in India. (See 1611.)

1627   Jahangir, weak from asthma and excessive drinks without food, died in Bhimbhar near Kashmir foothills on October 28. Since Shahjahan was in the Deccan then, he could not sit on the throne till February 4, 1628.

1628   Shahjahan was enthroned at Agra on February 4. (See 1627.) On the other hand Shahryar arrived at Lahore at the instance of his mother-in-law Noor Jahan and assumed the title of emperor. Being defeated he was thrown into prison and blinded. On Shahjahan's instruction Asaf Khan put to sword all the surviving male members of the royal house. Noor Jahan was pensioned off. She died in 1645.

1630 The seventh Sikh Guru Har Rai was born on February 5. (d. 1661).

Chhatrapati Shivaji, founder of the Maratha empire, was born on February 19 at Sivaner, Junner. The traditional date was April 6, 1627. (d. 1680).

1631 Mumtaz Begum died on June 7 at Burhanpur a few hours after the birth of a daughter. Mumtaz was married in 1612 and had given birth to eight sons and six daughters in 19 years.

Shahjahan expelled the Portuguese from their trading centre in Hooghly.

1632 Construction of Taj Mahal started as a mausoleum as well as the burial of Mumtaz (Arjumand Banu Begum). It was completed in 1653. Isa Effendi of Turkey was in charge of the construction and nearly 20,000 workers were employed. Experts were also brought from Europe.

Shahjahan forbade the building of new Hindu temples and ordered the demolition of any under construction, though he did not discriminate the Hindus in any other way.

Burton and Cartwright, two merchants, were the first Englishmen to come to Bengal. They stayed at Cuttack.

1633 On Mughal emperor's order indigo trade became a state monopoly. In 1636 normal trade was permitted, but imperial monopoly was reimposed again in 1655.

1634 The sacred Muslim relic, a hair from the beard of Prophet Muhammad, was brought from Medina to India by Syed Abdullah. It ultimately found its place in the newly constructed Hazratbal mosque in Kashmir, after its stints in Bijapur and Ajmer.

Shahjahan's famous peacock throne was completed by Bebadal Khan after seven years' labour. Shahjahan sat on that throne at Agra in March.

1636 Aurangzeb was appointed Viceroy of Deccan by Shahjahan on July 14. It ended in his dismissal in 1644.

1637 Diwan-i-Khas, the hall of private audience of Shahjahan in Delhi, was completed.

A.D.

1638 Shahjahan announced his desire to shift his capital from Agra to Delhi. (See 1646.)

Afzal Khan, Shahjahan's finance minister, died.

1639 Construction of Delhi's Red Fort started on April 29 and was completed on May 13, 1646.

Rajmahal (Akbarnagar), presently in Bihar, was made the capital of Bengal.

1640 Jean Baptist Tavernier came to India for the first time and then at intervals till 1667.

The British under Francis Day obtained permission from the ruler of Chandragiri on March 1 to establish a business centre in Madras. The name of the place gradually changed from Sri Ranga Raja Patnam to Chenna Patnam, then Madras Patnam, and lastly to Madras. But the fort was named St. George, which was later known as White Town. It was the first land to be held by the British in India. (See 1611, 1626 and 1726.)

The sixth Sikh Guru Har Govind had to leave Amritsar under the orders of Emperor Shahjahan. Sikhs were not allowed to visit Amritsar till 1708.

1641 The first Chogyal (ruler) of Sikkim was consecrated by the Lamas. (See 1975.)

1643 The Dutch opened another mint at Chaul. The mint was closed in 1740. (See 1611.)

1644 Construction of Jama Masjid of Delhi started. (See 1658.)

1645 Sikh Guru Har Govind passed away on March 28 (b. 1596). He nominated his grandson Har Rai as his successor and the seventh Sikh Guru.

Noor Jahan Begum, widow of Jahangir, died on December 17.

The Dutch established a factory at Kayal, south of Tuticorin. They also returned to Hooghly for business.

Gabriel Broughton, surgeon of ship Hopewell treated princess Jahanara Begum who was severely burnt. As a reward, Shahjahan granted Englishmen to trade throughout the Mughal empire free of any customs duty. She was more probably cured with a medicine prepared by a slave named Arif.

A.D.

1646 Shivaji started his adventurous career by capturing Torna fort from Bijapur at the age of 16.

The Red Fort of Delhi was completed on May 13. Ustad Hamid and Ustad Hira were the principal masons. (See 1639.)

Construction of Moti Masjid (Pearl Mosque) of Agra started. It was completed in 1653.

The capital was shifted from Agra to Delhi in a big procession along with Dara Shikoh. It was renamed Shahjahanabad which was the seventh Delhi capital and is presently known as Old Delhi. (See 1540 and 1911.)

1648 Shivaji raided Konkan area and plundered Mughal holdings. He imposed Sardeshmukhi (levy of 10 per cent) on the Mughal holdings to impose his authority.

1649 Saint Tukaram died. (b. 1608).

1650 *Padshahnama* was completed and dedicated to the emperor by Muhammad Amin Kaswini, comprising the history of the first ten years of Shahjahan's rule.

The East India Company made a settlement in Hooghly. Thus the Dutch and the English traded side by side in Hooghly.

The first adaptation of a Sanskrit work into a western language appeared. This was a collection of lyrics by the poet Bhartrihari, who died in 651. The adaptation was in fact a paraphrase in Dutch prose of a version in Portuguese.

The largest Indian diamond 'Great Mughal' was extracted from Kolar gold field. Its original weight was 785.5 carats. After cutting it was 280 carats.

1652 Construction of Se Cathedral at Goa with 80 mt long aisle and 14 alters, the largest church in India, was completed after 90 years.

1653 Taj Mahal was completed. It then cost more than Rs 4 crores and needed 500 kilos of gold. (See 1632.)

Madras was raised to the status of Presidency.

1655 Job Charnock, the so called founder of Calcutta, arrived in India. He obtained employment under the East India Company in Bengal as a junior member of the council at Kasimbazar, at a salary of £20 per annum. (See 1690 and 1693.)

A.D.

1656   The eighth Sikh Guru Har Kishan was born on July 14. (d. 1664).
Golconda was captured by Shahjahan under the command of his
son Aurangzeb.

1657   Dara Shikoh, the scholarly prince and a great admirer of Indian
culture completed the translation of sixty different *Upanishads* from
Sanskrit to Persian, before he got involved in the war of accession.
The western world came to know of the *Upanishads* when in 1801
Latin versions were printed of these Persian translations by a
Frenchman named Anquetil Duperron. (See 1270 B.C.)

On September 6 Shahjahan suddenly fell ill. His four sons Dara
Shikoh, Suja, Aurangzeb and Murad advanced towards Delhi to
capture the throne.

In Gujarat Murad proclaimed himself Emperor of India on
December 5. (See 1658.)

Raja Mukunda Rao founded the new city Bareilly. (See 1527.)

Indian tea was sold for the first time in England by Thomas
Garraway of London. It was then sold as a special drink. (See
1668 and 1861.)

1658   In the struggle for Delhi throne Suja, who crowned himself in
Rajmahal, was defeated by Dara Shikoh on February 14 in the
battle of Bahadurpur near Varanasi.

Jaswant Singh was sent by Shahjahan and Dara Shikoh to resist
Aurangzeb's advance towards Agra. But Jaswant Singh was
defeated at Dharmat on April 15. About 7,000 Rajput Rathors
sacrificed their lives for the emperor's cause.

Dara Shikoh in turn was utterly defeated by Aurangzeb on May 29
in the battle of Samugarh near Agra. Ten thousand supporters of
Dara fell in the fight which included nine Rajput and nineteen
Muslim imperial commandants of the highest rank. This battle really
decided the war of succession in favour of Aurangzeb.

Aurangzeb imprisoned Emperor Shahjahan in Agra fort on
June 8. Jahanara decided to remain with her father to share his
adversities. But Roshanara, who was greatly instrumental in
Aurangzeb's success, left the fort to join Aurangzeb in Delhi.

Murad was imprisoned by Aurangzeb on July 5. Aurangzeb all
along pretended that he wanted Murad to be the emperor, which

Murad believed to be true. Murad was invited in Aurangzeb's camp for formal announcement of accession. But Aurangzeb managed to put a pair of golden fetters on his ankles and at midnight he was packed off to Salimgarh fort in a closed Howdah on an elephant's back. (See 1661.)

Aurangzeb was informally enthroned on July 21. (See 1659.)

Jama Masjid, the largest mosque in the world, was completed, the construction of which was started by Shahjahan in 1644. The precincts are over 92 metre square and the minarets are 34 metre high and it has three snow-white marble domes.

Pratapgarh fort was constructed under Shivaji's instruction, which never fell.

1659 Suja was completely defeated by Aurangzeb in the battle of Khajwah on January 5. He was again defeated in Maksudabad near Malda on April 5. Suja left Bengal for Arakan in an Arakanese war vessel on May 12, 1660 and took refuge in Arakan capital Mrohang. Sandathudamma, the King of Arakan, barbarously murdered Suja and his whole family in 1661.

Dara Shikoh was finally defeated in the battle of Deorai on April 14.

Aurangzeb entered Delhi in May and his formal enthronement took place on June 5 with the title 'Alamgir'. (See 1658.)

On June 9, Dara Shikoh was treacherously handed over to Aurangzeb's army by Jiwan Khan, a Baluchi chief of Dadar, whose life was saved by Dara.

Dara Shikoh was beheaded on the order of Aurangzeb on August 30. It is reported that when Dara's head was taken to Aurangzeb, he put his foot on it and exclaimed, 'Behold the face of a would be emperor'. Aurangzeb then sent the severed head dressed in jewellery to Shahjahan in Agra fort. 'The trophy of war' was later hung on a pole outside the fort.

Shivaji killed Afzal Khan of Bijapur on November 10 near Pratapgarh fort by a clever but undignified move. It could be a preventive murder for Shivaji's own survival.

Muhammad Adil Shah of Adil Shahi dynasty expired. His mausoleum in Bijapur was built which is known as 'Gol Gombuz'.

Its great dome is 37.8 mt in diameter and 54.3 mt in height, the second largest in the world, being next to Vatican. The hall of the tomb is 41.2 mt square, covering an area of almost 1,704 sq mt which is the largest domed area, and the second largest floor area in the world.

1660 The famous Meenakshi temple of Madurai was consecrated.

1661 Medini Singh, Rajput prince of Garhwal, scared of Aurangzeb's threats, delivered Sulaiman Shikoh, the eldest son of Dara Shikoh, to the imperial force. On January 5 he was brought in chains to Aurangzeb's court and was imprisoned for life. He requested Aurangzeb to be spared of the usual loathsome beverage, causing a slow death. Aurangzeb took a solemn oath but never kept that oath. (See 1662.)

At the death of Guru Har Rai on November 8 (b. 1630) his second son Har Kishan became the eighth Sikh Guru at the age of 5 years 4 months. He died at the age of 7 years 9 months. (d. 1664).

After a mock trial for murder of Ali Naqi in 1657, Murad was beheaded on December 4 in Gwalior fort and was buried in the traitors' cemetery within its walls. (See 1658.)

On the occasion of the marriage of King Charles II of England with Princess Catherine de Braganza of Portugal on June 23, the British got Bombay as dowry from Portugal. But its occupation was withheld for four years on various pretences. King Charles II leased it out to the East India Company in 1668 for a loan of £5,00,000 at 6 per cent interest per annum for its upkeep and an annual rent of £10. (See 1665.)

1662 In March, Mir Jumla defeated the Ahom king Jayadeva Simha of Assam and entered Guwahati.

Dara Shikoh's handsome son Sulaiman Shikoh, who was captured by Aurangzeb in 1660 from Garhwal was beheaded in Gwalior fort in May. (See 1661.)

Aurangzeb got Dara's daughter Jani Begum married to his second son Azam. Dara's second son Siphir Shikoh was spared and was later married to the third daughter of Aurangzeb.

Francisco Xavier was canonised at Goa on December 2. (See 1542 and 1552.)

A.D.

1663 Cochin was captured by the Dutch.

1664 Shivaji started Surat campaign on January I and left Surat on January 9 after plundering the place. Thus for the first time the Indian and English troops came in direct conflict. (See 1670.)

Shivaji's father Shahuji died in January 23 after a fall while hunting. Shivaji took the title of Raja and began to mint coins in his own name.

Eighth Guru Har Kishan died of smallpox on April 6 (b. 1656) only at the age of 7 years 9 months in Delhi, where he was summoned by the Mughal emperor. Before his death Har Kishan nominated Tegh Bahadur, the second son of the sixth Guru Har Govind. He succeeded on August 11 at Bakala as the ninth Sikh Guru. Tegh Bahadur founded Anandpur in Punjab, the birthplace of the Khalsa, i.e., 'The Pure One'. (See 1699.)

Sultan of Bijapur granted land to the French to build Pondicherry, 'The New City'. (See 1673.)

A French East India Company namely 'La Campagine des Indes Orientales' was formed by Jean Baptiste Colbert.

Aurangzeb prohibited repairs of Hindu shrines and temples.

The first modern hospital was established at Fort St. George in Madras.

1665 After a siege for two months and outer fortifications destroyed from Mughal gunfire, Shivaji virtually surrendered at Purandhar fort. Treaty of Purandhar was signed on September 4 between Raja Jai Singh for the Mughals and Shivaji. It was an extremely humiliating treaty since Shivaji had to give up control of 23 forts to Aurangzeb and was allowed to retain only 12 minor ones. (See 1666.)

British got hold of Bombay. Humphrey Cooke signed the instruments of surrender in the house of Lady D. Ignez Miranda. (See 1661 and 1676.)

1666 On January 22, Shahjahan died in Agra fort as a state prisoner. Jahanara arranged that Shahjahan be laid to rest beside Mumtaz in Taj Mahal.

Shivaji arrived at Agra on May 12 as a part of Treaty of Purandhar. (See 1665.) Aurangzeb put Shivaji and his six-year old son

A.D.

Sambhaji under house arrest in Agra. Shivaji and Sambhaji escaped in two baskets of sweets on August 19. Shivaji returned to Raigarh on November 20 after pilgrimage to Varanasi and Gaya, with a view to avoid detection. Sambhaji was kept at Mathura under the care of three Deccani Brahmins – Kashi, Visaji and Krishnaji.

The tenth Sikh Guru Gobind Singh was born in Patna on December 26. (d. 1708).

1667   Aurangzeb was persuaded by his court to grant Raja title to Shivaji.

Aurangzeb abolished customs duty on Muslims, while that on the Hindus remained.

The Danes established a factory in Bengal.

The British East India Company established its independent port at Bombay.

1668   The first French factory and settlement were established at Surat by Francois Caron.

The first British Regiment namely '1st British European Regiment' was formed in India.

The first official consignment of Indian tea reached Britain after the East India company ordered for 100 lbs of best tea from India. (See 1657.)

Aurangzeb prohibited all Hindu religious fairs.

1669   Aurangzeb issued a general order on April 9 to the provincial governors to demolish all the schools and temples of the infidels. As a result temples of Varanasi, including that of Viswanath, were destroyed. (See 1776.)

Bengal Pilot Service was established at Hooghly to guide the ocean-going vessels to Hooghly port through the Hooghly river. The work started with a small vessel called the Diligence built in 1667 by the East India Company.

There was a serious uprising of Jats near Mathura under the leadership of Gokla of Tilpat. The rising was suppressed by Hasan Ali Khan. Gokla was captured and cut to pieces.

The blackstone Srinathji's image was brought to Nathdwara near Udaipur from Mathura to protect it from Aurangzeb's destructive impulses. (See 1497.)

A.D.

1670 Aggrieved at the destruction of Viswanath temple of Varanasi by Aurangzeb, Shivaji captured the prestigious Mughal fort Singhagarh on February 17 but he suffered the loss of his best comrade Tanaji Malusare. The Maratha troops climbed up the rock with the help of a rope ladder tied to the tail of a huge reptile trained for the job. The reptile was named Yashwanti by Shivaji which proved its prowess in no less than twenty-seven similar exploits. (See 1703.)

Shivaji plundered Surat from October 3 to 5 for the second time (see 1664). He collected huge ransom from the French and the Dutch, but very little from the British, because of the valour shown by them. Bohra Muslims had to pay a ransom far in excess of the others.

Aurangzeb ordered the destruction of the great Keshava Deva temple of Mathura. It was built by Bir Singh Bundela of Orchha during the reign of Jahangir, at the cost of Rs 33 lakhs. Aurangzeb ordered to erect a mosque at the site.

A second Danish East India Company was formed. (See 1612.)

1671 The naval port of Jinjeera of Bijapur was handed over to the Mughals. Aurangzeb ordered dismissal of all Hindu head clerks and accountants from service. (See 1677.)

1672 Court of Judicature was set up as directed by the East India Company and English law was for the first time introduced in India on August 1.

Satnami, a peaceful Hindu sect of Patiala and Alwar, region revolted and was ruthlessly suppressed by Aurangzeb. Very few escaped the slaughter.

Aurangzeb sent a powerful army of 40,000 men under Mahabat Khan against the Marathas. Mahabat was accompanied by 400 Afghan and Punjabi dancing girls. The army attacked the fortress of Salhir. Shivaji's army, under the able guidance of Moro Pant Pingle and Pratap Rao Gujar, completely routed the imperial army. Only 2,000 of 40,000 strong army could escape with Mahabat Khan. About 125 elephants, 6,000 horses and the entire supplies of Mughal army fell in the hands of the victors.

1673 Pondicherry was founded by Francois Martin (French) and ultimately it became the capital of French settlements in India. The mercurial history of Pondicherry had a constant background

A.D.

to the history of the East India Company. Its possession changed hands several times: 1683-93 French; 1693-97 Dutch; 1697-1761 French; 1761-63 British; 1763-78 French; 1778-83 British; 1783-93 French; 1793-1802 British; 1802-3 French; 1803-16 British; 1816-1954 French; 1954 within the Union of India. (See 1664.)

1674 Shivaji was crowned in Raigarh fort on June 6 to prove his sovereignty. He took the title 'Chhatrapati'. Henry Oxinden of Bombay was present as the representative of the East India Company. Ganga Bhatta, the renowned Brahmin Pandit of Varanasi, who was on a pilgrimage to Deccan, was invited by Shivaji to consecrate him as the lawful sovereign of Maharashtra, which the saintly and learned Pandit agreed. On July 12 a treaty of friendship was signed between Shivaji and the East India Company, who were allowed to establish factories at Hubli and Rajapur.

Death penalty was imposed by the East India Company for theft. (See 1677.)

A group of the British forces mutinied. It was suppressed. Corporal Fake was shot after court-martial and Capt. Shaxton was deported to England.

1675 Guru Tegh Bahadur, the ninth Sikh Guru (b. 1621), after five days of unspeakable torture, was beheaded on December 13 in Delhi by Aurangzeb for his refusal to embrace Islam. The site of his execution in Chandni Chowk of Delhi is marked by Sis Ganj Gurdwara (the place of the head). The site of cremation of Guru's body is Rikab Ganj, which is next door to Parliament House. The place where the head was cremated in Anandpur is also known as Sis Ganj. Guru Gobind became the tenth and last Guru in mortal frame. (See 1699.)

1676 The East India Company got the authority from the King of England on October 5 to mint coins in Bombay named 'rupee' and 'pice', and the first coin was minted there in 1678. (See 1542.)

1677 Shivaji arrived at Hyderabad in February when Abul Hasan Tana Shah, the monarch of Golconda, received him honourably and the two signed a treaty of defensive and offensive alliance against the Mughals. Shivaji then proceeded further south to capture Jinjee fort. He also captured Vellore fortress.

Aurangzeb stopped recruitment of the Hindus in public service. (See 1671.)

Aurangzeb poisoned to death his own son Muhammad Sultan, about 38 years old, whom he felt could not be trusted.

The East India Company disapproved death penalty for theft. (See 1674.)

1678 Rajputs revolted against Aurangzeb for the persecution of the Hindus. Aurangzeb's son prince Akbar went over to the Rajputs. (See 1681.)

Aurangzeb ordered destruction of temples in hill states.

Designation of Chief Justice was introduced in India by the British.

1679 The Jeziya tax, abolished by Akbar, was reimposed on the Hindus on April 2 by Aurangzeb to finance the spread of Islam. (See 1564.)

Aurangzeb attacked Bijapur ruled by Dilir Khan. Shivaji came to Bijapur's rescue. But his son Sambhaji went over to the Mughals and later came back to Shivaji again in November.

1680 Shivaji died at Rairi i.e. Raigarh fort on April 3. His son Sambhaji succeeded to the throne in May. (b. 1630). In Raigarh fort a mausoleum was constructed at the spot where Shivaji was cremated. Facing it a pillar was erected in memory of his favorite dog Vaghya, who apparently jumped to his master's burning funeral pyre and thereby met his death.

The elegant Rana Raj Singh of Mewar who put up a heroic resistance against the Mughal attack in June unexpectedly died on October 22. He was succeeded by his eldest son Jai Singh.

The East India Company established a trading centre in Calcutta.

St. Mary's Church was built in Madras. It was the first church in India and perhaps in Asia which was open to all. The church was financed by Elihu Yale in whose name the famous Ivy League Yale University of U.S.A. was established. Robert Clive got married in this church in 1735. The painting 'Last Supper' in the church is believed to be the work of the pupils of Raphael, in which he put his finishing touch. (See 1687.)

1681 Shivaji's son Sambhaji's coronation was held at Raigarh fort on January 16. (See 1680.)

Prince Akbar again revolted against his father Aurangzeb and fled to Sambhaji for protection. He left Sambhaji's court in 1688 for Persia where he died in 1706. (See 1678.)

A.D.

1682 By an order of November 14, 1681 of the East India Company, Bengal was made into a Presidency on July 17, 1682 independent of Madras.

Aurangzeb, for the first time, took the field against Sambhaji, son of Shivaji.

Slave trade was prohibited in Madras by the British. It was resumed in 1687 for a short spell and was again prohibited in the same year.

1683 The Charter of August 9 issued by the British Crown authorised the Company full power to declare and make war and peace with any of the nations in Asia, and to recruit such military forces as necessary.

1684 Aurangzeb sent his son prince Muazzam to conquer Konkan. He wreaked destruction all the way and reached Goa. Then he had to retreat to Ahmadnagar suffering from hunger and pestilence.

The Portuguese established a mint in Diu which functioned irregularly till 1859.

1685 The East India Company obtained approval from King James II so that the British could exert their own rights in India.

1686 Aurangzeb attacked Bijapur. Mudhuna Pant, the Maratha Brahmin minister of Bijapur, betrayed and went over to the Mughals. He was later assassinated in a people's uprising. A peace treaty was signed on October 15 between Aurangzeb and Bijapur. (See 1687.)

Job Charnock left Hooghly on December 20 after a skirmish with the Mughal troops and founded the first settlement at Sutanuti in Calcutta. But in 1688 he had to abandon it for a short period. (See 1690.)

King James II granted a Charter to the East India Company to establish a mint in Madras.

The East India Company's naval establishment changed its name to Bombay Marine (see 1612). The name changed several times thereafter to Indian Navy, His Majesty's Indian Marine, The Royal Indian Marine, The Royal Indian Navy. Since India's independence it is known as the Indian Navy. (See 1948.)

1687 Aurangzeb annexed Golconda on September 30 from the Qutub Shahi Sultan Tana Shah through the treachery of his General Panni. (See 1512.)

Madras was the first Presidency to be chartered on December 11 for a Municipal Corporation with a Mayor's Court. (See 1726.)

The Headquarters of the East India Company in western India was shifted from Surat to Bombay. (See 1613.)

Elihu Yale became the Governor of Fort St. George in Madras for five years. (See 1680.)

Inspite of the peace treaty signed with Bijapur in 1686, Aurangzeb again attacked Bijapur on the pretext that the Muslim ruler there committed a crime by employing a Hindu minister. After seven months' resistance Bijapur surrendered. With that 197 year old Adil Shahi dynasty of Bijapur extinguished.

1688   The French East India Company got the sanction from Aurangzeb to establish a settlement in Chandernagar of West Bengal. But it did not have the Charter of the French government. (See 1719 and 1951.)

As a result of dispute with the Mughal governor of Bengal the British left Bengal and went to Madras. (See 1690.)

In Bombay the East India Company enrolled two companies of Rajput soldiers, one hundred in each and were put under the command of their own Indian officers. Perhaps that was the first build-up of an Indian Army by the Company.

The first mention of the name Calcutta (later Kolkata), is found in the letter of Charles Eyre and Roger Braddyll to Job Charnock from Dacca on June 22. (See 2000.)

Shivaji's son Sambhaji was captured by Aurangzeb on December 28, while he was awakening from a drunken slumber at Sangameswar. Sambhaji's Brahmin adviser Kavi Kailash tried to defend single-handedly. He was severely wounded and both were taken prisoners.

1689   Sambhaji and his adviser Kavi Kailash dressed as buffoons, carrying rattles in their hands and chained to the camels, were paraded through the streets. They were brought before Aurangzeb at Tulapur, sixteen miles from Pune. The emperor gave the choice to Sambhaji either to accept Islam or death. Sambhaji regained his pride and regardless of consequences stated that on the day when the emperor would bestow upon him his daughter's hand in marriage, he would accept the faith of the prophet. Aurangzeb in a

A.D.

frenzy of vindictiveness ordered in the presence of the entire court that both Sambhaji and Kavi Kailash should be blinded, their tongues cut and then to be beheaded, which was done on March 11. Their heads were paraded as trophies in each Deccan city and their bodies thrown as food to the pariah dogs.

On October 19 Raigarh surrendered with Sambhaji's queen Jesubai and her child. Aurangzeb ordered the child to be brought up in Islamic faith. But at the request of the emperor's second unmarried daughter Zinnatunnisa, the emperor for the only time on record, yielded to a gentler emotion and named him Shahu or 'The good one'. (See 1708.)

1690 The British reconciled with the Mughal emperor and the city of Calcutta was founded by Job Charnock on August 24 in Sutanuti village. That happened on his third attempt. (See 1688 and 1698.)

The French laid the foundation stone of their famous settlement Chandernagar on a site granted by Shyesta Khan. (See 1949 and 1950.)

1691 Being continuously oppressed by the Mughals and to avenge the destruction of Keshava Dev temple at Mathura by Aurangzeb, the Jats under Raja Ram Singh attacked Akbar's mausoleum in Sikandra. Apart from looting it, they dragged out the bones of Akbar and burnt them.

Job Charnock established the first English factory in Calcutta on February 10.

1693 Job Charnock, founder of Calcutta, died in the same city on January 10 and he was laid to rest. The tombstone reads 1692, since there was the old practice of the new year beginning in April. His tombstone was made of Charnockite granite named after him. Reputedly it is the oldest masonry structure above ground level in Calcutta. (See 1655 and 1690.)

The Company got the grant of three villages adjoining Madras. In 1708 three other villages were added. In 1717 Emperor Farrukhsiyar confirmed rights of these village on the British Embassy of John Surman and Edward Stephenson.

Raja Jai Singh's observatory was built in Varanasi.

A.D.

1694 Madan Mohan temple of Bishnupur was consecrated by Malla King Durjan Singh. It is the most exquisite terracotta temple of India. (See 694 and 1587.)

1695 In May Aurangzeb forbade all Hindus, except Rajputs, to ride palanquins, elephants, thoroughbred horses and to carry arms.

1696 A fort was built in Calcutta by the British and was named Fort William to give compliment to the ruling British monarch. This fort was demolished later and the present fort was built in 1773. (See 1757.)

1697 The worst Muslim desecration of Jagannath temple of Puri took place on May 17 at the instance of Aurangzeb. (See 1131.)

1698 Jinjee fort, the seat of Maratha power, fell to Aurangzeb on February 17 after eight-year siege. Raja Ram, the Regent, escaped and selected Satara as his capital.

A rival East India Company was formed in England on September 5 with the approval of the House of Commons, under the style – 'The English Company Trading to the East Indies' (See 1599 and 1702.)

Prince Azim-us-Shah, subedar of Bengal and grandson of Aurangzeb, authorised the East India Company on November 10, the rights to collect revenue of three villages Kalikata, Sutanuti and Govindapur for a sum of Rs 1,300 only from Mohandev, Rambhadra, Ramchand Roy Chowdhuri and others of Sarbana sect of Barisha, These three villages formed the nucleus of present-day Kolkata. (See 1690.)

1699 Maharaja Jai Singh II of Jaipur sat on Amber throne on March 5. (See 1727 and 1743.)

On April 13 Guru Govind Singh baptised the first five chosen followers (Panch Pyare) at Anandpur Sahib in Punjab, to form the core of Khalsa (order of the pure) and were given five distinguishing characteristics – *kesh* (unshorn hair), *kangha* (comb), *kara* (steel bangle), *kachha* (shorts), and *kirpan* (sword). They were given the suffix 'Singh' meaning lion. They were named Dayaram Singh, Dharamdas Singh, Himmatrai Singh, Mokham Chand Singh and Sahib Chand Singh. He himself also followed the same characteristics and suffix. (d. 1708. See 1596.).

A.D.

Raja Ram at the head of 60,000 soldiers took offensive against the Mughals. Pune, Nasik and the entire Godavari valley were recovered by the Marathas.

Calcutta became the seat of Presidency and Charles Eyre was appointed resident of Fort William.

Aurangzeb prohibited 'sati' throughout the Mughal empire. (See 1829.)

1700 Raja Ram died of smallpox at Singhagarh on March 2. He was succeeded by his infant son Shivaji III. The Regency was taken up by Raja Ram's masterful widow Tara Bai, who led the Maratha counter-offensives against the Mughals. (See 1761.)

Belvedere House of Calcutta, later the National Library, was built by Prince Azim-us-Shah. It later became the residence of the Governor General of Bengal in 1802.

1701 John Norris, representative of King William III of Britain, had an audience with Emperor Aurangzeb at Parnela in South India on April 28. Norris came in a grand procession with immense attractive presents to impress upon Aurangzeb about William's prosperity.

1702 The old and new East India Company united on July 22 and was named 'United Company of Merchants of England Trading to the East Indies'. This name finally changed to the East India Company in 1833. (See 1698.)

Mir Zafar, son of a poor Brahmin of Deccan, purchased by a Persian merchant and converted into Islam, was appointed Dewan of Bengal in 1700 and eventually in 1704 made the viceroy of Bengal, Bihar and Orissa by Aurangzeb with the title Murshid Quli Khan. He founded Murshidabad the new capital of Bengal. (See 1706.)

1703 The Mughal army captured Singhagarh. (See 1670.)

1705 On February 8 Aurangzeb had his last campaign to siege the fortress of Wagingera which resisted violently. When on April 27 Aurangzeb's army entered the stronghold, they found it completely empty. The defenders escaped through a tunnel at night to join their Maratha allies. The emperor was forced to drink a cup of bitter humiliation.

1706 The French governor general and founder of Pondicherry Francois Martin died on December 30. (See 1673.)

The Danes sent the first Christian missionary Bartholomew Zeigenbalg, a Protestant, who confessed that his mission had little success.

Murshid Kuli Khan shifted capital of Bengal from Dacca to Murshidabad. (See 1717.)

Somnath temple was razed to the ground for the seventh and the last time by Aurangzeb. (See 1783 and 1951.)

1707 Aurangzeb died at Ahmadnagar on February 20. A testament was found under his pillow in which he made a division of his empire amongst his sons in a futile attempt to prevent fraticidal struggle. His son prince Muazzam (Shah Alam) succeeded to the throne on March 3 as Bahadur Shah I. But his second brother prince Azam opposed him. Bahadur Shah I fought a decisive battle on June 8 against his second brother near Jajau, south of Agra. Azam lost his life along with his two sons. Later Bahadur Shah I had to fight his third brother Kam Bakhsh at Hyderabad on January 13, 1709. Kam Bakhsh died of wounds.

In the fratricidal struggle of the Mughal princes the Jat leader Churaman Singh promised support to one party but looted the camps of both the princes.

Badan Singh succeeded the leadership of the Jats and did not approve the double-dealing of Churaman Singh. He laid the foundation of a new ruling house of Bharatpur, which was later consolidated by Maharaj Surajmal, born in the same year 1707. (See 1753 and 1763.)

1708 Shahu, son of Sambhaji, entered Satara after being released by Aurangzeb's son Azam in the previous year. Shahu was crowned as the Maratha ruler on January 12. On the other hand Tara Bai, Raja Ram's widow and Regent for Shivaji III, declared Shahu as an impostor. Thus a civil war began amongst the Marathas. (See 1689 and 1712.)

After the unfortunate stabbing on September 19 by an Afghan assassin Gul Khan, the tenth Sikh Guru Govind Singh died at Nanded on October 7 (b. 1666). Banda Bahadur Bairagi, also known as Lachman Das, became the temporal leader of the Sikhs and captured Amritsar from the Mughals. The Holy *Granth Sahib* was since then considered as the representative of the Sikh Gurus. (See 1716.)

A.D.

1709 Bahadur Shah I (Shah Alam I) defeated his third brother Kam
Bakhsh at Hyderabad on January 13 and consolidated his position
as the Mughal emperor. Kam Bakhsh and his two sons were killed
in the clash.

1712 Bahadur Shah I died at Lahore on February 28 at the age of 72.
His four sons fought for the throne and the only survivor took the
throne on April 20 as Jahandar Shah. He put to death all the princes
of royal blood. Only his nephew Farrukhsiyar escaped the massacre
since he was away in Bengal. (See 1713.)

Shivaji III, son of Raja Ram and Tara Bai, died young. His other
brother Sambhaji was put on Kolhapur throne. There were two
Maratha royalties – one at Satara and the other at Kolhapur. (See
1708 and 1713.)

1713 Farrukhsiyar captured the throne of Delhi from Jahandar Shah with
the assistance of two Sayyid brothers namely Hussain Ali Khan
and Abdulla Khan. Jahandar Shah was strangled to death on
February 13, 1719. (See 1712.)

Balaji Viswanath, a very remarkable man in Maratha history, was
appointed Peshwa on November 16 by Shahu. Since then Shahu's
ascendancy was secured. (See 1708.)

The first book printed in an Indian language from moulded types
came out in Tamil language. (See 1557.)

1715 The first Christian church in Calcutta was built, the steeple of which
fell in 1737. The church was destroyed in 1756 by the troops of
Siraj-ud-daula. The present St. John's Church built in 1787 stands
at the same place. (See 1784.)

Asaf Jah established himself as the subedar of the Deccan and
later became the viceroy of the Mughal emperor and the first Nizam
of Hyderabad. (See 1724.)

Sikh chief Banda Bahadur Bairagi surrendered at Gurdaspur on
December 17 to the Mughal army of Farrukhsiyar. (See 1716.)

1716 Sikh chief Banda Bahadur Bairagi was brought to Delhi in chains
at the end of February along with over seven hundred followers.
The execution of the followers began on March 5 and continued
for about a week. Lastly on June 19 Banda was first offered pardon
if he renounced his faith and accepted Islam. On his refusal to do

A.D.

so, his four year old son Ajai Singh was hacked to bits before his eyes. It was followed by the execution of Banda, five of his commanders and another batch of Sikh prisoners. (See 1715.)

Rana Sangram Singh II became the ruler of Mewar. He was an able opponent of Mughal ruler Muhammad Shah, and dismemberment of the Mughal empire started.

1717 J. Surman got the 'Firman' from Farrukhsiyar for acquisition of 24 Parganas of Bengal by the Company and the right of free trade in Bengal. Surman also got the rights of six villages around Madras. (See 1690 and 1693.)

Peshwa Balaji Viswanath tried to re-establish the Maratha power. He conducted Maratha convention and Shahu was acknowledged as the independent sovereign of the Marathas. (See 1730.)

Murshid Quli Khan became the first Nawab of Bengal. (See 1702.)

1718 Hussain Ali Khan, with the backing of the Marathas, marched to Delhi from Deccan. Farrukhsiyar was caught, blinded and privately assassinated ignominiously on February 19, 1719 by the Sayyid brothers.

1719 Two puppets were successively put on the throne of Delhi by the Sayyid brothers and probably killed soon after. Then Rustam Khan, grandson of Aurangzeb, was made the emperor with the title Muhammad Shah. He was the last real emperor of India of any authority. (See 1713.)

Murshid Quli Khan, governor of Bengal, got virtually an independent status. (See 1702 and 1717.)

France gave a charter to the French East India Company for the first time for trade with India. Between 1604 and 1719 the French sent five trading companies to India, but none got the charter of the French govt. (See 1688.)

1720 Peshwa Balaji Viswanath died on April 2 and was succeeded by his son Baji Rao I on April 21. Baji Rao I was a great soldier and general.

Muhammad Shah murdered Hussain Ali Sayyid, but spared the life of the other brother Abdulla Khan Sayyid, who was imprisoned and poisoned to death in 1721. Muhammad Shah then became a free monarch.

A.D.

Jai Singh II of Jaipur commissioned the largest cannon Jaivana of 6.09 mt barrel, 81.44 cm diameter, weighing 50 tonnes. The cannon had a firing range of a 100 kg cannon ball up to 35 km. It was test-fired only once and that too with a 50 kg ball.

1721 Cricket was played for the first time in India at Cambay of Gujarat between two groups of British sailors. (See 1802, 1886 and 1926.)

Hyder Ali was born in Budi Kota village in Kolar district of Maharashtra. (d. 1782).

1722 Bharatpur, popularly known as Lohagarh, was founded by Maharaja Badan Singh, the Jat ruler.

Calcutta Police Force as a separate body, was formed by J.Z. Holwell. Interestingly London Police Force came into existence hundred years later in 1822.

Joseph Francious Dupleix, the greatest enemy of the East India Company ever in India, arrived from France.

'Nawab of Oudh' family was established by Sadat Khan, a Khorasan merchant. The dynasty ended in 1856.

1724 Mir Qumar-ud-din Chin Kilich Khan defeated the Mughal viceroy of Deccan in the battle of Shakarkheta. The Mughal Emperor Muhammad Shah gave him the title Asaf Jah, who established independent Nizam dynasty of Hyderabad. He died in 1748. (See 1715.)

1725 Murshid Quli Khan of Murshidabad died and was succeeded by his son-in-law Suja-ud-Daula, who destroyed Ostend East India Company of Germany in Banki Bazar near Barrackpore on the Hooghly river opposite Chandernagar.

The Jantar Mantar observatory of Delhi was the first one built by Maharaja Jai Singh II of Jaipur. This consists of six huge instruments in masonry which were devised to study the movement of the sun, the moon and the planets. In all he established five observatories in Delhi, Jaipur, Mathura, Ujjain and Varanasi. The one in Jaipur is the largest one. (See 1728.)

1726 King George I of England empowered the Company on September 24 to establish Municipal Corporations and Mayor's courts in Bombay and Calcutta. Calcutta Mayor's court existed till 1774. (See 1687.)

A.D.

1727 Jaipur city was founded by Maharaja Jai Singh II of Amber on November 18. Vidyadhar Chakraborty of Bengal was the architect of the first planned city in India, which he took eight years to build and was based on the Hindu treatise *Shilpa Shastra.* (See 1743.)

1728 Jai Singh's astronomical tables were completely based on his own observations for seven years. His observatories were also based on his own calculations. Jaipur has the biggest sun-dial (Samrat Yantra) in the world with an accuracy of 15 seconds. (See 1725.)

1729 The first Freemasons' Lodge of India was established in Calcutta Fort William by Mr George Pomfret. The oldest lodge still functioning in 2005 is Lodge Star in the East Calcutta which was established in 1740 under the English constitution and the oldest outside the U.K. The oldest lodge under the Indian constitution is Lodge Anchor and Hope which was established in 1773 and has its pride of position as No. 1 in the register of Grand Lodge of India. (See 1961.)

Dupleix became the governor of Chandernagar.

1730 Shahu defeated Sambhaji and was acclaimed as the ruler of the entire Maratha territory, except a small area around Kolhapur. (See 1717.)

1731 The Swedish East India Company was formed on June 13 at the instance of King Fredrick of Sweden, who gave the Company a charter for 15 years.

King John V of Portugal formed a temporary Portuguese East India Company.

1732 Warren Hastings, the first governor of East India Co. in India, was born on December 6 in Churchill village of Oxfordshire in U. K. Surprisingly it was Winston Churchill, the then prime minister of U. K. in whose time serious negotiations started about India's independence, which happened two years later in 1947.

1733 Mughals captured Tripura. (See 1808.)

1736 Bombay Council decided to make a ship-building yard in Bombay under the control of Navji Nusserwanji Wadia, who came from Surat. Wadia is a distorted Gujarati word Vadia meaning ship-builder.

1737 The worst cyclone on record in India hit Calcutta on October 11 and 12 which was accompanied by a 12 metre high tidal wave as well as a violent earthquake. It took a toll of 300,000 lives and 20,000 vessels were cast away. (See 1999.)

A.D.

Nizam was defeated by Baji Rao I and the Marathas appeared as the paramount power in India. Baji Rao I marched up to Delhi.

1738   Suja-ud-daula died. Sarfaraj Khan became the governor of Bengal. But he was an incapable person. (See 1725 and 1740.)

Nadir Shah Quli, a Persian Turk, entered India in November.

1739   Nadir Shah entered Delhi. On March 22 enraged at the assassination of one of his soldiers, he gave the signal of the infamous general massacre of Delhi from Sunheri mosque. The massacre and pillage continued for 58 days in which 20,000 citizens perished. He returned to Persia with Shahjahan's famous peacock throne and Kohinoor diamond. His invasion left the Mughal empire bleeding and prostrate. The Mughal army virtually disintegrated thereafter. There is no trace of the peacock throne anywhere in the world. Afghanistan was separated from the Indian empire as a result of a treaty signed on May 26 between the Mughal Emperor Muhammad Shah and Nadir Shah.

Karikal was founded by the French.

1740   Peshwa Baji Rao I died on April 28 on the bank of the Narmada river near Khargon and his son Balaji Baji Rao was placed on his father's seat as the Peshwa.

Ali Bardi Khan, Sarfaraj Khan's brother and assistant in Bihar, ousted Sarfaraj in the battle of Giria on May 20 and captured the throne of Murshidabad. Ali Bardi was recognised as the viceroy of Bengal, Bihar and Orissa by the Mughal emperor. (See 1738.)

1741   The Marathas from Berar, also known as 'Bargis', started pillaging Bengal under Bhaskar Pandit for almost ten years and caused a lot of damage in Bengal. (See 1742 and 1744.)

1742   Nana Phadnavis, the Maratha master-diplomat, was born on February 12.

Nawab Ali Bardi Khan of Murshidabad gave permission to the British to dig a ditch around Calcutta, renowned as 'Maratha ditch' to protect the citizens of Calcutta from the 'Bargis'. Later the filled ditch was called 'Circular Road'. (See 1741 and 1744.)

Dupleix became the governor of Pondicherry ruling from Chandernagar. (See 1754.)

A.D.

The first Carnatic war began between the British and the French for supremacy in the south. It lasted for nearly six years. (See 1750.)

1743 Jai Singh II, the founder of Jaipur city and the most renowned ruler of Jaipur, died. (See 1699 and 1727.)

1744 Bhaskar Pandit, under whose leadership the Maratha 'Bargis' were pillaging Bengal, was invited by Ali Bardi Khan, the Nawab of Murshidabad, for a discussion. Bhaskar Pandit along with his nineteen officers were treacherously slaughtered. (See 1741, 1742 and 1745.)

Robert Clive entered the services of the East India Company. (See 1765 and 1767.)

1745 Raghoji Bhonsle of the Marathas pillaged Orissa and the most of Burdwan, as a reprisal of Bhaskar Pandit's murder. (See 1744.)

1746 De La Bourdonnais of France captured Madras from the British. (See 1748.)

1747 Ahmad Shah Abdali (Durrani) of Afghanistan entered India for the first time. He was opposed by the Mughal Emperor Muhammad Shah's son, also named as Ahmad Shah. Abdali invaded India for the ninth and the last time in 1767.

1748 Mughal Emperor Muhammad Shah died on April 27, succeeded by his son Ahmad Shah.

Nizam Asaf Jah, the ruler of Hyderabad and the mighty opponent of the Marathas, died in June.

On July 29 Admiral Edward Boscawen landed at Fort David, 25 km south of Pondicherry, to help the East India Company to fight the French. With him came a force of royal troops of British government. These were the first troops of the British army to serve in India for the British Crown, mainly against the French. (See 1948.)

Peace was declared between England and France after the war in Europe, on the basis of restitution of all gains in India to each other. Madras once again flew the English flag. (See 1746 and 1758.)

1749 Chatrapati Shahu, grandson of Shivaji, died on December 15. Raja Ram, a posthumous son of Shivaji II, was brought to Satara and solemnly crowned. (See 1750.)

A.D.

1750   Warren Hastings landed at Calcutta for the first time in January at the age of eighteen as a civil servant of the East India Company.

The second Carnatic war started and continued till 1754. (See 1742.)

Raja Ram was brought from Satara to Pune by Sangola Agreement. The chief offices of Maratha state were vested in Peshwa, who became the de facto Maratha ruler. Pune became the capital of Maratha empire instead of Satara.(See 1749.)

Tipu, son of Hyder Ali, was born at Devanhalli village near Bangalore on November 20. (d. 1799).

1751   Clive exhibited a heroic feat in capturing Arcot on August 30 from Chanda Saheb. The fame of English valour spread throughout India. (See 1752.)

Ahmad Shah Abdali (Durrani) of Afghanistan invaded India for the second time and annexed Punjab and Sind to Afghanistan.

A brilliant French leader Bussy started dominating affairs in Nizam's territory in Hyderabad until he was recalled by the French Governor Lally in 1758.

1752   Chanda Saheb, Nawab of Arcot, was finally defeated in the battle of Tiruchirapalli. After his surrender he was executed by the British forces under Clive. (See 1751.)

Ahmad Shah Abdali of Afghanistan invaded India for the third time and captured Kashmir. (See 1819.)

Gregorian calendar came to be used throughout Britain and the British Dominions. The date lag since 1582 was covered by naming the day after September 2, 1752 as September 14. Earlier in 1582 Pope Gregory XIII changed the Julian calendar introduced by Julius Caesar of Rome to the Gregorian calendar, when October 5 became October 15 and every fourth year a leap year.

1753   Maharaja Surajmal made himself rich by plundering Delhi between May 9 and June 4. His vandalism eclipsed those committed by Ahmad Shah Abdali. He became the richest potentate in the 18th century India. (See 1707 and 1756.)

The Nawab of Oudh virtually became independent of Mughal rule. (See 1856.)

Siraj-ud-daula was formally declared Ali Bardi Khan's successor in Bengal. He manifested a rather cruel disposition in his use of power. (See 1756.)

The poet Bharat Chandra Roy of Krishnagar wrote Annada Mangal in Bengali. It was a triology of three practically independent books.

1754 Dupleix left India in September. (See 1742.)

First Nizam of Hyderabad's grandson Sahabuddin, son of Emperor Jahandar Shah, more known as Gaziuddin, deposed and blinded Delhi Emperor Ahmad Shah as well as his mother. He took the throne with the title Alamgir II and became entirely independent of the Marathas.

1755 The principal Danish settlement was established in Serampore near Calcutta. (See 1845.)

1756 Ali Bardi Khan of Bengal died in Murshidabad on April 9. His youngest daughter's son Siraj-ud-daula succeeded him as the Nawab of Bengal at the age of 20 years. (See 1753.)

Jose Custodio Faria was born in Candolim of Goa on May 31. This Goan scientist-revolutionary fought in the French revolution. He was also known as Abbe Faria. The celebrated French writer Alexander Dumas has immortalised this man in his classic *Count of Monte Cristo*. He died in Paris on September 20, 1819.

Siraj-ud-daula attacked Calcutta on June 17 with 50,000 troops and captured it on June 21. 146 British prisoners including their commander John Zephenia Holwell and four women were locked up in a small room, infamous as 'Black Hole'. 123 people perished inside due to suffocation. Holwell, Mrs Carey, Mrs Bowers and Miss Ann Wood were amongst the 23 survivors. Calcutta was renamed Alinagar by Siraj-ud-daula. Clive sailed from Madras on October 10 with 5 battleships, 5 other vessels, 900 European soldiers and 1,500 Indian sepoys to recapture Calcutta.

Ahmad Shah Abdali of Afghanistan invaded India for the fourth time. He sacked Mathura, Brindavan and Delhi.

Suja-ud-daula became the Nawab of Oudh.

After Badan Singh's death his adopted son and successor Surajmal became the Jat chief. He made the Jats a very formidable power in Hindustan. (See 1753, d. 1763.).

The Danes took possession of Nicobar Islands for colonising purpose. (See 1847.)

A.D.

1757 The British recaptured Calcutta on January 2 under Clive.

Bandel was captured on January 12 by Captain Eyre Coote from the Portuguese.

Siraj-ud-daula advanced towards Calcutta with 40,000 troops. On February 4 Clive sent an envoy to him for negotiation. On February 9 a treaty was signed between Siraj and Clive conceding the British the right to fortify Calcutta, to establish a mint and reparation of losses, and renaming Alinagar as Calcutta. (See 1756.)

Clive succeeded in taking Chandernagar from the French on March 23.

On June 13 Clive started his march for Murshidabad with 900 Europeans of 39th Foot Regiment, 2,000 Indian soldiers and 8 pieces of cannon. Siraj-ud-daula assembled 15,000 cavalry and 35,000 infantry. On the way Clive captured Katwa on June 17. Siraj took the offensive on June 23 at Plassey of Bengal, lost the battle and fled on a camel. British casualty was 22 dead and 56 injured. Siraj-ud-daula did not lose more than 500 men.

On June 29 Mir Zafar was installed on the throne at Murshidabad as the Nawab of Bengal, Bihar and Orissa.

Siraj-ud-daula was captured and assassinated on July 2 by Muhammad Beg at the instance of Miran, son of Mir Zafar.

First rupee coin of the East India Company was minted in Calcutta on August 19.

Clive became the Governor of Bengal for the first time after 24 Parganas were ceded to the East India Company by Mir Zafar on December 20.

The famous Chowringhee Road of Calcutta was constructed.

The construction of present Fort William of Calcutta was started by Lord Clive and was completed in 1773. It is reputed to be the only fort in India which has never been besieged. No shot was ever fired from its ramparts or fortifications until the Second World War, when anti-aircraft guns were fired in 1942 and 1943 at Japanese planes. (See 1696.)

1758 King of England's charter of January 14 allowed the Company to keep any booty taken in wars against the enemies of the king and the Company.

Peshwa's brother Raghunath Rao or Raghoba captured Delhi and then Lahore and Punjab fell to him in April.

French General Bussy took leave of Nizam Salabat Jung on June 18 and left for Europe. With his departure the French influence in India gradually diminished.

Separate courts were constituted for the Indians and the Europeans by the East India Company.

Count de Lally, the French General, arrived at Pondicherry. He sieged Madras fort on December 12 then under British occupation. The siege ended with Lally's retreat on February 16, 1759.

1759 French siege of Madras, then under the British control since December 12, 1758 ended with French General Lally's retreat on February 16.

Emperor Alamgir II of Delhi was murdered by his minister Imad-ul-Mulk on November 30. Shah Alam II, grandson of Aurangzeb, became the Mughal emperor.

In Chinsura Clive defeated an expedition from United East India Company of the Netherlands to re-establish Dutch position in Bengal. That defeat marked the end of Dutch power in India.

Ahmad Shah Abdali on his fifth invasion reoccupied Punjab. (See 1751.)

1760 French General Lally capitulated and surrendered Pondicherry on January 14 to British Captain Eyre Coote.

After the victory of the British on January 22 in the battle of Wandiwash against the French, the British virtually had no European opponent left in India.

A large Maratha army under Sadashiv Rao Bhau completely defeated the Nizam on February 3 in the battle of Udgir. (See 1763.)

Clive left India on February 25. Clive's successors as governors in India were J. Holwell (February to July) and H. Vansittart from July 1760 to 1765. Clive came back to India again on May 3, 1765.

Maratha army under Sadashiv Rao Bhau and Vishvas Rao captured Delhi on July 3. But the army soon moved out of Delhi because of scarcity of food supplies and money.

A.D.

Mir Zafar's son Miran, who was responsible for the assassination of Siraj-ud-daula on July 2, 1757 was himself killed by a thunderbolt on July 4 on the bank of the Gandak near Patna. His countrymen heaved a sigh of relief on his death.

Mir Zafar was deposed and his son-in-law Mir Kasim became the Nawab of Bengal on September 27. He ruled till July 7, 1763.

1761 The third and last battle of Panipat took place on January 14 between the Marathas and the Afghan invader Ahmad Shah Abdali. The Marathas lost 28, 000 soldiers and were virtually routed. The Maratha leader Peshwa Balaji Baji Rao died a broken-hearted man on June 23. His 18 year old son Madhav Rao I became the Peshwa on July 20 with the assistance of his uncle Raghunath Rao or Raghoba.

The Afghans sacked Amritsar and the Golden Temple.

Rani Ahalya Bai took charge of Indore and maintained an idyllic regime till 1795.

Jat Raja Surajmal captured Agra fort and ensured absolute sovereignty of Bharatpur. (See 1763.)

Hyder Ali entered the government of Mysore and virtually took all powers out of Mysore Raja's hand. (See 1399 and 1799.)

Tara Bai of Pune died on December 9. (See 1700.)

1762 Ahmad Shah Abdali attacked India for the sixth time and the Sikhs were defeated near Ludhiana.

A detachment of the Madras army under the British captured Manila from the Spaniards. The Madras army also participated in overseas expeditions in 1795, 1810, 1811 and 1840. (See 1801.)

1763 Murshidabad was captured by the East India Company under Major Adams for the second time on June 24 and Mir Zafar was reinstated as the Nawab on July 7 deposing Mir Kasim (see 1760.) Mir Kasim fought the British at Katwa on July 19, at Giria on August 2, and at Udayanala near Rajmahal on September 5, and lost all the battles. Patna was captured by the British from Mir Kasim on November 6.

Nizam of Hyderabad was defeated by the Marathas under the leadership of Raghunath Rao at Rakshabhuvan on the banks of the Godavari in October. (See 1760.)

Najib-ud-daula, a Rohila chief and Nadir Shah's deputy, took control of Delhi. (See 1771.)

Sannyasi and Fakir rebellions started in Bengal against the foreign rule. They had effective control in north Bengal and north Bihar till 1774.

Jat Maharaja Surajmal of Bharatpur, while hunting, was killed by a freak Afghan raid by Najib-ud-daula's troops on December 25. His son Jawahir Singh succeeded him. (See 1761 and 1768.)

1764 Mir Kasim, with the backing of Delhi emperor, attacked Patna on May 3 but lost the battle. (See 1777.)

The European Bengal Regiment mutinied, which was followed by the first Indian Sepoy Mutiny against the British in Patna in May. Major Hector Monroe forced the mutineers to surrender and put many of them to death. (See 1765 and 1857.)

The combined forces of Mir Kasim, Emperor of Delhi and Nawab Suja-ud-daula (Oudh) were again defeated in the battle of Buxar on October 23. That victory made the British virtually the master of the entire Ganga valley from the Himalayas to the sea.

Raja Nanda Kumar was given the title 'Maharaja' by Shah Alam II. He was also appointed collector of Burdwan, Nadia and Hooghly. (See 1775.)

Ahmad Shah Abdali invaded India for the seventh time. He concluded a treaty with the Marathas and entrusted the Mughal empire to them.

1765 Clive returned to Calcutta from England on May 3 and became the Governor of Bengal for the second time, which continued till 1767. (See 1744 and 1760.)

On August 12 Clive, on behalf of the company took over 'Diwani', the position of revenue minister of Bengal, Bihar and Orissa from Delhi emperor by the Treaty of Allahabad. This action is a notable landmark in the political and constitutional history of British India, which is taken as the beginning of British rule. (See 1767.)

Marathas defeated Hyder Ali of Mysore. But he got favourable terms in treaty.

Mir Zafar died and his son Nizam-ud-daula succeeded him in Bengal.

A.D.

The revolt of the 15th Battalion of Bengal assumed serious proportions when they were ordered to board a ship for Burma which they refused. Their leaders Raghunath Singh, Umraogir Singh and Yusuf Khan were tied to a cannon mouth and blown away. (See 1764 and 1857.)

1766 British officers of the East India Company revolted against the reduction of the field allowance by order of the Court of Directors.

Official postal system was introduced by Lord Clive.

Chuar uprising covered five districts of Bengal and Bihar. It continued for six years and then again from 1795 to 1816.

A gold mohur equivalent to Rs 14 was put into circulation. (See 1769.)

Hyder Ali of Mysore invaded northern Malabar. The Zamorin of Calicut and all his relatives committed suicide.

1767 The battle of Changama took place on September 3 between the combined forces of Hyder Ali and Nizam and the British army. Thus started the first Anglo-Mysore war (1767-69). Col. Smith routed the combined forces.

Clive returned to England disheartened and sick. He probably committed suicide in 1774. (See 1744 and 1765.)

Ahmad Shah Abdali entered India again for the eighth and last time. He could not subdue the Sikhs, confessed defeat and left the Sikhs to themselves.

Amar Singh, who was a Sikh chief and a protege of Ahmad Shah Abdali, founded Patiala state.

Thyagaraja, the saint and composer, was born at Thiruvayur and was named after the deity of the great temple there. His 'samadhi' is in Thiruvayur on the bank of the Kaveri in Thanjavur district. His death anniversary is observed as 'aradhana' – a great musical festival. (d. 1847).

Bolts made an unsuccessful attempt to start a newspaper and a printing press in Calcutta. But he was deported by order of the Company. (See 1780.)

Survey of India was founded. It is thus one of the oldest scientific organisations of India. Mount Everest, the highest peak in the world was discovered by the Survey of India. One of its greatest

A.D.

achievements is execution of the great trigonometrical survey. (See 1818 and 1852.)

1768   Jat Raja Jawahir Singh was assassinated in June by a degraded soldier. Ratan Singh succeeded him. But Jat power declined until renowned Ranjit Singh appeared on the scene. (See 1780.)

Col. Smith signed a peace treaty with the Nizam on February 23 who accepted British supremacy.

1769   The first organised horse-racing in India took place at Akra near Calcutta on January 16, which continued till 1809, after which it moved to Calcutta Maidan. Calcutta hosted the first Derby in India in 1843-44 season and the winner took a princely purse of Rs 5,000. Originally the races were run in the mornings until 1876 when it was decided that afternoon races would be more attractive. (See 1819 and 1848.)

On March 17 the East India Company imposed various restrictions on weavers of Bengal to destroy the 'muslin' and textile industries in Bengal. (See 1790.)

In the first Anglo-Mysore war Hyder Ali dictated peace terms to the British under the walls of Madras on April 4 with mutual restitution of conquests. (See 1767.)

French East India Company was dissolved.

A new gold *mohur* equivalent to Rs 16 was introduced. (See 1766.)

1770   On Najib-ud-daula's death in October, his son Zabita Khan took over Delhi administration.

A great famine and plague epidemic in Bengal took the toll of one fifth of the total population of fifteen million.

The first financial bank under European direction namely Bank of Hindustan was established in Calcutta by Alexander and Co. (See 1809.)

The corridor of Rameshwaram temple was completed which took 30 years. The outer and inner corridors of the temple with 983 pillars have a total length of 1,220 metres. The outer east-west corridor being 210 metres long. Though the temple's anecdote connects Ramchandra and Sita of the Ramayana, the temple itself was actually built in the 17th century and came in the present form in the 19th century.

A.D.

1771 Madras race course was established which was the first race course in the country. A few races were held in April. (See 1769.)

Hyder Ali lost to the Marathas in the battle of Milgota Pass. Marathas pursued him until he reached the safety of his capital in May. Marathas captured Delhi and induced the Mughal Emperor Shah Alam II to return to Delhi after an absence of 7 years from the capital. He was then in Allababad under the British protection. Shah Alam II was installed on Delhi throne on December 25. (See 1763.)

The first proper light-house was built in Colaba near Bombay. (See 1821.)

1772 The Court of Directors of the East India Company appointed Warren Hastings as the Governor of their Bengal Council on April 13. He took the seat on April 28 and in October 1774 he became the Governor General of Bengal and continued till February 1785. Revenue business and treasury were removed from Murshidabad to Calcutta.

Ram Mohan Roy was born at Radhanagar in Hooghly district on May 22. He was a scholar of Sanskrit, Persian, Arabic, Greek, Hebrew and Latin. He founded Hindu College in 1817 and Brahmo Samaj in 1828. He was a protagonist for the abolition of 'sati' i.e. immolation of Hindu windows. (d. 1833).

The Company made the proposal for separate civil and criminal courts in districts on August 15. It is known as the first British Indian code. (See 1837.)

Peshwa Madhav Rao I prematurely died at the age of 28 on November 18. With his death the last hope of Maratha supremacy extinguished. His brother Narayan Rao became the Peshwa on December 13 at Satara.

Calcutta became the administrative headquarter of East India Co.

The first public court of the Portuguese was instituted in India.

Muslim personal law, based on Shariat, was first enacted by the British.

1773 Peshwa Narayan Rao was murdered on August 30 by his uncle Raghunath Rao or Raghoba, who proclaimed himself as the Peshwa. (See 1772 and 1774.)

A.D.

Within the Maratha confederacy a great change came in. Scindia of Gwalior, Holkar of Indore, Bhonsle of Nagpur and Gaekwad of Baroda virtually became independent of Peshwa's control.

The Regulating Act of 1772 was passed in the British Parliament to control the functionaries of the East India Co. at the instance of Lord North. This was the first parliamentary enactment relating to territorial possessions in India.

The imperial army of Shah Alam II, lead by Mirza Nazaf Khan, recovered Agra from the Jats. (See 1761.)

Jat ruler Nawab Singh of Bharatpur died. His younger brother Ranjit Singh captured Bharatpur with the aid of the Mughals, by ousting his other brother Naval Singh.

1774 On April 8 Narayan Rao's widow delivered a posthumous son, who was installed on April 18 as Peshwa Madhav Rao II only when 10 days old, as a challenge to Raghunath Rao or Raghoba. (See 1773, 1778 and 1796.)

The British, under command of Col. Chapman, captured Rohilakhand on April 23 after the battle of Miran Katra. Rohila chief Hafiz Rahmat Khan was killed and their territory was annexed to Oudh.

Under the Regulating Act of 1772 the Mayor's Court in Calcutta was replaced by the Supreme Court which functioned till 1862. The Supreme Court judges and the new members of the council landed at Calcutta on October 19 to purify the old Company administration. The new government was installed on October 20. Warren Hastings was appointed the first Governor General of Bengal. Earlier in 1772 his designation was Governor of Bengal Council. Calcutta was made the capital of British India by the East India Co. (See 1726 and 1912.)

Clive died, perhaps committed suicide, on November 2 in England at the age of 49, under strain of ill health and charges of his misdeeds in India.

The first licence for digging and selling coal was issued to two gentlemen Summer and Hetlay by the East India Co. (See 1775.)

1775 Treaty of Purandhar was signed on March 1 between the British and Nana Phadnavis.

A.D.

On March 6 Raghunath Rao signed Treaty of Surat with the British.

The British troops captured Barrackpore of Bengal, where the first shot of Sepoy Mutiny was fired on March 29, 1857.

Ordnance Board was constituted on April 8 by the Bengal Presidency as an independent body, thus recognising the important role ordnance played in the British expansion in India. Ordnance Services Corps consider this year as their date of foundation.

Maharaja Nanda Kumar was arrested on May 6. Record shows that Warren Hastings prophesied Nanda Kumar's death sentence on May 18, though the case against him was not tried until June. He was hanged in Calcutta on August 5 on the charge of forgery. He was the last Indian to die on a forgery charge. Surprisingly it is also clear that the provision of English statute of 1728 making forgery a capital offence was not legally in force in India.

In the first Anglo-Maratha war (1775-82) on May 17, the Marathas were badly mauled in the battle of Arras by Col. Keating.

Abdul Zafar Siraj-ud-din Muhammad Bahadur Shah II, the last of the Mughal emperors, was born. (See 1837 and 1857, d. 1862.)

Varanasi ceded to the British.

The first lot of coal was struck in a Raniganj coalfield. (See 1774.)

1776 Warren Hastings resigned from the position of Governor General of Bengal but later retracted it.

Nathaniel Brushy Halhead made the compilation of Hindu Dharma Shastra in England for the first time. It was printed in London.

Muslim fakirs under Majnun Shah increased disturbances in different parts of Bengal. Majnun Shah died in 1787. But his son Chirag Ali operated in concert with Bhabani Pathak and Devi Choudhurani.

The present Viswanath temple of Varanasi was built by Ahalya Bai of Indore and the gold plating of nearly 700 kg of gold was provided by Maharaja Ranjit Singh about 50 years later. (See 1806.)

1777 Mir Kasim, the ex-Nawab of Bengal, died in extreme poverty as a fugitive in Delhi. (See 1763 and 1764.)

Kunwar Singh, the hero of Sepoy Mutiny, was born at Jagdishpur.

Warren Hastings' house was built in Alipore in Calcutta. It was

A.D.

later made into an educational institution. It became famous as Hastings House.

1778   Revolution took place in Pune in favour of Raghunath Rao as the Maratha-head. It was followed by a counter revolution in which he was ousted from Pune.

For the first time Grenadiers were formed in the Indian Army. Six companies of Grenadiers were selected from different battalions of the Bombay army under Col. Egerton. It is a term vested with the highest traditions in martial history.

Swami Virjanand, the blind sage of Mathura, was born near Jalandhar. At the age of five he lost his eyesight after an attack of smallpox. He occupied a place of eminence as a scholar of Sanskrit. He established a 'Pathshala' at Mathura to spread the religious literature and the knowledge of Vedas. His noted disciple was Swami Dayananda Saraswati. Swami Virjanand expired on September 14, 1868.

The first European indigo factory was set up.

The first printed Bengali book, a grammar in Bengali script, was published by Nathaniel Brushy Halhead, which was released in 1779. The Bengali types were made by punch-cut process by Charles Wilkins and Panchanan Karmakar in Hooghly. For this production Halhead and Wilkins got a reward of Rs 30,000 from East India Company. (See 1801.)

1779   A confederacy was formed amongst Hyder Ali, the Nizam and the Maratha chiefs for expulsion of the British from India.

Schwartz Church was built by Raja Serfoji of Thanjavur as a token of affection for the Spanish missionary Rev. C.V. Schwartz, who was Raja's tutor. Possibly this was the first church built by a Hindu ruler.

1780   The first newspaper in India *Hicky's Bengal Gazette or the Original Calcutta General Advertiser* was published in English in Calcutta on January 29 by James Augustus Hicky assisted by William Hickey. It was a weekly paper published on Saturdays. The paper ceased to exist in 1783 when Augustus Hicky was imprisoned for defamation of dignitaries in their paper. (See 1767.)

Capt. Bruce captured Gwalior fort on August 3 under Major Popham.

A.D.

Warren Hastings and Philip Francis fought a gun duel in Calcutta on August 17 to settle personal and official quarrels. Francis was wounded but survived.

Maharaja Ranjit Singh was born on November 13. He raised a most powerful fighting force and for the first time in a thousand years of Indian history brought the traditional invaders of India to their knees, and commanded the entrance to Khyber Pass. It is hard to find another ruler who never took life in cold blood, yet built up such a large empire. He passed away at Lahore on June 27, 1839.

General Goddard captured Bassein fort near Bombay on December 11.

The second Anglo-Mysore war (1780-84) took place between Hyder Ali and the British. (See 1799.)

The first private printing press was started by the Baptist missionary in Serampore of Bengal. (See 1556.)

Warren Hastings established Muhammedan Madrasa in Calcutta for spread of Arabic education among the Indian people. It was perhaps the first government aided educational institution under British supervision. (See 1792.)

The first Writers' Buildings of Calcutta came up to accommodate the junior staff of the East India Company. The structure was completely rebuilt in 1880.

Calcutta Maidan was formed.

1781 Hyder Ali's progress was checked by Eyre Coote after the battles of Porto Novo on July 1, Pallilore on August 27, and Salangarh on September 27. The British supremacy was established and Hyder Ali was subdued.

Nagapatnam was captured by the British on November 12.

The *India Gazette* was published.

Europe first learnt of Kalidasa's *Shakuntala* from William Jones' translation published in Britain.

1782 The Treaty of Salby was signed by Anderson for the British and the Scindia for the Marathas on March 17, by which the Marathas were forbidden to have dealings with any nation other than the British.

A.D.

A powerful French squadron under Admiral de Suffrein appeared in the Indian Ocean to assist Hyder Ali, but to little effect.

Hyder Ali died on December 7 in a camp near Chittur. (b. 1721).

Hyder Ali's son Tipu became the actual ruler of Mysore above Chama Raja. (See 1795 and 1799.)

An office (Court of Wards) was established in Bengal to take care of the zamindaris of minors, females and incapables.

Begums of Oudh were forced to pay Rs 76 lakhs to the British.

The first home for the aged was started by an unknown village headman in Madras, and is still in existence. It is known as 'Monegar and Rajah of Venkatagiri Choultries'. The home, initially meant for paupers, is now open to destitutes and infirm people of above 60 years of age.

The great banyan tree of Indian Botanic Garden near Calcutta originated from a date palm as per Bentholl's book *Trees in Calcutta* The main trunk circumference of which measured 15.45 metres, was removed in 1925. On May 1, 1980 its ariel roots numbered 1,380, height 26.67 mt and overall circumference 414.24 mt (See 1787 and 1988.)

1783   Charles James Fox's India Bill for the improvement of administration in India was presented in the British Parliament on March 5 and it was defeated in the following year.

Tipu Sultan sieged Mangalore and the French came forward to assist him.

Commercial production of shellac for export was initiated by Lyall Marshall & Co. founded in Dhaka.

Court of Directors censured Warren Hastings and he resigned his chair.

Rani Ahalya Bai of Indore rebuilt the eighth Somnath temple. (See 1026, 1395 and 1951.)

1784   Asiatic Society of Bengal was established on January 15 by William Jones with Warren Hastings as the first patron, which later became Royal Asiatic Society and ultimately Asiatic Society since June 1951.

Pitt's India Bill was introduced in the British Parliament on August 13 for improvement of government rules for the management of

A.D.

Indian affairs and was passed. It was known as India Act of 1784. (See 1773, 1788 and 1844.)

The Gumbuz of Srirangapatnam was built by Tipu Sultan in the garden that Hyder Ali nurtured. Ultimately Tipu and his parents were buried inside the Gumbuz.

The first newspaper of Madras namely *The Madras Courier* was published by Richard Johnson.

Public lotteries were introduced in Calcutta expressly for the purpose of developing the city. The first public lottery was for raising fund for the construction of St. John's Church. Later Hare Street, Amherst Street, College Street and Strand Road were built by the money lotteries fetched. Government took over these lotteries in 1809.

The Preventive Detention Act was perhaps introduced for the first time in India. (See 1818.)

Nawab Asaf-ud-daula built the Bara Imambara in Lucknow as a famine relief measure. The interior vaulted hall measuring 50 mt long, 16 mt wide and 15 mt high, is one of the largest apartments of its kind. The zigzag intricate path inside the 5 mt thick walls of the hall is popularly known as Bhulbhulaiya.

1785 Zabita Khan, ex-Rohila chief, died in January. (See 1770.)

Warren Hastings attended the meeting of the Council for the last time on February 1 and left India on February 8.

On July 29 Wintle ascended in a balloon for the first time in India from Esplanade area in Calcutta. (See 1889.)

The *Bhagavad Gita* was translated into English for the first time by Charles Wilkins in London.

1786 First list of charges against Warren Hastings was placed in British Parliament on April 4 by Burke. Additional charges were put up on April 28 and May 5.

Lord Cornwallis was appointed Governor General as well as the Commander-in-Chief. He took office on September 12.

The first joint stock bank namely the General Bank of India was formed in Calcutta. (See 1770.)

In Patna a huge beehive-shaped building Gol Ghar was constructed for granery storage against possible famine by John Garstin under

A.D.

instructions from Warren Hastings. It was unusable since the door on the ground level opened inwards and could not be opened when the granary was full.

Bengal was divided into thirty-five districts by John Shore as territorial units, which virtually revived Akbar's system of 'Sirkar'. (See 1787.)

Sayyid Ahmed Barelwi, the preacher of Wahabi doctrine, was born at Rae Bareli.

1787 Indian Botanic Garden was founded near Calcutta on July 6 by Robert Kyd on 273 acres of land. It contains the famous banyan tree of unknown date of origin, but is taken as 1782.

35 districts of Bengal declared in 1786 were reduced to 23 districts. (See 1786.)

The famous Bengalee dacoit Bhabani Pathak of Bankim Chandra Chattopadhyay's *Devi Chaudhurani* fame was killed in July during a battle with the British near Jalpaiguri in north Bengal.

Vishnupada temple of Gaya was constructed on the bank of the Falgu river by Ahalya Bai of Indore.

1788 Pitt's Regulatory Act was introduced on February 2 to put further controls on the Government of India after the 1784 Bill and was passed on February 25.

The trial of Warren Hastings commenced on February 13 in the House of Commons, London which ended on April 23, 1795 with honourable acquittal of Hastings.

The *Calcutta Gazette,* presently known as *Gazette of Govt.* of *West Bengal,* was first published on March 4 by Francis Goldwin. The first advertisement in an Indian Language (Bengali) was published in the third issue of the same Gazette on March 25.

Ghulam Kadir, the infamous son of Zabita Khan, seized Delhi on July 15. He blinded the old monarch Shah Alam II on August 9 with his own dagger. The Monarch's wives, daughters and other female relatives were exposed and disgracefully dishonoured. He put up a puppet emperor Bedar Bakht. Ultimately Ghulam Kadir was captured by Scindia on December 21 and subjected to the most barbarous mutilations as a reprisal under which he died. Scindia controlled the affairs of Delhi till 1803 with the blind

A.D.

Mughal Emperor Shah Alam II on the throne, virtually as a figurative head.

Lt. Archibald Blair of Indian Navy and surveyor Lt. R. H. Colbrooke first surveyed the Andaman and Nicobar Islands starting on December 29. Port Blair got its name from Lt. Blair. The Andaman Islands have a cluster of 258 islands and 56 in Nicobar group. But only 34 islands are inhabited. (See 1858.)

British engineers Henry and George Jessop established Jessop & Co., India's oldest engineering company.

Tea plantation was first tried in Indian Botanic Garden of Calcutta. (See 1826.)

1789 On July 4 the East India Company signed a treaty with the Nizam and the Peshwa against Tipu Sultan on the understanding that a cavalry of 10,000 will be attacking Tipu's territory and the conquered area will be divided amongst the three. (See 1790.)

The first weekly newspaper of Bombay namely *Bombay Herald* came out.

Camerson brought bougainvillea plant in India. (See 1859.)

1790 The third Mysore war broke out and Dindigul was captured by the British army on August 21 under General Meadows, who then captured Palghat on September 21 with sixty guns. The indecisive war was concluded by the Treaty of Srirangapatnam in 1792.

Lord Cornwallis, by the regulation of December 3, took away from the Nawab of Murshidabad his power of administering criminal justice, and Sadar Nizamat Adalat was shifted to Calcutta.

Twelve Brahmin friends of Guptipara in Hoogly district of Bengal held the first community, i.e. 'Baro-Yari' (now means public) Jagadhatri Puja at the cost of Rs 7,000 collected from public subscription.

Export of fine 'muslin' cloth of Bengal was banned by the East India Company. (See 1769.)

Ram Mohan Roy, in a treatise antagonistic to Hindu idolatory, laid the foundation of a prose literature of the Bengali vernacular.

1791 Bangalore, under Tipu Sultan, capitulated to Lord Cornwallis on March 21. The British lost a gallant and accomplished soldier Col. Moorhouse. (See 1789.)

A.D.

After the battle of Arikera on May 13 Lord Cornwallis had to retreat back to Madras.

The *Bombay Gazette* came out.

Shah Abdul Kadir translated the Quran into Urdu.

1792 By the Treaty of Srirangapatnam in March, Tipu had to agree to surrender half of his territory. (See 1790.)

Banaras Sanskrit College (original name Queen's College) was set up by Jonathan Duncan, a resident of Varanasi. It was perhaps the second educational institution to be established by the British. (See 1780.)

The first modern observatory was established at Madras by the East India Co. But the telescope was first used for astronomical studies in 1689 by the Jesuit Father Richaud in Pondicherry.

The Cricket Club of India, the first cricket club, started on the grounds, presently Eden Gardens complex in Calcutta. The first Indian cricket club is the Oriental Cricket Club of the Parsees in Bombay, founded in 1848.

1793 Permanent Settlement Act was promulgated by Lord Cornwallis in Bengal and Bihar on March 22 to fix the revenue amounts to be paid once for all by the zamindars every year.

Lord Cornwallis decided to leave India's administration exclusively in the hands of the European covenanted staff of the Company, with complete exclusion of the Indians.

William Carey arrived in India. He built up the famous Serampore Mission in 1800. He laboured in India for first seven years without making a single convert, but did splendid work in promoting education and improving vernacular. He built in Serampore the first Theological College in Asia.

The Company's charter to trade in India was renewed.

1794 Vizieram Rauze, Raja of Vizianagram, raised the banner of revolt against the British and was killed in a battle. Later there were two more rebellions in the same region under Birabhadra Rauze (1830-33) and Jagannath Rauze (1832-34).

Lord Cornwallis planned amalgamation of the Crown's army with the Company's army. But the proposal was turned down by the Court of Directors of the Company.

A.D.

Dwarkanath Tagore, grandfather of Rabindranath Tagore, was born. (d. 1846).

1795 Warren Hastings was honourably acquitted of the charges on April 23. The trial continued for 145 working days and cost him £70,000. The East India Company gave him a grant of the money. (See 1788.)

On November 27 a packed house greeted the first performance of a Bengali drama *Kalpanik Sambadal* a translation by Golak Nath Das of M. Jodrell's book *The Disguise*. It was produced by Gerasim Stepanovich Lebedev, a Russian who came to India in July 1787, in his own theatre hall on Domtala street, now Ezra Street in Calcutta. (See 1883.)

Cochin was annexed by the British from the Dutch.

The East India Company ordered the 15th Battalion of Bengal Native Infantry to proceed to Malacca. While the battalion initially agreed, at the last moment they refused to board the two ships and started firing. Lt. Col. Erskin suppressed the rebellion by pounding them with a pair of cannon. Thereafter the 15th battalion was disbanded for ever and a new 37th battalion was raised. (See 1765 and 1824.)

Chama Raja, the titular sovereign of Mysore, died. Tipu Sultan eliminated the puppet king by imprisoning his family. (See 1782 and 1799.)

Rani Ahalya Bai of Indore died. Tukaji Holkar became the sole ruler. (See 1761.)

Measures were taken against infanticide in the sea off Sagar Island of Bengal in fulfilment of vows. (See 1803.)

Two mahogany plants were brought to India from West Indies.

1796 Peshwa Madhav Rao II committed suicide on October 22 by jumping from the terrace. The throne went to his cousin and Raghoba's son Baji Rao II on December 4, who was the last of the Peshwas.

1797 Lord Cornwallis was sworn in as the Governor General of India on February 1 in England for the second time. But he did not proceed to India until 1805. (See 1803.)

Poet Mirza Ghalib was born on December 27. (d. 1869).

A.D.

1798 Allahabad fort was made over to the East India Company and a permanent maintenance of 10,000 troops was agreed upon.

The Nizam of Hyderabad concluded a Treaty of Subsidiary Allowance with the British.

1799 In the fourth and last Mysore war which began in 1798, siege of Srirangapatnam by the British began on April 17. Major General W. Pomham and General Baird led the British troops. Tipu Sultan was killed in the battle on May 4. He was the only Indian king who died on the battlefield fighting the British. Tipu was cremated by the British with the pomp and splendour due to a sultan. Tipu had an infatuation about tigers and simultaneously an intense dislike for the British. At his instance a mechanised toy was developed by the French emanating a tiger killing a Briton, with all the sounds of roar and agony. The toy is now exhibited in Victoria and Albert Museum in London. (b. 1750).

Krishnaraja Udiyar, the infant descendant of the Hindu Raja of Mysore was reinstated on June 30 after Tipu's death on May 4. (See 1399, 1782 and 1795.)

Wajir Ali, Nawab of Oudh, was deposed by the British since he refused to toe the line and to pay the increased subsidy to the British.

Ranjit Singh of Punjab captured Lahore on July 7 from its Sikh rulers.

The famous Hawa Mahal Palace or Palace of Four Winds was built at Jaipur by Maharaja Pratap Singh.

1800 The great Maratha statesman Nana Phadnavis died on March 13.

Fort William College was established in Calcutta on August 18 by Lord Wellesly, who was made the commander-in-chief on August 7. This first college of India was abolished in 1854. (See 1812.)

The first English teaching school was established in Bhowanipore of Calcutta. Its name was Union School.

After Tipu's death in the previous year Coorg declared independence which was shortlived, since the British annexed it in 1834.

1801 The first Bengali version of the New Testament was published from Serampore in February.

A.D.

William Carey was appointed professor of Bengali language in Fort William College on April 12.

Bengal and Madras had Supreme Courts by the charter of December 26.

Karnataka was annexed by the Company.

The Bombay army went to fight in Egypt. It also went to Mauritius in 1810 and to Iran in 1856. (See 1762 and 1795.)

The first printed Bengali book *Pratapaditya Charita* written by Ramram Basu was published. In this year Carey's *Bengali Grammar* was also published. Both were printed in Serampore Press. (See 1778.)

1802 The first gun and shell factory was set up at Cossipore in Calcutta on March 18. It was then known as Gun Carriage Agency.

Peshwa Baji Rao II, after being defeated by Yashwant Rao Holkar, concluded a treaty of Subsidiary Allowance with the British on December 31. Thus he sacrificed his independence just to be a prince under British protection.

The first century in cricket was scored on Indian soil by Peter Vansittart for Etonians, against the Cricket Club of Calcutta. (See 1721.)

1803 Delhi was captured by Lord Lake on September 14 against the combined forces of the Sikhs and the Marathas in the second Anglo-Maratha war (1803-05). The blinded Emperor Shah Alam II (see 1788.) came under British protection from Scindia. In the treaty of Surji Arjangaon of December 30, the British acquired the control of Delhi, Agra, Broach and other territories. That was in fact the true end of the Mughal empire. (See 1857 and 1862.)

On September 18 the British captured Puri from the Marathas without any struggle.

In the Treaty of Deogaon with Bhonsle on December 15, Orissa along with Cuttack came under the Company's rule.

Calcutta had its first statue. That was of Lord Cornwallis. The full-size statue is now preserved in Victoria Memorial Hall. (See 1797 and 1881.)

Lord Wellesely suppressed the sacrifice of children in the sea off Sagar Island in fulfilment of vows. (See 1795.)

A.D.

1804 Holkar of Indore unexpectedly attacked Delhi with an army of 20,000 strong after capturing Mathura. After a 9-day siege, Lt. Col Burns and Lt. Col. Ochterlony repulsed the attack.

The Asiatic Society of Bombay began as the Literary Society with James Mackintosh as the president. (See 1830.)

1805 A permanent provision was made for the Mughal emperor of Delhi by an order issued on May 23 by the Governor General of India Lord Wellesley. (See 1803.)

Lord Cornwallis died on October 5 at Ghazipur in U P of sickness, only eight weeks after his arrival from England on July 30. A memorial was erected there in his honour. (See 1797 and 1803.)

William Carey published the first Marathi grammar. Later with the help of Marathi Pandit Vaijnath Sharma, the first Marathi to English dictionary was published. (See 1814.)

Lord Lake threw away his fame by failing to capture Bharatpur during the reign of Raja Ranjit Singh. Here the British suffered their first major setback.

The dome of Harmandir Sahib of Amritsar was plated with gold by Maharaja Ranjit Singh. It was later named 'Golden Temple' by the British. (See 1609 and 2005.)

1806 Indian forces at Vellore and Madras mutinied in July since they were forbidden to wear caste-marks and earrings during parade. The mutiny was speedily quelled by Col. Rolls Gillespie after slaying nearly 500 mutineers. (See 1824.)

Ranjit Singh captured Ludhiana.

Akbar Shah II became the Delhi emperor. He refused to meet Lord Hastings on equal terms in 1813 when he became the governor-general. But Akbar Shah II ultimately did so with Lord Amherst, who took over in August 1823. (See 1835.)

Pindari bandits of central India created a lot of disturbances. (1806-18)

1807 Junagarh state was annexed by the Company. (See 1948.)

1808 The Sikhs of Sirhind sent a deputation to the British for protection against Raja Ranjit Singh.

Tripura was taken over by the British. (See 1733.)

A.D.

1809 European army officers of the Company revolted against differential treatment meted out to them compared to the Royal Regiment officers.

Bank of Bengal, also known as Presidency Bank, was established which happened to be the pioneer in modern banking system. Bank of Bombay was established in 1840 and Bank of Madras in 1843. All three together were known as Presidency Banks. (See 1770.)

The present Kali temple of Kalighat in Calcutta, built by Santosh Roy Choudhury of Sabarna Roy Chowdhury family, was consecrated. The original temple was built around 1540 in Bhowanipore area.

1810 The famous Duncan Dock of Bombay was completed on June 23.

The East India Company acquired Delhi as a result of the second Maratha war.

Horse Artillery was first created in Punjab army.

1811 Thomas Manning was the first Englishman to enter Lhasa of Tibet. He started from Rangpur of north Bengal and went via Paro of Bhutan. He had to leave Lhasa on April 12, 1812 under orders from Peking.

Importation of slaves into India was forbidden.

1812 Pindari menace came to a peak under the patronage of some of the Maratha chiefs. (See 1806 and 1818.)

The East India Company established College of Fort St. George in Madras on the model of Calcutta Fort William College. (See 1800.)

1813 The first boat race in Calcutta took place on July 25, when seven sailing boats competed on the Hooghly river.

The Gujars of Saharanpur rose in revolt on account of the resumption for the enormous estate of Raja Ram Dayal Sharma by the British after his death.

The Burmese conquered Manipur. (See 1826.)

The first Town Hall in India was built in Calcutta by the citizens. The construction started in 1805.

Ranjit Singh got hold of Kohinoor diamond from the exiled king of Afghanistan Shah Suja-ul-Mulk, who was staying at Lahore.

A.D.

Semaphore system of communication was introduced between Calcutta and Chunar of U.P., and also between Calcutta and Sagar Island. (See 1839, 1851 and 1855.)

1814   Calcutta Museum was established on February 2 as a part of Asiatic Society at the suggestion of a Danish surgeon Dr Nathaniel Wallich, who was its first director also. The present building was opened to the public on April 1, 1878.

Coal mining first started in Raniganj of Bengal. (See 1775.)

Tantia Tope of Sepoy Mutiny fame was born. (d. 1859).

The Serampore Press (of Bengal) issued the first printed Marathi book *Simhasan Battisi.* (See 1805.)

1815   On May 8 General David Ochterlony captured Malaun of Nepal. The garrison gave themselves up to the British. It is in his honour Ochterlony Monument of Calcutta was erected in 1828.

The first iron smelter was established in Madras.

The Company started minting silver coins in India.

The first iron bridge was built by Jessop & Co. Ltd. over the Gomti river in Lucknow. (See 1788 and 1854.)

1816   Nepal signed a treaty with Governor General Lord Hastings and ceded Kumaon and Garhwal districts to India. Nepal also withdrew from Sikkim. (See 1975.)

Appa Saheb, Bhonsle of Nagpur, signed a treaty with the British. It not only deprived Nagpur of its independence, but also hastened the break up of the Maratha confederacy.

Gangadhar Bhattacharya and Hara Chandra Roy launched a Bengali Journal *Bengal Gazette* from Calcutta. This poineer effort for a Bengali journal was shortlived. (See 1821.)

1817   Ram Mohan Roy started Hindu College in Calcutta on January 20 with the help of Justice H. East David Hare, earlier a watchmaker, at 304 Chitpore Road in the house of Gora Chand Basak. This college was later renamed as Presidency College.

Devendranath Tagore, father of Rabindranath Tagore, was born on May 15. (d. 1905).

Syed Ahmad Khan was born. He started the Aligarh Movement and founded Muhammedan Anglo-Oriental School of Aligarh in 1875. (d. 1898).

A.D.

Mill's *History of India* was published for the first time.

Jabalpur was annexed by the British.

Ferdunji Naoroji was born. He was the leader of Young Bombay Party, which established several political, social and religious associations in the eighteen hundred fifties. (d. 1885).

The grandeur of Ajanta cave temples was a discovery of pure accident. Some British soldiers in pursuit of a tiger entered the ravine and were awestruck by the majestic beauty of Ajanta sculptures and frescoes. The artistic endeavours of chisel and brush attained their peak during the reign of Chandragupta II of Pataliputra. Started in 200 B.C. work was still in progress till 650 A.D. The complex contains 29 caves, of which 5 are temples and 24 are monasteries.

1818 The last battle between the Marathas and the Company took place in Rampura on January 10. The Marathas lost and they were completely decimated. Pune was captured by the British.

Rana of Udaipur and the British signed a treaty on January 13, by which a British envoy was appointed in Rana's court. The glorious House of Mewar thus went under complete British protection.

In February the Nawab of Bhopal concluded a Defensive and Subordinate Alliance with the Company.

On April 7 the British introduced Bengal State Prisoners Regulation III of 1818, for detention and deportation of political prisoners and revolutionaries without trial. This regulation lasted till India won her independence in 1947. (See 1784.)

The first vernacular newspaper *Samachar Darpan* was published on May 31 in Bengali language by Carey and Marshman from Serampore.

Pindari bandits, the unruly cavalry bands of central India and on friendly terms with Holkar and Scindia, were smashed. (See 1806 and 1812.)

India's first cotton mill was established in Calcutta. (See 1854.)

Sanchi was rediscovered by General Taylor of Bengal Cavalry, but restoration began only in 1912 by John Marshal.

The first missionary attempt in female education was made in Chinsurah by London Missionary Society School. (See 1819.)

A.D.

Trigonometrical Survey of India was founded. (See 1767 and 1852.)

Bhil uprising started and lasted till 1831.

1819   Serampore College in Bengal was established on June 1 by William Carey, Ward and Marshman.

Goa's revolutionary scientist Jose Custodio Faria died on September 20. (b. 1756).

Ranjit Singh conquered Kashmir from Dost Muhammad and expelled the Afghans from there. (See 1752.)

The first concerted effort for spread of female education was made by starting a school in Gauribari area by Calcutta Female Juvenile Society established by foreign ladies under the patronage of Baptist Mission. (See 1849 and 1879.)

The first Sanskrit to English dictionary was published by the Sanskrit scholar H. H. Wilson.

Madras Eye Hospital was established. It was the world's second eye hospital.

The first house of a Briton 'Kennedy House' was built in Shimla, which town in 1864 became the summer capital of India for six months in a year and continued to be so till 1939.

Calcutta Race Course, one of the finest in the world, was constructed. (See 1769 and 1847.)

1820   After a meeting held at Calcutta on September 14 the Agri-Horticultural Garden of Calcutta started functioning. (See 1830.)

Ishwar Chandra Vidyasagar (Banerji) who gave the Bengalees their first primer in 1855 was born on September 26 in Birsingha village in Midnapore district of Bengal. He was one of the makers of modern Bengal. He led the movement for widow remarriage and abolition of polygamy in Hindu society. (d. 1891).

1821   A Sanskrit college was opened in Pune by the Company to appease the sentiment of the higher class people who were then deprived of the patronage of Peshwa's durbar.

Ram Mohan Roy founded the first nationalist press with his Bengali paper *Sambad Kaumudi*. (See 1822.)

Burmese commanders conquered Assam.

The Church Missionary Society opened the country's first boarding school for girls in Tirunelveli of Tamil Nadu. (See 1820.)

A.D.

On the initiative of foreign artists, for the first time, lithographic printing of a picture was done in Calcutta.

Armenian College was founded in Calcutta on Free School Street.

India's oldest functioning lighthouse was set up on Sagar Island at the estuary of the Hoogly river. It was renovated in 1911. The original 27 mt high circular tower was still in use in 2005. (See 1771.)

1822 On July 1 the first Gujarat newspaper *Bombay Samachar,* original name *Moombaina Samachar,* came out of Gujarati Samachar Press (established in 1812) of Firduonji Marzaban. It became a daily paper in 1837 and is the oldest Indian newspaper still in existence. (See 1838.)

Miratul-Akhbar, the first weekly journal in Persian, was published by Ram Mohan Roy in Calcutta. (1821)

Bombay Native School and Book Society was formed. In 1827 the name was changed to Bombay Native Education Society.

The first water supply scheme for Delhi was formally opened on November 4.

Captain Young established Mussourie hill station.

Oriental Life Insurance Company was founded for undertaking life risks of Indians.

India's first Fire Brigade unit was set up in Calcutta. Five fire brigade engines were first imported in 1865. Of these three were horsedrawn and the other two drawn by men.

1823 The first steamship *Diana* – a gunboat, was built in Calcutta by Kyd & Co. She was launched at Calcutta on July 12.

The Company started Sanskrit College in Calcutta in a rented house in Bowbazar to teach traditional studies. The college shifted to its present site on May 1, 1826.

Bengal Chamber of Commerce was established in Calcutta to look after the interest of the European business community.

The first coffee plantation was opened.

Gopal Hari Deshmukh, a robust champion of social reform of Maharashtra, was born. He was famous by his pen-name 'Lokahitwadi'. (d. 1892).

The rule 'Keep to the left' on the road was introduced.

A.D.

John Adams, the acting Governor General, launched the first repressive measures against the Press. (See 1835.)

1824   The great Bengali poet Madhusudan Dutta was born on January 25 in Sagardari village of Jessore district, now in Bangladesh. He suddenly embraced Christianity on February 9, 1843 and Michael was added to his name. He was born a rebel and died a rebel on June 29, 1873.

A revolt of about 410 Indian soldiers of 47th Native Infantry troops broke out in November in Barrackpore as a protest against the order to go to Burma by sea, which they believed would lose their caste. Edward Page gave orders to fire on them when about 60 soldiers lay dead on the field; followed in the afternoon by two dozen executions either by hanging or by firing. (See 1762, 1795 and 1806.)

Nana Saheb alias Dhundu Pant was born. During the Sepoy Mutiny in 1857 while his own soldiers were sent to assist the British, he himself was forced by the mutineers to take the lead. (d. 1859).

On the death of Sivalinga Rudra, Rani Chenamma of Kittur brought in an uprising for its liberation from the British management.

Swami Dayananda Saraswati was born in Tankara in Gujarat. He became a disciple of the blind Swami Virjananda in 1860. During his stay in Bombay he founded the Arya Samaj on April 10, 1875. He died in Ajmer on October 30, 1883.

On November 24 the Calcutta merchants voted a lakh of rupees to the first person who would navigate a steamship to India. (See 1825.)

General Lodwick was the first Englishman to visit (old) Mahabaleswar, a tiny village with three temples. The place was considered so holy that Englishmen were not allowed earlier. The new town was founded by John Malcolm in 1828.

The small Dutch possessions in India were taken over by the British in exchange for Sumatra.

The first native girls' school (non-residential) was opened by the American Missionary Society in Bombay. (See 1821.)

1825   Dadabhai Naoroji was born on September 4. He was the first Indian to be elected a member of the House of Commons in England from Central Finsbury. A patriot at heart he was one of the founders

A.D.

of the Indian National Congress. He coined the word 'Swaraj'. (d. 1917).

On October 14 the Grenadier Company in Assam refused to march on the pretext of bad climate. The court martial sentenced all the ring leaders to death. (See 1806 and 1824.)

The first steamship *Enterprise,* under Captain Johnson, reached Calcutta via Cape of Good Hope on December 7. She was a 475 tonne vessel with 120 horsepower engine and started from Deptford in England on August 16. (See 1824.)

Rao Tula Ram, distinctive hero of the 1857 Sepoy Mutiny, was born on December 9. Under his instruction Rao Krishan Gopal attacked Meerut on May 10, 1857 and killed a large number of British troops. He marched at the head of the troops in Haryana area to crown the last Mughal Emperor Bahadur Shah II once again the Emperor of India. He died on September 23, 1863.

The first metalled road was built in Calcutta.

1826 The first Indian Barrister Gnanendra Mohan Tagore was born in Calcutta on January 24. (See 1862, d. 1809.).

Assam was annexed by the East India Company.

Tea plants were found in Assam by C.A. Bruce. (See 1788.)

Bharatpur was annexed by the Company after imprisoning the usurper Durjan Sal. A young raja was placed on the throne.

The first all-Hindi weekly newspaper *Udant Martand* was published on May 30 by Pandit Jugal Kishore Shukla of Kanpur. The paper survived for one and a half years only.

Vedanayakam Pillai, the writer of the first Tamil novel, was born. (d. 1889).

After the Indo-Burmese war, Manipur was incorporated into India. (See 1813.)

Rubber plant seeds were first brought to India from Brazil by Henry William. (See 1900.)

1827 Jyotirao Govindrao Phule was born. His was a florist family of Pune district. He was a great social reformer concerned with female education and pioneer in fighting for the rights of the non-Brahmins. (d. 1890).

A.D.

The first large-scale strike on record was that of the palanquin bearers of Calcutta in May in protest against (a) wearing the badge and (b) demand of fare on the basis of distance instead of the time they took to cover the destination, against a government order issued on May 12, published on May 21 issue of *Sambad Timir Nashak.* Calcutta's 2,900 palanquins came to a standstill, but only for a short period. (See 1862.)

Indians were permitted to sit as jurors in the court of law.

Bengal Club was established on February 1 in Gordon's Building of Esplande East in Calcutta. It is the second oldest club in India, and is still in existence. It was exclusively for the foreigners until 1958, when Indians were admitted. The first one was United Services Club.

1828   Brahmo Samaj was founded by Ram Mohan Roy. Its first session was held on August 20 in the rented house of Kamal Bose on Chitpore Road in Jorasanko area in Calcutta.

The Assamese rebelled and proclaimed Gomdhar Kanwar of Ahom royal family as the king. It was suppressed in October. The leader of the enterprise Dhananjay Borgohain, an ex-minister of the Ahom king, was imprisoned. (See 1858.)

An army naturalist exploring coal in Assam came upon streaks of oil. But he ignored it. It was finally discovered in 1867, only six years after its discovery in the world. (See 1889.)

Ochterlony Monument, later known as Shahid Minar since August 9, 1969 was built in Calcutta to the memory of David Ochterlony, hero of Nepal campaign. It is a Greek column on an Egyptian base, crowned with a Turkish dome. (See 1815.)

1829   Lord Bentinck abolished Sati i.e. burning of the Hindu widows with their husbands, by Regulation XVII of 1829 dated December 4. Anybody taking part was to be charged with culpable homicide. In Calcutta and its neighbourhood alone, there were 253, 289 and 441 cases of Sati in 1815, 1816 and 1817 respectively. The number of Sati officially reported in Bengal increased from 385 in 1785 to 839 in 1818. (See 1699 and 1832.)

Darjeeling proper was first located by Captain Lloyd who considered it to be a right place for develoing into a hill station.

A.D.

Darjeeling rose to international fame for two Ts – Tea and Tenzing Norgay, both of them climbed to the top of the world. (See 1840 and 1953.)

East India Company founded the Indian Navy. (See 1612. 1891 and 1934)

Col. James Todd wrote *Annals and Antiquities of Rajasthan.*

Royal Calcutta Golf Club was established. It is the oldest golf club outside Great Britain.

Water hyacinth, originally of Brazil and a menace today, is supposed to have been brought by a French traveller Victor Jacquemont.

1830 With the joint efforts of Alexander Duff and Ram Mohan Roy, General Assembly's Institution was established on July 13 with only five pupils, where teaching of the Bible took an important place. It took the name Scottish Church College in 1921.

Ram Mohan Roy sailed for England on November 15. He was the first Indian Brahmin (then a Brahmo) to go to England where he arrived on April 8, 1831 and died on September 27, 1833. He went as an envoy of Akbar II, the token Mughal emperor, to represent his miseries to King George IV. He was also the first Indian to travel in a railway train from Manchester to Liverpool.

Radha Kanta Dev of Sova Bazar, Calcutta founded the Dharma Sabha in opposition to Ram Mohan Roy's Brahmo Samaj. (See 1828.)

Capt. William Sleeman launched a campaign to exterminate 'Thugees' who were brought under control by 1837 and completely eliminated by 1860. Thugs claimed that they got their inspiration from the carvings of Ellora caves. The township Sleemanabad of Madhya Pradesh was established in his honour in 1860. It is on record that Behram, one of the most notorious 'Thugees', himself killed 931 persons by strangulation between 1790 and 1840. (See 1836.)

Iron and Steel were manufactured by modern methods in south Arcot of Madras. (See 1874 and 1908.)

The Bombay Public Library was opened under the patronage of John Malcolm, as a unit of the Asiatic Society. (See 1804.)

The first Flower Show in the country was organised by the Agri-Horticultural Society in Calcutta. (See 1820.)

A.D.

The first steam-driven paper-making machine was set up by William Carey in Calcutta. He printed the *Bible* in 31 languages, most of them in Indian vernacular. (See 1870.)

Ishwar Chandra Gupta started a Bengali journal named *Sambad Prabhakar.*

1831 The first Fine Arts Exhibition was held in the Public Library of Calcutta on February 1 by Brush Club. The pictures were all drawn by foreign artists. It is not known when the first work of an Indian was exhibited.

Ram Mohan Roy landed in England on April 8.

Mysore was taken over by the British on October 3.

Henry Louis Vivian Derozio died on December 26. (b. 1808).

The Kols of Ranchi, Singhbhum, Manbhum, Palamau and Hazaribagh rebelled since their land holdings were being transferred from Kol headmen, known as Mundas, to Sikh and Muslim farmers, which lasted till 1837. Thousands of them were massacred before British authority could be reimposed.

Sessions work were given to the district judges who handed over their magisterial power to collectors. (See 1829 and 1837.)

A monthly magazine in Tamil was started by missionaries in Madras.

1832 In January the Britishers visited Naga Hills for the first time and started to bring the Nagas under control. An administrative centre was started there only in 1877. (See 1881 and 1963.)

The British Parliament finally rejected on July 11 the appeal of Hindu puritans against 'sati' abolition. (See 1829.)

The first Marathi newspaper *Bombay Darpan* was started by Bal Shastri Jambekar.

Wilson College of Bombay was established by the missionaries.

1833 Ram Mohan Roy expired at Stapleton Grove in Bristol in England in the early hours of September 27. (b. 1772).

Savings Bank facility was initiated by Presidency Bank in Calcutta. Both British and Indian individuals were extended the facility.

Lord William Cavendish Bentinck was the first Governor General of India. Earlier his designation was Governor General of Bengal. (See 1858.)

A.D.

The British trading company in India got its final name East India Company. (See 1599 and 1702.)

Ice was imported for the first time. Frederick Tudor sent a shipload of 160 tonnes of natural ice of Wenham Lake from Boston under Captain Rogers. About 100 tonnes landed in Calcutta around September 6. This trade continued up to 1860s until ice-making machines were invented.

1834   Coorg was annexed by the East India Company on May 7 from Raja Veer Rajendra, after formally declaring a war.

Governor General William Bentinck changed the official language of the Courts of Justice from Persian to English.

Peshawar was taken by Raja Ranjit Singh.

The first Indo-British collaboration took shape in Carr Tagore & Co. under the Charter Act of 1833. There were four partners namely W. Carr, Dwarkanath Tagore, D. M. Gordon and W. Princep. (See 1843.)

The East India Company established Elphinstone Institute in Bombay to encourage English study.

Gulab Singh, the Dogra ruler of Jammu, sent a Dogra army under the command of Jorawar Singh and captured Ladakh. (See 1840.)

1835   Darjeeling was obtained by the East India Company from the King of Sikkim on February 1 for a consideration of Rs 3,000 per annum, subsequently raised to Rs 6,000 in 1846, which was stopped at the end of 1849 after the unfriendly attitude of the king of Sikkim. (See 1839.)

On February 2 Thomas Babington Macaulay opened the floodgate of western education in India by linking higher education with the English language. It was followed by the famous resolution of March 7 for promotion of European literature and science in India. English was introduced as the medium of instruction for the first time for higher studies.

Though work on Calcutta Medical College started on January 28, it was officially opened on February 20. It actually started full functioning from June 1 having fifty students with Dr M. J. Bramley as the first principal. (See 1836, 1839 and 1845.)

Rani Laskmi of Jhansi was born in Varanasi on November 16. Her original name was Manikarnika. (See 1858.)

A.D.

Homoeopathic treatment was first started in Calcutta by an amateur German S. F. Hanneman. He is different from the world famous Dr Samuel Hahnemann. (See 1881.)

The British stopped striking coins with Emperor Akbar Shah II's image on the twenty-ninth year of his rule. The British king's image was put instead. (See 1806.)

Vaman Abaji Modak, Marathi scholar and well-known educationist, was born. (d. 1897).

Freedom of press was established by Charles Metcalfe while he was the temporary Governor General. (See 1823.)

Corporal punishment in the native army was abolished by Lord William Bentinck.

Tea cultivation started in Assam near the confluence of the Brahmaputra and Kundil rivers.

1836　Munshi Newal Kishore, son of Jamuna Prasad Bhargava, a zamindar of Aligarh, was born on January 3. He tried to build up an integrated Indian society where perfect religious harmony could prevail. With that in view he founded 'Newal Kishore Press and Book Depot' in Lucknow, which is the oldest printing and publishing concern in Asia. His greatest tribute came from King Abdur Rahman of Afghanistan in 1885 when he said, "..I am thankful to the Lord that I have seen you. In India nothing had given me more pleasure than having seen you..." (d. 1895).

On January 10 Professor Madhusudan Gupta and four of his medical students Raj Krishan Dey, Uma Charan Sett, Dwarkanath Gupta and Nobin Chandra Mitra shook off all the tentacles of prejudice and dissected a dead body in Calcutta Medical College. The government even went so far as to fire a salute of guns from Fort William to mark the occasion. (See 1835.)

Ramakrishna Paramahanasa Dev was born in early morning on February 18 in Kamarpukur village in Hooghly district. (d. 1886).

The first public library, known as Calcutta Public Library, was opened on March 21 by Dwarkanath Tagore and Joachim Hayward Stoequeler, editor of the newspaper *Englishman,* at 13 Esplanade Row, residence of F. P. Strong. It was amalgamated with the Imperial Library on January 30, 1903. It became National Library in 1948.

A.D.

The Madras Chamber of Commerce and Industry was established on September 29.

Life imprisonment was imposed for association with the 'Thugees'. (See 1830.)

1837 Ramkrishna Gopal Bhandarkar, a reputed oriental scholar, was born in Malvan in Ratnagiri district on July 6. Besides a teacher, researcher and author, he was a social reformer and active member of Prathana Samaj of Bombay. (d. 1925).

On the death of Akbar Shah II his son Bahadur Shah II ascended the throne of Delhi on September 28 at the age of 62. His rule as the Mughal emperor as well as the Mughal dynasty ended with the Sepoy Mutiny of 1857. (See 1862.)

James Princep, Secretary of Asiatic Society, deciphered the ancient Brahmi and later Kharosthi inscriptions of India which had a great impact on the study of ancient history of India.

In Bengal it was decided to have a separate district judge and district magistrate in each district. (See 1772, 1829 and 1831.)

The Christian College was established in Madras.

Positive action started against human sacrifice in Orissa. It was extirpated in 1852.

The first political organisation of India was the Zamindari Association of Calcutta. It was principally a body of landlords, which in 1838 changed its name to Landholders' Association. The principal organisers were Radha Kanta Deb and Prasanna Kumar Tagore. The association was designed to defend landlords against what were believed to be propeasant tendencies of the government. It became defunct in 1851.

The first tea-estate was set up at Chabuwa in Assam by the East India Co.

1838 Bankim Chandra Chattopadhyay, the author of Vande Matram song and one of the first two Bengali graduates, was born on June 28. He was the most creative and powerful master of Bengali prose during the century. (d. 1894).

Keshab Chandra Sen was born on November 19. He joined the Brahmo Samaj in 1857 but seceded from it in 1866. He reorganised it into Bharatiya Brahmo Samaj during 1875-78. (d. 1884).

A.D.

The daily newspaper *Times of India* was published from Bombay. It is the oldest English daily newspaper still in circulation in 2005. (See 1822.)

Mirza Ghulam Ahmed, founder of the Ahmadiya sect, was born. (d. 1908).

1839   Jamshedji N. Tata was born on March 3. He founded the Tata Iron and Steel Company which was then one of the largest integrated steel mills in the world. He also set up textile mills in Bombay and Nagpur, and introduced sericulture in India. (d. 1904).

Calcutta Medical College Hospital was opened on April 1 with 20 beds only for male patients. (See 1835.)

Raja Ranjit Singh of Punjab died at Lahore on June 27. His imbecile son Kharag Singh succeeded him but he died the next year.

Nainital was discovered on November 18 by P. Barron, a British sugar merchant of Shahjahanpur. The Tal (lake) of the Goddess Naina Devi lay at an elevation of 1,938 metres at the foothills of the Himalayas. He built the house Pilgrim Cottage in 1840. It was destroyed in devastating rains in 1880.

Dr. Campbell came to Darjeeling as its superintendent, when its population was hardly one hundred hill people. He planned the town and virtually established Darjeeling as a hill station. (See 1835.)

Dr. William B.O' Saughnessy, the Irish professor of Calcutta Medical College, installed the first electric telegraph line 33.8 km long, from Calcutta towards Diamond Harbour with a 213.4 metre river crossing. (See 1813, 1851 and 1855.)

Reconstruction of Grand Trunk Road, now National Highway No. 2, started. (See 1538.)

1840   Lord Auckland bought a piece of barren land in Calcutta. His sisters Miss Emily and Fanny Eden converted it into a beautiful garden. Originally it was named Auckland Circus Gardens. Records do not reveal when its name was changed to Eden Gardens. The first cricket match was played in Eden Gardens itself in 1874.

Tea was grown experimentally in Darjeeling hills. The first commercialisation was done by Alubari Tea Company in 1856 which gave the impetus to establish tea gardens. (See 1850 and 1894.)

A.D.

Commander Jorawar Singh of Jammu & Kashmir captured Skardu of Baltistan and made an ambitious thrust into Tibet itself. In the midwinter of 1841 Jorawar Singh and his men were trapped at 4,600 mts (15,000 ft) above sea-level in Tibet. They including Jorawar perished like the armies of Napoleon and Hitler in Russia. (See 1834.)

Photographic cameras were introduced in Indian market. (See 1856 and 1897.)

Khajuraho was discovered by a British army engineer T. S. Burt while hunting. It was reclaimed and opened to the public in 1923.

Postmen (delivery peons with uniform and badge) were introduced for regular mail delivery.

Female missionaries for work with women and children arrived from Europe for the first time.

1841 A. Carsetji was the first Indian to become Fellow of the Royal Society.

A hospital for females, the first one in India, began to function in Calcutta. (See 1882.)

1842 Mahadev Govind Ranade was born on January 18. He was one of the first graduates of Bombay University and perhaps the most mature and influential Maharashtrian of his time. He was the chief architect of Bombay Prarthana Samaj. (See 1867, d. 1901.).

The first steamer of Peninsular and Oriental Steam Navigation Company came to India and touched Madras in December via the Cape of Good Hope. Surprisingly her name was *Hindustan.*

Surat was taken over by the British.

Lord Ellenborough brought back the sandalwood gates of Somnath temple from Ghazni. (See 1026.)

1843 Sind was annexed by the British in August after the Amirs were defeated in several battles.

Debendranath Tagore, father of Rabindranath Tagore, accepted Brahmo religion on December 22 at the hands of Ramchandra Vidyabagish.

Panambakkam Ananda Charlu was born in Kadamanchi village of Andhra Pradesh. He was a nationalist leader, prominent lawyer, and founder of Madras Mahajana Sabha. (See 1884, d. 1908.).

A.D.

Ambala military cantonment was laid out by the British.

British Indian Society was formed in Bengal by the British people for the welfare and just rights of all classes of Indian subjects. This Society merged with the British Indian Association formed in 1851.

Carr Tagore & Co. amalgamated with Elmore Humphrey & Co. to form Bengal Coal Co. It was the largest producer of coal for about 125 years. (See 1934.)

Vishnudev Bhave staged his play 'Sita Swayamvar' at the court of Sangli state. It was the beginning of Maratha theatre. (See 1880.)

The legal status of slavery was abolished by the British. (See 1811, 1848 and 1860.)

1844   Gooroodas Banerjee was born on July 26 in Calcutta. He was a judge of Calcutta High Court. In 1890 he became the first Indian vice-chancellor of a university which happened to be Calcutta University. (d. 1918).

W. C. Bonerjee, the first president of the Indian National Congress, was born of December 29 in Kidderpore, Calcutta. He joined the Bar in June 1867. He was the first Indian to act as the Standing Council. (d. 1906).

Mono Mohan Ghose was born. He was the first president of the Indian Association (1876) and founder of the *Indian Mirror* newspaper in 1861. (d. 1896).

Calcutta Christian Juvenile Society was established. It blossomed into Calcutta Y.M.C.A in 1857. (See 1873.)

Lord Ellenborough was recalled from the position of Governor General of India. It was the only instance where the Court of Directors used their power under the provisions of Act of 1784.

Abel Johnson Higginbotham opened the first bookshop in the country at Madras and ultimately it became the largest in India.

Bahai faith came to India from Iran. (See 1873 and 1986.)

1845   Serampore of Hooghly district and Balasore were bought by the East Indian Company from Christian VIII, King of Denmark on February 22 for a sum of Rs 12,50,000. That liquidated all Danish settlements in India's main land. (See 1755 and 1847.)

The first batch of four medical students of Calcutta Medical College namely Suryakumar Chakraborty, Bholanath Basu, Gopallal Seal and Dwarkanath Basu left for England for higher studies in surgery. (See 1835.)

The first newspaper in Hindi, the *Benares Akhbar* was published.

Pherozshah Merwanji Mehta was born on August 4. He was a great lawyer, social worker, and founder of the Bombay Presidency Association. (d. 1915).

The first Sikh war against the British broke out on December 11. Ultimately Punjab lost its independence in 1849.

Grant Medical College was established in Bombay.

Husain Husaini Aga Khan came to Bombay from Persia and was received by the Khoja community as their religious head.

1846 Lahore was captured by the British on February 20 and infant Duleep Singh was recognised as the ruler. At the age of 14 he abandoned his Sikh religion and became a Christian in 1853. He was the first Indian prince to do so. In later part of his life he became a Sikh again. (See 1849.)

Prince Dwarkanath Tagore, a Hindu philanthropist and grandfather of Rabindranath Tagore, died in London on August 1. (b. 1794).

By the Treaty of Amritsar on March 16, the British took the decision to establish a distinct Kashmir state under a Hindu prince in subordination, namely Raja Gulab Singh of Jammu, for one million pound.

Jalandhar was captured by the British from the Sikhs and virtually the Sikh kingdom as well in the next 3 years.

Urdu poet Akbar Allahabadi was born. He laid the foundation of a new school of Urdu poetry by writing humorous verse. (d. 1921).

1847 Royal Calcutta Turf Club was established on February 20. (See 1769 and 1819.)

Mrs Annie Besant was born in London on October 1. She landed at Tuticorin on November 16, 1893. Amongst her glorious services to India, she established Central Hindu College in Varanasi in 1898. She established Indian Boy Scouts' Association in 1917. She was one of the founders of Women's Conference. (d. 1933).

A.D.

Bishop Wilson built Wilson Church in Bombay in Gothic style. King George V attended divine services there in 1911 and so did Queen Elizabeth II in 1961.

The Nicobar Islands were abandoned by Denmark and were offered to England for £50,000 which the British turned down. The Islands were handed over to the British in 1868 absolutely free of any charge. (See 1756 and 1845.)

Raja of Tanjore set up a homoeopathy hospital. (See 1835 and 1881.)

Saint, poet and composer Thyagaraja died. (b. 1767).

1848 Raja Ravi Verma, the famous classic painter, was born in Kilimanoor of Kerala on April 29. He was a prolific painter. Maharana Pratap's portrait and Shakuntala writing a love letter to King Dushyanta are considered masterpieces in portrait painting. (d. 1906).

Surendra Nath Banerji, popularly known as Rashtraguru, was born on November 10. He passed his final ICS Examination in 1869 and joined in 1871. After a lawsuit on his exact age, he was posted in Sylhet as Assistant Magistrate under district magistrate H.C. Sutherland, an Anglo-Indian by birth, who got him dismissed on a false charge. He was not even allowed to enrol himself as a barrister. Then he devoted himself to the task of saving his hapless countrymen. Twice he became the president of the Indian National Congress. (See 1874 and 1875, d. 1925.).

Kandukuri Virasalingam of Andhra Pradesh, a radical visionary, protagonist of Hindu widow marriage and an architect of the renaissance of Telugu language, was born. (d. 1919).

The French abolished the slave trade in India.

The College of Civil Engineering was opened at Roorkee by Lt. MacLagan. (See 1854.)

1849 The second Anglo-Sikh war broke out in September 1848. The Sikhs again lost in Chillianwala on January 13. A treaty was signed on March 29 by Maharaja Duleep Singh vesting Punjab under direct British control. Duleep Singh got a pension of Rs 5,00,000 per annum. The Kohinoor diamond was set aside for Queen Victoria. The Sikh kingdom ended and the Sikh army was disbanded. (See 1845.)

A.D.

Bethune College of Calcutta started it activities for female education in the upper class families. It was established on May 7 under the name Calcutta Female School by Elliot Drinkwater Bethune and Ram Gopal Ghose with the patronage of Ishwar Chandra Vidyasagar. (See 1819 and 1879.)

1850 Bhartendu Harish Chander, a Hindi poet and dramatist, was born on September 9. He wrote a number of Hindi dramas following the English model. He is called the 'Father of modern Hindi literature'. (d. 1885).

The famous Kohinoor diamond, now the tenth largest in the world, left India for Queen Victoria of England. It became the property of the British Crown. (See 1849.)

The first Companies Act was passed. (See 1956.)

Kashinath Trimbak Telang was born. He was a scholar, reformer and politician, and founder-member of Bombay Presidency Association. He was also the first Indian vice-chancellor of Bombay University. (d. 1893).

Tea plantation began in Darjeeling. The first tea garden of Dooars was opened in 1862. (See 1840.)

The town of Matheron (Maharashtra) was built after Hugh Malet, collector of Thana, visited the site.

Alexander Hunter established the first art school in Madras. (See 1854.)

1851 The Geological Survey of India was established on March 5 in Calcutta.

The first official telegraph line was opened between Calcutta and Diamond Harbour on October 24. (See 1813, 1839 and 1855.)

The British Indian Association of Bengal was established on October 29 with Radha Kanta Dev as the president and Devendranath Tagore as the secretary. The Association demanded improvement of local administration. (See 1843.)

1852 Postal system for the general public was introduced in Karachi, the first time in Asia, on July 1. It was valid only in the district of Sind, and is now known as 'Scinde Dawk'. Its denomination was half anna (3 paise).

Radhanath Sikdar, working under Andrew Waugh, Surveyor General of Trigonometrical Survey of India, calculated the height of a peak as 8,839.8 metres (29,002 ft) and named it as Mount Everest, who was the predecessor of A.Waugh. Later, after correction of refractions, the peak was found to be 8,882.2 mts. (29,141 ft) high. But the survey department holds the figure as 8,839.8 mts. (See 1767.)

1853   Indian Railways started on April 16 when with a 21-gun salute, the first train of Great Indian Peninsular Railway with 3 steam-engines hauling 20 coaches with 400 people left Victoria Terminus (Bori Bunder) of Bombay for Thane, a distance of 33 km, at 3.30 P.M. This first passenger train in Asia took 57 minutes to cover the distance. A public holiday was declared in Bombay so that people could attend the function. (See 1854 and 1855.)

Saradamoni Devi (Shri Ramakrishna's spiritual consort) was born on December 22 in Jairambati of Hooghly district. (d. 1920).

Competitive examination for the Indian Civil Service (ICS) started in England, through the Charter Act of 1853, which in theory, threw it open to Indians as well. East India College in Haileybury in England was the exclusive recruiting ground. (See 1863.)

Nagpur and Berar lapsed to the East India Company.

Cinchona plantation first started in the Indian Botanic Garden, Calcutta with six plants. But those did not survive. 230 cinchona plants were sent to Mongpu in 1862 which ultimately became the prime producer.

First meteorological observations started in the survey office at Park Street in Calcutta. The meteorological office started functioning in Alipore in 1875 and Park Street station was closed.

1854   Lord Dalhousie annexed Jhansi on February 27 under the East India Company after refusing to recognise the adoption of 5-year old Ananda Rao (a descendant of Raghu Nath Rao I) by Rani Lakshmi Bai, widow of Raja Gangadhar Rao. (See 1858.)

East India Railway ran its first passenger train on August 15 between Calcutta and Hooghly. (See 1853 and 1855.)

India's first modern post office was established in Calcutta. The first stamp officially issued on May 4 from Calcutta was of half anna denomination with Queen Victoria's image in blue colour.

A.D.

The record shows that the first office for postal service was established on March 31, 1774.

Bombay Spinning & Weaving Co., the first Indian textile mill, was set up in July in Bombay by Cawasji N. Dewar. (See 1818.)

Engineering College was opened in Elphinstone College of Bombay, but soon it closed down due to lack of students. (See 1848, 1856, 1864 and 1880.)

The first railway bridge was built to cross the Thane creek in Bombay.

Fowles was the first real coffee planter who opened Marcara Coffee Estate in Coorg.

Letter boxes away from the post office were introduced in October in all major cities.

The Government School of Art was established in Calcutta. (See 1850.)

1855 Howrah station was opened and the formal inauguration of East India Railway was held on February 1, when the line was laid up to Raniganj from Calcutta, after earning some revenue from carrying coal. (See 1853 and 1854.)

The first long distance telegraph line between Calcutta and Agra, a distance of 1,300 km was opened on March 24. (See 1813, 1839, 1851 and 1867.)

Ishwar Chandra Vidyasagar's first Bengali primer *Varnaparichay* was published on April 1. (See 1820.)

Bhabatarini Kali temple of Dakhineswar was consecrated by Rani Rasmoni on May 21. Shri Ramakrishna Paramahansa Dev attained 'Siddhi' here and became immortal for his devotion to the Goddess.

Armed Santhal revolt against British oppression and moneylenders started on June 30 in Bhognadighi, now in Bihar. The rebels were led by Sidhu, Kanu, Chand and Bhairab. It ended in December. The revolt was crushed with severe ruthlessness. More than 15,000 Santhals were killed and many villages destroyed. Sidhu was betrayed, captured and killed in August. Kanu was accidentally arrested in February 1856. A special administrative system was introduced in a newly-formed district of Santhal Parganas.

The first jute spinning mill was set up in Rishra in Hooghly district by George Auckland and Biswambhar Sen. It wound up in 1868.

Sebastio Rodolfo Delgado was born in Goa. His Portuguese-Konkani dictionary is a standard work. He was the professor of Sanskrit in Lisbon University. (See 1907, d. 1922.).

1856   On February 7 Wajid Ali Shah, ruler of Oudh, was asked to abdicate by the British Resident on grounds of chronic misrule. Wajid Ali refused. Oudh was annexed on February 13. His wife Begum Hazrat Mahal remained in Lucknow with her minor son Birjis Qadir, while Wajid Ali was deported to Calcutta. The Begum fought the British during Sepoy Mutiny to re-establish the right of her son. She organised a women's brigade and led her troops from March 6 to 14, 1858 in the attire of a male army officer. After the mutiny she fled to Nepal and expired in Kathmandu in 1879. (See 1976.)

Lord Canning instituted a law on July 16 authorising the remarriage of Hindu widows under Hindu Widows Remarriage Act of 1856. Ishwar Chandra Vidyasagar, the protagonist, arranged the first widow marriage on December 7 between the child-widow Smt. Kalimati Devi and Siris Chandra Vidyaratna (Bhattacharya).

Bal Gangadhar Tilak was born at Ratnagiri on July 23. He is acclaimed as the 'Father of Indian Unrest'. He brought to the political arena a new kind of leadership which was highly intellectual. (d. 1920).

Sri Narayana Guru, a religious reformer and a living embodiment of 'Adwaita' was born on September 20 in Chempazhanthi village of Kerala (d. 1928).

Postal envelope was introduced for the first time on November 29.

Lady Charlotte Canning popularised photography in India. Many thousand photographs are known to have been taken by her in India or under her auspices, but only a handful survived. Curiously, Lady Canning's name lives in Bengal in the shape of an Indian sweetmeat known as 'Ladykeni'.

Swami Shraddhanand (Mahatma Munshi Ram) was born at Talwan in Jalandhar. He was a valiant warrior of the war of independence. He founded the Gurukul in 1902 at Kangri in Haridwar, a unique seat of learning in keeping with the ideals of the Vedic seers. In 1917 he became a 'Sannyasi'. He was assassinated on December 23, 1926 by a Muslim fanatic.

A.D.

The first All India Photographic Exhibition was organised by the Photographic Society of India in Bombay.

The Civil Engineering College was established in Calcutta and the classes were held in the Writers' Buildings. In 1864 it merged with Presidency College. The Bengal engineering College was established in 1880. (See 1848, 1856 and 1864.)

The first Bengali play *'Kulin Kula Sarvasya'*, composed by Ram Narayan Tarkaratna in 1855, was enacted by the Oriental Seminary.

Shri Ramakrishna Paramahansa Dev became the priest in Dakshineswar Kali temple.

1857 The Calcutta, Bombay and Madras Universities were founded on January 24, July 18 and in September respectively.

Troubles of Sepoy Mutiny first broke out in Baharampore of Bengal on February 26 in the 19th Bengal Infantry. But the first shot was fired on March 29 by Mangal Pandey (of Ballia, U.P.) of the 34th Bengal Infantry at Barrackpore of Bengal. Mangal Pandey was hanged at Barrackpore on April 8.

Real mutiny started on May 10 at Meerut, followed in Delhi the next day. The first British to lose his life was Col. Finnis in Meerut. On May 17 Bahadur Shah II was declared as the independent Mughal emperor of India by the sepoy mutineers, which ironically ended the rule of Mughal dynasty. Bahadur Shah II surrendered to Lt. W.S.R. Hodson on September 21 at Humayun's tomb in Delhi.

The British recaptured Delhi from the mutineers on September 20.

Four mutinies occured during the preceding 13 years in 1844, 1849, 1850 and 1852. But they were of minor significance. (See 1764 and 1765.)

The School of Tropical Medicine was established in Calcutta largely due to the enthusiasm of Leonard Rogers.

The Calcutta Y.M.C.A. was established. (See 1844 and 1873.)

Copyright Act was passed. (See 1952.)

Calcutta had the first city gas through pipeline for domestic cooking and street lighting.

The Alipore Bar Association of Calcutta was established, which happens to be the oldest Bar Association in India.

A.D.

Panchmari was discovered by Captain Forseith. It later became the summer capital of Central Province, now Madhya Pradesh.

1858   On February 26 Diwan Maniram Dutta and Piali Barua were hanged for their effort to place Kandarpeswar Simha, grandson of Purandara Simha, the last Ahom king of Assam, on the throne. The attempt of the Assamese nobility to regain their independence was crushed. (See 1828.)

J.P. Wallker sailed from Calcutta on March 4 with 200 convicts, mostly of the sepoy mutiny, along with four overseers and two doctors to start a new settlement in the Andaman Islands where they reached on March 10. In all about 3,000 mutineers were transported to Andaman and except for one, namely Mir Zafar Thaneswari, probably none could come back from there. (See 1879 and 1909.)

Lucknow mutineers surrendered on March 21.

On April 4 after a bitter battle with the British under Huge Rose, Rani Lakshmi of Jhansi slipped away from Jhansi to Kalpi and then towards Gwalior. She was killed by a stray bullet on June 18 while fighting in male attire in the battle of Kotah-ki-Sarai near Gwalior. (See 1835 and 1854.)

When India rose against British authority Kunwar Singh, an old lion of eighty years, fought a determined battle for about a year. He fought his last battle near Jagdishpur, his birthplace, in which the British forces were completely routed. He died on the next day on April 24, 1858 from severe injuries suffered in the battle.

Gwalior fort was captured by the British from the mutineers on June 20 and the Sepoy Mutiny officially ended on July 8.

On September 1, the last day of their authority, the Court of Directors of the East India Company held their final meeting at the East India House, Leadenhall St., London. Transfer of authority from Company to the British Crown was fixed on November 1, on the strength of the Government of India Act passed in British Parliament on August 2. On November 1 simultaneous proclamation was presented to the people of India in eighteen languages and read out at Calcutta, Bombay Madras, Lucknow, Lahore, Peshawar, Karachi and Rangoon. Lord Canning was then at Allahabad, near the centre of Sepoy Mutiny. A Durbar was held there inside the fort. The Union Jack was raised to the thuds of

A.D.

saluting guns. India became a part of the British empire. The administration by Indian Civil Service officers started. Governor General Lord Canning took the title Governor General and Viceroy.

Freedom fighter Bipin Chandra Pal was born in Sylhet on November 7. He was one of the renowned trio 'Lal-Bal-Pal', referring to Lala Lajpat Rai, Bal Gangadhar Tilak and Bipin Chandra Pal. (d. 1932).

The renowned scientist Jagdish Chandra Bose was born on November 30. (d. 1938, see 1895).

Bankim Chandra Chattopadhyay and Jadu Nath Bose were the first two Indians to be conferred Bachelor of Arts Degree from Calcutta University on December 11, with 7 grace marks in one of the six subjects. The examination result was out on April 18.

Peary Chand Mitra's *Alaler Gharer Dulal* was the first real novel in Bengali.

1859   Bahadar Shah II's trial started on January 7 and ended on March 29. He was found guilty of complicity in Sepoy Mutiny and was exiled to Rangoon in December, where he expired on November 7, 1862. (b. 1775).

Tantia Tope, a leader of Sepoy Mutiny, was captured in April, court-martialled and hanged at Sivapuri on April 18. His actual name was Ramachandra Raghunath Tope (b. 1814). His wife and daughter lost their lives in the battle of Kanpur.

Nana Saheb, alias Dhundu Pant, one of the top leaders of Sepoy Mutiny, died in Nepal on September 24. (b. 1824).

Indigo riots started by Bengal peasants to protest against the torture and exploitation of the British indigo planters. This gave the impetus for jute cultivation.

Bougainvillea plant was brought to Calcutta by Thomas Thompson, Superintendent of Indian Botanic Garden. The plant's name originated from Louis Antine de Bougainville, a French naval explorer, who discovered the plant in Brazil. (See 1789.)

1860   Dr W.M. Haffkine was born at Odessa in Russia on March 16. He came to India in March 1893. He popularised cholera vaccine in India which he invented at the Pasteur Institute, Paris. In 1896 when Bombay suffered an epidemic of bubonic plague, he arrived at the city on October 7, invented the plague vaccine at Grant

A.D.

Medical College and inoculated himself to prove its harmlessness. The bacteriological laboratory established by him is named Haffkine Institute to perpetuate his memory. (d. 1930).

Vishnu Narayan Bhatkhande, the great architect of the renaissance of Hindustani music, was born on August 10. (d. 1936).

M. Visveswarayya was born in Karnataka on September 15. He was a notable engineer and a maker of modern Karnataka. Many of his spectacular achievements include the scheme of Krishnaraja sagar reservior and construction of Hyderabad city. He died on April 14, 1962.

Indian Penal Code (Act XLV) was passed into law on October 6 and came into force on January 1, 1862. Its Section 302 provides for 'life sentence', but even till 1999 its was not clear about the length of imprisonement meant by life sentence. (See 1999.)

The first batch of Indian contract workers landed at Natal in South Africa on November 16.

Agostino Lourenco from Margao received his Doctorate in chemistry in Paris on December 4. He is possibly the first Indian to get a Doctorate from a foreign university.

British govt. levied licence tax on business firms, which in effect was the income tax. (See 1869.)

Keeping and trafficking in slaves were made punishable crimes under the British Penal Code. (See 1811, 1843 and 1848.)

Ishwar Chandra Vidyasagar was awarded with the first act for raising the age of consent of girls for marriage which was 10 years. (See 1891.)

Construction of Hill Cart Road to Darjeeling from Siliguri started and was completed in nine years.

Silchar Polo Club was established by Joseph Lavy and Robert Stewart. It was the world's first Polo Club. The game in the present form originated in Manipur. (See 1861.)

Double-decker railway coaches were introduced for the first time on Bombay-Baroda route. But they were not popular and were discontinued. Such coaches were reintroduced in 1978.

1861 Brahma Bandhav Upadhyay was born in Khanyan village of Bengal on February 11. His actual name was Bhabani Charan

A.D.

Bandyopadhyay. He took the pseudo name after embracing Christianity. He was a fiery national journalist, and amongst the first batch of teachers in Visva Bharati in Santiniketan. (d. 1907).

Motilal Nehru was born at Agra as a posthumous child on May 6. The family later shifted to Allahabad. The national movement benefited substantially from his dynamic leadership, large-hearted devotion, princely sacrifice and great qualities of organisation and inspiration. (d. 1931).

Rabindranath Tagore was born on May 7. (d. 1941).

Madame Bhikaji Cama was born on September 24 in Bombay. From an early age she took interest in social and political work. She believed in the principle of non-cooperation. She started her own newspaper *Vande Mataram* in U.K. She carried her campaign for India's political emancipation throughout Europe and America. She had to remain in exile from 1909 to 1935. She was allowed to return to India only when her health completely broke down in 1935. She died on August 30, 1936. (See 1902.)

Madan Mohan Malaviya was born at Allahabad on December 25. He was a giant among men and he built up the noble edifice of Indian freedom. His chief contribution was the founding of Banaras Hindu University. (d. 1946).

The first public auctions of tea were held in Calcutta on December 27.

Maximum rainfall in a year was recorded in Cherrapunji of Assam which was 22, 987 mm including 9,300 mm in July alone.

Small Causes Courts were established in commercial towns of Delhi, Amritsar, Lahore and Shimla.

Radha-Swami Satsang, an esoteric sect, was founded by Tulsi Ram, better known as Sib Dayal Saheb.

General Alexander Cunningham began regular archaeological exploration. (See 1862, 1864 and 1904.)

Paper currency notes of denominations of Rs 10, 50, 100, 1,000 and 10,000 were introduced as legal tender under the Paper Currency Act of 1861.

Indian Civil Service Act was passed. The maximum age of entry into I.C.S. was fixed at 22 years and one year's probation in

England, which in 1866 was reduced to 21 years and two years probation in England. This was further reduced to 19 years in 1878 to deprive the Indians. (See 1869.)

Times of India was amalgamated with the *Standard, Telegraph, Courier* and *Bombay Times*.

Calcutta Polo Club was established. It is the oldest Polo Club existent in the world. (See 1860.)

1862   Indian Penal Code and Code of Criminal Procedure passed on October 6, 1860 came into force on January 1.

Sambhunath Pandit was the first Indian to assume the office of the judge of a High Court (Calcutta) on February 2. He was a Kashmiri Brahmin domiciled in Calcutta.

Gnanendra Mohan Tagore passed the Barrister-at-Law examination from Lincoln's Inn on June 21. In November 1865 he was enrolled in Calcutta High Court as the first Indian barrister in the country. He was born in Calcutta on January 24, 1826. He embraced Christianity and expired in London on January 5, 1890.

Present Calcutta High Court was inaugurated on July 1. Original side and appellate sides were amalgamated. Foundation of the present building was laid in 1864 and completed in 1872. It is interesting to note that at least one case 'Basaks vs Setts', originally filed in 1850s and transferred to Calcutta High Court from the earlier Supreme Court, was still pending even in 2000.

Madras High Court was inaugurated on August 6.

Bombay High Court was inaugurated on August 14.

Sriniwas Shastri, a great patriot and politician, was born on September 23.

Bahadur Shah II, the last of the Mughal emperors, died on November 7 in captivity in Burma at the age of 87. He was buried on the same day. The British troops trampled on his grave and mounted guards just effaced it. (See 1837.)

The first industrial strike in India and the second industrial strike in the world was by about 1,200 workers of Howrah Railway Station in the first week of May. (See 1827.)

Director General of Commercial Intelligence and Statistics started working. But they observed their centenary in 1979.

Archaeological department was opened with General Alexander Cunningham as Director of Archaeology.

M.A. Degree was conferred for the first time by Calcutta University.

The Dahlia flower, a plant of South Africa, was first introduced in India by the Agri-Horticultural Society of Calcutta.

1863 Swami Vivekananda (Narendranath Dutta) was born in Calcutta on January 12. (d. 1902).

Satyendra Prasanna Sinha was born on March 24 at Raipur in Birbhum district West Bengal. He was an active member of Congress. He left Congress in 1919 along with other moderates. In the same year he was raised to the peerage as Baron Sinha of Raipur and was entrusted with piloting the Government of India Act of 1919 through the House of Lords in London. He was the first Indian to enter the Governor General's executive council. He died on March 5, 1928. (See 1919 and 1989.)

The Indian Navy was transferred to the British Admiralty on April 30.

Rao Tula Ram died on September 23. (b. 1825).

Satyendra Nath Tagore was the first Indian to be directly recruited in the Covenanted Civil Service, which was later renamed as Indian Civil Service. He entered the service in 1864. The direct recruitment was stopped in 1881. (See 1980.)

The Wahabi Movement started by Sayyid Ahmed of Rae Bareli for Muhammedan domination met the British forces in a great strength in Swat country and suffered a serious setback. (See 1786 and 1872.)

Devendranath Tagore purchased 20 acres of land and founded the core of Santiniketan. He dedicated the place to the public in 1888 as a place for meditation. (See 1910 and 1921.)

India's first passenger lift was installed in Government House at Calcutta. It is still functioning in 2005.

1864 Hari Narayan Apte, a well-known Marathi writer who popularised social and historical themes in his novels, was born on March 8. (d. 1919).

Asutosh Mukherji, the great educationist and lawyer of Bengal, was born on June 29. He was popularly known as 'Bengal Tiger'. He made Bengali a compulsory language in the University, thereby restoring it to a place of prestige. (d. 1924).

A.D.

Civil Engineering College, which was established in 1856 in Calcutta with classes held in Writers' Buildings, was merged with Presidency College. (See 1856 and 1880.)

Keshab Chandra Sen visited Madras and persuaded the people there to establish the Veda Samaj, which was changed to Brahmo Samaj in 1871 by K. Sridharalu Naidu. Then he went to Bombay. (See 1867.)

Alexander Cunningham's 'Archaeological Survey First Report' stated the year of the Battle of Kurukshetra of the Mahabharata as 1424 B.C. (See 1861.)

Bankim Chandra Chattopadhyay serially published *Rajmohan's Life* which happened to be the first English novel by an Indian. (See 1865.)

Shimla became the summer capital of India and continued to be so till 1939, after which it was discontinued because of the Second World War. (See 1819.)

1865   Lala Lajpat Rai was born in Dhudike village of Ferozepur district on January 28. The ruling passion of his life was the political emancipation of his people. His spirit revolted against injustice in any shape or form and always voiced his protest. (d. 1928).

As per the treaty with the Bhutan ruler on November 11, the British Government took over Dooars territories bordering Bengal and Assam. There were eighteen doorways leading to Bhutan under the control of its ruler. Eleven of these are now in Bengal and seven in Assam. That is how the name 'Dooars' originated.

The first incidence of fire in an underground mine took place in Raniganj coal-belt.

Kathiawar state of Saurashtra (later Junagarh) was the first native state to issue its own postage stamp. (See 1852 and 1854.)

The first full-fledged Bengali novel titled *Durgesh Nandini* was published by Bankim Chandra Chattopadhayay. (See 1864.)

The *Pioneer* made its first appearance in Allahabad. It was an Anglo-Indian newspaper.

1866   Gopal Krishna Gokhale was born in Kotluk village of Ratnagiri district of Maharashtra on May 9. The freedom fighter was the image of truth, full of humanity and one who called nothing his own. In 1905 he founded Servants of India Society. (d. 1915).

A.D.

The Allahabad High Court was inaugurated on November 25 with five judges, though it sat in Agra between 1866 and 1868. In 1869 it moved to Allahabad.

Oil was first really found on a commercial scale when Goodenough of McKillop Stewart Company drilled a well near Jaypur of Assam. . (See 1828 and 1889.)

1867 As a result of Keshab Chandra Sen's visit to Bombay in 1864, the Prarthana Samaj, i.e., prayer society was established there on March 31 by Ranade, Bhandarkar and others. (See 1842, 1864 and 1874.)

Dar-ul-Uloom (House of Learning) popularly known as Azhar al - Hind was founded by Maulana Muhammad Qasim Nanantawi and Maulana Rashid Ahmed Gangoni at Deoband of Uttar Pradesh on May 30. It is now a world renowned seat of Islamic studies. Nanantawi was the hero of the battle of Shamli, which was a precursor of the 1857 freedom struggle.

Gaganendranath Tagore was born at Calcutta on September 17. He was a prolific and versatile artist of rare originality. He was the pioneer of modern interior decoration of our country. (d. 1938).

Sister Nivedita (Margaret Elizabeth Noble) was born on October 28 at Dunganon in Ireland. She was a disciple of Swami Vivekananda. She made India her home and worked with revolutionary ardour for social and political reforms. (See 1898. d. 1911.)

The Calcutta-London telegraph line was conceived by Werner Von Siemens of Germany. He began erecting the line this year and completed the seven thousand mile line in 1869. It took 68,706 poles of pine, oak and iron and passed through Iran, Russia and many other European countries. It gave good and efficient service right up to 1931.

1868 The *Amrita Bazar Partika* was first published as a weekly issue in Bengali on February 20 by three Ghosh brothers namely Sisir Kumar, Basanta Kumar and Hemanta Kumar. In 1878 it became an English paper to circumvent the provisions of the Vernacular Press Act. It became a daily paper on February 19, 1891. (See 1994.)

Swami Virjanand expired on September 14. (b. 1778).

Lakshminath Bezbaruah of Assam was born on October 5. (d. 1938).

A.D.

Naikda rising against the British as their rulers took place in Gujarat.

Nicobar Islands were handed over to the British by Denmark free of charge. (See 1847.)

'Rasogolla', the well-known sweet of Bengal, was invented by twenty-two year old Navin Chandra Das of Baghbazar, Calcutta, who named the sweet himself. (See 1930.)

The photographic studio Bourne & Shepherd was established in Shimla in 1864 and shifted to Calcutta in 1868 and is probably the world's second oldest studio which operated till 2000, though not under the same ownership. A rich collection of historic photographs was gutted in a devastating fire in the studio on February 6, 1991.

1869 Mirza Ghalib expired on February 15. (b. 1797).

Income tax at the rate of one per cent was introduced in India for the first time from April 1 to meet the budget deficit of Rupees two and a half crores. (See 1860.)

A new Divorce Act came into operation on April 1.

Damodar Hari Chapekar, virtually the first terrorist of India, was born on June 24. (d. 1898).

Mahatma Gandhi (Mohandas Karamchand Gandhi) was born on October 2 at Porbandar in Gujarat. (d. 1948).

Kasturba, wife of Gandhiji, was born in the same year and at the same place Porbandar as Gandhiji. In Gandhiji's momentous public life she stood by his side, simple, serene and dauntless in the hour of trial and tragedy. She died on February 22, 1944 in Aga Khan Palace at Pune, as a political prisoner while under British rule.

For the first time four Indians, Surendra Nath Banerji, Romesh Chandra Dutta, Beharilal Gupta and S. B. Thakur were successful in the I.C.S. examination then held in U.K. only. (See 1848 and 1861.)

1870 Poona Sarvajanik Sabha was founded on April 2, when 95 founding members from different parts of Maharashtra assembled in Pune. The first president was the Chief of Aundh.

Dada Saheb Dhundiraj Govind Phalke, pioneer of Indian cinema, was born at Trymbak near Nasik on April 30. He started as a photographer and scene painter. Phalke's role as initiator of the cinematographic art stands unrivalled in the history of Indian cinema. He was the first director and 'Father of Film Industry'. (d. 1943. See 1913 and 1969.)

A.D.

On August 27 Sashipada Banerji of Calcutta, through his solo effort, established a labour organisation 'Sharmajivi Sangha' to look after the welfare of the labourers. (See 1884 and 1918.)

The affairs of Calcutta port came under the management of a statutory body on October 17 under the terms of Act V of 1870. Later it was consolidated under the Calcutta Port Act of 1890, and known as The Commissioners for the Port of Calcutta and later Calcutta Port Trust.

Chitta Ranjan Das, the nationalist leader, was born on November 5. He was the founder of Swarajya Party in 1922 within the freedom movement. He advocated fighting the British Raj from within the council chambers. (d 1925).

Dr. (Miss) Ida Sophie Schrudder, founder of Vellore hospital, was born on December 9. (d. 1960. See 1900.)

The first steamer from England via Suez Canal reached India.

Direct submarine cable line between India and England was established.

Ralli Paper Mills, the first one, was established. (See 1830.)

1871 Charles Freer Andrews was born in Newcastle-on-Tyne in U.K. on February 12. He was a real friend of India and made India his spiritual home. On March 20, 1904 Andrews came to India as a Christian missionary. Soon he found his goal amongst the poor and oppressed people of India. He was affectionately known as Deenabandhu, meaning friend of the poor. He died in Calcutta on April 5, 1940.

Abanindranath Tagore was born on August 7 at Jorasanko, Calcutta. The discerning eye of the artist in him found out some strange affinity between the two art friends – one indigenous and the other foreign. (d. 1951)

Lord Mayo organised the first population census in India and the figure 206 millions was perhaps a near estimate. Census is carried out every ten years thereafter. (See 1891.)

Steeple-chasing began in India with the formation of Ballygunj Steeplechase Association.

K. Shridharalu Naidu converted Veda Samaj of Madras into Brahmo Samaj. (See 1864.)

A.D.

Madhav Prasad Misra, writer of the first authentic Hindi short story, was born. (See 1904.)

John Paxton Norman, the officiating chief justice of Bengal, was fatally wounded due to stabbing in Calcutta on September 20 by a Muhammedan, suspectedly of Wahabi sect. The following year Lord Mayo met the same fate in Port Blair, by a prisoner of Wahabi sect.

1872   Lord Mayo, viceroy of India, was assassinated on February 8 in the Andaman Island by Sher Ali, an Afghan Wahabi prisoner, as a revenge for the punishment given to their leader Amir Khan. Sher Ali was hanged on March 12. (See 1863.)

Indians played football for the first time. Nagendra Prasad Sarbadhikary formed the first football club with his classmates of Hare School in April and established Sova Bazar Club. Later he joined Town Club. (See 1889 and 1890.)

Sri Aurobindo was born on August 15 in the house of Man Mohan Ghose, barrister, in Lower Circular Road, Calcutta. He passed the classical tripos at Cambridge University with first class honours, winning all the prizes in classics. He became successful in the I.C.S. examination. He relinquished all that and declared complete autonomy and freedom from British control. Later he became an ascetic in Pondicherry. (d. 1950. See 1908 and 1910).

Pandit Vishnu Digambar, a blind music revolutionary, was born on August 18. (d. 1931).

Prince Ranjit Singhji, of Ranji Trophy fame, was born on September 10. (d. 1933. See 1895).

Bhai Vir Singh was born in December at Amritsar. In 1894 he founded the Khalsa Trust Society for the propagation of Sikh culture and religion. He is also called the 'Father of Modern Punjabi Literature'. (d. 1957).

The Government of India passed the Native Marriage Act, popularly known as Civil Marriage Act, to legalise inter-religion and intercaste marriages. (See 1955.)

1873   On May 15 the resolution was taken in England to dissolve the East India Company on and from June 1, 1874.

Y.M.C.A. of India was established on June 20 in Calcutta. Actually the first one appeared in 1857 which made little headway and virtually disappeared in 1865. (See 1844.)

A.D.

Michael Madhusudan Dutta died on June 29. (b. 1824).

Swami Rama Tirtha was born at Murariwala village of Gujranwala district on October 22. He was a great social reformer, religious savant and poet. He attained 'Enlightenment' on the banks of the holy Ganga at Rishikesh. He left his mortal frame on October 17, 1906.

Vithalbhai Patel was born at Nadiad. He was a man of iron will with a magnificent political career. (d. 1933).

The first rubber plantation was established in Charduar in Assam. Tapping started in 1899.

1874 Horse-drawn tramcar started running in Bombay on May 9 and then in Madras. Calcutta had its first tramcar in 1881. The name 'tram' came from Outramway, the then new system of transport developed by Outram in Birkenhead town in U.K. (See 1907 and 1964.)

The East India Company was dissolved on and from June 1. (See 1599, 1833 and 1873.)

Assam was cut off from Bengal and was made a Chief Commissioner's province.

The first lady doctor Clara Swain, an American national, came to India at Calcutta. (See 1883.)

Prarthana Samaj Building was erected in Bombay. (See 1867.)

Sir Sturt Hogg Market commonly known as New Market of Calcutta was opened. Construction started in 1871.

S.N. Banerji was removed from Indian Civil Service on an inadequate ground of age limit, which was reduced to nineteen years in 1878 to prevent the Indians from joining the Indian Civil Service. (See 1848 and 1861.)

1875 Swami Dayananda Saraswati founded an Arya Samaj centre on April 10 in Bombay and in 1877 in Lahore. (See 1882.)

Syed Ahmed Khan established Aligarh Muhammedan Anglo-Oriental School at Aligarh on May 24. It got the status of a college in 1878 and was made Aligarh Muslim University in 1920.

On July 9 Bombay Stock Exchange, the first one in India, was formed under the shade of a large banyan tree.

A.D.

Mayo College of Indo-Saracenic architecture was established at Ajmer in October for education of children of noble families of India.

Vallabhbhai Patel, the 'Iron-man' of Indian National Congress was born at Nadiad on October 31. He spent long years in prison. His health broke down but spirit remained undaunted. His finest hour was when he accomplished the integration of the Indian states with the Union (d. 1950). His father Jhaveribhai Patel fought in the Sepoy Mutiny of 1857 under the flag of Rani of Jhansi. Jhaveribhai was wounded in the battle of Gwalior and as a prisoner spent many years in jail.

Tej Bahadur Sapru, the great Liberal leader, was born on December 8. (d. 1959).

Surendra Nath Banerji founded the first students' union based on politics. (See 1848.)

Calcutta Zoological Garden, the first zoo of India, was founded at the instigation of an Englishman of German descent, Karl Schwendler, who was an official in the Post and Telegraph Department. The first inmates were four huge Gallapagos tortoises. One of these was still alive in 2005.

The Indian Meteorological Department was established.

The game of snooker was first invented in Jabalpur by an army officer Col. Naville Chamberlain, later British prime minister. The rules were finalised in Ootacamund.

1876 On July 26 the Indian Association was founded in Calcutta to stimulate the political feeling amongst the middle class citizens in eastern India. The principal organiser Surendra Nath Banerji attended the function in spite of the death of his only son that morning. Mono Mohan Ghose was elected the president. (See 1848, 1883 and 1885.)

Science Association was established in Bowbazar Street of Calcutta on July 29 by Mahendra Lal Sarkar, which was later renamed as Indian Association for Cultivation of Science.

Bengali novelist Sarat Chandra Chattopadhyay was born on September 17 in Debanandpur village of Hooghly district. (d. 1938).

A.D.

Vande Mataram song was written on December 20 by Bankim Chandra Chattopadhyay. (See 1882, 1896 and 1950.)

Md. Ali Jinnah, founder of Pakistan, was born on December 25. (d. 1948).

Bhikoba Lakshman Chavan, one of the earliest and most selfless workers of Prarthana Samaj of Bombay, started the first night school there for Bombay's factory workers. (See 1867.)

Desika Vinayakam Pillai, a poet of the first rank, was born in Nanjil Nadu of Kanyakumari district. He was conferred the affectionate title 'Kavimani'. (d. 1954).

Publication of Civil and Military Gazette started.

Large areas of Mysore, Maharashtra, Punjab, Madhya Pradesh and Uttar Pradesh were under the grip of a severe famine till 1878.

The entire city of Jaipur was given a pink wash in honour of Prince Albert's visit leading it to be known as 'Pink City'.

1877 By the act of Parliament passed on April 3, 1876 Queen Victoria was proclaimed 'Queen and Empress of India' on January 1 in Delhi Durbar (Imperial Assemblage), presided over by Lord Lytton I. (See 1948.)

Sir John Lawrence a passenger steamer of McLean & Co. of Calcutta, perished off the Orissa coast on May 25 in a cyclone with 732 pilgrims. The steamer started from Calcutta in spite of a storm warning. An aristocrat family of Sova Bazar area of Calcutta lost 33 family members in the disaster. (See 1948.)

Ulloor S. Parameswara Iyer, popularly known as Ulloor, was born on June 5 at Changanacherry, Kerala. He was a staunch patriot and a great poet. (d. 1949).

Pandit Gopa Bandhu Das, a bright luminary of Orissa, was born in Puri on October 9. Apart from his dedication to the freedom movement, he was a poet and an author. (d. 1928).

Md. Iqbal was born on November 9 at Sialkot. He came of Kashmiri Brahmin stock. He was unrivalled in the fields of Persian and Urdu poetry. He died in Lahore on April 21, 1938 and was buried in the compound of the famous Badshahi mosque built by Aurangzeb.

1878 Mother of Sri Aurobindo Ashram in Pondicherry Miss Mira Alfassa, later Mrs Mira Richer, was born in Paris on February 21.

She permanently settled down in Pondicherry on April 24, 1920. (d. 1973).

On March 13, the Vernacular Press Act was passed to control vernacular press and publications. The *Amrita Bazar Patrika* from Bengali language overnight became an English newspaper. (See 1868.)

Calcutta Museum in the present building was opened to public on April 1. It happened to be the largest museum in Asia. (See 1814.)

On April 27 Calcutta University allowed women to appear in the entrance examination. Srimati Kadambini Ganguli (nee Bose) was the first Indian lady to appear in the entrance examination in December. (See 1879 and 1883.)

On May 15 the younger group of Brahmo Samaj rebelled and started Sadharan Brahmo Samaj under the leadership of Sivanath Shastri and Ananda Mohan Bose.

The Madras newspaper *The Hindu* first came out on September 20, as a weekly issue with only 80 copies, with G.S. Aiyer as its editor. It became a daily paper on April 1, 1889.

Muhammad Ali Jauhar, one of the founders of Jamia Millia Islamia, was born in Rampur on December 10. (See 1920.)

Mukunda Das was born in Banari village in Dhaka of Bangladesh. His real name was Yajneswara De. He plunged into the Swadeshi movement in 1905 and turned a worshipper of Goddess Kali. He was known as Charan Kabi or bard of Swadeshi movement. (d. 1934).

Vallathol Narayana Menon, a great poet of Kerala of international fame, was born. (d. 1958).

Khaki was introduced in Indian Army's dress replacing red coat. The idea was conceived by Lt. Harry Lumsden. (See 1946.)

1879 The poetess in English and nationalist leader Sarojini Naidu was born of February 13. She was acclaimed as the Nightingale of India. In 1947 she became the governor of Uttar Pradesh. She was the first lady to hold that position. She chaired the Asian Relations Conference held in Delhi 1947. (d 1949).

Bethune College of Calcutta, the pioneer of women's college education in India, was established on March 4. Perhaps it was then the only women's college in the British empire outside Great Britain. The first lady to pass Fine Arts from there was Kadambini Ganguli (nee Bose). (See 1849.)

Narayana Malhar Joshi, the father of Indian trade union movement, was born on June 5. He started the India Trade Union Congress in 1921. (d. 1955).

Postcard of one pice was introduced by the Post and Telegraph Department on July 1.

Siliguri-Darjeeling mountain train, popularly known as Toy Train, started operating between Siliguri and Tindharia, a distance of 29 km, in August. It was finally extended to Darjeeling on July 4, 1881. The oldest surviving railway engine on show in Rail Transport Museum in New Delhi, is of this section.

E.V. Ramaswami Naicker was born of September 17 at Erode in Tamil Nadu. He was the most distinguished leader in the Dravidian Movement of Tamil Nadu. He believed in direct action to overthrow the British. (d. 1972. See 1949.)

Sadhu T. L. Vaswani was born on November 25 in Hyderabad of Sind. He was the founder of Mira Movement. (d. 1966).

Jatindra Nath Mukherji was born in Jessore on December 8. He was better known as 'Bagha Jatin', because as a young man he had tackled a Royal Bengal tiger single-handed and killed it with a knife. (See 1915.)

C. Rajagopalachariar, the philosopher-nationalist leader, was born on December 10. He was the only Indian as well as the last Governor General of India. He founded the Swatantra Party in 1959 which merged with the Janata Party in 1977. (d. 1972).

The great Saint Ramana Maharishi was born in Tiruchuzhi near Madurai on December 30. He spread his message of inward peace and realisation and insisted that the real Maharishi was not his body but lies in the earnest search for 'Truth'. (d. 1950).

The construction of the ill-famed cellular jail of the Andaman Island started with bricks brought from Burma. It contained seven wings radiating from a central tower having a total of 756 cells each measuring 4 mt by 2.75 mt. (See 1858 and 1909.)

Basudev Balwant Phadke of Maharashtra, who with a band of young men revolted against the British rule, was arrested on July 3 in

A.D.

Buddhist monastery near Bijapur. On October 22 the first treason case against British rule was filed. He was the first freedom fighter to conceive Indian Republic. He died in a prison in Aden on February 17, 1883.

In U.P. the first nationalist paper in English *Indian Herald* was published by Pandit Ayodhyanath.

Calcutta Branch of Theosophical Society was established. Madame Helena Petrovna Blavatsky and Col. Henry Steel Olcott first founded the society in U.S.A. in 1875. It was popularised in India by Mrs Annie Besant. (See 1882 and 1893.)

Mono Mohini Bandyopadhyay, daughter of Rev. Krishna Mohan Bandyopadhyay, was the first Bengali and probably the first Indian lady to be a government employee.

Mahalakshmi Race Course of Bombay was constructed.

1880   Money order system was introduced on January 1.

The first issue of *Illustrated Weekly of India* was out on January 3. It actually came out as a weekly edition of the *Times of India,* which was by then 42 years old. At that time its name was *The Times of India Overland Weekly Edition.*

Keshab Chandra Sen introduced 'Nababidhan' on modernisation of Brahmo Samaj and fraternity amongst religions on January 25.

C.Y. Chintamani, the renowned journalist, was born on April 10. (d. 1941).

Annasaheb Kirloskar presented the first musical play in Marathi 'Sangeet Sakuntal' on October 3 in Anandodbhav Auditorium in Pune. (See 1843.)

The water reservoir of Bombay and its terraced garden known as the Hanging Garden was constructed. It was renovated in 1921. The actual name is Pheroz Shah Mehta Garden.

Systematic exploitation of gold started in Kolar gold mines in Mysore by John Taylor and Sons.

Hand-pulled rickshaw first appeared in Shimla. Calcutta had its rickshaw in 1900.

Bengal Engineering College of Sibpur was established. (See 1856 and 1864.)

1881 St. Stephen's College was founded in Delhi on February 1 by Cambridge Missionaries. Presently it is the oldest college in Delhi with a continuous history. It was first affiliated to Calcutta University, then to Punjab University and finally with Delhi University after the establishment of the University there in 1922.

The first Homoeopathic Medical College and Hospital was established in Calcutta on February 14 by Rajendra Lal Dutta and M. M. Basu. (See 1835 and 1847.)

The first statue of an Indian, that of Ram Nath Tagore, the youngest brother of Dwarkanath Tagore and a social reformer, was unveiled in Calcutta Town Hall on March 11 by Ashley Eden. (See 1803 and 1977.)

The Toy Train reached Darjeeling on July 4. (See 1879.)

Calcutta had its first horse-drawn tramcar. Three Englishmen Dilwyan Parrish, Alfred Parrish and Robinson Sautar started Calcutta Tramways Co. First horse-drawn tram ran on Sealdah-Armenian Ghat track on November 1. (See 1902.)

India had its first telephone exchange in Calcutta with 50 lines, only after 5 years of its invention. (See 1913.)

Nagaland was declared a district of Assam. (See 1832 and 1963.)

In Punjab a newspaper *The Tribune* was sponsored by Sardar Dayal Singh Majithia.

Vinayak Chatre of Kolhapur started the first Indian circus namely Chatre Circus.

The first Factory Act was passed, which was followed by one in 1911 and another in 1934. The first act stipulated that no child under 7 years could be employed in a factory and children under 12 years were not to be employed for more than 9 hours a day.

1882 The Postal Savings Bank system was introduced on April 1.

Eden (maternity) Hospital was opened in Calcutta on April 19 in the name of A. Eden. The first patient was admitted on July 17. In the first year 41 European and 82 Indian ladies were admitted. (See 1841.)

Bidhan Chandra Roy was born on July 1 and he died on the same date in 1962. By an extraordinary feat he qualified both for M.R.C.P. and F.R.C.S. in England in the same year 1911.

A.D.

Nandalal Bose was born of December 3. He was one of the great masters of Indian art who appeared in the wake of Bengal renaissance. His passing away on April 15, 1966 marked the end of an era.

Bankim Chandra Chattopadhyay's novel *Ananda Math* was published on December 12. But the song *Vande Mataram* itself was published in *Banga Darshan* earlier. Jadunath Bhattacharya was the first person to compose the music. It was first sung on December 28 in the 1896 session of Indian National Congress in Calcutta.

The headquarters of the Theosophical Society was established in December in Adyar near Madras. (See 1879.)

The Indian branch of the French social organisation Little Sisters of the Poor was established.

A cow protection association was formed as a part of Arya Samaj programme, which led to serious communal troubles off and on. (See 1875.)

Arya Mahila Samaj, a women's organisation, was founded by Pandita Rambai under the roof and with the active cooperation of the Prarthana Samaj of Bombay. (See 1867 and 1875.)

Subramaniam Bharati was born. The zamindar of Ettayapuram in Tamil Nadu, where he was born, conferred the title of Bharati on young Subramaniam. The burning desire for freedom brought him under British displeasure. He spent some time in Pondicherry with Sri Aurobindo. (d. 1921).

1883 On February 17 Basudev Balwant Phadke expired in Aden prison. (See 1879.)

Vinayak Damodar Savarkar was born on May 28 at Bhagur village near Nasik. His life is a story of resistance, struggle, suffering and sacrifice for the cause of political, social and economic emancipation of India. In 1904 he founded an organisation Abhinav Bharat to wrest freedom from the British rulers, if necessary, by the use of arms. He founded the Hindu Mahasabha in 1927. (d. 1966).

India's first public theatre hall namely Star was opened on July 21 at Calcutta on Beadon Street. On that day 'Daksha Yagna' drama was staged. It shifted to its later site on Bidhan Sarani on May 25,

A.D.

1888 and the symbolic star was lit up every evening since then until the employees went on strike, followed by a lockout on December 1, 1987. In an accidental fire the hall was burnt to cinder on October 12, 1991.

Swami Dayananda Saraswati, the founder of Arya Samaj, died on October 30 in Ajmer. (See 1875, b. 1824.).

Under Surendra Nath Banerji's leadership the political group of Bengal held a national conference from December 28 to 30 under Bharat Sabha. They pressed for wider employment of Indians in various public fields as well as for political concessions. (See 1876 and 1885.)

Tarapada Banerjee of Krishnagar originated the idea of collecting a national fund to assist the sufferers for national cause, as a memento of Surendra Nath Banerji's imprisonment for two months on May 5, who was found guilty of contempt of court. Surendra Nath Banerji was the first Indian to go to jail in performance of his duty as a journalist.

India's first International Exhibition was opened in Calcutta in December by Lord Ripon.

Kadambini Ganguli (nee Bose) and Chandramukhi Basu were the first two Indian women to pass the B.A. examination from Calcutta University. Chandramukhi became the first woman M.A. (in English) in 1884 and joined Bethune School of Calcutta as a teacher. Kadambini studied medicine and got 'Graduate of the Medical College of Bengal' diploma, but not 'Bachelor of Medicine' degree. She became the first Indian lady doctor in 1888 and joined Eden Hospital of Calcutta. (See 1874, 1884 and 1889.)

1884 Keshab Chandra Sen died on January 4. (b. 1838).

The director general of post offices launched the scheme of postal insurance on February 1.

Madras Mahajana Sabha, a political organisation, was founded in Madras in May by P. Ananda Charlu.

India's first President Rajendra Prasad was born in Jiradei village of Bihar on December 3. He was a brilliant student and never stood second in any examination. (d. 1963).

The political group of Madras held a conference attended by theosophists from various parts of India. (d. 1885).

A.D.

Conventional history of labour movement derived its starting point from the meeting of Bombay mill workers, convened by a local editor N. M. Lokhande. (See 1870 and 1918.)

Reply post cards were introduced.

The first boxing match in India was held in Calcutta.

1885 Jatindra Mohan Sen Gupta, a nationalist leader, was born on February 22. (d. 1933).

As the outcome of 1876, 1883 and 1884 political conferences in Bengal and Madras, the Indian National Congress, then known as the Indian National Union, was founded by Allan Octavian Hume, a Scotsman and as ICS officer who voluntarily retired in 1882. It held its first meeting on December 28 in Bombay Tejpal Hall with 72 delegates from all over India. W. C. Bonerjee was the president. Actually Hume started the Congress with the blessings of the then Viceroy Lord Dufferin.

King Thibaw, the last king of Burma, lost to the British. He was kept a captive at Ratnagiri in the west coast of India. He expired in 1915 and was buried in Baharampore (Bengal).

Bharatendu Harishchandra died. (b. 1850).

Bombay Institute for Deaf and Mute was established which was the first institute of its kind in India.

1886 The great revolutionary Rash Behari Bose was born on May 25. He secretly left India for Japan in May 1915. He died in Tokyo on January 21, 1945. (See 1943.)

S. Muthulakshmi Reddi was born on July 30. She was a nationalist, social worker, educationist, physician and a selfless public worker. She had many firsts to her credit. In 1926 she became the first woman legislator (member of Madras Legislative Council), first woman alderman (in Madras Corporation 1937), first woman deputy president of a legislature in the world.

Maithili Saran Gupta was born on August 3 at Chirgaon near Jhansi. He drew his poetic inspiration and themes mainly from India's ancient history, culture and traditions. He died in Chirgaon in December, 1964.

Ramakrishna Paramahansa Dev expired in the early morning of August 16. (b. 1836).

A.D.

The great revolutionary Raja Mahendra Pratap was born on December 1 at Mushran in U.P. He escaped from India in 1914 and became the head of the provisional Indian government in Kabul in 1915. (d. 1979).

On Christmas eve Vivekananda and his collegues assembled at Atpur village and took the vow of 'Sannyas'.

Public Service Commission was first appointed under the chairmanship of Aitchison, governor of Punjab. (See 1926.)

Maharaja of Bikaner was the first person to switch on electric light in our country. He illuminated Bikaner palace with the help of engineer Robinson. (See 1897 and 1899.)

Anandibai Joshi became the first Indian woman physician on graduating from Women's Medical College in Pennsylvania of U.S.A. (See 1883.)

The first Dayanand Anglo-Vedic College (DAV) was opened in Lahore.

The first complete Bengali version of the *Quran* was written and published by Giris Chandra Sen.

The first cricket team of India consisting of 16 Parsee youths toured England. (See 1721, 1926 and 1932.)

1887 Manabendra Nath Roy (actually Narendra Nath Bhattacharya) was born on March 21 in Arbelia village of 24-Parganas of West Bengal. (See 1916, d. 1954).

Artist Jamini Roy was born on April 11. (d. 1972).

Gandhiji sailed for Great Britain on September 4 for his Bar-at-Law degree.

Govind Ballabh Pant was born in Khunt in Almora district on September 10. He had a brilliant academic career and built up a flourishing practice at Nainital bar. He abandoned it and plunged into active politics. He was an outstanding parliamentary figure in his days. He was awarded Bharat Ratna in 1959. (d. 1961).

Srinivas Ramanujam was born on December 22. He was one of the greatest mathematicians India has ever produced. (d. 1920).

K. M. Munshi, founder of Bhartiya Vidya Bhavan, was born on December 30. (d. 1971).

Troilanga Swami expired in Varanasi. He was born in Vazianagram. His original name was Sivaram and later Ganapati Saraswati. People of Varanasi called him Troilanga Swami since he came from Telengana region.

The Bengal National Chamber of Commerce & Industry was established. It was the first national chamber of commerce. (See 1823.)

Kadambini Gaguli (nee Boss) became the first lady doctor and joined Eden Maternity Hospital. She along with Jyotirmoyee Devi (daughter of Dwarkanath Tagore) were the first women councillors of Calcutta Corporation. (See 1883 and 1886.)

Sharp Memorial School for the Blind was establisted in Dehradun. It was the first of its kind in our country. (See 1963 and 1988.)

1888   Freedom fighter Trailokyanath Chakraborty was born on May 5. (d. 1970).

Present Victoria Terminus station (Bori Bunder) of Bombay was completed in May. It was built in Italian-Gothic style. (See 2004.)

Allama Mashriqi was born on August 25. He had a brilliant career. In 1931 he organised Khaksar Party (Servants of God) in Hyderabad. He started as a communalist, but during the first half of the 1940s he propagated Hindu-Muslim unity, and later he became the chief exponent of racial and communal hatred in Hyderabad. He died also on August 25 in 1963 in Pakistan.

Sarvepalli Radhakrishnan, the renowned philosoper and the second president of India, was born at Tiruttani near Madras on September 5, which is now observed as Teachers Day', since he himself was a professor. (d. 1975).

C.V. Raman, the Nobel Prize winner in physics, was born at Tiruchirapalli on November 7. (See 1930. d. 1970).

Abul Kalam Azad, a freedom fighter, was born in Mecca on November 11. (On June 5 as per his application for a passport in 1923). Apart from his contribution to the Indian national struggle, Maulana Azad was an outspoken champion of rationalism and progressiveness in all spheres of Indian life. (d. 1958).

The renowned historian Romesh Chandra Majumdar was born on December 4. (d. 1980).

A.D.

Acharya J. B. Kripalani, a renowned freedom fighter, was born in Hyderabad, Sind. (d. 1981).

Vishnu Gopal Pingle was born. (d. 1915).

Durand Footbal Tournament was introduced in Shimla only for the military teams. The venue was shifted to Delhi in 1940 due to the Second World War. It is the second oldest football trophy in the world, the oldest being the F. A. Cup of England. The trophy was named after Mortimar Durand, who established the once famous Calcutta Football Club.

The theory that Hindus and Muslims are two nations was first clearly spelt out by Syed Ahmed Khan. (See 1875.)

The first houseboat 'Victory' was built at Dal Lake in Srinagar.

1889 Some Assamese youths educated in Calcutta brought out their own literary journal *Jonaki* on January 13 from 10 Armenian Street which stressed the linguistic identity of Assamese language.

Weekly *Hindu* of Madras was converted into a daily newspaper on April 1.

Ram Chandra Chatterjee, wrestler and director of Great India United Circus, was the first Indian to ascend in a balloon namely the 'Viceroy' on April 10 from the compound of Oriental Gas Co. in Narkeldanga of Calcutta, along with his preceptor Percival Spencer. On May 4 he made the solo flight from the same place in his own balloon namely 'The city of Calcutta' and reached a height of 1,200 metres. (See 1785 and 1890.)

The first Indian team Sova Bazar Club to play in a football tournament was in Trades Cup against St. Xaviers Club on July 11. It happened to be the first All India Tournament. (See 1872, 1888 and 1890.)

British Indian Committee, the branch of Indian National Congress, was opened in London on July 27 by Dadabhai Naoroji, W. S. Caine, William Digby and William Wedderburn.

Mohan Bagan Athletic Club was established in August. In 1989 the club President Umapati Kumar (93 years), who joined the club in 1917, had the unique privilege and distinction of participating in the club's Golden Jubilee, Diamond Jubilee and Centenary celebrations. (See 1911.)

A.D.

Sarat Chandra Bose, the elder brother of Subhas Chandra Bose, was born on September 6. He joined Calcutta bar in 1913. Drawn in early life to a political career under the leadership of C. R. Das, after whose death he became a stalwart of the Congress in Bengal. In 1946 he resigned from the Congress and formed a new party called the Republican Socialist Party. (d. 1950).

The first successful oil well was sunk at Digboi on October 19 where oil was struck at 200 metres. It was the world's oldest continuously running oil field till 2005. (See 1828 and 1866.)

Jamnalal Bajaj, a freedom fighter, was born on November 4 in Kashi-ka Bas village near Jaipur. He became the grandson and heir by adoption of Bachhraj Bajaj, a religious-minded philanthropist of Jaipur. He settled in Wardha. He earned immense wealth, but never stooped to unclean business practices. Bajaj Group of Industries had grown into a huge organisation. (d. 1942).

Jawaharlal Nehru, India's first prime minister, was born on November 14, which is now observed as Children's Day. (d. 1964).

Khudiram Bose of Muzaffarpur Bomb Case was born on December 3. (See 1908.)

Vedanayakam Pillai died. (b. 1826).

Ahmadiya Movement was founded by Mirza Ghulam Ahmed. It described itself as the standard bearer of Muslim renaissance.

Bidhu Mukhi Bose and Mary Virginia Mitter were the first two ladies to get the Bachelor of Medicine degree from Calcutta University. (See 1883 and 1884.)

Pandita Ramabai, who earlier started Arya Mahila Samaj with little success, became a Christian and started 'Sharada Sadan', a school and residence for child widows.

Acharya Narendra Deo was born at Sitapur in U.P. He gave of his best to attain freedom of the country. He was the vice-chancellor of Kashi Vidyapith from 1927 to 1947.

Prince Albert (later King Edward VII) laid the foundation of Glass-House in Lal Bagh Garden in Bangalore on November 30, which is really the Horticultural Exhibition Building.

1890   Barrister Gnanendra Mohan Tagore died on January 5. (b. 1826).

A.D.

Ram Chandra Chatterjee was the first person to make a descend by parachute from a balloon at Calcutta on March 22. (See 1889 and 1940.)

On July 24 Sova Bazar Club was the first Indian team to beat an English (military) football team East Surrey by 3 goals to 2. (See 1872 and 1889.)

National Professor Suniti Kumar Chatterjee was born on November 26. (d. 1977).

Jyotirao Govindrao Phule died. (b. 1827).

Bicycle made its appearance in India. (See 1938.)

Kesarbai Kerkar, Goa's most precious bequest to Hindustani music, was born. It was one of the monumental voices of the century in north Indian tradition. (d. 1977).

1891 The *Amrita Bazar Patrika* became a daily paper on February 19. (See 1868.)

Age of Consent Bill was passed on February 19. (See 1860.)

Bhimji Ramji Ambedkar was born of Mahar (untouchable) parents in Mahu village in western Maharashtra on April 14. He was the prime architect of the Constitution of Independent India. In 1924 he started an organisation in Bombay named 'Bahiskrit Hitakarini Sabha' for the upliftment of the untouchables. In April 1942 he formed a political party called Scheduled Castes Federation. He embraced Buddhism on October 24, 1956. (See 1947, d. 1956).

Ishwar Chandra Vidyasagar died on July 29. (b. 1820).

Senapati Tikendrajit, Prince of Manipur, was hanged along with his brothers Agnesh Sena and General Thangal on August 13, shortly after a British officer was publicly beheaded in Manipur, who was sent there to suppress the revolt. Manipur lost its independence.

The first effective census was taken. India's population figure was 27,94,46,000. (See 1871.)

Mahabodhi Society of India was established by revolutionary Anagarik Dharmapal.

Direct recruitment for Indian Civil Service was stopped. (See 1863.)

Rovers Cup Tournament started in Bombay.

Indian Marine was named Royal Indian Marine. (See 1829 and 1934.)

A.D.

Mahatma Gandhi was declared a barrister as a member of the Inner Temple, where he was admitted as a student on November 6, 1888. But he was debarred as a barrister at a parliament of the Inn held on November 10, 1922 for 'exciting dissatisfaction towards the British Raj' The journal *Young India* in its issue of November 30, 1922 had written, 'A time will surely come when the Inner Temple will reassert as an honour the fact that the greatest man of our times belonged to her'. That truly happened sixty-six years later. On November 6, 1988 Inner Temple honoured itself by readmitting Gandhi as a 'Bar-at-Law', on the centenary of his enrolment as a student there.

1892   Viceroy Lansdowne opened the new Bombay Tansa Water Works on March 13 designed by Major Tulloch.

Miss Meera Behn was born as Madeleine Slade in England. She landed at Bombay on November 6, 1925 and was at Sabarmati Ashram the next day. She loved India and joined in India's struggle for freedom. She left India for good on January 18, 1959 and settled down in a small village near Vienna.

Swami Vivekananda sojourned on the rock in the midst of the sea off Kanyakumari for three days on December 25, 26 and 27. (See 1970.)

Calcutta Muslim Orphanage was established.

Calcutta Orphanage was established by the Brahmo community under the leadership of Pran Krishna Dutta.

Deaf and Dumb School was established in Calcutta.

The principle of indirect election was first introduced by the British. But popularly elected representatives entered the legislatures only in 1909. (See 1952.)

Gopal Hari Deshmukh alias Lokahitwadi died. (b. 1823).

The first automobile was imported by Maharaja of Patiala. It was a French-made De Dion Bouton car. It got pride of place with its licence plate number 'O'. (See 1904.)

1893   Surya Sen, alias Masterda, of Chittagong Armoury Raid case, was born on March 22. (d. 1934).

Prasanta Chandra Mahalanobis, founder of Indian Statistical Institute, was born on June 29. (See 1931, d. 1972)

A.D.

Swami Vivekananda attended the World Parliament of religions at Chicago and delivered a speech on the opening day on September 11. His famous soul-stirring speech was delivered on September 19. In America he was branded as the 'Cyclonic Hindu'. His extempore speeches raised him to a great height.

Annie Besant landed at Tuticorin on November 16 and from that day she took India by storm, preaching the doctrines of the Theosophical Society. (See 1879.)

The free coinage of silver ceased and a gold standard was introduced.

Bal Gangadhar Tilak reorganised the old Maharashtrian Ganapati festival and gave it a political character by organising lectures, singing parties and processions. He was a great source of inspiration to Gandhiji's freedom struggle.

Kashinath Trimbak Telang died. (b. 1850).

The I.F.A. (Indian Football Association) Shield, the blue riband of Indian football, was introduced in Calcutta (See 1980.)

1894   National Professor Satyendra Nath Bose was born on January 1. For some time he worked with Albert Einstein. (See 1974, d. 1974).

Meher Baba, Indian saint of Persian origin and gifted with psychic powers of prediction, was born on February 25.

Novelist Bankim Chandra Chattopadhyay died on April 8. (b. 1838).

V. V. Giri, the fourth president of India, was born at Berhampore of Orissa on August 10. He was one of the patriarchs of trade union movement of India. (d. 1980).

Pous Mela festival of Santiniketan was inaugurated by Rabindranath Tagore on December 23.

The first medical conference was held in Calcutta between December 24 and 29. It was opened by Viceroy Lord Elgin II

The Philatelic Society of India held the first philatelic exhibition in December in Calcutta.

Punjab National Bank, the first purely Indian bank, came into being.

In the Dooars region of Bengal tea was first cultivated at the foothills of the Himalayas at Gazaldoba. (See 1840 and 1850.)

A.D.

1895   Munshi Newal Kishore died on February 19. (b. 1836).

Bal Gangadhar Tilak inaugurated the Shivaji festival at Raigarh on April 15 to revive the spirit of adventure, heroism and to reawaken the desire to liberate the country from foreign yoke.

Vinoba Bhave (real name Vinayak Narahari Bhave) was born in Gagoda village of Maharashtra on September 11. He was the staunchest spiritual heir to Gandhiji. The Bhoodan and Sarvodaya Movements and rehabilitation of the Chambal valley dacoits gave him world fame. As a freedom fighter he went to prison several times. Gandhiji selected him to lead the Individual Satyagraha in 1940. He breathed his last on November 15, 1982 in his Paunar Ashram in Madhya Pradesh. He was posthumously awarded Bharat Ratna on January 25, 1983. He was the first recipient of Magsaysay Award in 1958.

Prince Ranjit Singhji was the first Indian to play in English country cricket on behalf of Sussex. In his first match against M.C.C. he scored in two innings 77 runs not out and 150 runs. The next year he played for England in the Test match against Australia, when he scored 62 runs and 154 runs not out. He was the captain of Sussex from 1899 to 1904. In all he played 163 first class matches in England. (See 1872.)

The first railway steam engine was built at Ajmer Works of Rajputana Malwa Railway for Bombay-Baroda and Central India Railway. (See 1950.)

Beighton Cup, the blue riband of Indian hockey, was introduced in Calcutta.

J.C. Bose successfully transmitted wireless signals, a year before Marconi.

1896   Swami Paranabananda Brahamachari, the founder of Bharat Sevashram Sangha, was born in Bajitpur village of Faridpur district (now in Bangladesh) on January 29. He took 'Sannyas' in 1924. (See 1929, d. 1941.)

Morarji Desai, India's fourth prime minister, was born on February 29. The first non-congress prime minister expired on April 10, 1995 only 10 months short of his birth centenary.

Cinema first came to India on July 7, when a team of agents of Lumiere Brothers of France began showing short cinematographic

A.D.

films titled, Entry of Cinematography, Arrival of A Train, The Sea Bath, A Demolition, Workers Leaving the Factory, and Ladies and Soldiers on Wheels, at Watson Hotel in Bombay. The total duration of these six films was less than one hour. (See 1899 and 1913.)

'Vande Mataram' was first sung in the Indian National Congress session in Calcutta on December 28. (See 1876.)

Durand Line was drawn to define the boundary between India and Afghanistan.

Anandamoyee Ma of universal fame was born on April 30. Her childhood name was Nirmala Sundari Devi. (d. 1982).

Mono Mohan Ghose died. (b. 1844).

1897 Netaji Subhas Chandra Bose was born in Cuttack on January 23. At the age of 23 he ranked fourth in the I.C.S. examination in London. The great nationalist leader escaped from India in 1941 and fought against the British with his Azad Hind Fauj in the Second World War. (d. 1945).

Zakir Hussain, the third president of India, was born at Hyderabad of Andhra Pradesh on February 8. Through his efforts Jamia Millia Islamia came into existence on October 29, 1920. On his death on May 3, 1969 he was laid to rest at Jamia Millia Islamia in New Delhi.

Swami Vivekananda established Ramakrishna Mission at Belur on May 1, which was registered under the Society Act XXI of 1860 on May 4, 1909.

On June 22, the Diamond Jubilee Day of Queen Victoria's Coronation, Damodar Hari Chapekar (b. 1869), a Deccan Chitpavan Brahmin, shot at Charles Rand, Plague Commissioner and Ayerest, District Magistrate of Pune. While Ayerest died on the spot, Rand expired on July 3. That was the first terrorist act in India. Damodar went to gallows on April 18, 1898. His brother Balkrishna Chapekar (b. 1873) was put to death on May 12, 1899 for the same offence. Another brother Vasudev Chapekar (b. 1879) was executed on May 8, 1899 for killing the traitor who disclosed their identity. All the three brothers were hanged in Yervada Central Jail.

The world's first fingerprint bureau was set up in June in Calcutta. Edward Richard Henry and his assistants Azizul Haque and Hem

Chandra Bose devised the first known method of fingerprint classification.

Bal Gangadhar Tilak was for the first time arrested on July 27 and sent to eighteen months rigorous imprisonment for publication of poem entitled 'Shivaji's Utterances' in *Kesari* magazine of June 15.

Ronald Ross discovered malaria parasites in the anopheles mosquito in Calcutta Presidency General Hospital (now SSKM Hospital), on August 20, and got Nobel Prize in 1990.

The first power-house, incidentally a hydroelectric station, was set up at Sidrapong in Darjeeling with installed capacity of 130 kw. (See 1899.)

Maharaja Prodyot Kumar Tagore was the first Indian to be made a member and next year the Fellow of Royal Photographic Society of U.K. (See 1840 and 1856.)

Vaman Abaji Modak died. (b. 1835).

1898 Sister Nivedita (Margaret Elizabeth Noble), an Irish lady of Scottish descent, came to India on January 28 and on March 25 she was initiated to Brahmacharya by Swami Vivekananda. (See 1867.)

Damodar Hari Chapekar was the first terrorist to go to the gallows. He was hanged in the Yervada Central Jail on April 18. (See 1897, b. 1869.)

Belur Math of Calcutta was consecrated on December 9. The monks started living there from January 2, 1899. (See 1938.)

Central Hindu College was established at Varanasi by Mrs Annie Besant. It formed the nucleus of Banaras Hindu University.

Society for the Protection of Children was established in Calcutta.

The first Indian music was produced on gramophone record in Calcutta factory of Gramophone and Typewriter Ltd. (See 1902.)

Syed Ahmad Khan died. He started the revival of Urdu as the language of the Muslims in India. (See 1875, b. 1817.).

Calcutta Football League started only amongst the European teams. The first two Indian teams Mohan Bagan (estd. 1889) and Aryans (estd. 1884) were allowed to play in the Second Division in 1914. Mohan Bagan got into the First Division in 1915. (See 1889 and 1911.)

A.D.

1899 On January 2 monks started living in Belur Math. (See 1898.)

Calcutta was the first city to go electric on April 17 with a thermal plant with an installed capacity of 100 kw. It was the world's third city after London and New York.

Rebel Bengalee poet Nazrul Islam was born on May 25 in Churulia village of Burdwan district. (d. 1976).

Smt. Kamala Nehru, wife of Jawaharal Nehru, was born on August 1. (d. 1936).

Bengal Chemicals and Pharmaceuticals Ltd. was established by Prafulla Chandra Roy.

The last insurrection of the heroic Mundas took place around Ranchi of Bihar under their leader Birsa Munda.

The first Indian to make a film was Harischandra Bhatvadekar when he exhibited his own short items 'The Wrestlers' and 'Man and Monkeys'. (See 1896 and 1913.)

1900 General Cariappa, the first Indian commander-in-chief of the Indian Army, was born on January 28. (d. 1993).

Shrimati Vijayalakshmi Pandit, the first woman president of the United Nations General Assembly, was born on August 18. (d. 1990. See 1936.).

The renowned dancer Uday Shankar was born of December 8. (d. 1977).

North West Frontier Province (now in Pakistan) was created.

Pasteur Institute was established in Kasauli for the treatment of persons bitten by rabid animals.

Regular rubber plantation was set up in Kerala. (See 1826 and 1873.)

Norman Pritchard was the first Indian athlete to win medals in the Olympic games. He won a silver medal in the 200 metre sprint in 22.8 secs and another in 200 metre hurdles in 26.6 secs. in Paris Olympic. As per the Olympic rules then, he represented individually and not as an Indian. (See 1952 and 2004.)

The internationally famous Vellore hospital had a very modest beginning in a small room by Dr. (Miss) Ida Sophia Schrudder (born on December 9, 1870), an extraordinary medical visionary. She passed away on May 24, 1960.

A.D.

Dr. Graham's Home was founded in Kalimpong by Dr. John Anderson Graham.

Kamlabai Gokhale, India's first film actress, was born. (d. 1992. See 1913.)

1901   Mahadeo Govind Ranade died on January 16. (b. 1842).

At the beginning of twentieth century whole India's population was 29,43, 65,056 as on March 1. (See 2000.)

Mahakavi G. Sankara Kurup, the first winner of the coveted 'Janapith Award', was born on June 3. (See 1965, d. 1978.)

Shyama Prasad Mukherji, a great champion of Hindu Mahasabha, was born on July 6. He was the founder of Bharatiya Jana Sangh. (d. 1953).

Rabindranath Tagore established his Brahmacharya Ashram, the core of Visva Bharati University, on December 12 with only 5 students, including his son Rathindranath Tagore and as many teachers. It was formally opened on December 22. (See 1863 and 1921.)

India's first women's magazine *The Indian Ladies Magazine* was started by Smt. Kamala Swaminathan in Madras.

V.D.Paluskar set up the first musical school Gandharva Mahavidyalaya at Lahore.

Smt. Kadambini Ganguli was the first Indian lady to address an open session of the Indian National Congress held in Calcutta, when she moved the Vote of Thanks.

Gandhiji for the first time attended the Indian National Congress session held at Calcutta. But he joined the organisation in 1915. (See 1935.)

Digboi Oil Refinery, the oldest in India, started its operation. In 2005 it was the oldest running refinery in the world. (See 1889.)

Sriramulu Potti was born in Madras. He was a follower of Gandhiji and worked for the propagation of cottage industries and Khadi. From October 19, 1952 he undertook a fast unto death for the formation of a separate Andhra state. He went through the ordeal for fifty-eight days and finally laid down his life on December 16, 1952. (See 1953.)

A.D.

1902   Anusilan Samiti, a revolutionary organisation of Bengal, was formed on March 24.

Swami Vivekananda died on July 4. A brilliant career came to a sudden end at the age of 39. (b. 1863).

Jayaprakash Narayan was born on October 11 in Sitabdiara village of Bihar. (d. 1979).

Madame Bhikaji Rustam K. R. Cama left India to carry her message of freedom in Europe and America against the British rule. She is known as the 'Mother of Indian Revolution'. She propagated militant nationalism. On August 22, 1907, in the second International Socialists Congress held at Stuttgart in Germany she unfurled India's national flag, the first time in an international conference. This flag was saluted by the delegates which included Lenin and was the precursor of the present tricolour national flag after several changes in its design and colour. (See 1861.)

Calcutta and thereby India had her first electric tram. (See 1881.)

The first Indian to record a song was Miss Sashimukhi of Classic Theatre of Calcutta. It was made by Gramophone and Typewriter Ltd. on a 25 cm one-sided disc featuring the song 'Kanha Jeevan Dhan' from the play Srikrishna. (See 1898.)

The first wireless communication was established between Sagar Island and Sandheads in Diamond Harbour near Calcutta.

1903   King Edward VII was declared Emperor of India on January 1. Lord Curzon staged Delhi Durbar to mark the splendid apotheosis of his own viceroyalty.

Lord Curzon opened the Imperial Library in Metcalfe Hall in Calcutta on January 30. (See 1836 and 1948.)

Kamaladevi Chattopadhyay was born on April 3. She was a stalwart for women's emancipation, took part in the freedom struggle and devoted herself to rural development of arts and crafts. (d. 1988).

Gandhiji started legal practice in South Africa on April 26. He set up British Indian Association in Transvaal in South Africa.

The famous Tajmahal Hotel of Bombay was opened. It was however completed in 1904 at a cost of £50,000.

1904   C. F. Andrews arrived in India on March 20. (See 1871.)

A.D.

The great singer Kundanlal Saigal was born in Jammu on April 4. (d. 1947).

Jamshedji N. Tata, founder of the House of Tatas, died on May 19. (b. 1839).

India's second Prime Minister Lal Bahadur Shastri was born on October 2. (d. 1966).

Jatindra Nath Das, the freedom fighter, was born in Calcutta on October 27. He died of hunger strike in 1922.

Automobile Association of Bengal (now Automobile Association of Eastern India) the first of its kind, was established in Calcutta with 60 motor cars. Maximum permissible speed limit was fixed at 32 km per hour. Under its auspices the first car rally was held on August 28 between Calcutta and Barrackpore. Eleven cars and four motorcycles with one lady competitor Mrs Acatos participated in the rally. (See 1892.)

The first cross-country motor car race was inaugurated on December 26 between Delhi and Bombay, a distance of 1,425 km to be covered in seven days. It was organised by Motor Union of Western India. 33 cars participated and 21 finished the race.

Automobile Association of South India was formed after a meeting at Udhagamandalam.

The first Sikh migrants went to Canada. (See 1914.)

Co-operative Societies Movement started. (See 1912.)

The first authentic short story in Hindi 'Ladki Ki Bahaduri' (portraying a girl's heroic struggle against Calcutta pimps) was published in a Hindi magazine *Sudarshan*. It was written by Pandit Madhav Prasad Misra. An earlier story 'Indumati', written by Kishorilal Vajpayee and published in the *Saraswati* in 1900, bore a distinct resemblance to Shakespeare's *Tempest*. (See 1871.)

The Lion Capital of Ashoka's pillar was found at Sarnath. and is kept in Sarnath Museum. It is made of sandstone, 210 cm in height and is dating the third century B.C. (See 1950.)

1905   Devendranath Tagore died on January 19. (b. 1817).

India Home Rule Society was formed on February 18 in London by Shyamji Krishnavarma.

A.D.

India's fifth President Fakhruddin Ali Ahmed was born on May 13. (d. 1977).

Veteran Maharashtrian classical vocalist Hirabai Barodekar was born on June 14.

The first partition of Bengal was approved by the Parliament on July 20 and was effected by Lord Curzon on October 16. (See 1911 and 1947.)

As a protest against Bengal's partition, the Indian National Congress declared boycott of British goods for the first time on August 7 and advocated to buy Swadeshi. Earlier on July 16 a resolution was adopted in a public meeting in Bagerhat (now in Bangladesh) to boycott British goods at the suggestion of *Sanjivani,* a Bengali weekly of Calcutta, published on July 13.

Hockey wizard Dhyan Chand was born on August 29. (d. 1979. See 1995.).

Sheikh Muhammed Abdullah of Kashmir was born on December 5 in Soura of Kashmir. In May, 1946 he launched Quit Kashmir campaign challenging the Maharaja's right to rule Kashmir. The same year he was elected President of All India State Peoples' Conference. The people of Kashmir called him Lion of Kashmir. (d. 1982).

Associated Press of India was established. (See 1913 and 1949.)

G. K. Gokhale founded the Servants of India Society, the first secular organisation for the welfare of the underprivileged, rural and tribal people.

The Prince of Wales (later King George V) visited India and laid the foundation stone of Bombay's Prince of Wales Museum built in the 16th century Muslim architecture.

Henry Phips of America established the nucleus of Agricultural Research Institute at Pusa in Bihar, which was shifted to Delhi after Bihar earthquake in 1934.

Victoria Memorial, a marble monument fashioned after Taj Mahal, was proposed to be built in Calcutta by Lord Curzon in memory of Queen Victoria. (See 1906 and 1921.)

The exploration of Rajgir, the old Magadha capital, began. (See 519 B.C.)

1906 On January 4 the Prince of Wales (later King George V) laid the foundation stone of Victoria Memorial Hall of Calcutta. It was designed by William Emerson with some modifications by R. N. Mukherji. (See 1905 and 1921.)

W. C. Bonerjee died on July 21. (b. 1844).

Chandrashekhar Azad was born on July 23. (See 1931.)

The earliest tri-colour Congress flag was of green, yellow and red stripes. The green stripe was with seven lotuses as the symbol of seven provinces of India. The yellow stripe was inscribed with Vande Mataram in Devnagari and the red stripe had a sun and a crescent moon. This flag was hoisted by S. N. Banerji in Calcutta on August 6. (See 1902.)

Chitta Ranjan Das, Bipin Chandra Pal and Subodh Chandra Mullick founded *Vande Mataram* newspaper on August 6, with Aurobindo Ghose as the editor.

Raja Ravi Verma died on October 2. (b. 1848).

Swami Rama Tirtha expired on October 17. (b. 1873).

All Indian Muslim League was formed under the leadership of Aga Khan to divert the Muslim mind from the national political movement. On December 30 Nawab Salimullah Khan of Dhaka became its founder president.

Howrah Station, the largest railway station in India, was built.

1907 Electric tram was introduced in Bombay on May 7 and the last one ran in that city on March 31, 1964. (See 1874 and 1900.)

Revolutionary Bhagat Singh was born on September 27 at Banga in West Punjab. He was the first revolutionary to raise the slogan 'Inquilab Zindabad', after throwing a bomb in the Central Assembly in Delhi. This slogan meaning 'long live revolution' later became the war cry of India's independence struggle. (d. 1931).

Brahma Bandhav Upadhyay died on October 27. (b. 1861).

The first terrorist dacoity related to freedom struggle took place in Chingripota railway station (now in Bangladesh) on December 6. The iron safe of the station yielded only Rs 700.

Gandhiji had his first taste of imprisonment in December in Johannesburg jail. There he had to wear a cap being a coloured prisoner. This type of cap was later renowned as Gandhi cap and became one of the great symbols of freedom fighters in India.

A.D.

W. W. Pearson came to India. He joined Santiniketan in September 1913.

Jim Corbett shot the Champawat tigress in Kumaon region, which took a toll of 436 human lives (about 200 in Nepal), a gruesome record amongst maneaters. (See 1926 and 1935.)

Sebastio Rodolfo Delgado became the professor of Sanskrit in Lisbon University and thus he was the first Indian to hold the chair of Sanskrit in any European University. (b. 1855, d. 1922).

Two Indians K. G. Gupta and Syed Hussain Bilgrami were for the first time admitted to Privy Council of India.

Madhav Prasad Misra died. (b. 1871).

The first cinema house Elphinstone Picture Palace was opened by J. F. Madan in Calcutta.

Boy Scout Movement (later converted to Bharat Scouts and Guides in 1949) started in India. (See 1917.)

In the Congress annual session at Surat, the party was split into Moderates and Extremists.

Mysore Maharaja's new palace, built in Indo-Saracenic style, was completed on the foundations of the old one, which was partly destroyed by fire in 1897. The palace was partially opened to visitors in 1975. It is one of the finest palaces in the world.

1908 Tata Iron & Steel Co., the first steel company of India, was established on March 1. Production started in 1911.

Khudiram Bose of Midnapur and Prafulla Chaki of Rangpur threw boumbs in Muzaffarpur of Bihar on April 30 with the idea to kill the District Magistrate Kingsford. By mistake the bomb was aimed at a wrong carriage. Mrs Kennedy and Miss Kennedy were killed instead. Khudiram was hanged on August 11 at the age of 19 (b. 1889). That was the first hanging for political terrorism in the twentieth century. He was the youngest to die on the gallows for freedom of India. Prafulla committed suicide on May 1 by his own pistol. (See 1897.)

Sri Aurobindo was arrested in connection with Manicktola Bomb Case on June 2.

The Calcutta Stock Exchange was opened on June 15 through the efforts of Baldeodas Daduawala and Overend.

Ram Dhari Singh, a Hindi poet, better known as Dinkar, was born on September 30. (d. 1974).

P. Ananda Charlu died. (b. 1843).

Bal Gangadhar Tilak was exiled to Mandalay for 6 years for sedition. He is considered as the 'Father of India's Freedom Struggle'.

Nihal Singh was the first Indian to take part in Wimbledon Tennis Tournament. (See 1929 and 1950.)

Mirza Ghulam Ahmed, founder of the Ahmadiya sect, died. (See 1889, b. 1838.).

1909 E. M. S. Namboodiripad was born on June 14 in Palghat in Kerala. In 1957 he formed the first communist government in India in Kerala state. (d. 1998).

William Hutt Curzon Wyllie, a Scotland Yard officer and political aide-de-camp to the then secretary of state for India and unintentionally Dr Cowas Lalkaka, a Parsee physician, were killed on July 1 by revolutionary Madan Lal Dhingra in the Imperial Institute of London. Madan Lal was hanged in Pentonville prison in London on August 17. He was the first Indian revolutionary to be hanged in U.K. His remains were brought to New Delhi on December 12, 1976.

Conjeevaram Natarajan Annadurai was born on September 15 in a weaver community of Kanchipuram. He started the Dravida Munnetra Kazhagam (Dravidian Progressive Federation) on September 17, 1949. (d. 1969).

The first batch of ten political prisoners connected with Alipore Bomb Case in the struggle for independence were deported to the Andaman Cellular Jail. The last batch of political prisoners sailed back to the mainland for good on January 18, 1938. The penal settlement was officially abolished in 1945. As per available records, between 1909 and 1938, a total of 499 political prisoners were deported there—370 from Bengal, 84 from Punjab, 20 from U.P., 18 from Bihar, 3 each from Madras and Bombay and one from Delhi. (See 1879.)

Renowned nuclear scientist Homi Bhabha was born on October 30. At his initiative the Tata Institute of Fundamental Research was founded in 1945. (d. 1966).

A.D.

The great scholar Ramesh Chandra died on November 30.

Minto-Morley Reform, for the first time, tried to introduce a representation and a popular element in the government. This also provided for the first time separate Muslim representation of the Muslim community in the election.

S. P. Sinha was the first Indian to be appointed to the viceroy and Governor General's (then Lord Minto II) Executive Council as a law member.

Elected representatives entered the legislatures for the first time. (See 1892 and 1952.)

The Indian Institute of Science started functioning at Pune, which owes its origin to J. N. Tata.

Sakhawat Memorial School was established by Begum Rokeya Sakhawat Hussain for the emancipation of Muslim women of Calcutta.

1910 Ram Manohar Lohia, a prominent socialist leader, was born at Akbarpur in U.P. on March 23. (d. 1967).

Sri Aurobindo left politics and reached Pondicherry on April 4 where he made the seat of his yoga.

Mother Teresa (Agnes Gonxha Bojaxhiu) was born on August 26 of Albanian parents in Skopje of Yugoslavia. (d. 1997. See 1929.)

President Ramaswami Venkataraman was born on December 4. (See 1987.)

On April, 16 Malayala Manorama of Kerala started a children's page – the first one in India. It only had a break between 1938 and 1947 during the freedom struggle.

Gitanjali, a collection of poems, was published by Rabindranath Tagore, who got the Nobel Prize in 1913 in literature for this book. (See 1912.)

1911 The world's first official airmail flight with 5,500 letters and post cards was made on February 18 between Bamrauli near Allahabad and Naini, a distance of 6 miles across the Ganga, by a Frenchman Henry Picquet in a Humber Sommer biplane in 13 minutes. (See 1920 and 1932.)

Sachchitanand H. Vatsyayan, an outstanding Hindi poet-journalist, a freedom fighter and the winner of Jnanpith Award of 1979, popularly known as Agyeya, was born on March 7. (d. 1987).

A.D.

The overhead reservoir at Tallah Pumping Station of Calcutta was commissioned on May 16. It is the largest overhead tank in the world with a capacity of 9 million gallons erected 29 metres above the ground. The depth of the tank is 5 metres.

Mohan Bagan was the first Indian football team to win the I.F.A. Shield on July 29. The barefooted team defeated East Yorkshire Regiment by 2 to 1 goals. This boosted the inspiration for national emancipation. Mohan Bagan was allowed to play in the Second Division of Calcutta Football League in 1914 and was promoted to First Division in 1915. (See 1889 and 1898.)

Sister Nivedita died on October 13. (b. 1867).

King George V and Queen Mary, the first ever British King and Queen, landed in Bombay on December 2. The Gateway of India was erected in 1924 in Bombay to commemorate the occasion. In Delhi Durbar on December 12 the King announced that Delhi was to be made the new capital (eighth city). The King also annulled the partition of Bengal. (See 1905.)

'Jana Gana Mana....', now India's national anthem, was first sung on December 27 at the Indian National Congress session at Calcutta. (See 1950.)

Girl Guide Movement (founded by Lord Baden Powell in 1910) was introduced in India at Jabalpur, where a company was formed in 1929. All India Girl Guides Association then became a full member of the World Association. This Association was amalgamated with Bharat Scouts and Guides in 1951.

1912   King George V and Queen Mary left India for England on January 10.

The capital on India was officially shifted from Calcutta to Old Delhi on April 1 and the province of Delhi was declared by a proclamation. (See 1774 and 1931.)

On May 18 R.G. Torney and N.G. Chitre's 'Pundalik' was released at Coronation Cinematograph in Bombay. Though this was the first real attempt at an Indian silent feature film, it was shot by foreign technicians and was only of 12 minutes duration. (See 1913.)

Viceroy Lord Hardinge II entered New Delhi mounted on a tusker for the initiation of the new capital on December 23. A bomb

A.D.

explosion marred the occasion since the viceroy was injured and became unconscious. (See 1931.)

The Botanical Survey of India was founded.

The Cooperative Societies Act was passed. (See 1904.)

Bihar and Orissa were separated from Bengal. (See 1935.)

Panchayats were first established in villages under the Panchayat Act, but with little success until 1952, when a new Panchayat Act revived the system. It is a three-tier structure of local self-government at the village, block and district levels.

Rabindranath Tagore published *Gitanjali* in English. (See 1910 and 1913.)

Oxford University Press, the oldest publishing house in the world (estd. 1478), came to India when E.V. Rieu opened an office in Bombay. (See 1978.)

Mounted Police was formed in Calcutta, primarily as bodyguards for the viceroy and the governor. The horses were brought from Australia.

1913 The first fully Indian four-reel silent feature film 'Raja Harischandra' (1,130 mt) was produced by Dhundiraj Govind Phalke or more popularly known as Dadasheb Phalke. The film was shown in Coronation Cinematograph in Bombay on May 3. (See 1870, 1896, 1899, and 1972.)

Neelam Sanjiva Reddy, the sixth President of India, was born on May 19. (See 1977, d. 1996.)

Ghadar Movement was initiated on November 1 at San Francisco by Indian immigrants under the instance of Tarak Nath Das to enlist support from the west for India's freedom struggle. (See 1914 and 1915.)

Rabindranath Tagore got the Nobel Prize on November 13 in literature for his collection of poems *Gitanjali,* after its English translation was published in 1912. The message reached Calcutta on November 15. He was the first Asian to get the Nobel Prize. (See 1910.)

The first automatic telephone system was installed at Shimla with 700 lines. (See 1881.)

A.D.

Kamalabai Gokhale and her mother Durgabai were the first women to appear in a film, which was Phalke's second film 'Mohini Bhasmasur'. (See 1900.)

The Indian Companies Act came into effect. (See 1956.)

Marwari Relief Society was established by Jugal Kishore Birla.

The Associated Press of India was amalgamated with Reuters, which came to India in 1860. (See 1905 and 1949.)

1914   On March 28 *s. s. Komagata Maru* sailed from Hong Kong to Vancouver with 351 Sikh and 21 Punjabi Muslim youths, under the leadership of Gurjeet Singh, as a part of Ghadar Movement. This trip was basically meant to challenge the colour bar in Canada. The steamer reached Vancouver on May 13, but was forced to leave Vancouver on July 28 for its return journey to India, which ended at Budge Budge near Calcutta on September 29, when 17 youths were shot dead and 202 sent to jail for challenging the British Raj. (See 1904, 1913 and 1915.)

Mother of Sri Aurobindo Ashram came to India for the first time on March 29. (See 1921.)

Sam Hormuj Framji Jamshedji Manekshaw, India's first Field Marshal, was born on April 3. (See 1973.)

Madras port was bombarded by German light cruiser Emden on September 22.

Tenzing Norgay was born. (d. 1986. See 1953.).

MacMahon made the alignment to show the north-eastern boundary of India, which is internationally known as the McMahon Line to demarcate the boundary between India and China. The Shimla Agreement accepted McMahon Line as the traditional boundary for the two countries. (See 1962.)

Snehalata, a Bengali girl, burnt herself to death when she learnt that her father had to mortgage their house to meet dowry and marriage expenses. The whole country was shocked and the anti-dowry movement started but with little success. (See 1961.)

Bengalee revolutionaries waylaid a cartload of 50 Mauser pistols and 46,000 rounds of ammunition while being unloaded at Calcutta port on August 26. Rodda & Co.'s employee Haridas Dutta took

A.D.

delivery of the consignment in guise of a bullock-cart driver. (See 1918.)

Sepoy Khudadad Khan of the 129th Baluch Regiment was the first Indian to be awarded the Victoria Cross for his gallantry in Belgium in the First World War.

Indian Science Congress held its first session in Calcutta with Ashutosh Mukherji as the President.

1915 On January 1 Gandhiji was awarded *Kaiser-e-Hind* Gold Medal by the British government for his services in South Africa for war efforts. He surrendered the award on August 1, 1920.

On January 9 Gandhiji landed in Bombay on his return from South Africa for good. That year he became a member of the Indian National Congress. (See 1901 and 1935.)

Gandhiji visited Santiniketan on February 17 for the first time while Rabindranath Tagore was abroad. In a letter to C.F. Andrews, Rabindranath wanted to know whether 'Mahatma' had arrived at Santiniketan. Their first meeting took place soon after on March 6, when Gandhiji visited Santiniketan for the second time. Incidentally Brahma Bandav Upadhyay, the first teacher to join Rabindranath in his Brahmacharya Ashram, referred to Rabindranath as 'Gurudev' at its very inception in 1901. He also hailed Rabindranath as the 'World Poet' in an article in the English magazine *Sophia,* even before he personally knew the poet.

Gopal Krishna Gokhale died on February 19. (b. 1866).

The Defence of India Act was passed on March 18.

Revolutionary Rash Behari Bose bade adieu to his motherland on May 12 on board the Japanese ship *Sanuki Maru* for Japan, under the assumed name P. N. Tagore. (See 1943, d. 1945.).

Rabindranath Tagore got the Knighthood ('Sir' title) from the British government on June 3. He relinquished it in 1919 after the Jallianwala Bagh massacre.

As a sequel to Ghadar Movement, an armed insurrection was planned by the Bengali revolutionaries. Jatin Mukherji (Bagha Jatin) was intercepted by the British on September 9 at Kaptipada on the banks of the Buri Balang river in Orissa. He died of bullet injuries on September 10 in Balasore Hospital. His associate Hardayal escaped to Berlin to organise an uprising from Kabul. (See 1879, 1913 and 1914.)

Pheroz Shah Mehta died on November 4. (b. 1845).

Vishnu Gopal Pingle was hanged on November 17 in Talegaon prison of Pune for organising a rebellion amongst Indian Army. (b. 1888).

The provisional government of India was established in Kabul in exile with Raja Mahendra Pratap as its head. (See 1886.)

Gandhiji founded the Satyagraha Ashram on the outskirts of Ahmedabad on the Sabarmati river. It is popularly known as Sabarmati Ashram. (See 1917 and 1930.)

First apple trees from California were planted in Kotgarh village, 52 miles from Shimla, by an American missionary Samuel Evens Stokes, who later became a Hindu and took the name Satyanand. (b. 1882, d. 1946. Also see 1875).

Exploration of Nalanda monastery site began. (See 672.)

1916 The Banaras Hindu University was opened on February 3 under the guidance of Madan Mohan Malaviya. (See 672.)

The seventh President Gyani Zail Singh was born on May 5 in Sandhawan village, now in Pakistan. (d. 1994).

Sreemati Nathibai Damodher Thackersey (SNDT) Indian Women's University, the first women's university and the fifth Indian university, was established at Pune on June 20 by D. K. Karve.

The Zoological Survey of India was established on July 2.

Mrs Annie Besant in cooperation with Bal Gangadhar Tilak founded Home Rule League on August 1 with Dadabhai Naoroji as its president.

Narendra Nath Bhattacharya changed his name to M. N. Roy (Manabendra Nath Roy) in June at the advice of Dhan Gopal Mukherji, in the campus of Stanford University, U.S.A. to avoid detection and arrest as a revolutionary.

Indian National Congress placated Muslim League by accepting the system of separate electorate. (See 1919 and 1920.)

A.D.

1917 On April 18 Gandhiji defied section 144 of Criminal Procedure Code in Champaran of Bihar which was one of his first testing grounds of Satyagraha. He was arrested but the case was later withdrawn. There firmers testified against the indignities suffered by them at the hands of the British indigo planters.

Hriday Kunj of Sabarmati Ashram in Ahmedabad became Gandhiji and Kasturba's home from June 17. When Gandhiji started his Dandi march on march 12, 1930 he vowed not to return to Sabarmati Ashram till India was free. (See 1915 and 1933.)

Dadabhai Naoroji died on June 30. (b. 1825)

Indira Gandhi, India's third prime minister, was born on November 19. (d. 1984).

J. C. Bose founded Bose Research Institute at Calcutta on November 20.

The demand for reorganisation of states on linguistic basis first originated.

First Bengali feature film 'Nala Damayanti' was produced by J. F. Madan. (See 1913.)

The South Indian Liberal Federation, more popularly known as Justice Party, was inaugurated in Madras, basically for anti-Brahmin movement.

Mrs Annie Besant was the first woman president of the Indian National Congress in its 33rd session in Calcutta in December.

Indian Boy Scouts' Association was established by Mrs Annie Besant. (See 1907 and 1949.)

Women's Indian Association was established by Mrs Annie Besant which became All India Women's Conference in 1926.

1918 Montague-Chelmsford Report on reforms of Indian constitution was published on July 8. Lord Montague was the Secretary of States for India and Lord Chelmsford was the Viceroy.

Sidney Rowlatt submitted a report on July 19 on Indian administration advocating rigorous steps. (See 1919.)

Indra Lal Roy was the first pilot to get the Distinguished Flying Cross (DFC). He was the first ace pilot having shot down at least nine German planes in the First World War. He was the first Indian airman killed in an air-battle with German planes over London on July 22, 1918.

President Shankar Dayal Sharma was born on August 19. (d. 1999).

Sai Baba of Shirdi expired on October 15. He was born in a Brahmin family in Patri village in Hyderabad. In his childhood he was brought up by a Sufi Muslim *fakir*. There was a controversy over his funeral and he was ultimately buried in Shirdi mosque in Maharashtra. (See 1926.)

Gooroodas Banerjee died on December 2. (b. 1844).

Nabibala Debi, a widow of Bengal, was arrested for giving shelter to revolutionaries who waylaid Mauser pistols of Rodda & Co. in 1914. She was thus the country's first female political prisoner. (See 1914.)

King's Commission of Indian Army was opened to the Indians. Field Marshal K. M. Cariappa was amongst the first group to receive the King's Commission. (See 1949 and 1986.)

The great influenza epidemic took a heavy toll of life throughout the world and affected 5 million people in India.

The first labour union in India namely Madras Labour Union was organised by B. P. Wadia. (See 1870 and 1884.)

1919   On March 1 Gandhiji announced his desire to start Satyagraha against proposed Rowlatt Act meant to curb civil and political liberties. The date for the first countrywide *Hartal* was fixed on March 30 and then shifted to April 6.

Hari Narayan Apte died on March 3. (b. 1864)

Osmania University of Hyderabad was inaugurated on March 15.

On March 18 Rowlatt Act became law of the land.

Modern Indian shipping started on April 5 with the maiden voyage of Scindia Steam Navigation Company's 5,940 tonne ship *Liberty*. (See 1948.)

On April 10 Miss Mercia Sherwood, an English school teacher, was assaulted by a mob in Amritsar. Brig. Gen. R. E. H. Dyer issued the infamous crawling and flogging order.

On April 13 Brig. Gen. R. E. H. Dyer (born in Shimla in 1864) opened fire on an unarmed assembly of people in Jallianwala Bagh of Amritsar protesting against Rowlatt Act. The force consisted of 25 rifles of the 9th Gurkhas, 25 rifles from the detachments of 54 Sikh F.F. and 59th rifles F.F. making a total of 50 rifles and 40

A.D.

Gurkhas armed with kukris. While 1,650 bullets were fired in 6 minutes, 379 people were killed and 1,208 were wounded. Michael O'Dwyer was then the governor of Punjab who naturally defended the action. (See 1940.)

Rabindranath Tagore renunciated his Knighthood on May 30 as a protest against the Jallianwala Bagh massacre. (See 1915.)

Vikram Ambalal Sarabhai, the renowned nuclear scientist, was born on August 12. (d. 1971).

The first meeting of the Rotary Club of Calcutta was held on September 26 at Peliti's Restaurant with a membership of 20 people. R. J. Coombes, a businessman, took the initiative after his return from a business trip to U.S.A. It got the charter from International Association of Rotary Clubs of U.S.A. on January 1, 1920.

Gandiji's *Navajivan* magazine appeared on October 7 and *Young India* on October 8.

King's proclamation was made on December 23 that the new reforms of Government of India Act would offer some sort of self government. But it evoked little interest amongst Indian politicians.

Satyendra Prasanna Sinha was made a Baron and he was since then known as Lord S. P. Sinha of Raipur, which place is in Birbhum district of Bengal. The last hereditary Indian Baron Lord Sudhindra Prasanna Sinha died on January 6, 1989. (See 1916 and 1863.)

Western India Automobile Association was established. (See 1904.)

Madras entered the film industry with 'Keechaka Badham'. (See 1913.)

M. N. Roy established the Communist Party in Mexico, which was the first one outside Russia. (See 1916 and 1920.)

K. Virasalingam expired. (b. 1848).

1920   On January 1 Rotary Club of Calcutta got the charter from International Association of Rotary Clubs of U.S.A. (See 1919.)

On January 10 India became a member of the League of Nations.

Organised air transport began in India on January 23 by two Royal Air Force planes between Karachi and Bombay. It also carried airmail. The postage was 8 annas (50 paise) and was closed within seven weeks because of lack of support. (See 1911 and 1932.)

The great sitar maestro Ravi Shankar Bhattacharya was born on April 7.

The mathematician Srinivas Ramanujam died on April 26. (b. 1887).

Sarada Ma, wife of Shri Ramakrishna Dev, expired on July 21. (b. 1853).

Bal Gangadhar Tilak died in the early hours of August 1. (b. 1856).

Gandhiji renounced the *Kaiser-e-Hind* medal on August 1 which was vested upon him in 1915.

Gandhiji secured the control of the Indian National Congress by preaching the doctrine 'Swaraj within one year' and Non-Cooperation Movement started formally on August 1.

Anglo Oriental College of Aligarh was converted into Aligarh Muslim University on September 9. It was the first university to use the regional language (Urdu) as the medium of instruction.

Communist Party of India was formed at Tashkent on October 17 with seven members including M. N. Roy, Birendra Chattopadhyay and Abani Mukherji. (See 1916 and 1919.)

Jamia Millia Islamia was founded at Aligarh on October 29 as an integral part of the policy animating the Khilafat and the Non-Cooperation Movement. In 1925 the Jamia moved from Aligarh to Delhi. It is now an educational and cultural institution.

The inaugural session of the All India Trade Union Congress was held in Bombay on October 31. (See 1926.)

The Indian Red Cross Society was founded on November 5 by Bengal Act VIII. Its activities were directed towards improvement of health, prevention of diseases and mitigation of suffering. St. John Ambulance Association is a wing of this society.

The Indian National Congress boycotted elections under the new reforms of Government of India Act of 1919.

Gandhiji started to work against untouchability,

Justice Saadi Lal was the country's first Indian Chief Justice, when he was designated in Lahore High Court.

Rafiuddin Ahmed founded the first Dental College in the country at Calcutta.

A.D.

Women were for the first time in India allowed to vote in Madras Province.

India, for the first time, officially participated in Olympic games held at Antwerp. The participants were Purna Chandra Banerji (sprinter) of Bengal and Chowgule, Datar and Kahijadi of Maharashtra. (See 1900 and 1924.)

Gandhiji joined the All India Home Rule League and became its president. (See 1916.)

The Ali brothers, Muhammad and Saukat started the Khilafat Movement to force the British government to restore the Turkish Sultan to his former position taken away from him by the Treaty of Sevres.

The Indian National Congress supported the Khilafat Movement led by the Ali brothers in favour of Sultan of Turkey, who was removed by the British.

Mysore state announced the scheme for the largest artificial lake Krishnarajasagar, along with a dam and a beautiful garden called Brindavan Garden. (See 1936.)

Jinnah parted company with Congress.

Bijoli was the country's first film magazine (Bengali Weekly) edited by Nalinikanta Sarkar.

Associated Chamber of Commerce was the first central organisation to come into being comprising only of British Chambers. (See 1926.)

Bombay's Marine Drive was built on reclaimed land from Back Bay. It is dubbed as Queen's Necklace because of the dramatic curve of the streetlights at night.

Blessington opened India's first ice-skating rink at Shimla.

1921 The Chamber of Princes was inaugurated on February 8 by a Royal Proclamation. Out of a total of 562 states, rulers of 108 states were members of Chamber of Princes. Rulers of 127 states were represented by 12 nominees. The third category of 327 were really landlords and remained unrepresented. (See 1947, 1971 and 1972.)

Gandhiji and Motilal Nehru inaugurated Kashi Vidyapith on February 10 at Varanasi towards nationalist education with Bhagwan Dass as the Principal. The entire staff and students

A.D.

participated in the freedom movement throughout its career. On July 21, 1962 Kashi Vidyapith got the status of a university.

Duke of Connaught laid the foundation stone of India Gate in New Delhi on February 10 commemorating the bravery of Indian soldiers who died in the First World War. 13, 516 names are engraved on the arch.

The Indian National Congress flag was adopted on March 31. It was hoisted for the first time during the Vijaywada conference.

Netaji Subhas Chandra Bose submitted his resignation from the Indian Civil Service on April 22 for service to the nation. (See 1897.)

Mother of Pondicherry Ashram settled down in Pondicherry permanently on April 24. (See 1878 and 1914.)

The world famous film director and a very popular short-story writer Satyajit Ray was born on May 2. He was awarded the highest honour 'Legion d Honeur' of France in 1989. (See 1991 and 1992.)

One of the important uprisings of India, namely Mopla Revolt by the Muslims of Malabar region of Kerala started on August 20, which was stamped out by December after 1,826 persons were killed, 1,500 wounded, 5,400 captured and 14,000 surrendered. It is still debated whether it was a peasants revolt or a political uprising or a fanatical outburst of communalism.

Gandhiji made a bonfire of foreign clothes on August 22.

President K. R. Narayanan was born on October 27.

On November 20 an incident resembling Calcutta's Black Hole tragedy occurred. 60 Moplahs were found asphyxiated in a closed goods wagon when the wagon was opened at Podanur in Kerala. (See 1756.)

Prince of Wales (later king Edward VIII) landed at Bombay on November 21. Congress observed all India strike.

Rabindranath Tagore formally inaugurated Visva Bharati at Santiniketan on December 24 with Brojendra Nath Seal as the chief guest, though actually founded in 1918. (See 1863 and 1901.)

Prince of Wales (later King Edward VIII) opened Victoria Memorial Building at Calcutta on December 28, which was finally completed in 1934. (See 1906.)

A.D.

At a meeting of students that Gandhiji addressed in Madurai, they aired the complaint that 'Khadi', the uniform of national movement, was too costly to wear. Gandhiji's answer to that was, the solution lay in wearing less clothes and from that day, as an example, he discarded the dhoti and kurta and switched over to the loin cloth.

Urdu poet Akbar Allahabadi died. (b. 1846).

Subramaniam Bharati expired. (b. 1882).

India, for the first time, participated in the Davis Cup Tournament in tennis. The participants were L. S. Deane, A. A. Fyzee, S. M. Jacob and M.Sleem. The team reached the third round and lost to Japan. Since then India reached the final thrice. While in 1966 and 1987 India lost to Australia and Sweden respectively, in 1974 India refused to play against South Africa because of that country's apartheid policy. (See 1982.)

Imperial Bank of India, later named State Bank of India, was started by unifying the three Presidency Banks of Calcutta, Bombay and Madras. (See1955.)

The British government announced that the entrance examination of the India Civil Services (ICS) conducted only in England could be held in India as well.

The excavation of Harappa in Punjab (Pakistan), the site of Indus valley civilisation, started.

Krishnarajasagar Dam of Mysore was completed. It was the brainchild of M. Visveswarayya and the construction started in 1911. (See 1936.)

1922 On February 1 Gandhiji wrote to the then Viceroy Lord Reading to inform him that he was intensifying his action and non-cooperation was to be escalated to civil disobedience.

The unfortunate incident of Chauri Chaura of U.P. happened on February 5, when the mob attacked the police station and killed 22 policemen. Gandhiji persuaded the Congress Working Committee after fasting for 5 days in penance to pass the resolution on February 12 ending the Civil Disobedience Movement. Incidentally, in the 1942 August Movement at the same place 30 policemen were overwhelmed and burnt alive.

A.D.

Gandhiji was arrested for the first time in India on March 10, by the order of Viceroy Lord Reading, near Sabarmati Ashram in Ahmedabad. (See 1944.)

Sebastio Radolfo Delgado, ex-professor of Sanskrit of Lisbon University, died. (b. 1855, see 1907).

Chitta Ranjan Das and Motilal Nehru unitedly formed Swarajya Party.

Excavation of Mohenjodaro of Sind (Pakistan) started.

1923   Singaravelu Chettiar first observed 'May Day' on May 1 in India. 'May Day' had its origin in Chicago of U.S.A. in 1886. Labourers there demanded 8 hours of labour, 8 hours of social and cultural activities and 8 hours of rest.

Radio Club of Bombay broadcast its first programme in June.

The first socialist weekly magazine *The Socialist* was started in Bombay by S. A. Dange.

Cornelia Sorabji became the first woman advocate when she was admitted in the Allahabad High Court Bar. She was the first woman graduate of Bombay University. She was also our country's first woman law graduate (from England) in 1894. But she was not allowed to practice till this year.

Two young men from Gujarat learnt the art of making safety matches and set up a small unit in Sivakasi of Gujarat. In the same year Swedish manufacturers set up a safety match factory in India, which later came to be known as Wimco.

1924   Ashutosh Mukerji died on May 25 in Dumraon of Bihar. (b. 1864).

On July 31 broadcasting was pioneered by Madras Presidency Club Radio. It continued for 3 years. (See 1927.)

The first All India Athletic Competition was held in Delhi by the Olympic Association of India to choose the Olympic team for the Paris Olympics. (See 1900 and 1920.)

Satyabhakta, a left wing Congressman, established the Communist Party of India in Kanpur in July. The first All India Communist Conference was held in Kanpur from December 25 to 27 with Singaravelu Chettiar as the president.

Atal Behari Vajpayee was born on December 25.

A.D.

Open competitive examination started for recruitment of Indians in Indian Police Service. (See 1948.)

About 1,50,000 workers of Bombay textile mills were on strike between January and March demanding bonus.

Gateway of India of Bombay was completed. (See 1911.)

1925 The first electric train service started on February 3 between Victoria Terminus of Bombay and Kurla.

Chitta Ranjan Das died on June 16. (b. 1870).

Surendra Nath Banerji died on August 6. (b. 1848).

Hindustan Socialist Republican Association, who opted for violent overthrow of the British, looted the government treasury from the mail van near Kakori railway station on August 9. Chandrasekhar Azad was the commander-in-chief. (See 1931.)

Ramakrishna Gopal Bhandarkar expired on August 24. (b. 1837).

Miss Madelein Slade (Meera Behn), the daughter of a British Admiral, came to Sabarmati Ashram on November 7. (See 1892.)

K. B. Hedgewar founded Rastriya Swayamsevak Sangha (RSS) with the dream of a Hindu Rashtra, by unfurling 'Bhagwadhwaja' – a saffron flag, at a camp in Amaravati for military training of the Hindus.

The Shiromoni Gurudwara Prabandhak Committee (S.G.P.C.) was constituted by law to look after Sikh Gurudwaras following a prolonged agitation to liberate them from the control of the Mohants, i.e., professional priests.

Raghunath D. Karve opened the country's first family planning clinic in Bombay and possibly second in the world after Marie Stopes opened such a clinic in London. (See 1952.)

An act was passed abolishing Devadasi system in temples. (See 1947.)

1926 On May 1 Jim Corbett killed the notorious man-eating leopard of Rudraprayag at Gulabrai village. The leopard created a reign of terror in Rudraprayag area between 1918 and 1926 having killed 125 people. A memorial stands on the exact spot where the leopard was shot as a respectful homage to Jim Corbett. (See 1907 and 1935.)

A.D.

The first motor bus service started in Bombay on July 15. The cruising speed was 32 km per hour and each bus could carry 24 passengers seating and two standing.

Shri Satya Sai Baba was born on November 23. (See 1918.)

Sri Aurobindo attained Purna Siddhi i.e. full enlightenment, on November 24.

Swami Shraddhanand was killed on December 23 by a revolver shot, fired by a young Muslim named Abdul Rashid. (b. 1856).

First Public Service Commission was established as provided for by the Government of India Act of 1919. (See 1886.)

Indian School of Mines and Applied Geology was opened at Dhanbad.

Indian plastic industry had its beginning when combs, soap boxes, ashtrays of plastics were manufactured for the first time in India.

Trade Union Act was passed to confer a legal and corporate status of a registered workers' union. (See 1920.)

All India Women's Conference was established. It played a leading role in emancipation of women in India. It really started in 1917 with the deputation led by Smt. Sarojini Naidu to Lord Montague, the then Secretary of State for India. (See 1917.)

Rash Behari Bose founded India Independence League in Japan. (See 1942.)

Indian cricket team played the first unofficial cricket Test match against the first M.C.C. visiting team from U.K. (See 1886 and 1932.)

In Calcutta bus service (after Bombay) was introduced by Calcutta Tramways Company. (See 1874.)

Fatma Begum set up Fatma Film Corporation and produced as well as directed *I-Bulbule Paristan,* in which she herself along with her three daughters Zubeida, Sultana and Sahazadi also acted.

S. Muthulakshmi Reddy became the country's first woman legislature being elected in the Madras Legislative Council. (See 1886.)

1927 Regular broadcasting in India first started in Bombay on July 23 and later in Calcutta by Indian Broadcasting Co. on August 26. (See 1924 and 1932.)

A.D.

On November 5 Viceroy Lord Irwin met Gandhiji, S. Shriniwas Iyengar (Congress President) and M.A. Ansari at New Delhi. He announced the impending visit by an official British Commission led by John Simon. (See 1928.)

Uttar Pradesh (then United Provinces) Automobile Association was formed on December 19.

The Federation of Indian Chambers of Commerce and Industry was formed with 27 Indian Chambers. (See 1920.)

Dufferin, originally a troopship, was inaugurated as a training ship for merchant navy cadets. It was decommissioned in 1972, and replaced by 'Rajendra'.

Parliament House was opened in New Delhi.

Burmese Buddhists rebuilt the Nirvana Stupa at Kushinagar, which was built by Samudragupta in the 4th century.

V. D. Savarkar formed the Hindu Mahasabha.

The Free Press News Service was established.

Sarat Kumar Roy of Krishnagar in West Bengal joined Rawson MacMillan's Arctic expedition as a geologist, attached to Natural History Museum of Chicago. He happened to be the first Asian to go to the North Pole. In Alaska a mountain peak was named Mount Sarat in his honour. (See 1982 and 1989.)

1928 On February 12 Gandhiji gave the signal to resume Satyagraha in Bardoli which was abandoned after Chauri Chaura massacre in 1922.

The new Satyagraha was led by Vallabhbhai Patel and Abbas Tyabji. Vallabhbhai was honoured with the popular title 'Sardar' because of his great leadership during the movement. (See 1929.)

Lord S. P. Sinha died on March 5. (b. 1863).

C. V. Raman discovered 'Raman Effect' of scattered light on February 28, which earned him the Nobel Prize in physics. (See 1930.)

Pandit Gopa Bandhu Das died on June 17. (b. 1877).

As an after-effect of the lathi-charge in Lahore on October 30 for protesting against the Simon Commission, Lala Lajpat Rai succumbed to his injuries on November 17, reported to have been inflicted by Scott, superintendent of police. (b. 1865. See 1929.).

A.D.

The first talkie film 'Melody of Love' was shown on December 28 at Elphinstone Picture Palace in Calcutta.

National Hockey Championship was inaugurated in the form of an all-India trial for raising funds to send the Indian hockey squad to Amsterdam Olympic. United Provinces became the champion and only certificates were awarded. In 1936 Bengal became the first province to win a shield presented by the Maoris of New Zealand. But this ill-fated trophy won by Punjab shortly before partition was never returned. In the early fifties when Madras hosted the tournament, a South Indian daily newspaper donated the trophy Rangaswamy Cup to perpetuate the memory of one of its former editors.

India got a gold medal in hockey for the first time in the Amsterdam Olympic, which she retained till 1960 when she went down to Pakistan in the Rome Olympic. Hockey was introduced in Olympic in 1908 when England won the first gold medal. (See 1980.)

Judo sport of Japan was introduced in India.

The first flying club was officially founded in Bombay, though Behala Flying Club of Calcutta was opened in December 1927.

P. M. Kabali of Bombay obtained the first commercial 'B' licence for flying in U.K. (See 1929, 1930 and 1931.)

Religious reformer Sri Narayana Guru died in Sivgiri Math of Barkala. He propagated removal of caste system. Through his untiring efforts ultimately the Maharaja of Travancore made the Temple Entry Proclamation. (b. 1856. See 1936.)

Tree plantation as a festival (Vriksha-ropan Utsav) was first introduced by Rabindranath Tagore at Santiniketan. (See 1949.)

1929   Bharat Sevashram Sangha was established by Swami Pranabananda Maharaj in February in Bajitpur village of Bangladesh. (See 1896.)

J. R. D. Tata was the first Indian to secure a pilot's licence for passenger planes on February 10. (See 1928.)

The first commercial aviation reached India on April 7, when Imperial Airway's London-Cairo weekly service was extended up to Karachi. The first internal passenger service (along with airmail) started on December 30 from Karachi to Delhi with stoppages at Hyderabad (Sind) and Jaipur. The name of the company was Indian

A.D.

State Air Services and was fully owned by the Government of India.

India's first air cargo service started on May 21 between Calcutta and Bagdogra (Siliguri) by Bengal Air Transport. It operated only for one week.

Jatindra Nath Das died in Lahore Central Jail on September 13, on the 63rd day of hunger strike which he commenced on July 13, as a protest against the rude behaviour of the jail authorities with the undertrial political prisoners. (b. 1904).

Child Marriage Restraint Bill (popularly known as Sarda Act) was passed on September 23. (See 1860, 1891, 1930, 1955 and 1978.)

Lata Mangeshkar, the great movie playback singer, was born on September 28. She held the unique world record of more than 30,000 gramophone records to her credit till 1992. (See 1942 and 1984.)

On Gandhiji's birthday (October 2) he made a public trust of the Navajiban Karyalaya, a property worth one lakh of rupees at that time.

Calcutta Electric Supply Corporation started digging a mansize tunnel on December 16 under the Hooghly river which was completed in September 1931. The tunnel is 27 metre deep, 1.8 metre in diameter, and 631 metres long and carries electric cables from Calcutta to Howrah. Calcutta Telephones also use this tunnel for their own cables. This underwater tunnel was constructed long before the Calcutta Metro Railway was conceived. (See 1972.)

To avenge the death of Lala Lajpat Rai, Bhagat Singh shot dead Saunders, a head constable of police on December 17, who was mistaken as Scott. (See 1928 and 1931.)

Gandhiji was received by Viceroy Lord Irwin on December 23. Although only a few hours earlier an attempt on Irwin's life was made by the revolutionaries (See 1927.)

At the stroke of midnight on December 31, Gandhiji led Congress members in Lahore to take a vow for Swaraj – nothing less than full independence. Jawaharlal Nehru was then the Congress president. (See 1930.)

Board of Control for Cricket in India was establihsed after it had its actual foundation in December 1928.

A.D.

Vallabhbhai Patel earned the title Sardar for his leadership of the peasants' revolt at Bardoli against increased taxes. (See 1928.)

Gandhiji started the Harijan Movement and defined Harijan as children of God. (See 1933.)

An English lady Miss Joan Page was the first woman to fly an aeroplane in India at Calcutta. She had her training in Behala Flying Club.

Miss Jennifer Sandeson, an Anglo-Indian girl, was the first woman participant in Wimbledon Tennis Tourament. (See 1908.)

Mother Teresa came to India and settled down in Calcutta. (See 1931 and 1950.)

A set of six airmail stamps was issued for the first time in the world.

Rashtrapati Bhavan of Delhi was completed. It contains 340 rooms, 37 salons, 74 lobbies, 1 km of corridor, 18 staircases, 37 fountains and 130 acres of Mughal Garden, the largest accommodation of any president or king in the world then.

1930   Rabindranath Tagore visited Gandhiji's Sabarmati Ashram on January 18.

January 26 was for the first time observed as Swaraj Day. (See 1929.)

Gandhiji started Civil Disobedience Movement on March 12 by refusing to pay taxes to the government. (See 1922 and 1932.)

Gandhiji commenced his Dandi march for Salt Satyagraha on March 12, a distance of 388 km from Sabarmati Ashram of Ahmedabad, with his 78 ashramites. They reached Dandi on April 5 and broke the salt law—a master stroke in political strategy. He was arrested at 01.10 A.M. on the morning of April 6. Gandhiji promised not to return to Sabarmati Ashram until independence was achieved. That opportunity never came except for a five-day visit in 1933. (See 1915.)

Age of Consent Act of 1891 was further modified from April 1 by raising the marriageable age of girls to 14 years and of boys to 18. This was popularly called the Sarda Act, because the original bill was introduced by Harbilas Sarda. It was pointed out that as per the 1921 census, the number of Hindu widows were 612 under

A.D.

one year of age; 2,024 under 5 years; 97,857 under ten years and 332,024 below fifteen years of age. (See 1891.)

The new steel-rope bridge of 136-metre span of Lachchmanjhula in Rishikesh was opened to the public on april 11. The old coir-rope bridge of 86-metre span installed by Surajmul Jhunjhunwala was washed away by the great floods of 1924. The present one was donated by his son Shew Prasad Tulshian to perpetuate his father's memory. It was the first motorable suspension bridge in the country. (See 1986.)

The Punjabi daily newsaper *Desh Darpan* was first published on Baisakhi Day in April (the New Year Day of Bengal) from Calcutta. It is perhaps the oldest Punjabi newspaper conceived by Ghadar Party leader Munsha Singh and edited by Niranjan Singh Talib.

Chittagong Armoury raid took place on the night of April 18 by the terrorist group of about 62 men of the Indian Republican Army, under the leadership of Surya Sen alias Masterda. The incident aroused great national aspirations in the country. The battle of Jalalabad hill took place on April 22. Twelve fighters lost their lives. (See 1934.)

Simon Commission report was published in May. It received no sympathy from the Congress.

The first deluxe train was introduced between Victoria Terminus of Bombay and Pune on June 1. It was named Deccan Queen with accommodation of 61 first class, 156 second class and 19 attendant seats. It was also India's first vestibule train.

Dr. W. M. Haffkine died on October 26 at Paris. (b. 1860).

The first Round Table Conference opened in London on November 12 and ended on January 19, 1931 without the participation of Indian National Congress. 16 Indian princes, 56 Indian and 13 British representatives attended the conference. (See 1931.)

Red Shirt Movement was launched in North-West Frontier Province (now in Pakistan) by Khan Abdul Ghaffar Khan, popularly known as Badshah Khan as well as Frontier Gandhi, in support of Congress.

Muhammad Iqbal, the poet-philosopher of Punjab, made a proposal for the amalgamation of Punjab, North-West Frontier Province, Sind and Baluchistan in a single autonomous state within the

A.D.

framework of Indian Federation. Pakistan was conceived later. (See 1933.)

C.V. Raman got the Nobel Prize in physics for the discovery of the Raman Effect on scattered light. (See 1928.)

Tinned Rasogolla was introduced by Krishna Chandra Das, son of Nabin Chandra Das. (See 1868.)

1931   Motilal Nehru, father of Jawaharlal Nehru, died on February 6. (b. 1861).

On February 9, a set of six stamps were issued on the inauguration of New Delhi. Those were the first pictorial as well as commemorative stamps.

The capital of India shifted from Old Delhi to New Delhi, the ninth city. The formal inauguration took place on February 10. The city was designed by Edward Edwin Lutyens (son-in-law of Viceroy Lord Hardinge) and Herbert Baker. (See 1912.)

After several meetings between them commencing on February 17 in Viceregal Lodge, Gandhi-Irwin Pact was signed on March 5 with the understanding the Civil Disobedience Movement would be called off, political prisoners would be released, salt manufacture would be permitted and Congress would attend the next Round Table Conference.

Winston Churchill described Gandhiji as a 'Half naked seditious fakir'. In this context it is interesting to note that while in internment in Aga Khan Palace after 1942 August Movement, Gandhiji wrote to Churchill on July 17, 1944:

> Dear Prime Minister, you are reported to have a desire to crush the simple 'naked fakir' as you are said to have described me. I have been long trying to be a fakir—and that naked—a more difficult task. I therefore regard the expression as a compliment though unintended. I approach you then as such and ask you to trust and use me for the sake of your people and mine and through them those of the world. (See 1930.)

During an encounter with the British police in Alfred Park of Allahabad, Chandrashekhar Azad of Hindustan Republican Army ended his life with his own pistol on February 27. (See 1906 and 1925.)

India's first talkie film 'Alam Ara' (Hindi) was produced in Imperial Film Studio of Bombay by Ardeshir B. Irani and was released on March 14 at Bombay's Majestic Cinema Hall.

A.D.

Bhagat Singh along with his associates Sukhdev and Sivaram Rajguru were hanged on March 23 on the charge of murder of Saunders, a head constable whom they mistook to be Scott, responsible for Lala Lajpat Rai's death. (See 1907 and 1929.)

Former Prime Minister V. P. Singh was born on June 25.

Pandit Vishnu Digambar, the blind musician of Maharashtra, died on August 21. (b. 1872).

The second session on Round Table Conference was held between September 7 and December 1 with Gandhiji as the representative of the Indian National Congress. (See 1930 and 1932.)

Political prisoners in Hijli detention camp (near Kharagpur) were fired upon on September 16 by prison authorities. Two prisoners Tarakeswar Dutta and Santosh Mitra died and many more were injured.

Indian air force came into existence on October 9 with Andrew Skeene as the chairman. The first batch consisted of Subroto Mukherji, Amarjit Singh, Bhupinder Singh, A. D. Awan, Sankar and Tandon. The first batch of these six officers was commissioned on October 8,1932. With six officers and twenty-two Hawai Sepoys it took to wings on April 1, 1933 at Drigh Road, Karachi with 4 Westland Wapiti aircrafts. (See 1933.)

In the history of the Indian revolutionary movement, for the first time, two school girls Shanti Ghose (later Das) and Suniti Ghose (later Choudhury), alias lla Sen and Mira Devi, both students of class VIII of Faizunnisa Girls School, used revolvers to shoot and kill C. G. B. Stevens, magistrate and collector of Comilla on December 14. As the accused were young, instead of being sent to the gallows, they were sentenced to transportation for life.

First Bengali talkie film 'Jamai Sasthi' was released five weeks after 'Alam Ara'. In the same year, there were twenty-two Hindi talkie films, three in Bengali and one each in Tamil and Telugu.

Calcutta Probhat Studio's 'Sairindhri' was the first Indian coloured film which was coloured in Germany. (See 1951.)

The first Indian Gliding Association was formed by P. M. Kabali in Aundh of Satara district of Maharashtra. (See 1928.)

Agnes Gonxha Bojaxhiu took her vows in Darjeeling and adopted her name Teresa. (See 1950 and 1979.)

The first National Billiards Championship was held in Calcutta.

Frank Smythe, a mountaineer, discovered Valley of Flowers at an altitude of 3,352 metres in the Garhwal hills.

Bratachari Movement was initiated by Gurusaday Dutta.

Indian Statistical Institute was founded by Prof. Prasanta Chandra Mahalanobis. (See 1893.)

Bata India Ltd. started shoe manufacture in Konnagar of West Bengal.

1932   Freedom Fighter Bipin Chandra Pal died on May 20. (b. 1858).

Indian cricket team visited U.K. and played the first official Test match on June 25 against England at Lords in U.K. under the captaincy of Col. C. K. Naidu. (See 1886 and 1926.)

Ramakrishna Mission Seva Pratisthan was established on July 24 for the service of the sick.

Pritilata Waddedar was the first woman terrorist martyr to sacrifice her life for her country's freedom. She committed suicide on September 24 by taking poison, after leading an armed raid on the European Club in Chittagong, now in Bangladesh, killing one European woman.

Indian air force was commissioned on October 8. In the Second World War it was awarded the prefix Royal. (See 1931.)

India's first airliner service by Tata Sons Ltd. started on October 15. J. R. D. Tata himself flew a Puss Moth plane from Karachi to Bombay. (See 1911, 1920 and 1933.)

The third and last Round Table Conference was held between November 17 and December 24. (See 1930 and 1931.)

The second Civil Disobedience Movement started. (See 1930.)

The government of India took over broadcasting at the initiative of Lionel Fielden and it was named Indian State Broadcasting Service. (See 1927 and 1936.)

The Act regulating partnership business was passed.

Gandhiji founded the All India Harijan Sevak Sangh for social reform and education of the depressed class.

A.D.

Background music was first introduced by Deboki Bose in a movie in New Theatre Studio's Bengali film 'Chandidas'.

The first Marathi talkie film 'Ayodhyeche Raja' was screened.

Bengal Lamp Works manufactured the first indigenous electric lamp in their Calcutta factory.

Indian Military Academy was set up at Dehradun on October 1.

1933 Rahmat Ali Chaudhuri, an Indian Muslim graduate in Cambridge read out a four and a half page note on January 28 proposing division of India in Waldorf Hotel in London. Therein for the first time, the name of the Muslim majority state was proposed as Pakistan, which means 'Land of the Pure'. P stood for Punjab, A for Afghania – Rahamat Ali's name for North-West Frontier Province, K for Kashmir, S for Sind and 'tan' of Baluchistan. When the word Pakistan is written in Urdu, there is no 'i' in it. (See 1930, 1940 and 1947.)

Gandhiji's *Harijan Weekly* came out from Pune on February 11. According to Gandhiji, the word Harijan was first coined by a poet-saint of Gujarat. (See 1929.)

Indian air force took to wings on April 1 at Drigh Road, Karachi. (See 1931.)

The great cricket player Ranjit Singh died on April 2 (b. 1872). Ranji trophy was introduced in 1934 to perpetuate his memory. The original gold trophy was donated by Maharaja of Patiala, which is now in Pakistan. The present one is a silver trophy, an exact replica of the gold one, and was donated by Maharaj Kumar of Vizianagram.

Nationalist leader Jatindra Mohan Sen Gupta died on July 22 in internment at Ranchi. (b. 1885).

Gandhiji went back to Sabarmati Ashram on July 26 after his release from jail, with the idea to disband the Ashram. He left the Ashram for good at the midnight of July 31. The British arrested him and his 32 followers there. At the suggestion of Gandhiji, the Ashram was renamed as Harijan Ashram. (See 1930 and 1936.)

Annie Besant, the great social worker and founder of Home Rule Movement, died on September 21. (b. 1847).

Indian National Airways started India's first daily passenger air service on December 1 between Calcutta and Dhaka. (See 1932.)

Chameli Basu was the first lady to pass M.Sc Examination. She did it in physics from Calcutta University.

Ancient Monument Preservation Act was passed by the central legislature.

Vithalbhai Patel died. (b 1873).

1934   Surya Sen alias Masterda, leader of the Indian Republican Army, who masterminded the Chittagong Armoury Raid, was hanged in Chittagong Jail on January 12, alongwith his lifelong comrade Tarakeswar Dastidar. Their dead bodies were disposed off at the bottom of the Bay of Bengal from the British battle cruiser *HMS Epingham*. (See 1930, b. 1893).

The great earthquake of Bihar on January 15 took a toll of 20,000 lives. Monghyr town was razed to the ground.

'Charan Kabi' Mukunda Das died on May 18. (b. 1878).

Jayaprakash Narayan took the lead to form the Congress Socialist Party on October 21. At one time he was the brightest star on the firmament of Indian socialism.

All India Village Industries Association, with Gandhiji as its patron, was launched on October 26.

Mohammedan Sporting Club was the first Indian team to be the champion of First Division Football League of Calcutta.

Ranji Trophy, in honour of the great cricket player Ranjit Singhji (d.1933), was started for the National Cricket Championship. Bombay became the first champion and Northern India the runners-up in the final played early in 1935. (See 1933.)

Reserve Bank of India Act was passed. (See 1935.)

Royal Indian Marine was renamed Royal Indian Navy. (See 1829 and 1891.)

United Press of India was established.

First playback in movie film came into operation in New Theatre's 'Bhagya Chakra' (Bengali), and 'Dhup Chhaon' (Hindi), both directed by Nitin Bose. In fact he was one of the world's pioneers in this playback technique.

'Seetha' (Hindi) produced in this year by East India Film Co., Calcutta and directed by Debaki Bose was the first film to win an international laurel. It was shown in the third International

A.D.

Exhibition of Cinematographic Art in Venice in 1935 and was awarded a Gold Medal.

'Seeta Bibaha' was Oriya cinema's first feature film.

'Sati Sulochana' was the first Kannada talkie film to be released, though 'Bhakta Dhruva' was made earlier.

1935 Reserve Bank of India came into existence on April 1 and was nationalised in 1947. (See 1934.)

Indian Postal Order was introduced on April 1.

Quetta earthquake took a heavy toll of life on May 21. Government of India restricted the news as well as the volunteer services.

Government of India Act 1935 got the Royal assent on August 4. The main principles were an All India Federation, Provincial Autonomy and responsibility with safeguards. It defined an Anglo-Indian as 'A European with a European male progenitor, but the female is a native Indian.'

In September the Doon School of Dehradun, India's first public school, was established. It owes its existence to Satish Ranjan Das, one of preindependent India's most prominent barristers and a member of the Executive Council of Viceroy of India. Unfortunately S. R. Das could not see the fulfilment of his dream, which was brought into reality through the untiring efforts of his wife and devoted friends who collected the funds to start the school.

Gandhiji retired from Indian National Congress and politics in order to devote himself to village welfare. But nevertheless he continued to guide Congress policy from behind the scene. (See 1915.)

India's first national park was established on Delhi-Nainital road and was named as Hailey National Park. After 1947 it was known as Ramganga National Park. Two years after Jim Corbett died in 1955 it was decided to rename an enlarged area of 52,880 hectares of forest in the foothills of the Himalayas as Corbett National Park (See 1926.)

The first Assamese film 'Joymati' was produced.

In the first general elections in British India, Indians were elected on a restrictive basis to the central and provincial legislative assemblies.

1936 Kamala Nehru, wife of Jawaharlal Nehru, died in a sanatorium near Lausanne in Switzerland on February 28. (b. 1899).

Orissa was separated from Bihar as a new state on April 1. (See 1912.)

Gandhiji decided to take up residence at Sevagram Ashram on April 30 after a visit to Segaon village near Wardha on Jamnalal Bajaj's invitation. It was ultimately closed on March 17, 1955. (See 1933.)

Lord Brabourne laid the foundation-stone of Brabourne Stadium of Bombay on May 22, the first real stadium.

The name All India Radio, 'AIR' was adopted on June 8. It was later changed to Akashvani in 1958. (See 1932.)

Madame Bhikaji Cama died on August 30. (b. 1861).

Vishnu Narayan Bhatkhande expired on September 19. (b. 1860).

Shakuntala Devi, the human calculating machine, was born on November 4. On June 1980 she took only 28 seconds to compute the 23rd root of a 201 digit number, while the then world's fastest computer 'Univac' at Bureau of Standard of Washington D.C. in USA took well over a minute. She was thus the only person to outdo a computer.

All India Kisan Sabha of the peasants was established. It held its first session in December in Faizabad.

Vaikom Satyagraha in Travancore (now Kerala) led eventually to throwing open all government temples in the state on November 12 to all Hindus irrespective of their caste. (See 1928.)

The first automotive tyre manufacturing plant was set up in Sahaganj of West Bengal by Dunlop Rubber Company of India Ltd.

Brindavan garden of Krishnarajasagar Dam was opened to the public. It was contemplated by Mirza Ismail, the then Dewan of Mysore. Its unique musical dancing fountain was installed by Philips of Holland in 1984. (See 1920.)

Vijayalakshmi Pandit became India's first woman cabinet minister when she took over health portfolio of Uttar Pradesh government.

Air-conditioned railway coaches were introduced for the first time.

Kabbadi featured as a demonstrative sport in Berlin Olympics. But it never got the olympic status even up to 2004. (See 1952.)

A.D.

1937 Federal Court of India was created which was the highest judicial authority in the country. It became the Supreme Court of India on January 26, 1950.

Administration of India's provinces under the new Government of India Act of 1935 was enforced on April 1.

The great scientist Jagdish Chandra Bose died on November 23. (b. 1858).

Indian National Congress, for the first time, participated in provincial and central legislatures.

Lalita of Madras qualified as a civil engineer and was thereby the first woman engineer. (b. 1919).

Burma was separated from India.

1938 The new temple of Belur Math of Ramakrishna Mission near Calcutta was consecrated on January 14. (See 1898.)

Bengali novelist Sarat Chandra Chattopadhyay died on January 16. (b. 1876).

The last batch of political prisoners sailed back to the mainland on January 18 from the ill-famed Andaman Cellular Jail. (See 1909.)

Urud poet Muhammad Iqbal died on April 21. (b. 1877).

The first National Planning Committee was constituted at the instance of the then Congress President Subhas Chandra Bose. It supended its activities at his instance when the Second World War broke out in September 1939. (See 1951.)

Woodlands Hotel was opened in Madras, the first of Woodlands chain, India's first hotel chain, by K. Krishna Rao.

Bharatiya Vidya Bhavan was founded by K. M. Munshi.

Revolutionary Socialist Party was formed.

Lady Ratan Tata Cup was introduced for the women's national hockey championship. (See 1928.)

Gaganendranath Tagore died. (b. 1867).

The first bicycle factory was set up in Calcutta. (See 1890.)

Lakshminath Bezbaruah, the Assamese literary all-rounder, died. (b. 1868).

The first advertising film was made for Hindustan Lever's product 'Dalda' at Bombay Talkies studio by S. Mukherji, under the agency of Lintas, which was the first agency to venture into this business.

1939   Ramakrishna Mission Institute of Culture was founded on January 29, which was conceived in 1936 as a part of Shri Ramakrishna's first centenary programme.

Netaji Subhas Chandra Bose, the then president of the Indian National Congress, differed widely with Congress viewpoint. He resigned from the Congress on April 29 and formed Forward Bloc on June 22.

The foundation stone of Mahajati Sadan conceptualised by Subhas Chandra Bose was laid by Rabindranath Tagore on August 19.

U. N. Brahmachari established the first blood blank in September in Calcutta which was the second one in the world.

1940   On March 13 in Caxton Hall of London, Udham Singh alias Muhammad Singh Azad, an engineer shot dead Michael O'Dwyer, who was the governor of Punjab in the dark days of Jallianwala Bagh in 1919. It was a historic belated revenge. Udham Singh was hanged in London on June 13. His ashes were brought to Delhi on July 19, 1974. (See 1919.)

'Pàkistan' resolution was adopted by Muslim League on March 23. (See 1933 and 1947.)

The world's longest marriage of 86 years (since 1853) of Bombay's Temulji Bhikaji Nariman and Smt. Nariman ended with the death of the former in August at the age of 91 years 11 months. Both were married at the age of five. (See 1999.)

As a symbolic protest to the British rule, 'Individual Satyagraha' was launched on October 17 by Gandhiji, who selected Vinoba Bhave to be the first person to court arrest by shouting anti-war slogans. Jawaharlal Nehru was the second choice. The total number of such persons who courted arrest was 23,223. The movement was suspended on December 17.

In Bombay conference of radical group of Congress from December 20 to 22, M. N. Roy announced formation of Radical Democratic Party. (See 1920.)

The nucleus of aircraft industry was founded at Bangalore by a private orgnatisation namely Hindustan Aircraft Ltd. It was taken over by the government of India in 1945. (See 1951.)

Col. A.G. Rangaraj of Army Medical Corps was the first person to carry out a modern parachute descend. He jumped again on August

A.D.

10, 1992 of the age of 75 after a lapse of nearly 40 years. (See 1890 and 1959.)

1941   Swami Pranabananda, founder of Bharat Sevashram Sangha, passed away on January 8. (b. 1896).

Subhas Chandra Bose escaped from his Calcutta residence, then under house arrest, in the early hours of January 17 and reached Berlin on March 28 through Afghanistan. In Berlin Subhas Bose raised Indian Legion (Free Indian Army) on November 2. The army addressed him as Netaji which stuck since then. He got every Indian in Germany to accept Jai Hind as the national greeting and Tagore's song 'Jana gana mana...' as the national anthem, which free India eventually accepted. (See 1943 and 1950.)

A modern shipyard was established at Vishakhapatnam by Hindustan Shipyard Ltd. The first ship *Jala Usha* was launched from the shipyard on March 11, 1948.

C.Y. Chintamani died on July 1. (b. 1880).

Rabindranath Tagore breathed his last on August 7. (b. 1861).

The idea of Indian National Army was first conceived by Mohan Singh in Malaya, who was taken a prisoner in Malaya by the Japanese on December 15, while retreating with the British army. It was formed but disbanded after sometime because of difference of opinion with the Japanese. (See 1943.)

National Football Championship in the form of Santosh Trophy, after the name of Maharaja of Santosh, was inaugurated. In the first year 14 teams participated. Bengal became the champion and Delhi the runners-up.

1942   Jamnalal Bajaj passed away on February 11. (b. 1889).

Stafford Cripps Mission arrived in India on March 22 to find out a political formula for transfer of power to Indians. But it was unsuccessful since Congress rejected the proposal on April 2.

During the Second World War Japanese ships and planes touched Port Blair on March 22.

First Japanese air-bombing on India's mainland took place on April 6 at Visakhapatnam. The first one on Calcutta took place on December 20. (See 1943.)

On August 8 in Bombay Congress session 'Quit India' resolution was passed and Gandhiji gave the 'Do or Die' call for independence struggle. As a sequel top Congress leaders were arrested in the early morning of August 9. The whole country went into mass upheaval, which is known as August Movement. According to the White Paper published by the British government in 1943, the people destroyed 250 railway stations, burnt and damaged 800 post offices, cut telephone and telgraph lines at 3,500 places and burnt 155 police stations and government buildings. The actual figures were probably much higher. Police and military opened fire on 538 occasions. Six times people were machine-gunned from low-flying aircrafts. By November official statistics showed 1,028 killed and 3,125 seriously injured. 60,000 people were arrested, 26,000 convicted and 18,000 detained under Defence of India Act.

Rash Behari Bose organised Indian National Army on September 1 comprising of 50,000 Indian officers and soldiers, who surrendered to the Japanese in Singapore. (See 1926, 1941 and 1943.)

Matangini Hazra, local pet name Gandhi Buri, a 72 year old widow of Tamluk town in Midnapur district became immortal by bravely facing the police bullets on September 29 while leading a procession in Tamluk during the August Movement. (See 1977.)

Sri Aurobindo Ashram School started on December 2 which was later known as Sri Aurobindo International Centre of Education.

Dr Dwarkanath Kotnis died in China on December 10.

Hindustan Motors Ltd., the first motor car manufacturing unit of India, was incorporated. (See 1898 and 1948.)

Lata Mangeshkar first appeared as an actress and a singer in the Marathi film 'Pahali Mangalagaur'.

1943 Subhas Chandra Bose left Germany in a German U-Boat (submarine) from Kiel on February 8 along with his secretary Major Abid Hasan. They changed over to a Japanese submarine near Madagascar on April 28 and reached Tokyo by air from Sabang island on June 13. (See 1941.)

Dada Saheb Phalke, the father of Indian cinema, passed away on February 16. (b. 1870).

The 450-metre cantilever Howrah bridge (Rabindra Setu) connecting Calcutta and Howrah across the Hooghly river was completed and opened on February 28 replacing the old pontoon

A.D.

bridge inaugurated on October 17, 1874. It was then the world's third largest cantilever bridge. (See 1972.)

Indian Independence League of Japan sent fourteen men to spread the seed of revolt amongst the Indian Army. Four of them were executed in Madras fort on September 9.

Indian National Army or Azad Hind Fauj was handed over to Netaji Subhas Chandra Bose by Rash Behari Bose at Singapore on July 7. Netaji founded Azad Hind Government there on October 21 and declared war on U.K. and U.S.A. on October 23. (See 1941 and 1942.)

Rani of Jhansi Brigade (women's wing of INA) was formed on October 23.

On November 6 Japan handed over the Andaman and Nicobar Islands to Azad Hind Government and their names were changed to Shahid and Swaraj Dweeps.

The only daylight air-raid on Calcutta by the Japanese planes took place on December 5. (See 1942.)

A terrible famine in Bengal took a toll of 2.7 million lives.

'Kismet' film of Bombay Talkies began its run of 3 years and 8 months at Roxy cinema hall in Calcutta, – the longest running Indian film so far. (See 1981.)

Dr M. C. Mody opened the first free eye camp at Tirupati. In 1968 he operated upon 833 cataract patients at a stretch which was a world record even in 1989, by which time he performed 5, 95,019 eye operations, which was also unique in the world.

Indian Peoples' Theatre Association was formed by Communist Party of India to strengthen the anti-Fascist movement. It was inspired by Puran Chand Joshi, the then general secretary of Communist Party of India.

1944 Kasturba Gandhi, Gandhiji's wife, died in internment in Aga Khan Place of Pune on February 22. (b. 1869).

Three brigades of Azad Hind Fauj (INA) under the Japanese army crossed Burma border and invaded north-eastern India on March 18 and hoisted the national flag on March 19 on Indian mainland. They fought their crucial battle at Bishenpur, south of Imphal, and that is the farthest INA reached inside India.

A.D.

The ammunition ship *S.S. Fort Stikine* with 1,318 tonnes of explosives exploded in Shed No. 1 of Victoria Dock of Bombay on April 14, causing extensive damage including destruction of 12 ships and over 1,200 lives. The catastrophic fire claimed 231 lives of Bombay Port Trust, fire brigade, army, navy and police while fighting the fire. It took 45 days to contain the conflagration. Since then April 14 is observed as the Fire Services Day.

On May 6 Gandhiji was released from Aga Khan Palace in Pune, his last confinement. In all he spent 2,089 days in Indian prisons and 249 days in South African prisons. When Mahatma Gandhi was released, Netaji broadcast a special message to him on July 6 from Singapore asking his blessings and concluded by Christening him 'Father of the Nation' – a honorific that stuck.

M. V. Dhurandhar, master painter of Maharashtra, passed away on June 1.

Rajiv Gandhi was born on August 20. (d. 1991).

Tara Singh, a shrewd old Sikh leader, issued a formal call for a sovereign Sikh nation for the first time. (See 1947.)

1945 The great revolutionary Rash Behari Bose expired in Tokyo on January 21. (b. 1886).

'Kali Yuga' era ended on February 18, which as per Aryabhatta, began on February 18, 3102 B.C.

First air letter form was issued in May.

On June 14 Lord Wavell broadcast the desire to meet India's top politicians in Shimla on June 25. Immediately he released all the political leaders who were in prison without trial since August 9, 1942.

Netaji Subhas Chandra Bose reportedly got seriously injured and badly burnt in a Japanese plane crash in Taihoku airport in Taiwan on August 18 at about 2 P.M. He expired in the nearby Japanese military hospital between 8 and 9 P.M. (b. 1897).

India, though still under the British rule, was made one of the 46 original members of the United Nations on October 30. The U.N.O. came into existence on October 24.

The trial of Indian National Army prisoners began in Red Fort of Delhi on November 5 and continued till December 31. (See 1946.)

A.D.

The Tata Institute of Fundamental Research was founded through the initiative of Homi Bhabha, who was its first Director.

1946   On January 3 the three Indian National Army heroes, Col. Shah Nawaz Khan, Col. G. S. Dhillon and Col. P. K. Sehgal, who were under trial in Red Fort of Delhi in 1945, were released by Gen. C. Auchinleck, Commander-in-Chief, under irresistible pressure from the Indian public.

On February 18 about 1,100 naval ratings of the Royal Indian Navy on *HMIS Talwar* in Bombay went on strike in protest against low pay. Soon they were joined by about 20,000 ratings from other establishments. British troops had to be called to suppress the mutiny when Indian soldiers refused to fire on the ratings. On February 23 the ratings surrendered on the advice of the Congress leaders, but with a declaration that 'We surrender to India and not to Britain'.

British Cabinet Mission, led by Lord Pethick Lawrence, arrived in India on March 24.

On April 22 the army was instructed for complete change over from khaki to olive green uniform. The army of free India continues to wear the olive green even in 2005. (See 1878.)

First Satyagraha campaign for Goa's liberation from the Portuguese was launched on June 18. (See 1510 and 1961.)

As a result of Direct Action on August 16 by Muslim League, 'Great Calcutta Killing' took a toll of 5,000 lives with 15,000 injured and more than one lakh were rendered homeless.

On September 2, Jawaharalal Nehru became the Prime Minister of the interim government of undivided India. Muslim League proclaimed it as a 'Day of Mourning'. (See 1947.)

In November British Prime Minister Clement Attlee summoned Jawaharlal Nehru, Baldev Singh, Muhammad Ali Jinnah and Liaquat Ali for an extraordinary conference at 10 Downing Street, London, the residence of the British prime minister.

Madan Mohan Malaviya expired on November 12. (b. 1861).

Home Guard Organisation was founded on December 6.

The Constituent Assembly started its session on December 9 in the Constitution Hall and Rajendra Prasad was elected as the Chairman on December 11.

A.D.

Telengana uprising started and continued till 1952. The peasants of nine districts led by the communists began their struggle on economic issues such as grain tax, forced labour and eviction. But soon it developed into an uprising against the feudal rule of the Nizam. It cost nearly 2,000 lives. About 10,000 active members were arrested.

Orissa government decided to shift its capital from Cuttack to Bhubaneswar. (See 1949.)

The first National Lawn Tennis Championship was held and Sumanta Mishra won men's singles title.

1947 On January 6 All Indian Congress Committee accepted partition of India by a majority vote of 99 in favour and 52 against the resolution.

The great popular singer Kundan Lal Saigal died in Jalandhar on January 18. (b.1904).

On February 20 the British Prime Minister Clement Attlee announced in the House of Commons that the British would leave India by a date not later than June 1948. Simultaneously it was announced that Lord Louis Mountbatten, the great grandson of Queen Victoria, would succeed as the twentieth and the last Viceroy of India.

Lord Louis Mountbatten arrived in India on March 22 and was installed as the last Viceroy on March 24.

The Indian Standards Institution was established on May 29. The name was changed to Bureau of Indian Standards on April 1, 1987.

On June 2 Lord Louis Mountbatten declared the British decision on partition of India and Indian leaders accepted it on June 3.

The India Independence Act was placed before the British Parliament on July 5 and passed on July 18. It immediately got the Royal assent.

India's National Flag was adopted by the Constituent Assembly on July 21. It was designed by Badr-ud-din Tyabji.

On August 14 India was divided and Pakistan was created with full independence. (See 1933 and 1940.)

On August 15 India (after partition) was declared independent of British rule with New Delhi as its capital, a city which was the seat

A.D.

of 21 dynasties and grave of 17 empires. Out of a total of 562 princely states in undivided India, 532 were within the new geographical limits of India. 529 states acceded to the Indian Union except Hyderabad, Junagarh and Kashmir. Interestingly 286 states were concentrated in Gujarat area, and the smallest was Bilbari with a population of only 27 and annual revenue of Rs 80.

On August 15 Pandit Jawaharlal Nehru was sworn in as the first Prime Minister of free India by Lord Louis Mountbatten. (See 1946.)

On August 15 awards for gallantry in combat with the enemy were instituted in the form of Param Vir Chakra, Maha Vir Chakra and Vir Chakra.

The first contingent of British troops, the second battalion of the Royal Norfolk Regiment, and part of 1st Battalion of Wiltshire Regiment sailed home in *S. S. Georgic* on August 17. (See 1948.)

Vallabhbhai Patel was appointed deputy prime minister of India on August 23, which position was abolished with his demise in 1950. (b. 1875).

On August 29 a drafting committee with B. R. Ambedkar as Chairman was appointed to draft the Constitution of India. It was submitted to the Governor General on February 21, 1948. The Constitution was finalised on November 26, 1949 and came into force on January 26, 1950 when India became a Republic.

Indian Standard Time was introduced on September 1. Clocks all over India were set to IST in 1965.

Kashmir was invaded by Pakistani tribesmen on October 24 under the banner of Azad Kashmir forces, with a view to annex it to Pakistan. Maharaja Hari Singh of Kashmir appealed for help to India on October 25. He signed the Instrument of Accession to India on October 27. (See 1965, 1971 and 1999.)

Major Somnath Sharma of Kumaon Regiment was the first recipient (posthumously) of the highest gallantry award Param Vir Chakra for his heroism in Badgaon in Kashmir on November 4, that saved Srinagar.

On November 21 the first post-independence postage stamp was issued. It was of 3½ annas denomination depicting India's national flag with Hindi inscription Jai Hind.

The word Khalistan referring to independent Sikh state was coined by Kapur Singh, an advisor to Maharaja of Patiala and a professor of comparative religion in Oxford University. (See 1944.)

Indian cricket team for the first time toured Australia under Lala Amarnath as its captain. Australia's captain was Don Bradman. Australia won four Tests and one Test was drawn. (See 1956.)

Sarojini Naidu became the Governor of Uttar Pradesh, the first woman Governor.

Vijaylakshmi Pandit became the first woman ambassador of India when she was posted in Russia.

Devdasi Act abolished the dedication of girls to temple service. (See 1925.)

1948   On January 1 a complaint was lodged in the Security Council of United Nations by India on Kashmir invasion by the so-called Pakistani tribesmen.

Gandhiji commenced his seventeenth and the last fast unto death on January 13 to bring about Hindu-Muslim unity. He broke his fast on January 18 after the leaders promised accord.

Gandhiji was assassinated on January 30 (b. 1869) in Birla House prayer meeting in New Delhi through revolver shots by Nathuram Vinayak Godse. Since then January 30 is observed as Martyrs' Day. (See 1949.)

The draft of Constitution of Independent India was presented to the President on February 21. (See 1947.)

The last British soldiers, 1st Battalion of Somerset Light Infantry, left Indian soil at Gateway of India of Bombay on February 28. (See 1748, 1911 and 1947.)

Air India International was established on March 8 for overseas services.

The first modern Indian ship *S. S. Jala Usha* was launched on March 11 from Visakhapatnam. (See 1941.)

Himachal Pradesh was created on April 15 by the merger of some 30 small ruling hill states.

India to United Kingdom weekly air service via Cairo and Geneva was inaugurated on June 8. (See 1953.)

A.D.

C. Rajagopalachari became the first and the only Indian Governor General of India on June 21, and the last Governor General as well. (See 1950.)

On June 22 His Majesty the King of United Kingdom relinquished his title 'Emperor of India'. (See 1877.)

H.M.S Achilles, formerly of Royal Navy, was commissioned as *HMIS Delhi* on July 5 in U.K. and became the first flagship of Indian Navy. It arrived at Bombay on September 15. After India became a Republic on January 26, 1950 it became *INS Delhi* with Capt. A. K. Chatterji as its first Indian Commanding Officer. On May 13, 1978 *INS Delhi* was decommissioned and her ensign and commissioning pennant were lowered for the last time on June 30, 1978.

The first public corporation, namely Damodar Valley Corporation, was formed on July 7.

On July 17 the government removed all discriminations against women in matter of employment. They were made eligible for any public service including administrative service and police service. (See 1975.)

Calcutta State Transport Corporation was inaugurated on July 31 and thus the first state-controlled road transport system was introduced.

Md. Ali Jinnah, founder of Pakistan, died on September 11. (b. 1876).

Due to internal anarchy by the Rajakars, the militant youths within Hyderabad state, the Indian troops entered the state on September 13 and annexed Hyderabad to Indian territory on September 17. On the Indian side there were only 10 casualties but nearly 1,200 Rajakars were either killed or injured.

Prime Minister Jawaharlal Nehru delivered his maiden speech in the U.N. General Assembly on November 3. (See 1977.)

In view of the undesirable activities of the Nawab and his ministry, Junagarh state was annexed to India on November 9. (See 1807.)

In the great river tragedy on November 18 nearly 500 people were drowned when the ferry steamer *Narayani* capsized and sank in the Ganga near Patna. (See 1877.)

A.D.

The National Cadet Corps was first organised on November 27 for the student community. (See 1963.)

Ismail Porter, a labourer, was the only civilian to be awarded Maha Vir Chakra. In 1948 Kashmir operations he rescued army personnel with utter disregard to his own safety.

Uday Shankar took four years to complete his film 'Kalpana', – a dance spectacular.

An all India service, IAS (Indian Administrative Service), was instituted to man senior positions in the states and at the Centre. The ICS was technically wound up and amalgamated with IAS. (See 1863 and 1980.)

For security reasons North East Frontier Agency was brought directly under the Union Government. (See 1972.)

Employees' State Insurance Act was passed for the first time to provide certain benefits in case of sickness and injury. (See 1955.)

West Indies cricket team visited India for the first time. (See 1952.)

Mother Teresa took Indian citizenship. (See 1950 and 1979.)

The first India-made Hindustan 10 motor car moved out of Hindustan Motors Ltd's assembly line. (See 1898, 1942.)

The name of Imperial Library was changed to National Library. (See 1903.)

Films Division of the Ministry of Information and Broadcasting was set up. It started releasing newsreels and films in 1949.

The Minimum Wages Act 1948 was passed to provide fixation of minimum wages in certain employments.

1949 Ceasefire was declared in Kashmir on January 1. (See 1947.)

Lt. Gen. K. M. Cariappa became the first Indian Commander-in-Chief. Indian Army came under him on January 15. Since then this date is observed as Army Day. (See 1986.)

Night airmail service was inaugurated on January 30.

Associated Press of India, owned and operated by Reuter, was transferred to Indian ownership on February 1 and was named as Press Trust of India. (See 1905 and 1913.)

Sarojini Naidu expired in Lucknow on March 2. (b. 1879).

Present Rajasthan state came into being on March 30 with Jaipur as its capital.

A.D.

On April 1 Institute of Chartered Accountants of India was constituted as a statutory body under a special Act of Parliament.

On April 5 Boy Scouts and Girl Guides were unified and renamed as Bharat Scouts and Guides. (See 1907, 1911, 1917, and 1921.)

On May 17 the Indian Constituent Assembly approved with only one dissent vote to remain within the Commonwealth of Nations.

On June 19 people of Chandernagar, the French Indian Settlement, decided by plebiscite in favour of Settlement's merger with the Indian Union. (See 1690 and 1950.)

For the first time in Asia, Youth Hostel Movement was launched in Mysore in July with a good-will grant of Rs 500 from the University of Mysore. Maharaja's College Hostel was the first hostel to be used as such. Incidentally while the Youth Movement first originated in Germany in 1909, the idea of Youth Hostels was developed only in 1932.

Bhubaneswar was declared the capital of Orissa on August 19. (See 1946.)

Hindi was declared as the National Language of India by the Constituent Assembly of India on September 9.

Dravida Kazhagam of E.V. Ramaswamy Naicker had a split and C. N. Annadurai formed the Dravida Munnetra Kazhagam in Tamil Nadu on September 17 with the basic idea of serving the non-Brahmins. (See 1879.)

The first devaluation of rupee after independence took place in September. (See 1966.)

Foundation-stone of National Defence Academy was laid at Kharakvasla by Jawaharlal Nehru on October 6. It was then the only military institution of the world where cadets of all the three services, the army, navy and the air force, were trained. It was officially opened on January 16, 1955.

Territorial Army was formed on October 9.

In October the Abolition of Privy Council Jurisdiction Act was passed and thus Federal Court of India (later Supreme Court) became the highest judicial authority in India. Nobody could appeal to Privy Council of U.K. any more. (See 1950.)

A.D.

Nathuram Vinayak Godse and Narayan Dattatreya Apte were hanged in Ambala Jail on November 15 for Gandhiji's murder. (See 1948.)

The Constitution of India was adopted on November 26 by the Constituent Assembly and it came into force on January 26, 1950.

Muthamma Chohivia Beliappa was the first woman to pass the Indian Administrative Service examination. She opted for Indian Foreign Service. (See 1951 amd 1970.)

National Cadet Corps services were extended to women also. (See 1948.)

Women were inducted in the Calcutta Police Force in November.

Malayalam poet Ulloor S. Parameswara Iyer died. (b. 1877).

Vanamahotsava (afforestation) programme was initiated. (See 1928.)

1950 'Jana gana mana...' was adopted as the National Anthem of India on January 24. 'Vande Mataram...' was adopted as the National Song with the same status of 'Jana Gana Mana...' Herbert Murril's orchestra tune of the National Anthem was accepted after an international competition. (See 1911 and 1941.)

On January 26 India was declared a sovereign democratic republic. (See 1947.)

Rajendra Prasad was elected the first President of India (Rashtrapati) on January 24. He took office on January 26 from the Governor General C. Rajagopalachari. (See 1948.)

The government of India adopted the National Emblem on January 26. It is the replica of the Lion Capital of Ashoka's pillar at Sarnath. The words *Satyameva Jayate* from Manduka Upanishad are inscribed below the emblem in Devanagari script. The original Lion Capital is 210 cm in height and is now in Sarnath Museum. (See 1904.)

The industrial colony of Chittaranjan Locomotive Works was inaugurated on January 26. The first steam locomotive came out of the assembly line on November 1. (See 1895 and 1963.)

Supreme Court of India was inaugurated on January 28 with Justice Hiralal J. Kania as the first Chief Justice of India. (See 1949.)

Sarat Chandra Bose, elder brother of Netaji, died on February 20. (b. 1889).

A.D.

Maharshi Ramana breathed his last on April 14. (b. 1879).

Bhoodan Movement was started by Vinoba Bhave on April 18 on receipt of 80 acres of land in Pachampalli village of Telengana in Andhra Pradesh, offered by V. Ramachandra Reddy.

Chandernagore was taken over from the French on March 2. (See 1949.)

Shyama Prasad Mukherji was the first central cabinet minister (industries and supplies) to resign on April 19.

Mother Teresa founded 'Missionaries of Charity' in Calcutta on October 7. (See 1948 and 1979.)

Sri Aurobindo died on December 5. (b. 1872).

Vallabhbhai Patel, the first deputy prime minister of independent India, died on December 15. (b. 1875).

Planning Commission was established by Government of India on December 15. (See 1938.)

Both India and Pakistan accepted the award of Indo-Pakistan Boundary Dispute Tribunal under the Swedish Chairman Bagge.

A total of seven coins – one rupee, half rupee, quarter rupee, two anna, one anna, half anna and pice were introduced after independence. The Lion Capital appeared on the coin for the first time.

The country's first air crash of a passenger plane took place on July 17 when a DC 3 aircraft crashed near Pathankot killing all 22 persons on board.

Dilip Bose was the first Indian to be seeded in Wimbledon Tennis Tournament. His seeding was 15th. (See 1982.)

1951 Prem Mathur was the first woman pilot to get a commercial pilot's licence on January 24. She joined Deccan Airways on June 13 and flew as a co-pilot on a scheduled flight on October 24. (See 1984.)

Enumeration work of the first census of free India started on February 9. The census revealed 720 languages and dialects. The Constitution of India recognised fourteen major tongues for official, national and provincial uses. Incidentally in 1967 Nagaland adopted English as the medium of instruction. The census also revealed over 2,300 recognised castes, creeds and sects.

On March 4 eleven countries and 489 male and female athletes participated in the first Asian Games held in Old Fort of New Delhi. (See 1982.)

The new Somnath temple, built at the site of the fifth one of 1169, was opened by President Rajendra Prasad on May 11. This is the ninth temple, since the first seven were destroyed one after the other by the invaders. The eighth one built in 1783 by Rani Ahalya Bai still exists. (See 1026.)

Taraporewala Aquarium of Bombay was inaugurated on May 27 by President Rajendra Prasad.

The first Five-Year Plan (1951-56) was prepared and published by the Planning Commission on July 9. (See 1938 and 1950.)

The first aircraft designed and manufactured in India is Hindustan Trainer 2, i.e., H.T. 2. It had its maiden Flight on August 13. (See 1940 and 1961.)

Indian Institute of Technology, the first of its kind, was opened on August 18 in Kharagpur, West Bengal. The disreputed cellular jail building of Hijli detention camp constructed by the British formed the nucleus of the institute. (See 1931.)

Shyama Prasad Mukherji founded Bharatiya Jana Sangh on October 2.

Artist Abanindranath Tagore expired on December 5. (b. 1871).

Salar Jung Museum was established at Hyderabad on December 16 with about 47,000 items – the individual collection of Mir Yusuf Ali Khan (Salar Jung III).

Bharat Sevak Samaj, a semi-government and non-political organisation, was established with a view to rouse the enthusiasm of people for social work.

Karan Singh (nearing 21 years), then the Regent of Jammu and Kashmir, passed B.A. examination from Jammu and Kashmir University as a private candidate. He missed a first division by six marks only. In 1949 as the Regent of the state, he became the Chancellor of the University. Thus, probably he was the first Chancellor in world history to be a graduate – by appearing as an examinee in a regular examination hall – from his own university.

Visa Bharati University was taken over by Government of India.

A.D.

Monotosh Roy was declared 'Mr Universe' in the Body Building Contest in London. He demonstrated 17 yogic asanas in 30 seconds in the agility test which carried 20 marks. That enthralled the spectators so greatly that he exceeded the time frame with the rhythmic mythological poses of his muscles. Then the time-keeper forgot to ring the bell at 30 seconds till someone pointed out to her that it was well past time. (See 1952 and 1988, d. 2005).

Central Film Censor Board was formed. (See 1952.)

The first police dog squad was set up in Madras. Dogs are believed to have been used for crime detection as far back as in the Vedic age. The Rig Veda speaks of how a dog named Sarma located the sage Brihaspati's stolen cow.

'Jhansi Ki Rani' of Sohrab Modi was the first full technicolour film of India. Earlier V. Santaram's 'Shakuntala' was hand tinted. (See 1931.)

Anna Rajan Malhotra nee George was the first lady to join as IAS officer in India proper. Her first assignment was as a sub-collector of Hosur district in Tamil Nadu. She later became the first lady Chairperson of Nhava Sheva Port Trust, and thereby probably in the world too. (See 1949.)

1952   The first International Film Festival was inaugurated in Bombay on January 24.

India had its first ever cricket Test victory on February 2 at Chepauk Stadium, Madras against the visiting M.C.C. team. (See 1926, 1932 and 1971.)

Employees Provident Fund and Miscellaneous Provisions Act was passed on February 23.

Sindri fertilizer factory in Bihar was formally inaugurated on March 2. It was the first government-owned, factory.

The first session of free India's Parliament began on May 13.

The first world convention on copyrights was signed on September 8 at Geneva by 35 nations including India. (See 1857 and 1958.)

The Community Development Programme was launched on October 2.

A.D.

Sriramalu Potti commenced fasting on October 19 and died on December 16 for a separate Andhra state for Telugu-speaking people. (See 1953, b. 1901.).

Saifuddin Kitchlu was the first Indian to get Lenin Peace Prize of U.S.S.R. on December 21.

The world's first official Family Planning Programme was launched. (See 1925, 1956 and 1961.)

The first general election on adult franchise basis was held in India under the new constitution. (See 1892 and 1909.)

Monohar Aich became 'Mr Universe' in short height category in Body Building Contest in London. (See 1951.)

Kashaba D. Yadav won a Bronze Medal in wrestling in Bantamweight (57 kg) freestyle category in Helsinki Olympic. That was India's first official Olympic medal in athletics. (See 1900, 1996 and 2000.)

Cinematograph Act to differentiate between 'Adult' movies and movies for 'Universal' exhibition came into effect. (See 1951.)

Indian cricket team visited West Indies for the first time under Captain Lala Amarnath. (See 1948.)

Pakistan cricket team visited India for the first time. (See 1954.)

All India Handicrafts Board was established by the Government of India to help the craftsmen.

Atul Products, the pioneer in the dyestuff industry, started its operation with a small tonnage of sulphur black and azo dyes.

Ashoka Chakra, a gallantry award for bravery other than in the face of the enemy, was instituted.

Kabbadi was declared India's National Game. (See 1936 and 1990.)

1953 Sangeet Natak Akademi was set up on January 29 for developing Indian drama, dance and music.

All India Khadi and Village Industries Board was constituted on February 2.

Sherpa Tenzing Norgay of Darjeeling and Edmund Hillary of New Zealand conquered Mount Everest for the first time on May 29. The success came on the eleventh assault; the first one was in 1921. (See 1965 and 1984.)

A.D.

Shyama Prasad Mukherji died on June 23. (b. 1901).

All airlines of India were nationalised on August 1 by Air Corporation Act. Two separate corporations Indian Airlines and Air India were formed for domestic and international services respectively. (See 1948 and 1994.)

Andhra Pradesh became a separate state of India on October 1 with Hyderabad city as its capital. (See 1952.)

Chandigarh city was founded on October 7 as the new capital of Punjab. It was the creation of a French architect Le Corbusier. (See1967.)

Estate Duty Act of 1953, generally known as Death Duty, came into effect from October 14. (See 1985.)

The University Grants Commission was constituted.

Vijayalakshmi Pandit became the President of the 8th General Assembly Session of the United Nations. She was the first Indian as well as the first woman to get the exalted position.

Archbishop Valerian Gracias was the first Indian to be created as a Cardinal by the Vatican.

Indian Institute of Social Welfare and Business Management was founded under Calcutta University. It is the first government recognised management institute in the country. (See 1956.)

Madras Motor Sports Club organised the first All India Motor Race meet in October at Sholavaram, about 25 km from Madras. (See 1989.)

1954 M. N. Roy (actually Narendra Nath Bhattacharya) died on January 25. (See 1916, b. 1887.).

A great tragedy occurred in Kumbh Mela at Allahabad on February 3 when more than 500 people were trampled to death in a stampede on the river bank at the Mela site.

Sahitya Akademi was inaugurated on March 12 for enhancement of Indian literary pursuits. (See 1956.)

National Gallery of Modern Art was inaugurated on March 29 at Jaipur House in New Delhi.

Air Marshal Subroto Mukherji became the first Indian air chief on April 1. He suddenly died in Tokyo on November 9, 1960.

On April 1 South Point School, a co-educational one, was founded in Calcutta with only 17 students. It became the largest school in the world with 11, 683 regular students as on April 30, 1988. (See 1999.)

India recognised Tibet as the region of China on April 29.

On May 8 the Government of India decided to integrate Chandernagar (earlier under French possession) with West Bengal. (See 1951.)

Jawaharlal Nehru opened the then world's largest canal of Bhakra Nangal Hydroelectric Project in Punjab on July 8.

French territories Pondicherry, Mahe, Karikal and Yanon were handed over to the Government of India on November 1. A new state Pondicherry was formed comprising of these territories.

Himalayan Mountaineering Institute was established in Darjeeling on November 4.

Lalit Kala Akademi (National Academy of Arts) was inaugurated with Debi Prasad Roy Chowdhury as its first chairman.

The Government of India introduced personal civil decorations Bharat Ratna, Padma Vibhusan, Padma Bhushan and Padma Shree. In 1954 the first recipients for the highest honour 'Bharat Ratna' were C. Rajagopalachari, S. Radhakrishnan and C.V. Raman. (See 1977 and 1980.)

National Development Council was established with the Planning Commission members and chief ministers of all the states.

National Film Award was introduced. In the first year films produced in 1953 were considered for the award. The President's Gold Medals went to the Marathi feature film 'Shyamchi Aai' by P. K. Atre and to the documentary film 'Mahabalipuram' directed by Jagat Murari. (See 1975.)

The Special Marriage Act of 1954 legalised inter-caste, inter-region and inter-religious marriages as also divorce by mutual consent.

Air Commodore P. C. Lal, Group Captain H. Mulgaonkar and Wing Commander Roshan Suri were the first Indians to break supersonic speed barrier. They achieved this feat in a Super Marine Swift aircraft.

The 14-storey New Secretariat building in Calcutta was the first high-rise building in the country.

A.D.

Indian cricket team visited Pakistan for the first time. (See 1952.)

Poet Desika Vinayakam Pillai of Tamil Nadu died. (b. 1876).

Institute of Cost and Works Accountants was established.

1955 India's first newsprint factory started production on January 11 at Nepanagar in Madhya Pradesh.

Kharakvasla Defence Academy was officially opened on January 16. (See 1949.)

Indian Standard Institution (Certification Marks) Regulation Act 1955 came into force on March 17.

Sevagram Ashram of Gandhiji at Wardha was closed on March 17. (See 1936.)

N. M. Joshi died on May 30. (b. 1879).

Children's Film Society of India was set up in May.

Untouchability (Offence) Act came into force on June 1.

Imperial Bank of India was nationalised on July 1 and was renamed as State Bank of India. (See 1921.)

President Rajendra Prasad announced on July 15 the conferment of the highest national honour Bharat Ratna on Prime Minister Jawaharlal Nehru along with Bhagwan Das and M. Visveswaryya.

On July 25 it was announced in the Lok Sabha that the Government of India had asked the Portuguese Government to close its legation in New Delhi. (See 1961.)

The Integral Coach Factory at Perambur was inaugurated on October 2.

On November 14 the President inaugurated Employees' State Insurance Corporation. (See 1948.)

Top Soviet leaders Nicolai Bulganin and Nikita Khrushchev came to Delhi for the first time on November 18.

Indian Golf Union was formed on December 20.

Manufacture of motorcycles, scooters and three-wheelers started.

Hindu Marriage Act fixed the minimum age of a girl as 15 years and that of a boy as 18 years. It enforced monogamy, also provided for divorce and judicial separation. (See 1929, 1955 and 1978.)

Filaria Control Programme was taken up.

A.D.

National Chess Championship was officially instituted at Eluru, Andhra Pradesh. R.C. Sapre of Maharashtra and D. Venkaiya of Andhra Pradesh were joint winners. (See 1978.)

The New Zealand cricket team visited India for the first time. (See 1967.)

The new Karnataka state was created.

Lothal dock, a prehistoric site in Ahmedabad district of Gujarat, was discovered.

Central Coal Mining Research Institute was established in Dhanbad.

Industrial Credit and Investment Corporation of India was formed.

The first computer HEC-2M was installed in Calcutta.

Narinder Kapany of Imperial College of London University invented optical fibre.

Bharat Petroleum started making LPG gas and selling it in cylinder.

National Leprosy Eradication Programme started.

1956   Indian Companies Act of 1913 was revised and Companies Act of 1956 came into force on April 1. (See 1850.)

On May 24 the 2,500 anniversary of Buddha's birth was celebrated.

State Trading Corporation was set up in May.

Hindu Succession Act was passed on June 18 which recognised the right of inheritance of the women, along with the male successors, when some property was left without a will.

India's first nuclear research reactor 'Apsara' was commissioned on August 4. (See 1957.)

National Highways Bill was passed on August 13.

On August 31 the President gave his assent to the States Reorganisation Bill.

Life insurance business was nationalised on and from September 1 and Life Insurance Corporation was inaugurated. (See 1973 and 1999.)

Oil and Natural Gas Commission (ONGC) was established on September 17.

Central Family Planning Board to control the population increase was set up in September. (See 1952 and 1961.)

A.D.

B. R. Ambedkar and about two lakh scheduled caste men and women embraced Buddhism in Nagpur on October 14.

Ashok Hotel of Delhi was opened on October 30. It was the first 5-star Deluxe hotel in India, built to accommodate delegates of the UNESCO at its first out-of-Europe session. (See 1962.)

Indian states were reorganised on linguistic basis. On November 1 India's biggest state Madhya Pradesh was created. Delhi became a union territory. The Andaman and Nicobar Islands with a cluster of 314 islands were constituted into a union territory. Also the Laccadive, Minicoy and Amindivi Islands were made into a union territory. It is interesting to note that Pygmalion Point, presently known as Indira Point in the Nicobar Group, is the southernmost tip of India. (See 1973.)

Chou En-lai, Prime Minister of Communist China, arrived in India on November 28.

B. R. Ambedkar died on December 6. (b. 1891).

In Bombay Sulochona Modi became the Mayor, a first for any woman in India. But it was only for three months. (See 1957.)

Hero Cycle started with the production of only 25 cycles per day at Ludhiana which turned out to be the world's largest producer of 18,500 cycles per day in the year 2000.

The first open prison was inaugurated in the campus of Government Agriculture and Research Centre in Jaipur. Prisoners could live with their families and earn their livelihood outside.

The first Sahitya Academy award winner was Amrita Pritam for her collection of Punjabi poems *Sunahre*. (See 1954.)

Nehru, Tito and Nasser met at Brioni in Yugoslavia and founded the Non-Aligned Movement of the world. (See 1983.)

India's second Five-Year Plan (1956-61) was launched.

Andhra University was the first one to start a 2-year Master of Business Administration (MBA) Degree course. (See 1953.)

Lionism came to India when the first Lions Club was formed in Bombay, followed by Calcutta in the next year.

Australian cricket team visited India for the first time. (See 1947.)

National Atlas and Thematic Mapping Organisation of India was established.

A.D.

All India Institute of Medical Sciences was established in New Delhi.

Karnataka Vidhan Soudha in Bangalore, built in neo-Dravidian style, is one of the finest in India, having both the state legislature and the secretariat in the same building.

Travancore, Cochin and Malabar areas were merged to form Kerala state.

1957 Central Sales Tax Act of 1956 came into force on January 5.

India's first atomic research reactor 'Apsara' was inaugurated on January 20. (See 1956.)

National Calendar was adopted on March 22, which happened to be 1st Chaitra, 1879 Shaka. It is 78 years behind Christian era. (See 78.)

As the initiation of decimal coinage, 'Naya Paisa' was introduced on April 1. (See 1964.)

Postage stamps and sale of postage stationery in decimal system were also introduced on April 1.

The world's first communist government by election in a state was installed in Kerala on April 5. (See 1909.)

Janata Insurance Policy was launched in Bombay on May 26.

Export Risk Insurance Corporation of India (Private) Ltd. was formed on July 30 and inaugurated on October 4.

National Book Trust was set up on August 1 to encourage production of good literature and to make it available at moderate prices.

Indian Polo Team won the World Polo Cup in France on August 25.

Wealth Tax Bill was passed in the Rajya Sabha on September 5.

Jawaharlal Nehru's birthday on November 14 was officially announced as the 'Children's Day' of India.

Delhi War Memorial was unveiled in November in memory of 25,000 Indian soldiers and airmen who gave their lives during the Second World War.

India's second general election was held.

Bhai Bir Singh expired. (b. 1872).

A.D.

Bhabha Atomic Research Centre was established at Trombay near Bombay (See 1970.)

Central Warehousing Corporation started operating.

Sarah Cherian became the Mayor of Madras Corporation and thus considered the first regular woman Mayor of the country. (See 1956.)

India's first computer called TIFRAC was designed and assembled at the Tata Institute of Fundamental Research at Bombay. (See 1955.)

1958 The Copyright Bill passed on May 27, 1957 came into force on January 21, 1958. (See 1857 and 1952.)

Maulana Abul Kalam Azad died on February 22. (b. 1888).

Admiral R. D. Katari became the first Indian Chief of the Naval Staff on April 22. (d. 1983).

Gift Tax Act received President's assent on May 15.

Three-men Indian mountaineering team climbed Mt. Trishul 7,120 mt (23,360 ft) high peak in the Garhwal range on June 4. (See 1960.)

Mihir Sen was the first Indian to swim across the English Channel from Dover to Calais, a distance of 34 km on September 27 in 14 hours 45 minutes. (See 1959 and 1966.)

India began to switch over to metric system of weights on October 1. (See 1957 and 1962.)

Indian Explosive Ltd's factory at Gomia, the first explosive factory in India, was inaugurated on November 11.

On December 11 Wilson Jones became India's first individual World Champion in any international competitive sport by winning the Amateur Billiards Championship. He beat his Indian compatriot Chandra Hirjee by 4,655 to 2,887 points in the eight hour tie in Calcutta. (See 1977, 1984 and 1985.)

Supreme Court building was built in an Indo-classical style and completed this year. It has a central dome of 35.7 mt high and a total floor space of 1,85,800 sq mt.

Vinoba Bhave became the first recipient of Magsaysay award. (See 1895.)

Vallathol Narayana Menon expired. (b. 1878).

1959 Miss Meera Behn let India for good on January 18. (See 1892 and 1925.)

Tej Bahadur Sapru died on January 20. (b. 1875).

The foundation-stone of the first College of Engineering and Technology was laid on January 27 in New Delhi.

Anna Chandy was the first Indian woman judge when appointed in Kerala High Court on February 6. She became the first woman munsif in 1937.

Press Club of India was founded in New Delhi on February 21.

Oil India Limited was formed in February.

Dalai Lama XIV fled from Tibet and reached India on March 17 and was given political asylum on March 31. He settled down in Dharamsala in Uttar Pradesh, 425 km from Delhi.

India's first polyethylene plant, that of Alkali & Chemicals Corporation of India Ltd., was opened on May 2 at Rishra of West Bengal.

On June 4 C. Rajagopalachari announced formation of Swatantra Party. It merged with Janata Party on April 17, 1977.

On July 6 the first successful open heart surgery was performed by Dr N. Gopinath and Dr P. H. Betts in Vellore hospital, on a 12-year-old girl Beulah (later Mrs Samuel).

The first television centre was commissioned in New Delhi on September 15 as a UNESCO-aided programme.

Arati Saha successfully swam the English Channel on September 29. She was the first Asian lady to achieve the feat. (See 1958.)

National Council of Women's Education was inaugurated in New Delhi on October 16.

An agreement on the Gandak Irrigation and Power Project was signed between India and Nepal on December 4. The project was inaugurated by the King of Nepal on May 4, 1964.

President Dwight D. Eisenhower of the U.S.A. arrived in India on December 12. He was the first U.S. President to do so.

Gita Chanda became the first woman paratrooper and got the rank of Flight Lieutenant in Indian Air Force. (See 1940.)

A.D.

1960 Air India entered the jet age on April 20, when Boeing 707 Gaurishankar went into service for the first time to London. On May 14 it flew to New York. Thus India was the first Asian country to operate over the Atlantic. (See 1982.)

National Defence College in New Delhi for senior defence officers was inaugurated on April 27.

Bombay state was bifurcated into Maharashtra and Gujarat on May 1.

International Telex Service was introduced on May 16 between India and U.K.

Dr (Miss) Ida Sophie Schrudder, the founder of Vellore hospital, expired in Kodaikanal on May 24. (See 1900.)

Feroz Gandhi, a prominent member of the Lok Sabha and husband of Indira Gandhi, died on September 8 in New Delhi.

The first officially organised All India Mountaineering Expedition conquered Nanda Ghunti peak in the Kumaon Hills on October 20. The height is 6,580 mts., i.e., 21,690 ft. (See 1958 and 1964.)

Air Marshal Subroto Mukherji, India's chief of air staff, suddenly died on November 9 in Tokyo. (See 1954.)

Subscriber Trunk Dialling (STD) system of telephone was first introduced between Kanpur and Lucknow on November 26.

National Museum was inaugurated on December 18 in New Delhi.

Hindustan Photo Films Manufacturing Co. Ltd. was incorporated in November for making raw photographic film and X-ray film, in collaboration with Eta Banchet & Co. of France.

Jawaharlal Nehru resettled some of the Gadia Lohars in Chittorgarh area. They had been wandering ever since they lost in the historic battle of Haldighati between Rana Pratap and Akbar. The Lohars promised to lead the nomadic life until Chittorgarh was liberated from the Mughals. (See 1576.)

Manuel Aaron became India's first International Master in chess. (See 1987.)

Ram Charan, an officer of Indian Navy's education branch, was the first Indian to reach Antarctica as one of the members of an Australian expedition. (See 1977 and 1982.)

A.D.

Diners' Club International, a wholly-owned establishment of the U.S. based Citibank, introduced for the first time the credit card system on an all India basis. (See 1981 and 1998.)

Film & Television Institute of India was established in Pune. It started functioning in 1961. Its activities included three-year Diploma Course in Cinema, which was withdrawn after seven years.

Govind Ballabh Pant University of Agriculture and Technology was established at Pantnagar in U.P., which happened to be the first agricultural university in the country.

1961 Fertilizer Corporation of India was formed on January 1.

Queen Elizabeth II of Great Britain and the Duke of Edinburgh arrived in New Delhi on January 21 and left India on March 2.

Foundation-stone of the first HMT watch factory was laid on January 28 in Bangalore.

On February 24 the Government of Madras decided to rename Madras state as Tamil Nadu. (See 1968.)

India's first aircraft carrier *INS VIKRANT* was commissioned on March 4 in Belfast.

India's first financial daily *The Economic Times* was launched by the Times of India group in Bombay on March 6.

Govind Ballabh Pant expired on March 7. (b. 1887).

On April 5 Indian Drugs and Pharmaceuticals Ltd. was registered to implement four projects, namely (a) Antibiotics at Rishikesh (b) Synthetic Drugs at Hyderabad (c) Photochemicals at Kerala and (d) Surgical Instruments at Madras.

The first India-made supersonic fighter Marut (HF 24) took to air on June 24 at Bangalore. (See 1940 and 1951.)

Shipping Corporation of India Ltd. was formed on October 2.

Passenger plane AVRO HS748 had its maiden flight on November 1. (See 1967.)

The Grand Lodge of Ancient, Free and Accepted Masons of India was inaugurated on November 24. (See 1729.)

Yuri Gagarin of Russia, the first cosmonaut of the world, came to India on November 29.

The Government of India took military action in Goa in the early hours of December 18, which resulted in the liberation of Goa,

A.D.

Daman, Diu and Nagar Haveli from Portugal on December 19. That ended the longest colonial rule of over 450 years. (See 1510, 1946 and 1955.)

India's third Five Year Plan (1961-1966) was launched.

It was not until the third Five Year Plan that family planning in India was taken up in right earnestness. In the third Plan a substantial amount was alloted. (See 1952 and 1956.)

Arjuna Award to the best sportsmen of the year in various fields was introduced. (See 1963.)

The Government of India put into effect Maternity Benefit Act for the married women employees. (See 1986.)

Dowry Prohibition Act was passed. But it gave little redress to the suffering brides. (See 1914 and 1985.)

1962 Metric weights were fully adopted all over the country on April 1. (See 1958.)

M. Visveswarayya died on April 14. (b. 1860).

S. Radhakrishnan became the second President of India on May 13.

Bidhan Chandra Roy expired on July 1. (b. 1882).

President Radhakrishnan's birthday September 5 was declared as 'Teachers' Day'.

The Chinese made their first incursion into Indian territory in the eastern sector by violating the MacMahon line on September 8. (See 1914.)

Birla Planetarium, the first one in Asia and second largest in the world, was opened in Calcutta on September 29 with 689 seats.

China mounted a massive attack in NEFA and Ladakh on October 20, which resulted in Chinese advance well inside Assam. Ceasefire was declared by China on November 21.

On October 22 Jawaharlal Nehru dedicated Bhakra-Nangal Multipurpose River Valley Project to the nation. The quantity of cement required for Bhakra Dam was three times the total material that went to make up all the seven large pyramids of Egypt.

On October 26 the President made a proclamation of Emergency and Defence of India Ordinance, the first of its kind, consequent to the Chinese aggression of India. (See 1968 and 1975.)

Keeping in view the Chinese aggression, the Gold Bond Scheme was announced on November 3 and National Defence Council was set up on November 6.

K.C. Dey, the well-known blind singer of Bengal, died on November 28.

India's third general election was held. The indelible ink on the voters' finger nail was used for the first time.

The Smallpox Eradication Programme was launched. (See 1975.)

Hotel Classification Committee was appointed. (See 1956.)

Delhi University introduced correspondence courses, first time in India by a university.

The plan for central schools of the Government of India was finalised essentially for the children of the defence forces.

Syndicate Bank's Seshadripuram Branch at Bangalore was set up and was staffed entirely by women.

1963 Gold Control Measures of Government of India was announced on January 9 and came into operation on January 10. (See 1962 and 1968.)

The National Library for the Blind, the first of its kind, was set up at Dehradun on January 22. (See 1887.)

Peacock was declared as the National Bird on January 31.

Rajendra Prasad, the first president of India, expired on February 28 at Patna. (b. 1884).

The first passenger locomotive of Chittaranjan Locomotive Works was commissioned on March 11. (See 1950.)

Arjuna Award was announced for the first time on March 13 in recognition of outstanding performance in various sports. The first awards were for the year 1962. (See 1961.)

Centenary of Indian Red Cross was celebrated on May 8, the birthday of its founder.

Rohini, a glider made at the Aircraft Manufacturing Depot of the IAF, was first successfully flown on May 22 at Kanpur.

National Telex Service was inaugurated on June 24 linking four metropolitan centres Bombay, Calcutta, Delhi and Madras.

Kashi Vidyapith was raised to a university on July 21. (See 1921.)

Allama Mashriqi died on August 25. (b. 1888).

A.D.

India's space programme began with the launching of an equatorial rocket from Thumba on November 21.

Nagaland state came into existence as the 16th state of India on December 1. (See 1832 and 1881.)

Sucheta Kripalani became the Chief Minister of Uttar Pradesh and thus was the first woman chief minister of any state.

National Cadet Corps was made compulsory for all able-bodied male college students. (See 1948.)

N.C. Laharry, who joined Calcutta Rotary Club in 1926, became the first Asian president of Rotary International.

1964 The first diesel locomotive of Varanasi Diesel Locomotive Works came out of assembly line on January 4. It however had an imported engine.

Unit Trust of India started functioning on February 1.

On March 22 the first Vintage Car Rally was organised by the Statesman at Calcutta in which fifty cars participated.

The electric tramcar ran for the last time in Bombay on March 31.

National Maritime Day was observed for the first time on April 5. Earlier in 1962 India crossed the one million-tonne mark on GRT and thus attained majority.

Communist Party of India was split on April 11 between CPI and CPI (M) on ideological differences at the international level. CPI (M) had a further split in 1969 into CPI (M) and COI (M-L), i.e., Communist Organisation of India (Marxist-Leninist).

Jawaharlal Nehru, India's first prime minister, expired on May 27. (b. 1889).

As per Nehru's own wish, his ashes were strewn from aeroplanes on June 11 over the Himalayas and on the farms and fields and in the plains all over the country.

Naya paisa introduced in 1957 was renamed as paisa on June 1.

Lal Bahadur Shastri became the second Prime Minister of India on June 9.

Teen Murti House, the official residence of the prime minister of India, became Nehru Memorial Museum on June 27.

Industrial Development Bank of India was set up on July 1.

On October 25 the military tank produced at Avadi was named 'Vijayanta'. (See 1965.)

Renowned Hindi Poet Maithili Sharan Gupta died on December 12. (b. 1886).

First Indian jet trainer HJT-16 made its inaugural flight on December 12.

The All Women Indian Expedition led by Joyce Duneseth climbed Mrigthuni peak 6,855 mt (22,490 ft) high, the first peak to be climbed by women only. The sumitters were Rani Bhagwan Dass, Durga Gurung and Usha Sapre. (See 1960.)

The first two commemorative coins were introduced in honour of Jawaharlal Nehru. These were nickel coins of one rupee and fifty paise denominations.

The first synthetic rubber plant of Asia, namely Synthetics & Chemicals Ltd., was commissioned at Bareilly in U.P.

The National Film Archives of India was established.

Pope Paul VI visited India to attend the International Eucharistic Congress in Bombay. He was the first Pope to come to India.

1965   The Food Corporation of India was set up on January 15 at Madras, to ensure remunerative prices to the farmers and easy availability of foodgrains to the consumers at a fair price.

India's first alloy and steel plant in the public sector – Durgapur Alloy and Steel Plant Ltd. was commissioned on January 23.

Fighting broke out in Rann of Kutch on April 9 between Indian and Pakistani troops, which developed into a large scale war when Pakistani army invaded Chhamb and Dewa regions on September 1. Ceasefire was agreed upon on September 23. (See 1948, 1971 and 1999.)

The first Indian team ascended Mount Everest on May 20 under the leadership of Commander M. S. Kohli. On that day Capt. A. S. Cheema and Nawang Gombu reached the summit, followed by Sonam Wangyal and Sonam Gyatso on May 22, C. P. Vora and Ang Kami on May 24, Capt. H. S. Ahluwalia, H. C. Rawat and Phu Dorji on May 29. Incidentally, Sherpa Nawang Gombu thus reached the summit for the second time,—the first man in the world to do so. Gombu's first ascent was on May 1, 1963 with Jim Whittekar of America. (See 1953 and 1984.)

National Cadet Corps College for women was inaugurated at Gwalior on July 10.

Border Security Force came into existence on December 2.

The first India-made military tank Vijayanta rolled out of the assembly lines on December 12 at the Avadi Heavy Vehicles Factory near Madras. (See 1964.)

India's first eye bank was opened in Calcutta Medical College Hospital.

Philips India Ltd pioneered the concept of 'son-et-lumiere' show in India with the installation of such a lighting and electro-accoustic system at Red Fort in Delhi. It was set up by A. S. Jaspal with Melville D'Mellow.

Payment of Bonus Act was enforced.

The astounding Malayalam poet G. Sankara Kurup was the first recipient of the prestigious 'Janapith Award' for his collection of poems *Otakkuzhal* or 'Flute'. (See 1901.)

Payment of Gratuity Act was passed for payment of gratuity to the employees as a social security.

1966 Taskhent peace talk between India and Pakistan began on January 4.

Lal Bahadur Shastri, India's prime minister, suddenly expired at Tashkent on January 11 at 01.32 A.M. (See 1965, b. 1904).

Sadhu T. L. Vaswani breathed his last on January 16. (b. 1879).

Indira Gandhi became the third Prime Minister of India on January 23. (See 1967.)

Air India's Boeing 707 crashed in the Alps in Switzerland on January 24. All the 117 persons on board including the renowned nuclear scientist Homi Bhabha (b. 1909) perished in the crash.

Vinayak Damodar Savarkar died on February 26. (b. 1883).

Mihir Sen became the first Indian to achieve many remarkable swimming feats during this year. On April 6 he swam across the 35 km Palk Strait separating India and Ceylon in 25 hours 36 minutes, and on August 24 the 40 km Strait of Gibraltar in 8 hours 1 minute. He was the first person to swim the 64 km Dardanelles in 13 hours 55 minutes on September 12. Soon thereafter he crossed 26 km Bosphorus Channel on September 21. He was also the first man to swim across the entire length of 96 km Panama Canal on October

31 in 34 hours 15 minutes. The *Guiness Book of Records* hailed him as the unique long distance swimmer. (See 1958.)

Artist Nandalal Bose died on April 15. (b. 1882).

Rupee was devalued on June 6 by 36.5 per cent. (See 1949.)

Production of MIG (Russian) air force plane started at Nasik on June 10. (See 1970.)

Indian Parliament approved bifurcation of Punjab and creation of two states Punjab and Haryana on September 10. (See 1967.)

Reita Faria, a medical student of Bombay was elected Miss World on November 17 in a beauty contest held in London. (See 1994.)

India's largest rose garden was opened in Chandigarh on December 15 with over 36,000 rose plants.

Precision Instrument Factory at Kota was formally commissioned on December 16.

Srila Prabhupada founded International Society for Krishna Consciousness (ISKCON) in New York for the spread of Sanatan Dharma. He returned to India in 1970 with some disciples. He passed away on November 14, 1977 in Brindavan.

The favourable verdict in Balasaheb Patloji Thorat case in Pune ended the world's most protracted litigation. The suit was filed 761 years earlier in 1205 by his ancestor Maloji Thorat.

1967   The fourth general election of the Lok Sabha was held on February 15.

Indira Gandhi became the Prime Minister of India for the second time on March 12. (See 1966.)

Zakir Hussain became the third President of India on May 13.

India made AVRO aircraft HS 748 was handed over to the Indian Airlines on June 27. It was built in Aircraft Manufacturing Dept. of Kanpur. AVRO had its maiden flight on November 1, 1961.

Nagarjunasagar Dam, the world's longest masonry dam, was commissioned on August 4.

Central government, for the first time since independence, suffered a token defeat in the Lok Sabha on August 8.

Nagaland adopted English as the medium of instruction of the state on September 18. (See 1951.)

A.D.

India Tourism Development Corporation was set up on October 1.

Ram Manohar Lohia died on October 12. (b. 1910).

On October 12 the Working Committee of Jammu and Kashmir National Conference unanimously voted in favour of permanent accession of the state to India.

Punjab, after first partition in 1947, was again bifurcated on November 1 into two new states, Punjab and Haryana, on linguistic basis. Both had its capital at Chandigarh, which itself was made into a union territory. (See 1953, 1966 and 1969.)

All India Radio started its first commercial advertisements on November 1 from Bombay, Nagpur and Pune.

The first Indian developed rocket 'Rohini RH75' was launched from Thumba on December 4.

India had its first (Russian) submarine *INS Kalvari* commissioned on December 8 and arrived on July 5, 1968. (See 1984.)

After the completion of India's third Five Year Plan there was a Plan holiday for 3 years.

The country's first 'open' quiz contest was hosted in a small parish hall under Neil O'Brien, who was later known as Father of Quizzing in India. The winning team got a live duck as the prize.

Indian cricket team visited New Zealand for the first time under the captaincy of Nawab of Pataudi. (See 1955.)

Naxalbari, a collection of 60 odd villages at the foothills of the Himalayas in West Bengal, was the scene of an armed peasant uprising for land reforms. This led to a new political movement all over India and was branded as Naxalite Movement. (See 1969.)

1968 Dr Prafulla Kumar Sen with others performed the first heart transplantation in Asia on February 20 in K.E.M. Hospital of Bombay. He was the third surgeon of the world to do so.

Auroville, the international township of Sri Aurobindo Ashram, was inaugurated on February 28 with the assistance of all the states of India, UNESCO and 121 countries of the world, who poured soils from their respective lands into a lotus-shaped urn to symbolise universal oneness. It was the brain-child of the Mother and was designed by the French artist Rogar Anger.

A.D.

Public Provident Fund Bill was passed by the Lok Sabha on May 2.

Dara Singh won the world wrestling championship title on May 29. He defended the title till 1983 and in the process never lost the title though he had a drawn contest a number of times.

The first two stage rounding rocket ROHINI MSV 1 was successfully launched from Thumba on August 31.

On October 16 Hargovind Khorana (American citizen) shared the Nobel Prize for medicine and physiology on man-made synthetic gene. By birth he was the third Indian to get the Nobel Prize after Rabindranath Tagore and C.V. Raman. (See 1913, 1930 and 1979.)

Lok Sabha approved renaming of Madras state as Tamil Nadu on November 22. (See 1961.)

India's first meteorological rocket 'MENAKA' was successfully launched at Thumba on December 23.

Emergency declared in 1962 was withdrawn. (See 1975.)

Gold Control Act came into force. (See 1963 and 1990.)

1969 Madras state was offically renamed as Tamil Nadu. (See 1961 and 1968.)

The two-man rowing expedition to the Andamans set out from Calcutta on February 1 with Pinaki Chatterji and George Albert Duke. They reached the Andamans on March 5.

C. N. Annadurai died on February 3. (b. 1909).

The first superfast train Rajdhani Express was introduced on March 1 between New Delhi and Howrah with an average speed of 130 km per hour.

Indian Navy's first Helicopter Squadron was commissioned in Goa on March 15.

Indian Petrochemicals Corporation, the first public sector petrochemicals organisation, was inaugurated on March 22.

India's first atomic power station at Tarapore became operational on April 1. Its two boiling water reactors of 210 MW capacity each were commissioned in April. The plant was put into commercial operation seven months later. (See 1983.)

President Zakir Hussain expired on May 3. (b. 1897).

Lion was chosen National Animal of India on July 9 by the Board of Wildlife. (See 1972.)

A.D.

On July 19 the Government of India by an ordinance, nationalised the fourteen major commercial banks of India, whose deposits exceeded Rs 50 crores each.

On August 9 the name of Ochterlony Monument of Calcutta was changed to Shahid Minar. (See 1828.)

V. V. Giri was elected on August 20 as the fourth President of India. He was sworn in on August 24.

Armstrong and Aldrin, the Apollo 11 astronauts and the first men to land on the moon, arrived at Bombay on October 26.

Darshan Singh Pheruman died in Amritsar on October 27, i.e., on the 74th day of fasting, on his demand for inclusion of Chandigarh in Punjab state. (See 1967.)

Moon-rock collected by Armstrong and Aldrin was kept on exhibition in New Delhi on December 23.

India's fourth Five-Year Plan 1969-1974 was launched.

Indian National Congress suffered a major split followed by further splits in 1977 and 1979 when its very existence posed a problem.

The Naxalites formed a new political party called the Communist Organisation of India (Marxist-Leninist). (See 1967.)

'Dada Sahab Phalke' award was announced on his birth centenary year. The first recipient of this highest film award was Devika Rani Roerich for her contribution to film industry. (See 1913.)

Gir reserve forest, the last remaining habitat of the Asian lion, was established covering an area of 1,516 sq km. In 1913 the number of lions came down to 20.

1970 The foundation-stone of India's first and the world's largest coal-based fertilizer plant was laid at Talcher in Orissa on February 3.

The first off-shore oil well was inaugurated on March 19 in the Gulf of Cambay.

Meghalaya was inaugurated as an autonomous hill state within the state of Assam on April 2. (See 1972.)

All India Trade Union Congress was formally split on May 28.

Monopolies and Restrictive Trade Practices Act passed in 1969 came into force on June 1.

The first woman career-diplomat Muthamma Chohivia Beliappa was appointed as the Ambassador to Hungary on August 2. (See 1949.)

Freedom fighter Trailokyanath Chakraborty died on August 9 in Delhi while visiting India from Bangladesh. He spent 30 years in prison during the British rule. (b. 1888).

Vivekananda Rock Memorial at Kanyakumari was inaugurated by President V. V. Giri on September 2. (See 1892.)

The first sewage water reclamation plant of India for commercial use was commissioned on September 29 by Union Carbide India Ltd. in Bombay.

Bhabha Atomic Research Centre produced Uranium 233 on October 9. (See 1957.)

Indian Air Force got the first India-made Russian supersonic combat aircraft MIG 21 on October 19. (See 1966.)

Famous dancer Shambhu Maharaj, the Kathak King of India, died on November 4.

Scientist C. V. Raman expired on November 21. He was cremated within the premises of the Institute which he founded and nursed assiduously in his later life. (b. 1888).

On November 29 Haryana was the first state to achieve hundred per cent electrification of the villages.

Farakka barrage of West Bengal was completed. (See 1975.)

Prof. H. B. Mathur of the Indian Institute of Technology, New Delhi carried out of the first successful test in India on an alcohol-fuelled motorcar engine.

Nagendra Singh became the first Indian President of International Court of Justice.

Food and Drug Administration was introduced in Maharashtra. Thus Maharashtra was the first state to create a separate agency to control the quality of food, drugs, cosmetics, disinfectants and prices of drugs.

1971 Himachal Pradesh became a full-fledged state on January 25, the 18th state of the Indian union.

A.D.

For the first time in India's air history, an Indian Airline's Fokker Friendship aircraft *Ganga* was hijacked to Lahore on January 30 and it was destroyed by the hijackers on February 2. (See 1976.)

K. M. Munshi, a constitutional authority and founder of Bharatiya Vidya Bhavan, expired on February 8. (b. 1887).

India established the first satellite communication link via Arvi Earth Station wih Goonbilly in Great Britain on February 18.

Air India's first Jumbo jet plane Boeing 747 namely Emperor Ashoka landed at Bombay on April 18. (See 1978.)

India won the first ever cricket Test 'Rubber' when West Indies was defeated on April 20. (See 1952.)

India's first submarine base of Indian Navy was commissioned on May 19 at Visakhapatnam and was named Vir Bahu.

A 20-year Treaty of Peace, Friendship and Cooperation between India and Soviet Russia was signed on August 9.

Gandhi Sadan of Delhi, formerly Birla House, where Gandhiji was shot dead on January 30, 1948 was dedicated to the nation by President V. V. Giri on October 2.

National Committee on Science and Technology was set up on October 25.

Indo-Pakistan war broke out again on December 3 after the previous one in 1965 and the President declared national emergency. The war ended when the Pakistani army in East Pakistan surrendered on December 16 to the Indian Army after its assault on Dhaka. As a result, East Pakistan emerged as a sovereign independent country Bangladesh with its capital at Dhaka. (See 1948, 1965 and 1999.)

Parliament approved the Constitution (26th Amendment) Bill on December 12 abolishing privy purses and privileges of the princes and depriving them of recognition from January 1, 1972. 278 princes got privy purses and privileges that annually cost 6 million dollars to national exchequer. The benefits ranged from the largest of 3,50,000 dollars to Maharaja of Mysore to the lowest of 25 dollars to Talukdar of Kotadia. (See 1921 and 1972.)

Vikram Sarabhai, the famous nuclear scientist, died on December 30 in Trivandrum. (b. 1919).

A.D.

Medical Termination of Pregnancy Act was passed by the Government of India.

India's fifth general election took place. It was in fact an interim one after the general election of 1967, as the next one was due in 1972.

1972   Privy purses and privileges of the previous rulers of Indian states were abolished from January 1. (See 1971.)

Institute of Criminology and Forensic Science, the first of its kind in Asia, was inaugurated in New Delhi on January 4.

On January 9 India attained the top position in film production in the world with a record number of 433 feature films produced in 1971.

On January 20 Meghalaya got statehood and Arunachal Pradesh (earlier name North East Frontier Agency) became a Union Territory. (See 1948, 1970 and 1987.)

On January 21 states of Manipur, Tripura and Union Territory of Mizoram were inaugurated.

On January 26 Amar Jawan, a national memorial to the soldiers, was installed at India Gate in New Delhi.

International Airports Authority of India was set up on February 1. (See 1986.)

Vikram Earth Satellite Station at Arvi near Wardha was dedicated to the nation by President V. V. Giri on February 26.

The first World Book Fair was inaugurated in New Delhi on March 18.

Indo-Bangladesh 25-year Peace and Friendship Pact was signed on March 19.

The first International Sanskrit Conference was opened by President V. V. Giri on March 26. Over 500 delegates from India and 25 foreign countries attended the conference.

The renowned artist Jamini Roy expired on April 24. (b. 1887).

All coking coal mines were nationalised on May 1. (See 1973.)

Foundation-stone of the second Howrah bridge was laid by Indira Gandhi on May 20. (See 1943, 1979 and 1992.)

INS Nilgiri the first British designed Indian built modern warship of the Leander class, was commissioned on June 3 at Bombay. (See 2003.)

A.D.

India's first fully air-conditioned luxury passenger cum cargo ship *Harshavardhana* was launched at Mazagaon Dock of Bombay on June 10.

The noted historian D. G. Tendulkar died on June 12.

Prof. P. C. Mahalanobis, the founder of Indian Statistical Institute, breathed his last on June 28. (b. 1893).

Shimla Agreement between Indira Gandhi of India and Zulfikar Ali Bhutto of Pakistan was signed on July 2. (See 1971.)

Charu Majumdar, who masterminded Naxalite Movement and the founder President of C.O.I. (M-L) died on July 27. (See 1969.)

In July Kiran Bedi became the first woman I.P.S. officer. She was inducted in Delhi cadre.

Postal Index Number (PIN) code of 6 digits was introduced on August 15. The first digit indicates the zone, the second and third the sorting unit, and last three the particular post office.

Wildlife Preservation Act was passed on August 21 to protect various wild species from extinction including tigers and lions.

On August 28 Lok Sabha passed the General Insurance Business Nationalisation Bill. It came into effect from January 1, 1973. (See 2000.)

The first multi-role helicopter SA 315, manufactured by Hindustan Aeronautics Ltd., was test flown on October 18 in Bangalore.

On November 18 Board for Wildlife chose the tiger as the National Animal in place of the lion which had been enjoying the honour since 1969. (See 1969 and 1973.)

On December 13 Hindustan Aeronautics produced the first agricultural aeroplane named 'Basant'.

C. Rajagopalachari, the only Indian Governor General and the founder President of Swatantra Party, expired on December 25. (See 1948 and 1959, b. 1879.).

The work on Metro Railway in Calcutta started on December 29. (See 1929, 1981 and 1984.)

Indira Gandhi was the fifteenth recipient of the highest civilian award Bharat Ratna.

1973 General Insurance was nationalised on January 1. (See 1956 and 1999.)

A.D.

On January 2 General S.H.F.J. Manekshaw was promoted to the rank of Field Marshal. (See 1914 and 1986.)

The largest ship in the Indian merchant fleet 88,000 DWT super tanker *Jawaharlal Nehru* was inaugurated on February 4.

April 5 was declared as National Maritime Day for the Merchant Navy. (See 1964.)

All non-coking coal mines were nationalished on May 1, which including coking coal mines added up to 425 mines. (See 1972.)

Foundation-stone of the new capital of Arunachal Pradesh was laid at Itanagar on May 7. (See 1979.)

In October the first all-women police station in the country was set up at Calicut.

Laccadive, Minicoy and Amindivi Islands were constituted into a union territory, separated from Maharashtra. It was renamed Laskhadweep on November 1 and is the smallest union territory, being only 32 sq km. (See 1956.)

The name of Mysore state was changed to Karnataka on November 1.

India's first International Philatelic Exhibition was opened in New Delhi on November 11.

The Holy Mother of Sri Aurobindo Ashram of Pondicherry breathed her last on November 18. (b. 1878, See 1921.).

Govind Das, MP, was felicitated on November 21 in the Central Hall of Parliament, on completing 50 years as a Parliamentarian, an unprecedented record.

E. V. Ramaswamy Naicker, founder leader of Dravida Kazhagam, died at Vellore on December 24. (b. 1879).

Project Tiger was initiated to protect the tigers which were nearing extinction. The 1972 census showed only 1,827 tigers in India.

Test Pilot School of the Indian Air Force was opened in Bangalore.

A modern lighthouse was installed at Pygmalion Point (later named Indira Point) in Nicobar Island, the country's southernmost land's end.

National championship of women's cricket started and Bombay became the champion in the inaugural year. (See 1934.)

A.D.

1974   President V. V. Giri dedicated to the nation the Nehru Memorial Museum at Teen Murti House, New Delhi on January 27.

Satyendra Nath Bose, the great physicist, national professor and discoverer of sub-atomic particles (named Bosons after him) died on February 4. (b. 1894).

The leading Hindi poet Ramdhari Singh alias 'Dinkar' died on April 24. (b. 1908).

India's first nuclear detonation took place 107 mt underground at Pokhran in the Rajasthan desert on May 18 at 8.05 A.M. (See 1998.)

Udham Singh's ashes were brought from London to Delhi on July 19. (See 1940.)

Fakhruddin Ali Ahmed became the fifth President of India on August 24.

India's fifth Five-Year Plan 1974-79 was launched. It was finalised on September 25. But the Janata government ended it in 1978, one year before its expiry.

INS Satavahana the first establishment to give submarine training, was commissioned at Visakhapatnam on December 21.

On December 25 Air India Jumbo 747 was hijacked on its flight to Rome. The air crew themselves overpowered the lone hijacker. (See 1971 and 1976.)

1975   On February 12 India was declared one of the countries in the world that has eradicated smallpox. The last victim was Saiben Bibi (May 24). The world's last case was Ali Mao Moalin in Somalia (October 26, 1977). The programme was launched in 1962.

Bhanubhai Shah established the first kite museum of India named Shankar Kendra in Ahmedabad on February 26. It was the second in the world since Japan established the first museum only a few days earlier.

S. Radhakrishnan, India's second President, expired on April 17. (b. 1888).

India's first satellite ARYABHATTA, designed by Indian Space Research Organisation having a payload of 360 kg, was launched in the USSR with the help of a Soviet rocket on April 19. India took control of Aryabhatta on April 22. The satellite was named after the astronomer who was born in 476. (See 1979.)

A.D.

The 2,500 anniversary of Lord Mahavir's Nirvana was observed on April 24. Mahavir was the 24th Tirthankar.

India's first electric typewriter was produced on May 9 by Hindustan Teleprinters Ltd., a public sector undertaking.

The 26-mile feeder canal from Farakka to the Bhagirathi river, meant to protect Calcutta port from silting, was formally inaugurated on May 21. (See 1970.)

As a revolt against the Sikkim king by his subjects Sikkim became the 22nd state of India on May 16. The bill of accession was passed on the Parliament on April 26. (See 1641 and 1816.)

It was announced on June 7 that national film awards will be known as National Film Festival with the lotus, i.e. 'Kamal', the National Flower, as its symbol. (See 1954.)

On July 1 Indira Gandhi announced Prime Minister's 20-point Programme to realise national expectations. (See 1982.)

On August 1 Durba Banerjee became the first professional lady pilot in the world to command a commercial passenger flight, when she flew a 40-seater Fokker Friendship turbojet aircraft of Indian Airline's Flight IC 255 on Calcutta-Silchar-Imphal-Silchar-Calcutta route. While she took to flying in 1958 as a pilot of the Air Survey of India, she joined Indian Airlines in 1966 and was thus the world's first lady pilot of a scheduled passenger airline. She was also the world's first lady pilot to get Airbus endorsement in 1987 and became the co-pilot of Airbus. She retired from service on November 30, 1988 after 18,500 flying hours. (See 1984 and 1986.)

Equal Remuneration Ordinance for equal payments for male and female workers was promulgated on September 26. (See 1948.)

On October 24 the Ordinance promulgating abolition of bonded labour system was issued,which came into effect the next day.

India's worst coal-mine disaster occurred on December 27 in Chasnala mine near Dhanabad. 372 people inside the mine perished in a freak flood as a result of caving in of a protective wall inside the mine.

The first All India Kite-flying Contest was held in Calcutta. Kites were introduced in India by Mughal Emperor Shah Alam I i.e. Bahadur Shah I at the beginning of the eighteenth century.

A.D.

Packaged Commodities Regulation Act was passed.

The first women post office was opened in Pune to mark the International Women Year.

Gir Lion Sanctuary in Saurastra was declared a national park for the rare Asian lions.

Shireen Kiyash when selected for Indian women cricket team against Australia, she became the only person to have represented India in three different sports – basketball, hockey and cricket. In 1970 she played for India in the Asian Women's Basketball Championship in Kuala Lumpur. In the same year she played for India in the third Asian Women's Hockey Tournament in New Delhi. Her name featured in Limca Book of Records as the most versatile sports person in India.

1976 Commercial advertisement was introduced in TV programmes on January 1.

The lost city of Kapilavastu (Nepal) where Gautam Buddha spent 29 years of his life, was found in an excavation on January 23.

India's integrated national news agency Samachar was launched on February 1. But it disintegrated in 1978.

Offshore oilfield Bombay High went into commercial production on February 20.

Television was separated from Akashvani (radio). A separate corporation called Doordarshan was set up on April 1.

Antiquities and Art Treasures Act 1972 came into effect on April 5.

Four Indians successfully skied down the slope of Trishul peak (7,120 mt) on May 17 and put India on top of the ski map of the world.

Major General Gertrude Ali Ram, the first woman General in the Indian Army, took over as the first Director of Military Nursing Services at the Army Headquarters on August 27.

Poet Nazrul Islam died on August 29 while on a visit to Dhaka of Bangladesh. (b. 1899).

For the second time, an Indian Airline's Boeing 737 aircraft was again hijacked to Lahore on September 10. The aircraft was later released unharmed. (See 1971.)

A.D.

International (long distance) direct dialing telephone link was established between Bombay and London on October 9.

Madan Lal Dhingra's remains were brought to New Delhi on December 12 from U.K. (See 1909.)

The Hazrat Mahal Trophy for the women's national football championship was introduced. (See 1856.)

Nek Chand Saini's rock garden was inaugurated in Chandigarh. It is considered as a unique piece of art from discarded waste for which Nek Chand was universally commended.

1977   Janta Party was formed on January 23.

India's Naval Coast Guard Force was set up on February 1 to guard the country's 6,083 km coastline, one of the longest in the world. This force's operation is basically meant for civil defence of the coastline in close cooperation with army, navy and police.

President Fakhruddin Ali Ahmed expired on February 11. (b. 1905). B. D. Jatti was sworn in as acting President.

Internal Emergency declared on June 25, 1975 was withdrawn by Indira Gandhi on March 21 after the announcement of midterm general election whose results went very much against herself and her party. (See 1975.)

India's sixth general election was held. India got the first non-Congress (Janata) government at the Centre since independence. Morarji Desai was sworn in as the fourth Prime Minister on March 24. (See 1980.)

Government revoked the national emergency on March 27 which was proclaimed on December 3, 1971.

Swatantra Party merged with Janata Party on April 17. (See 1959.)

National professor and eminent linguist Suniti Kumar Chatterji passed away on May 29. (b. 1890).

Major Prem Chand and Naik Nima Dorji Sherpa were the first Indians, belonging to the army expedition team, to reach on May 31 the summit of the Kanchenjunga (8,547 mt), which is the third highest peak in the world.

On July 13 the Government of India withdrew personal civil honours like Bharat Ratna, Padma Vibhushan, Padma Bhushan and Padma Shree. (See 1954 and 1980.)

A.D.

Neelam Sanjiva Reddy was elected the sixth President of India on July 21. He was sworn in on July 25.

Edmund Hillary's Ocean to Sky 2,525 km long expedition on jetboats started from Haldia to the Himalayas up the Ganga on August 25. It was abandoned at Nandaprayag on September 28 because of strong current.

The great singer Kesarbai Kerkar died at Bombay on September 16. (b. 1890).

On September 22 the 27-member Cosmos soccer team of USA, led by the world famous football player Pele, arrived in Calcutta for playing two exhibition football matches.

Uday Shankar, the famous exponent of Indian dance, breathed his last on September 27. (b. 1900).

Indira Gandhi was arrested on October 3 on charges of corruption. She was released unconditionally the next day. This was the first instance of arrest of a former prime minister. (See 2000.)

On October 4 External Affairs Minister A. B. Vajpayee addressed the U.N. General Assembly in Hindi, the first ever address in this language. (See 1948.)

Srila Prabhupada of ISKCON breathed his last on November 14 at Brindavan. (See 1966.)

Michael Ferreira won both the World Amateur as well as Open Billiards Championships in Melbourne. He was the first Indian to achieve the double. He also scored world's highest break of 1,149 under the new rules on December 13 in the National Billiards Championship. (See 1958 and 2005.)

World's largest open-air theatre 'Drive In' was opened in Bombay on december 29 with a capacity of 893 cars and 2,000 seats.

Meher Moos was the first Indian women to touch Antarctica. (See 1960.)

India declared a 200 mile marine area around her territories as an exclusive economic zone.

Ashapurna Devi was the first lady to get the coveted Jnanapith Award for 1976 for her Bengali novel *Pratham Pratishruti*. (See 1965.)

Federation Cup, the national team championship of football, was introduced by All India Football Federation. I.T.I. (Indian Telephone Industries) of Bangalore lifted the trophy in its inaugural year.

Mohan Bagan became the first Indian team to exclusively win all the three major football trophies IFA Shield, Durand Cup and Rovers Cup without being a joint holder of any one of the three trophies. (See 1911.)

In Calcutta the first statue of an Indian lady, that of Matangini Hazra (b. 1870), was installed. She was shot dead on September 29 in 1942 at the age of 72 while leading the Congress procession as its standard-bearer in Tamluk of Midnapur district during the August Movement of 1942.

1978 Air India's big air disaster took place on January 1 when Emperor Ashoka, its first Jumbo jet Boeing 747, fell into the Arabian Sea off Bombay coast only a few minutes after take off. All 213 persons on board perished in a watery grave. (See 1971 and 1985.)

The President promulgated an ordinance on January 15 demonetising currency notes of values Rs 1,000, Rs 5,000 and Rs 10,000.

Mahakavi G. Sankara Kurup, the first recipient of Jnanpith Award died on February 3. (See 1965, b. 1901).

The renowned Bengali singer Pankaj Kumar Mullick expired on February 19.

India's sixth Five-Year Plan commenced on April 1. (See 1980.)

India's first double-decker train Singhagarh Express made her maiden run from Victoria Terminus of Bombay to Pune on April 12. (See 1860.)

Sobha Singh, builder of modern New Delhi, died on April 18 at the age of 90.

India's first flagship *INS Delhi* was decommissioned on May 13 and her ensign as well as the commissioning pennant were lowered for the last time on June 30. (See 1948.)

On September 15 Ararat Erevan of Armenia (Soviet Union) was the first overseas team to win IFA Shield jointly with Mohan Bagan. The scores were two goals each.

A.D.

The Child Marriage Act was further amended on October 1, which enhanced the marriageable age of a girl to 18 and that of a boy to 21 years. (See 1929 and 1955.)

Dr Subhas Mukhopadhyay claimed the credit of India's first and the world's second test-tube baby Durga Agarwal, a daughter of Bela Agarwal, born at 11.14 A.M. on October 3 in Belle Vue Nursing Home of Calcutta. It was not officially recognised then. It happened only 68 days after the first one, also a girl named Louise Joy Brown in London on July 26. Dr S. Mukhopadhyay committed suicide out of frustration. (See 1986.)

Fifteen-year-old Rohini Khadilkar made chess history when she became the National Chess Champion on October 10, the first woman to achieve the honour. (See 1955.)

Indian section of Oxford University Press celebrated the 500th year of existence in U.K. Their first book *Apostle's Creed* written by Tyrannius and published in London in 1478, wrongly printed the author's name as St. Jerome and the year as 1468. (See 1912.)

Alfredo Nobre Costa, a Goan descendant from one of the oldest families of Margao, became the Prime Minister of Portugal.

1979   India's first Jumbo passenger train Tamil Nadu Express was flagged off on January 29 from New Delhi railway station for Madras. It was also known as 'Double-headed' train since it had two engines with 21 coaches for carrying 951 passengers.

Arunachal Pradesh's new capital Itanagar was formally opened on February 10. (See 1973.)

On February 18 the ambassador of U.S.A. in India handed over a cheque of Rs 16,640 million to the Government of India, the largest amount paid by a single cheque in world's banking history. This amount was the accumulated payment for PL 480 food supplies to India and was released for agricultural and social welfare work.

A naval museum was opened in Bombay on April 5, which is the National Maritime Day of the merchant navy. This museum was the first of its kind in India.

Freedom fighter Raja Mahendra Pratap died on April 29. (b. 1886).

India's second satellite BHASKARA I was launched on June 7 from Bears Lake in U.S.S.R. The 444 kg experimental satellite was designed and built by Indian Space Research Organisation. (See 1975.)

The actual work of the main second Howrah bridge, cable-stayed type, the first of its kind in India and then the longest span of this type in the world, started on July 3 when the first well curb on the Calcutta bank had been constructed. The foundation stone of the bridge was laid by Prime Minister Indira Gandhi in 1972. (See 1992.)

The Janata Party suffered a major split. Morarji Desai resigned from the prime ministership. He was the first Indian prime minister to resign. Charan Singh became the fifth prime minister on July 28. But he also had to resign on August 20 only after 23 days.

India's first Satellite Launching Vehicle (SLV-3), a 22-metre long and 17 tonne rocket with solid fuel, was launched from Sriharikota at 7:58 A.M. on August 10 with a 40 kg technological payload. But it plummeted into the Bay of Bengal along with its payload only after 5 mts. 15 secs. (See 1980.)

President Neelam Sanjiva Reddy dissolved the Lok Sabha (Parliament) on his own on August 22 for the first time in its history since he felt that no party was capable of forming a stable ministry at the Centre. The next general election was recommended at the end of the year.

Maulana Abdul Ali Moudoodi, founder leader of Jamait-e-Islam died on September 22 in U.S.A. He was born in Aurangabad in 1903, but later migrated to Lahore in Pakistan.

Jayaprakash Narayan passed away on October 8. (b 1902).

Mother Teresa got the Nobel Prize for peace on October 17. (See 1931 and 1950.)

Rachel Thomas was the first civilian woman to jump out of an aircraft to become the first civilian skydiver. Up to November 12, 2000 she recorded 651 jumps.

Hockey wizard Dhyan Chand expired on December 3. (b. 1905. See 1995.).

Prakash Padukone became the World Champion in the first World Open Badminton Tournament held in London, by beating Morten Frost-Hansen of Denmark in straight sets of 15-4 and 15-11 (See 1980 and 1981)

A.D.

India's seventh general election was held. Indira Gandhi came back to power as the Prime Minister with a thumping majority. (See 1977.)

1980   Personal civil honours like Bharat Ratna, Padma Vibhushan, etc. which were withdrawn by the Government of India in 1977 were reintroduced on January 25 after Indira Gandhi again became the prime minister of India on January 14. (See 1954.)

Mother Teresa was awarded Bharat Ratna on January 25. (See 1979.)

The biggest ship built in the country *Rani Padmini* – 76,384 dwt bulk carrier, was floated on January 28 from Cochin Shipyard.

Romesh Chandra Majumdar, doyen of Indian historians, expired on February 11. (b. 1888).

On March 31 the last I.C.S. officer Nirmal Mukherji retired from service as cabinet secretary. He was the last on the list of 416 I.C.S. officers who formed the nucleus of administrative machinery in independent India on August 15, 1947. (See 1863.)

Positional Astronomy Centre was established in Calcutta on April 26. It was the first of its kind in India.

May 4 was declared as the Coal Miners' Day.

Sanjay Gandhi, the dynamic person to lead Youth Congress, General Secretary of Congress (I) and younger son of Indira Gandhi, died in a plane crash on June 23.

President V. V. Giri expired at Madras on June 24. (b. 1894).

Oil was struck in the Bay of Bengal on June 26.

Indian-built second Satellite Launching Vechicle SLV-3 was successfully blasted off on July 18 at 8:03:45 hours at Sriharikota, with a 35 kg satellite named ROHINI. The satellite was catapulted at an altitude of 285 km in a near earth orbit at a velocity of 28,000 km per hour. SLV-3 was a 17-tonne four-stage rocket powered with solid fuel. (See 1997 and 1981.)

The first experimental colour telecast was made from Madras TV Centre on July 18 for one hour in the afternoon. The telecast was watched simultaneously in Delhi also. (See 1982.)

India regained the gold medal in hockey on July 29 in the Moscow Olympic, which they lost in 1960.

Md. Rafi, the superstar playback singer of Hindi films for about forty years, died on July 31.

The IFA shield tournament in Calcutta was abandoned on October 1 for the first time in its 87 years of football history. Simultaneously the First Division Football League was also abandoned unfinished, due to an unfortunate loss of several lives in a stampede in Mohan Bagan-East Bengal league tie, resulting from soccer violence.

The first 5,377.9 km Himalayan Car Rally was flagged off from Brabourne Stadium, Bombay on October 18 with seventy-four starters. Shekhar Mehta of Kenya driving on Opel Ascona car won the first rally which was terminated at Narkanda instead of New Delhi on October 24.

Renowned badminton player Prakash Padukone was the first Indian to get the award of Fairplay Trophy and Diploma of International Fairplay Committee. (See 1979 and 1981.)

Aswini Kumar, the newly-elected member of the executive of the International Olympic Committee and former president of Indian Hockey Federation became the first Indian to award Olympic medals at a ceremony in Moscow. He distributed hockey medals to India (gold), Spain (silver) and USSR (bronze).

The sixth Five-Year Plan 1980-85 was launched. The original sixth Plan was scheduled for 1978-83 period, but abandoned.

1981 On January 6 scientists of the National Institute of Oceanography succeeded in collecting polymetallic nodules from the depth of 4,300 metres of the Indian Ocean bed on their 1,900 tonne research ship *Gavesani.* Indian became the seventh nation to develop this technology.

Vayudoot air service began with a lone flight of a F27 aircraft taking off from Guwahati airport on January 26.

The first-ever night cricket match was played on May 10 at the floodlit ground of Wilson College Gymkhana, Bombay between Blue Star Club and Fort Club. The former team won.

The worst-ever railway accident took place on June 6, when 416DN Samastipur Passenger train plunged into the Bagmati river in Bihar. While 268 dead bodies were recovered, an estimated 500 passengers lost their lives, since no proper counting was possible.

A.D.

unprecedented event in independent India – when Lok Sabha rejected a motion of confidence by a vote of 346 to 142. (See 1989.)

Chandra Shekhar took the Oath of Secrecy on November 10 as the eighth Prime Minister, again to form a minority government.

Vijaylakshmi Pandit expired in Dehradun on December 1. (b. 1900).

The INSAT ID geo-stationary satellite was put into orbit to replace INSAT IB. (See 1983.)

Manoj Kothari became the World Amateur Billiards Champion. (See 1958 and 1977.)

Kabbadi was introduced in eleventh Asian Games in Beijing. India won the gold medal. (See 1936 and 1952.)

Bombay-Delhi Rajdhani Express was the first fully air-conditioned train.

Har Prakash Rishi, Amarjeet Singh and Navjot Chaddha of Delhi created biking history when they rode their Kinetic Honda DX 100 cc scooter nonstop for 1,001 hours, covering 31,000 km. The engine was not shut off even during refuelling and when the riders changed. They thus broke the earlier record of 560 hours set in Italy in 1986.

Prasar Bharati Bill 1989 was unanimously passed in the Lok Sabha this year that granted autonomous status both to Akashvani (Radio) and Doordarshan (Television).

The eighth Five-Year Plan for 1990-95 was deferred and was decided to be operative from April 1, 1992

1991   On January 2 Thiruvananthapuram (Trivandrum) airport was updated to international airport, the first one to attend that status after independence. It was the fifth one after Bombay, Calcutta, Delhi and Madras. Ahmedabad was upgraded to that status on January 26.

On March 6 Prime Minister Chandra Shekhar resigned. As a result Lok Sabha was dissolved by the President on March 13. (See 1990.)

On April 18 Kerala was the first state to be declared hundred per cent literate. (See 1990.)

In a deserted island named Barren, about 130 km north of Port Blair in Andaman Group, a volcano erupted on April 30. As per records earlier eruptions were in 1795, 1803 and 1875. Probably this is the only live volcano in the country.

India's tenth general election took place between May 20 and June 15.

Former Prime Minister Rajiv Gandhi was killed in a bomb explosion (b. 1944) in Sriperumbudur near Madras on May 21 night where he went on an election campaign. Sixteen other persons also perished in that ghastly incident.

P.V. Narasimha Rao took oath as the tenth Prime Minister of India and formed a Congress ministry on June 21, being the largest party in the Parliament but lacked absolute majority.

Mrs Justice Leila Seth, a Judge of Delhi High Court, was sworn in as the Chief Justice of Himachal Pradesh High Court on August 5 and was thus the country's first lady Chief Justice.

In September Ocean Engineering Centre of the Indian Institute of Technology, Madras achieved a breakthrough when they started a 150 kw capacity pilot plant in Vizhinjam fishing harbour in Kerala harnessing sea-waves to generate electricity.

On October 10 India won the team title in the World Carrom Championship.

Salauddin and his wife Neena Chowdhury broke their own world record by travelling through six continents covering 40,538 km in 39 days 20 hrs 15 mts in a Nissan car starting on November 7 and completing on December 17. (See 1990.)

Prime Minister P.V. Narasimha Rao won Nandyal Parliamentary seat of Andhra Pradesh by a margin of 55,80,297 votes, a record in electoral history.

CNN was the first satellite TV channel available in India. (See 1992.)

The highest motorable bridge in the world was opened near Khardungla at a height of 5,650 mt above sea-level, in Ladakh region in Kashmir. (See 1988.)

1992   The first indigenously built submarine *INS Shalki* joined the navy on February 7. The name comes from a fish in the Andaman Sea. (See 1984.)

A.D.

On March 30, Satyajit Ray was conferred Honorary Oscar at Calcutta for his lifetime achievement in the film world. In the same month he was declared Bharat Ratna by the Govt. of India. He was thus the first person to get all the four coveted civilian honours, Padmashree, Padma Bhushan, Padma Bibhushan and Bharat Ratna.

The eighth Five-Year Plan for 1992-97 was launched on April 1.

Satyajit Ray breathed his last on April 23.

Rohit Mehta, an industrialist of Ahmedabad, was elected President of Lions Club International, at the 75th annual convention held in Hong Kong from June 23 to 26, and thus the first Indian to have that honour.

Shankar Dayal Sharma became the ninth President on July 25

On October 3 Geet Sethi won the World Professional Billiards Championship. (See 1991.)

Rapid Action Force, a central body, was raised on October 7, to quell communal and intercaste riots anywhere in India.

The second Howrah (Hooghly) bridge, officially named as Vidyasagar Setu, was opened on October 10. It was the first cable-stayed bridge in India, the largest in Asia and the third largest in the world. (See 1972.)

In October Zee TV launched the first private television channel. (See 1991.)

On December 6 Hindu fundamentalists completely destroyed Babri Masjid at Ayodhya, which was supposed to have been built by Emperor Babar. That resulted in the worst communal violence all over the country since independence. Over 1,150 lives were lost, more than 5,000 were injured with immense destruction of properties.

India's first hovercraft service became operative on December 10 between Surat and Gogha near Bhavangar in Gujarat. (55 nautical km.)

Indian Airforce inducted the first batch of women trainees in non-technical branch. They were commissioned as pilot officers after the training at the Airforce Academy. (See 1959 and 1999.)

On December 12, one of the world's largest monolithic statues of Lord Buddha, 17.2 mt tall and weighing 320 tonnes, was installed in the middle of Hussain Sagar lake in Hyderabad city.

A.D.

1993   On March 12 Bombay reeled under a series of eleven RDX bomb-blasts scattered around the city killing nearly two hundred fifty-seven and six hundred eighty four persons injured. It also caused a massive destruction of properties.

On May 10 Santoshi Yadav became the first woman in the world to reach Everest peak for the second time. Two other women of the same team Kunga Bhuti and Dicky Dolma (19 years) also reached the summit. Dicky was the youngest woman in the world to achieve the feat. (See 1984.)

Field Marashal K. M. Cariappa passed away in Bangalore on May 15. (b.1900).

On July 31 a floating maritime museum, the first of its kind, was inaugurated on steamer 'River Ganga' in Calcutta.

On September 30, a devastating earthquake struck Maharashtra and adjoining states killing 7,582 people. Nearly 15,000 persons were injured and about 70,000 houses over a wide area were razed to the ground or badly damaged.

Tamil Nadu appointed the first woman bus driver in the country M. Vasantakumari, hailing from Kanyakumari district.

In a great social orientation 73rd Constituent Amendment Act stipulated that 30 per cent seats in village Panchayats and local bodies were to be reserved for women.

J.R.D. Tata, the doyen of Indian industry, passed away in Geneva.

1994   On January 29 the Govt. of India repealed the Air Corporation Act of 1953 paving the way for restructuring Air India and Indian Airlines as public limited companies.

On February 8 Kapil Dev broke the world record by taking the 432nd wicket in Test cricket in the third Test match against Sri Lanka at Ahmedabad. He surpassed the earlier record of Sir Richard Hadlee of New Zealand.

On April 15 at Marrakesh, India along with 124 other nations, signed the world's biggest ever commercial agreement named General Agreement of Trade and Tariff (GATT), to usher a new era of prosperity and trade harmony. On January 1, 1995 World Trade Organisation was supposed to succeed GATT.

On May 21 Miss Sushmita Sen, an eighteen year old model from New Delhi was crowned Miss Universe in the beauty contest held at Manila. She was the first Indian to bag the title. (See 1966.)

A.D.

On July 27 Jaspal Rana won the World Shooting Championship in Milan.

Tushar Kanti Ghose, editor of Amrita Bazar Patrika for 64 years, died on August 29. He held the world record as an editor of the same newspaper.

On October 15 Polar Satellite Launch Vehicle launched from Sriharikota, placed a 870 kg remote-sensing satellite IRS-P2 in orbit. It was a significant step forward in self-reliance in satellite launching.

The first catamaran service started operating between Bombay and Goa on November 14. The distance of 225 nautical miles was covered in 6½ hours.

On November 19 Aishwarya Rai, a 21-year old model and a student of architecture of Bombay, was crowned Miss World 1994 in the beauty contest held in Sun City of South Africa. Thus in this year both Miss Universe and Miss World titles were won by Indian beauties. (See 1966.)

Former president Zail Singh expired on December 25. (b. 1916).

Karnam Malleswari of Andhra Pradesh was declared world champion in 54 kg class in the Women's Weight-lifting Championship held in Istanbul in November, both in clean and jerk as well as in total, by lifting 197.5 kg. She won two gold medals and one bronze medal, the highest achievement by any Indian in any world event, though not included in Olympic disciplines. (See 1995 and 2000.)

1995   Morarji Desai expired on April 10. (b. 1896).

In the early morning of May 11 the fifteenth century holy shrine of Sufi Sheikh Nooruddin Noorani at Charar-e-Sharif, 30 km from Srinagar, was set on fire by the militants which virtually destroyed the town as well.

On July 5 Industrial Development Bank of India opened the largest ever issue of 182.42 million shares of a total value of Rs 23,714.6 millions. The share of face value of Rs 10 was issued at Rs 130 each.

In one of the worstever train accidents, on August 20 over 302 people were killed and 363 admitted in a hospital when Delhi bound Purusattam Express rammed in the rear of the stationary Kalindi Express near Faizabad station in U.P. (See 1981 and 1999.)

The first cellular phone was commercially introduced by Modi Telstra on August 23 in Calcutta under the name Mobile Net.

August 29 was for the first time declared National Sports Day, it being the 90th birthday of hockey wizard Dhyan Chand.

Whole India was gripped in a devotional frenzy on September 21 that idols of Hindu pantheon, specially Ganesha, were 'consuming' milk offered to them. The satellite communication link rapidly turned it into a global phenomenon. Scientists soon proved it to be a hoax with practical demonstrations of capillary action.

On September 21 Jyortimoyee Sikdar was the first girl to win a gold medal in an international track event when she won 800 mt sprint in 2mt 06.75 secs in Asian Track meet. She also won a silver medal in 4x400mt relay.

On September 27 Calcutta Metro Railway ran between Dum Dum and Tollygunj—the first commercial run of the full length of 23 km. Dum Dum thus had the unique distinction of operating three railway systems which are Eastern Railway, Circular Railway and Metro Railway.

The first indigenously built tailless single engine Light Combat Aircraft rolled out of assembly hanger of Hindustan Aeronautics Ltd., Bangalore on November 17.

On November 19 Karnam Malleswari set a world record in the World Weight-lifting Championship when she lifted 113.00 kg in clean and jerk. She took all the three gold medals in her body-weight category. (See 1994 and 2000.)

A purely communication satellite INSAT 2C was successfully launched on December 7 from Kourou of French Guyana for a geo-stationary slot 36,000 km above earth.

An unidentified aircraft dropped a large quantity of arms and ammunitions near Purulia of West Bengal on December 18 night.

On December 23 in Mandi Dabwali of Haryana a disastrous fire broke out in a hall where students and parents assembled to participate in the Annual Day function of DAV Centenary Public School. 360 people perished on the spot and hundreds had to be hospitalised where within the next 72 hours another 62 persons succumbed to burn injuries.

A.D.

1996 Squardon leader Sanjay Thapar of Indian air force became the first Indian to parachute down to the geometric North Pole and unfurl the Indian flag on April 21. Incidentally this jump earned him the distinction of joining the elite group of 600 in the world who had so far accomplished this feat.

Eleventh general election took place between April 27 and May 7. Incidentally the election for Modakurichi seat of Tamil Nadu with 1,033 contestants had to be deferred to June 1. (See 1985.)

In the fourth week of April, a unique water park was inaugurated in Borivli in Mumbai. The Club Aquaria is based on British 'White Water' technology and offers interesting experiences like Water Slide, Water Pool, Lazy Water, etc.

Atal Behari Vajpayee assumed the charge as the tenth Prime Minister on May 16. But he resigned on May 28. (See 1998 and 1999.)

H. D. Deve Gowda was sworn in as the Prime Minister on June 1.

Ex-President Neelam Sanjiva Reddy expired on June 1. (b. 1913).

In August Anita Sarkar (33 years) of Calcutta became the first qualified woman football coach.

On November 12, a Saudi Arabia Jumbo jet and a Kazakhistan IL-76 airliner collided in the mid-air near Charki Dadri in Haryana sky killing all the 351 people aboard in the two planes.

On November 28 Capt. Indrani Singh of Indian Airlines became the first woman pilot to command a wide-bodied Airbus A300 jet aircraft.

In November A. Katashamma of the Good Samaritan Evangelical Lutheran Church became Asia's first woman Bishop when she succeeded her husband Paul Raj in Bhadrachalam of Andhra Pradesh. (See 1989.)

National Football League was inaugurated on December 17 in Calcutta with a match between East Bengal and Mohammedan Sporting, the two glamourous outfits of Calcutta.

In 1966 cricket World Cup tournament seating accommodation of Eden Gardens was raised to 1,08,000 which made it the world's largest cricket stadium.

India produced the first battery-operated motor car in Bangalore and named it REVA. The car needs to be recharged at least 8 hours for every 80 km run.

In Atlanta Olympic games Leander Paes won the bronze medal in the men's singles tennis. (See 1990, 1952 and 2000.)

For the first time in India, Miss World Beauty Contest was held in Bangalore. Miss Greece won the title with a cash prize of Rs 2.2 millions and one REVA car, the first battery-operated motor car made in India.

The Supreme Court upheld Kerala High Court's judgement on 'bandhs' called by the political parties as illegal.

1997 Delhi was the first city to use propane gas as vehicular fuel when 50 three-wheeler auto-rickshaws started plying on a trial basis on January 21.

An 18 year old college girl Sumita Sinha of Dhanbad probably set a world record in Thane on April 2 when a 3,200 kg truck passed over her. Sumita, who was 163 cm in height and weighed 55 kg broke her earlier record of passing an Ambassador car over her three years ago.

On April 20 Inder Kumar Gujral was appointed as the twelfth Prime Minister after the resignation of H. D. Deva Gowda.

India's new telecom Satellite 2D went into orbit on June 4 from Kourou in French Guyana.

On June 7 Mahesh Bhupathi became the first Indian to win a Grand Slam in tennis, pairing with Rika Hiraki of Japan in the mixed doubles in the French Open. (See 1999.)

On July 1, Prime Minister Inder Kumar Gujral inaugurated India's first 'Science City' in Calcutta. It was a Rs 60 crore scientific fantasia spread over 50 acres of former garbage dump, and the brain child of Saroj Ghose, Director-General of National Council of Scientific Museums.

K. R. Narayanan was sworn in on July 25 as the tenth President of the country.

On September 5 Mother Teresa, the founder of Missionaries of Charity, breathed her last in Calcutta.

On September 22 the Urdu farce *Adrak-ka-Panja* by Babbar Khan was staged 9,000th times. It was the world's longest running one-man show since 1964. It had been translated in 27 different languages.

A.D.

On September 29 the indigenous PSLV-C1 successfully lifted off ISRO's fourth remote-sensing satellite IRS-1D and was thus the first one to be put in space by an Indian vehicle.

Karnal-born aerospace engineer 37 year old Kalpana Chawla was the first Indian woman to go into space aboard US space-shuttle Columbia on November 19, from Kennedy Space Centre. (See 1984 and 2003.)

On November 22 Diana Hayden (24 years) of Hyderabad became the third Indian to be crowned Miss World, after Reita Faria and Aishwarya Rai, in the glamorous ceremony in Mahe of Seychelles Islands. (See 1966, 1994, 1999, and 2000.)

Nirad C. Chaudhuri, the renowned author, completed 100 years of his life on November 23. His first creative writing was *Autobiography of An Unknown Indian* in 1951. The pen did not stop thereafter even on the centenary year. (d. 1999).

Prime Minister I.K. Gujral submitted his resignation on November 28. The President dissolved the Parliament and ordered for general election.

1998   The twelfth general election was held in February.

On March 1 the draft of the ninth Five-year Plan for 1998-2003 was released.

Atal Behari Vajpayee became the Prime Minister for the second time on March 19 to form a B J P led coalition government. (See 1996 and 1999.)

Veteran CPM leader E.M.S. Namboodiripad expired on March 19. (b. 1909).

On May 11 three underground nuclear tests were conducted in Pokhran which included a hydrogen bomb. Two more smaller explosions followed on May 13. (See 1974.)

Pinaka, the multibarrel rocket system, was test-fired at Chandipore in Orissa on May 20.

Anti-tank Nag missile was test-fired on July 5 at Chandipore.

Country's first Dolphin City was inaugurated with five dolphins and two sea-lions on July 5 at Mahabalipuram by Amusement and Picnic Resorts Pvt. Ltd.

In one-day cricket on July 7 Sourav Ganguly and Sachin Tendulkar created the world record of 252-run opening partnership while playing against Sri Lanka in Colombo in Independence Cup Final, which India won. (See 1999.)

Indore became the first city in the country to have a private sector-run telephone service provided by Airtel.

Pilotless training aircraft Nishant was successfully flown on September 2 at Chandipore test range.

On September 26 Sachin Tendulkar notched up a record 18th one-day cricket century cracking an unbeaten 127 runs against Zimbabwe at Bulawayo.

Amartya Sen won Nobel Prize in economics for his contribution to welfare economics. He spent his student days in Santiniketan and Calcutta.

Opposite to credit card, the debit card was first introduced by Citibank, followed by HDFC Bank. (See 1960 and 1981.)

1999 In the first week of February Anil Kumble took all the ten wickets of Pakistan in the second innings of the second cricket Test match held in New Delhi. He thus equalled the world record of Jim Laker of England against Australia in 1956. It so happened for the second time in 1,445 test matches in 122 years.

On February 18 Supreme Court's verdict acknowledged the right of guardianship of minor children of mother as well.

On February 20 Atal Behari Vajpayee took a bus trip to Lahore and on February 21 signed Lahore Declaration with Pakistan Prime Minister Nawaz Sharif.

Jagbir Kaur Bengowal became the first woman president of Gurudwara Siromoni Prabandhak Committee on March 16.

On April 3 India broke into the global telecommunication services market with the successful launch of its first commercial telecom satellite INSAT IE by Europe's Ariane rocket from Kourou in French Guyana.

On April 8 Prime Minister A. B. Vajpayee sought a vote of confidence in Lok Sabha on President K. R. Narayanan's directive. Vajpayee lost by a single vote – 269 votes in favour and 270 against. Lok Sabha was dissolved on April 26 since the opposition failed to form a ministry.

A.D.

Agni II, described as the improved version of nuchear missile carrier was test-fired an April 11 at Chandipore, after a five year self-imposed embargo in testing the Agni series.

In one-day cricket on May 26 Sourav Ganguly and Rahul Dravid created a world record of 318-run partnership against Sri Lanka in World Cup Tournament. (See November 8 in 1999.)

India crossed an important milestone on May 26 when ISRO successfully put into orbit three satellites from the same rocket in its first commercial mission from Sriharikota – India's remote-sensing satellite IRS P2 along with the German and South Korean satellites. India was thus the fifth country after America, Russia, France and China, to launch more than one satellite.

Pakistani infiltrators backed by the army crossed the Line of Control in Kargil sector to cut off Srinagar – Leh highway in Kashmir. A massive response by the Indian Army in early May and also under diplomatic pressures Pakistan was forced to withdraw its forces by July 17. This was Pakistan's highest offensive since 1971 war. The Indian casualties were 519 killed and over 600 seriously injured.

On June 6 Leander Paes and Mahesh Bhupathi made history for India when they won first Grand Slam in French Open Tennis Tournament. The pair won Wimbledon Doubles also on July 4. On the same day Leander partnered USA's Lisa Raymond to win Wimbledon's Mixed Doubles title.

Nedunbassery International Airport near Kochi – the first such private venture – became commercially operational on June 10 with the landing of an Air India flight from Dahran of Saudi Arabia.

In end June Flight Officer Srividya Rajan was the first Indian woman pilot to participate in active service when she flew a helicopter in Kargil sector of Kashmir for crucial target spotting during Kargil conflict. (See 1992.)

Nirad C. Chaudhuri, the renowned author, passed away on August 1 in his Oxford sojourn. (b. 1897, see 1997.)

In the early morning of August 2 in one of the queer railway accidents Brahmaputra Mail collided head-on with Awadh-Assam Express at Gaisal in north Bengal. Both the trains were running in full speed on the same line in opposite directions. 288 bodies were recovered on the accident site and nearly 500 passengers were injured.

A.D.

On August 27 Sonali Bandyopadhyay of Allahabad became the first marine engineer in the country.

Atal Behari Vajpayee took the oath as Prime Minister for the third time on October 13. (See 1998 and 1999.)

On October 26 Supreme Court ruled that a convict punished with life imprisonment has to undergo the actual imprisonment of 14 years and thus put an embargo of any reduction of 14 years of actual physical imprisonment. (See 1860 and 2005.)

On October 29 a super-cyclone with windspeed of 260 km per hour – the highest on record in India – devasted the entire coastline of Orissa. Jagatsinghpur district was particularly affected. Over 10,000 people lost their lives and about ten million people became homeless. (See 1737.)

In October Najma Heptulla, deputy chairperson of the Rajya Sabha, was elected President of Inter-Parliamentary Union of 138 nations in Berlin. She was the first woman president in its 110 years of history.

On November 8 Rahul Dravid and Sachin Tendulkar's second wicket stand of 331 runs in Hyderabad against New Zealand broke the earlier world record set on May 26 this year.

The world's largest Giant Metrewave Radio Telescope was formally opened on November 30 at Narayangaon, about 90 km from Pune.

Insurance Regulatory and Authority Bill was passed in the Lok Sabha on December 2, which reopened the insurance sector to private companies. (See 1956 and 1973.)

On December 5 Miss Yukta Mookhey, a 20 year old zoology student of Mumbai, was crowned Miss World in London Olympic Theatre. (See 1966, 1994 and 1997.)

On December 24 an Airbus of Indian Airlines on its flight from Kathmandu to New Delhi with 178 passengers and 11 crew was hijacked by five armed terrorists. One passenger was stabbed to death. The ordeal ended at Kandahar on December 31 afternoon with an exchange of three terrorists detained in Kashmir.

On December 26 ex-president Shankar Dayal Sharma expired. (b 1918).

City Montessori School of Lucknow, established 40 years earlier, with 22, 612 students on its roll this year, entered the *Guiness Book of Records* as the world's largest school. (See 1954.)

A.D.

Lakshman Ksheerasagar and Lakshmibai of Athani – 180 miles from Hubli in Karnataka – completed 100 years of their marriage. The 102 year old barber was married in 1899 at the age of two years to his one year old wife who is presently 101 years. This couple thus enjoys the unique distinction of wedding centenary, perhaps a record to stay for ever. (See 1940.)

90 year old Hiralal Maniar, presently an accountant, served continuously for 70 years in K. Worah & Co. Pvt. Ltd. in Dhanbad since 1929. It earned him a mention in the *Guiness Book of Records* as the world's longest career in the same organisation.

2000 Photo idendity card was ordered compulsory for the first time on February 22 in Haryana State Assembly election.

INSAT 3B was launched from Kourou in French Guyana on March 22. It became operational in third week of April.

India's population figure reached one billion mark at 12.56 P.M. on Thursday, May 11 as per India's population clock. (See 1891.)

On May 13 Miss Lara Dutta was crowned Miss Universe. She was a 21-year-old economics graduate of Bangalore. Thus she was the second Indian to be crowned Miss Universe. (See 1994.)

In chess 3 times national champion, 21 year old S. Vijayalakshmi became the first woman Grand Master of the country

On July 29 Seema Bhadoria, a 17 year old college student pulled a plane weighing 3,390 kg with her teeth in Bhopal hoping to enter the *Guiness Book of Records.*

Karnam Malleswari became the first Indian woman to win an Olympic medal (bronze) on September 19. In Sydney she lifted a total weight of 240 kg in weight-lifting in 69 kg category.

On October 12 for the first time a former prime minister namely P. V. Narasimha Rao was convicted on a criminal charge. A lower court sentenced him to 3 years rigourous imprisonment and a fine of Rs 2 lakhs for bribing 10 Jharkhand Mukti Morcha members of parliament to bail his government out of a no-confidence motion tabled in July 1995. He was acquitted on appeal.

On November 1 Chhatisgarh state was carved out of Madhya Pradesh as the 26th state of India.

A.D.

Direct-to-home (DTH) telecast service was approved by the government for viewing any television programme of the world with a proper receiver.

Jyoti Basu (86 years) resigned on November 6 on health ground from chief ministership of West Bengal with the longest record of 23 years of uninterrupted rule with a nine-party coalition.

On November 9 a new state Uttaranchal came into being as the 27th state comprising of the hilly region of Uttar Pradesh.

Jharkhand, the 28th state of India, was born on November 15, which was carved out of Bihar's southern districts.

On November 30, Priyanka Chopra (18 years) of Barielly was crowned Miss World in London's Millenium Dome. Thus this year both the crowns Miss Universe and Miss World went to the Indian beauties for the second time. (See 1994.)

On December 23 Calcutta was officially renamed Kolkata. (See 1687.)

On December 24 chess Grand Master Vishwanathan Anand was crowned World Chess Champion (FIDE) defeating Grand Master Alexei Shirov of Spain in Teheran.

2001 A.D. Onwards

2001   On January 4 indigenously built Light Combat Aircraft (LCA) successfully completed its maiden flight at Bangalore. Each such supersonic aircraft would cost about Rs 90 crores. India is the eighth nation to develop this technology.

Agni II missile, India's most potent weapon delivery system was successfully test-fired on January 17 for the second time from Chandipore. The 16 tonne missile was lifted with 'solid motor' for the first time and was capable of carrying a nuclear war-head up to a distance of 2,000 km. (See 1999.)

On January 26 a devastating earthquake virtually destroyed all the buildings in towns and villages around Bhuj. It took a toll of nearly 19,000 people dead and 1,60,000 injured. The intensity in Richter scale was 7.9, the highest ever recorded in India.

In January Abhinav Brinda created a world record in air-rifle event at Luxemburg National Championship. His 702.2 points were better than that of Russia's Harji Bekoff's old mark.

On March 11 Pulella Gopichand of Hyderabad virtually became the world champion in badminton by winning all England men's singles title, thereby repeating the feat of Prakash Padukone in 1979. In the process Gopichand disposed off both the Olympic champion Ji Xinpeng of China in semi-final as well as the world number one Peter Gade of Denmark in final.

20 year old Harbhajan Singh became India's first bowler to achieve a hat-trick on March 11 in Test cricket. The great feat was achieved in Eden Gardens in Kolkata in the second Test against Australia. He was thus the 26th bowler in the world and hat-trick number 29.

March 18 was declared Ordnance Factory Day in India on the 200th anniversary of the first Ordnance Factory established in this country in 1801 in Cossipore of Kolkata

P. N. Bhagawati, an eminent jurist and the former chief justice of India, was appointed Chairman of New York based Human Rights Commission of March 26. He was thus the first Indian to chair the Commission.

On March 31 Sachin Tendulkar became the first cricketer in the world to score 10, 000 runs in one-day International, while playing against Australia in Indore.

On April 18 ISRO's Rs 1,400 crore project Geosynchronous Satellite Launch Vehicle (GSLV–DI) weighing 401 tonnes successfully took off from Shriharikota and placed the 1,540 kg experimental satellite 17 minutes later in a Geosynchronous Transfer Orbit. India thus joined the GSLV Club of Russia, Japan, China and France–led European Space Agency.

On June 12 defence scientists tested the Brahmos, a supersonic cruise missile at Chandipur. The name was coined by combining the two rivers Bhramaputra and Moscow. The 6.9 mt missile is capable of hitting a target at a distance of 280 km in 300 secs.

On October 24 while playing against Kenya in South Africa, Sachin Tendulkar and Sourav Ganguly broke their own world record by scoring 256 runs in opening wicket. That was the duo's 16th century partnership – another world mark. (See 1998.)

On December 13 India watched its worst horror experience as five terrorists of Pakistan based outfits fired indiscreminately inside the Parliament complex in New Delhi. They killed nine brave Indians (eight security personnel and one gardener) and thereby shaking a billion hearts. All the five terrorists were shot down by valiant policemen. The incident crossed the limit of tolerance of India and brought the country on the verge of war with Pakistan.

2002 On January 24 ISRO's 2,750 kg satellite INSAT-3C was successfully launched at Kourou of French Guyana. It was injected into a geosynchronous transfer orbit 21 minutes after lift-off.

On January 25 Air Chief Marshal Arjan Singh was made the first Marshal of IAF in recognition of his extraordinary services.

On February 27 at Godhra railway station near Ahmedabad, a mob of nearly 2,000 Muslim miscreants set fire in a railway compartment of Sabarmati Express, which was carrying Ram Sevaks – devotees of Ramchandra (of Ramayana). 57 men, women and children perished inside the compartment. In the terrible Hindu backlash in Gujarat, more than 700 Muslims were put to death, mostly burnt alive.

A.D.

On July 18 A.P.J. Abdul Kalam was elected eleventh President of India and was installed on July 25.

In November Smt. P. Bandopadhyay became the first lady vice-Marshal of the Indian Air Force.

On December 24 Delhi Metro-rail was inaugurated – the second one in India. A distance of 5 km from Seelampur to Tis Hazari was covered in 13 minutes. The system is supposed to go underground in about 3 years.

2003 Kalpana Chawla embarked on her second space voyage on January 16 in U.S. space shuttle Columbia. That flight had a tragic end while returning to earth. Columbia exploded in the sky on February 1, killing all the seven crew astronauts. (See 1997.)

On April 10 ISRO's satellite INSAT 3A weighing 2,958 kg was successfully launched from Kourou by Ariane 5 launch vehicle. Its purpose was to improve telecommunication, television broadcasting, meteorology, and satellite-aided search and rescue services.

The first indigenously built 'stealth' warship was launched on April 18 at Mazagaon Dock. Armed with awesome anti-missile defence capabilities, the warship was equipped with state-of-the art stealth features. (See 1972.)

On May 1 Sumeet Mukherji, Judge of Delhi High Court, was the first High Court Judge to be arrested and produced in court on allegations of undue favour for property allocations.

Chandan Thakur and Dipti Pradhan created a new record on June 23 when they tied their nuptial knot 4 metres under water for 35 minutes as per Maharashtrian Hindu rites. Even the sacred fire was there as the witness in Mumbai's Marine Central Pool. Earlier world record was held by a Thai couple whose under-water marriage was conducted in 10 minutes.

On July 6 Sania Mirza of Hyderabad became the first woman to win a Grand Slam in tennis, when she triumphed in Wimbledon Ladies Doubles event partnering Alisa Kleybanov of Russia for a 2–6, 6–3, 6–2 victory in the final. On a previous occasion Rita Davar finished runner-up in Wimbledon singles in 1952.

On July 21 Ajoy and Monisha of Chandigarh solemnised their marriage in Panchkula adhering to the traditions and rituals of four religions – Hindu, Muslim, Sikhism and Christianity. In turn a

Pandit, Moulavi, Granthi and Father performed their religious functions. The couple wore the traditional dresses while marrying in each style.

On July 26 East Bengal became the first Indian Club to win an international tournament on foreign soil, when they beat favourites BEC Tero Sasana of Thailand 3-1 in Jakarta to annex LG Cup Asean Club Football Championship.

On August 31 Chaitali Dhenki of Chinsurah Swimming Club became the first woman to win 81 km swimming contest of Mushidabad – the longest stretch in the world – in 11 hours 24 mts and 26 secs. Thereby she broke into the male bastion held by them. (See 1934.)

On September 28, India's most advanced communication satellite 2, 775 kg Insat 3E, with an operational life of 15 years, was launched from Kourou.

2004   Virender Sehwag became the first Indian to score a triple century (309) in Test cricket on March 29, while playing against Pakistan in Multan.

On April 7 Indian Airlines had its first woman check pilot for Airbus A320 in Capt. Sangeeta K. Bangar (39 yrs) with over 8,000 flying hours.

The fourteenth general election of Lok Sabha was held between mid-April and mid-May. Electronic voting machines were used for the first time in all the constituencies.

On May 22 Manmohan Singh (b. 26.09.1932) was sworn in as the thirteenth Prime Minister to head a coalition government under the name United Progressive Alliance led by Indian National Congress since no single political party could amass sufficient strength.

On May 29 'Saras', the first prototype of India's indigenous civil aircraft, made its maiden flight successfully at HAL airport in Bangalore.

In July Chhatrapati Shivaji Railway Terminus of Mumbai (earlier Victoria Terminus), built in 1853 to 1888 – the world's only working railway station and the first colonial building in India – got the World Heritage site status in UNESCO's 788 strong World Heritage list. (See 1888.)

A.D.

On August 17 shooter Rajyavardhan Singh Rathore of Indian Army created history by fetching India its first-ever Olympic silver medal at Athens in post-independence era. (See 1900.)

In September, Major General (Dr.) Punita Arora became the first woman in Indian Army to don the highest rank Lt. General, when she took over as commandant of the Armed Forces Medical College, Pune.

2005 It was declared that from March 3 the Sikhs' holiest shrine Golden Temple (British name) to be referred to as Harmandir Sahib.

National Champion Pankaj Advani (19 years old) lifted his maiden World Billiards crown at Malta on March 16. This win also made Advani the second cueist in the world to have won both the billiards and snooker amateur titles. (See 1977).

Women's National Champion Amiya Thakur (22 years) clinched World Ladies Billiards Championship crown in England on April 7.

On April 29 Bula Chowdhury created history to become the world's first woman swimmer to conquer five continents by crossing from Three Anchor Bay to Robben Islands near Cape Town in South Africa. Earlier on August 20, 2004 she became the first woman to cross seven seas.

On May 3 some sort of a record perhaps in the whole world was created of the shortest adult couple when 35 years old Arjun Mondal (92 cm in height) of Nungi near Kolkata got married to Manashi Ghose (79 cm in height) of Dumka in Rakshakali temple of Suri, Birbhum. Not only the marriage was solemnised according to Hindu rites, but was also officially registered.

Polar Satellite Launch Vehicle PSLV C6 blasted off on May 5 from Sriharikota to place two Indian satellites CARTOSAT (1,560 kg) and HAMSAT (42.5 kg) into a high polar orbit. This was the 20th satellite launch and ninth flight of the country's space organisation.

On May 6 Dola Banerjee won the first international gold medal for India in the women's recurve category in archery at the 18th Golden Arrow Grand Prix Championship in Turkey.

A.D.

On a single day July 26, Mumbai received 94.4 cm rain, the highest ever recorded in courtry's history, which caused more than 900 deaths. (See 1861.)

In July India's first bone bank was set up at Goverment General Hospital, Chennai.

On August 29, Parliament passed the bill, giving Hindu women equal rights in heritence of property. Thus a daughter has the same rights as the son. It came into force on September 9.

A tripartite agreement was signed in August between the Centre and State governments of Uttar Pradesh and Madhya Pradesh to connect Ken and Betwa rivers.

In September Supreme Court stated that 'imprisonment for life' should be treated as whole of the remaining period of convict's life and not 14 years in jail. (See 1860 and 1999.)

PART B
EVENTS BY DATES

PART B
Events By Dates
(Up to 2000 A.D.)

In 1582 Pope Gregory XIII changed Julian calendar to Gregorian calendar, when October 5 was called October 15 and every fourth year a leap year. In 1752 the Gregorian calendar was introduced throughout the British Dominion including India. The date lag since 1582 was covered by naming the day after September 2, 1752 as September 14.

JANUARY

January 1

1399 Timur left Delhi on his way back to his own territory in central Asia. He captured Delhi on December 18, 1398 and took the title 'Emperor of India'.

1664 Shivaji started Surat campaign.

1862 Indian Penal Code and Code of Criminal Procedure passed on October 6, 1860 came into force.

1877 In Delhi Durbar Queen Victoria was proclaimed as Empress of India.

1880 Money order system was introduced.

1894 The renowned scientist and national professor Satyendra Nath Bose was born.

1903 King Edward VII was declared Emperor of India.

1915 Gandhiji was awarded *Kaiser-e-Hind* gold medal by the Viceroy for the services rendered by him in South Africa.

1920 Rotary Club of Calcutta got the charter from International Association of Rotary Clubs of U.S.A.

1948 India lodged complaints against Pakistan to the U.N. for sending Pakistani raiders into Kashmir territory.

1949 Ceasefire was declared in Kashmir.

1961 Fertilizer Corporation of India was founded.

1972   Privy purses and other privileges of previous rulers of Indian states were abolished.

1973   General Insurance was nationalised.

1976   Commercial advertisement was introduced in TV.

1978   Air India's first Jumbo jet Boeing 747 namely Emperor Ashoka plunged into the sea off Bombay coast with 231 people aboard, all of whom perished.

1988   B. P. Jha was sworn in as the Chief Justice of Patna High Court, only to retire on the same day.

1998   Maharashtra was the first state to launch anti-smoking and anti-spitting campaign.

January 2

1757   Robert Clive recaptured Calcutta from Nawab Siraj-ud-daula.

1899   Monks of Ramakrishna order started living in Belur Math of Calcutta.

1973   Gen. S.H.F.J. Manekshaw was promoted to rank of Field Marshal.

1991   Tiruvananthapuram airport was updated to international airport status.

January 3

1836   Munshi Newal Kishore was born.

1880   The first issue of the *Illustrated Weekly of India* was published in Bombay.

1846   The three top-ranking Indian National Army (Azad Hind Fauj), heroes of the Second World War, were released by Gen. Claude Auchinleck.

January 4

1604   Prince Salim submitted to Akbar after his rebellion collapsed.

1884   Keshab Chandra Sen died.

1906   The Prince of Wales (later King George V) laid the foundation stone of Victoria Memorial Hall of Calcutta.

1964   The first diesel locomotive of Varanasi Locomotive Works came out of assembly line.

1966   Indo-Pakistani summit between Lal Bahadur Shastri and General Ayub Khan began at Tashkent after 1965 conflict.

1972   Institute of Criminology and Forensic Science was inaugurated in New Delhi.

January 5

1592   Mughal Emperor Shahjahan was born.

1659   In the battle of Khajwah, Shah Suja was defeated by Aurangzeb.

1890   Barrister Gnanendra Mohan Tagore died.

1957   Central Sales Tax Act came into force.

1988   First indigenously built Braille shorthand machine was released.

January 6

1316   Sultan Alauddin Khilji died, probably poisoned by Malik Kafur.

1947   All India Congress Committee accepted partition of India by a majority vote of 99 in favour and 52 against.

1981   National Institute of Oceanography succeeded in collecting polymetallic nodules from the Indian Ocean bed.

1989   Satwant Singh and Kehar Singh, the two convicts in Indra Gandhi murder case, were hanged.

       The last Baron Lord Sudhindra Prasanna Sinha died.

January 7

1859   The trial of Emperor Bahadur Shah II started for his complicity in Sepoy Mutiny.

January 8

1026   Sommath temple was completely ransacked and destroyed by Sultan Mahmud in his fourteenth and last expedition to India.

1941   Swami Pranabananda Maharaj, founder of Bharat Sevashram Sangha, died.

1984   The first woman pilot Susama Mukhopadhyay died.

January 9

1664   Shivaji left Surat after its plunder.

1915   Gandhiji landed in Bombay on his return from South Africa.

1963   Gold control measures were announced.

1972   It was announced that in the world, India produced the highest number of feature films (433) during 1971.

1982   The first Indian scientific expedition team landed on Antarctica.

January 10

1616   Sir Thomas Roe, the British ambassador, presented himself at Jahangir's court at Ajmer.

1692   Job Charnock, founder of Calcutta, expired in Calcutta.

1818   The third and last battle between the Marathas and the British took place at Rampura and the Maratha forces disintegrated thereafter.

1836   Professor Madhusudan Gupta and four of his students were the first people to dissect a dead boy.

1912   King George V and Queen Mary left India.

1963   Gold Control Scheme of Government of India came into operation.

1987   The first sailing boat expedition around the world completed its mission at Bombay.

January 11

1613   Jahangir granted imperial Firman to the East India Company to establish factories in Surat.

1955   India's first newsprint production started.

1966   Lal Bahadur Shastri died in the early hours of the morning at Tashkent, where he was engaged in a summit conference with Pakistan.

January 12   NATIONAL YOUTH DAY

1708   Shahu was crowned as the Maratha ruler.

1757   Bandel of West Bengal was captured from the Portuguese by the British under Captain Eyre Coote.

1863   Swami Vivekananda (alias Narendra Nath or Bireswar Dutta) was born.

1934   Surya Sen (Masterda) was hanged in Chittagong Jail.

1984   Swami Vivekananda's birthday was declared as National Youth Day.

January 13

1709   Bahadur Shah I (Shah Alam I or Prince Muazzam) defeated his third brother Kam Bakhsh at Hyderabad, who died of wounds.

1818   Rana of Udaipur signed a treaty with the British for British protection of Mewar state.

1849   The famous battle of Chillianwala of the second Anglo-Sikh war took place.

1889   Assamese youths started their own literary journal *Jonaki*.

1948   Gandhiji commenced fast unto death, his last one, in Calcutta insisting upon communal harmony between the Hindus and the Muslims. He broke the fast on January 18.

January 14

1758 By the charter of the King of England, the East India Company was allowed to keep any booty taken in any battle in India fought against the enemies of the Company and the King.

1760 French General Lally capitulated and surrendered Pondicherry to the British Captain Eyre Coote.

1761 The third battle of Panipat was fought between the Marathas and Ahmad Shah Durrani (Abdali).

1938 Belur Math (new) of Ramakrishna Mission was consecrated.

1969 The name of Madras state was changed to Tamil Nadu.

1982 Indira Gandhi expounded a new 20-point Economic Programme.

January 15   ARMY DAY

1784 Asiatic Society of Bengal was established.

1934 Earthquake in Bihar took a toll of 20,000 lives. Monghyr town was razed to the ground.

1949 Indian Army came under the first Indian Commander-in-Chief K. M. Cariappa. Since then this date is observed as the Army Day.

1965 Food Corporation of India was set up.

1978 The President promulgated an Ordinance demonetising currency notes of Rs1,000 and above.

1986 Gen. K. M. Cariappa (Retd.) was made Honorary Field Marshal for life.

1986 For the first time Indian Airlines had an all women crew on a commercial passenger flight.

January 16

1681 Shivaji's son Sambhaji's coronation took place at Raigarh fort.

1769 The first organised horse-racing took place at Akra near Calcutta.

1901 The great scholar Mahadeo Govind Ranade died.

1938 The famous Bengali novelist Sarat Chandra Chattopadhyay died.

1955 Kharakvasla Defence Academy was officially opened.

1966 Sadhu T. L. Vaswani expired.

1989 Prem Nazir (originally Abdul Khadar), holding the world record in appearing in lead role of more than 600 films, expired.

January 17

1601   Emperor Akbar entered Asirgarh fort which was renowned for its invincibility.

1941   In the early hours of the morning Subhas Chandra Bose escaped from his Calcutta residence for Germany via Moscow.

1987   Tata Football Academy was opened.

1989   Col. J. K. Bajaj was the first Indian to reach South Pole.

January 18

1842   The great Maharashtrian scholar Mahadeo Govind Ranade was born.

1930   Rabindranath Tagore visited Sabarmati Ashram of Gandhiji.

1938   The last batch of political prisoners sailed from Port Blair of the Andaman Islands for the mainland.

1947   The great singer Kundan Lal Saigal died at Jalandhar.

1959   Miss Meera Behn (Madeleine Slade) left India for good.

January 19

1597   Rana Pratap Singh of Mewar died.

1905   Debendranath Tagore breathed his last.

1987   Narain Dutt Ojha was sworn in as a Supreme Court Judge at 10.00 P.M. only to retire two hours later.

1990   Rajneesh, the Osho godman, expired in Pune.

January 20

1817   Calcutta Hindu College (presently Presidency College) was established at the house of Gora Chand Basak at 304 Chitpore Road, Calcutta.

1957   India's first atomic reactor 'Apsara' was inaugurated in Trombay.

1959   Tej Bahadur Sapru died.

1972   Arunachal Pradesh (formerly North East Frontier Agency) became Union Territory and Meghalaya got statehood.

January 21

1945   The great revolutionary Rash Behari Bose died in Tokyo, Japan.

1958   Copyright Act came into force.

1961   Queen Elizabeth II and Duke of Edinburgh arrived in New Delhi.

1972 Manipur, Mizoram and Tripura became full-fledged states of India.

1983 The first Indian Admiral R. D. Katari died.

1996 Some auto-rickshaws in New Delhi started plying on propane gas on trial basis.

January 22

1666 Shahjahan died in Agra fort at the age of 74 as a captive of Aurangzeb.

1760 The British won the battle of Wandiwash in south India against the French.

1963 National Library for the Blind was set up at Dehradun.

January 23

1565 In the great battle of Tellikota, the prosperous Hindu kingdom of Vijayanagar was extinguished.

1664 Shivaji's father Shahuji expired.

1897 Netaji Subhas Chandra Bose was born in Cuttack.

1920 Air transport and airmail services started.

1965 Durgapur Alloy Steel Plant was commissioned.

1966 Indira Gandhi became the third Prime Minister of India.

1976 The lost city of Kapilavastu of Gautam Buddha was found after excavation.

1977 Janata Party was formed by combining several political parties for fighting general elections against Congress led by Indira Gandhi.

January 24

1826 The first Indian Barrister Gnanendra Mohan Tagore was born.

1857 Calcutta University was founded.

1950 'Jana gana mana...' was adopted as the National Anthem of India. Rajendra Prasad was elected the first President of the Republic of India.

1951 Prem Mathur was the first woman pilot to get a commercial licence.

1952 The first International Film Festival was held in Bombay.

1966 Air India's Boeing 707 crashed in the Alps in Switzerland in which 144 people perished including the nuclear scientist Homi Bhabha.

January 25

1824 Bengali poet Michael Madhusudan Dutta was born.

1880 Keshab Chandra Sen introduced Nababidhan to modernise Brahmo Samaj.

1954 Manabendra Nath Roy (alias Narendra Nath Bhattacharya) died.

1971 Himachal Pradesh became a full-fledged state.

1980 Civil honours like Bharat Ratna, Padma Vibhushan, etc., were reintroduced after they were withdrawn on August 8,1977.

Mother Teresa was awarded the civil decoration Bharat Ratna.

1983 Vinoba Bhave was posthumously awarded Bharat Ratna.

January 26   REPUBLIC DAY

1556 Mughal Emperor Humayun expired from a fall on the staircase.

1930 For the first time observed as the Swaraj Day, i.e., independence day of India while under the British rule.

1950 India was declared as a Sovereign Democratic Republic when the new constitution of independent India came into force. Since then it is observed as the Republic Day of India.

C. Rajagopalachari relinquished the office of the last Governor General of India and Rajendra Prasad became the first President of India.

Ashoka's Lion capital was adopted as the National Emblem.

The Federal Court of India created in 1937 became the Supreme Court of India.

Chittaranjan, the locomotive town and a model industrial colony, was inaugurated.

India's flagship *HMIS Delhi* became *INS Delhi*.

1972 A national memorial Amar Jawan was installed at India Gate in New Delhi.

1981 Vayudoot air service started.

1982 Railway's *Palace on Wheels* was inaugurated.

January 27

1959 The foundation-stone of the first College of Engineering and Technology was laid in New Delhi.

1974 President V.V. Giri dedicated to the nation the Nehru Memorial Museum at Teen Murti House, New Delhi.

1988 The first-ever helicopter mail service was inaugurated.

January 28

1835 Calcutta Medical College started working.

1865 Lala Lajpat Rai was born.

1898 Sister Nivedita arrived at India.

1900 General K. M. Cariappa, the first Indian General, was born.

1933 Rahmat Ali Chaudhuri, an Indian Muslim graduate in Cambridge, coined the name PAKISTAN of the Muslim majority states of India.

1950 Hiralal J. Kania took over as the first Chief Justice of the Supreme Court of independent India.

1961 Foundation-stone of the first HMT watch factory was laid in Bangalore.

1980 The biggest bulk-carrier Rani Padmini was floated.

January 29

1528 Mughal Emperor Babar captured Chanderi fort from Rana Sanga's most distinguished lieutenant Medini Rai.

1780 India's first newspaper *Hicky's Bengal Gazette or the Calcutta General Advertiser* was published by James Augustus Hicky in English language.

1896 Swami Pranabananda Maharaj, the founder of Bharat Sevashram Sangha, was born in Bajitpur village in Bangladesh.

1939 Ramakrishna Mission Institute of Culture was founded.

1953 Sangeet Natak Academy was set up.

1979 India's first Jumbo passenger train with two engines 'Tamil Nadu Express' was flagged off from New Delhi railway station for Madras.

1994 Government of India repealed the Air Corporation Act of 1953.

January 30   **MARTYRS' DAY**

1530 Rana Sangram Singh of Mewar expired.

1903 Lord Curzon opened the Imperial Library (National Library in 1948) in Metcalfe Hall in Calcutta.

1948 Mahatma Gandhi was assassinated by Nathuram Vinayak Godse in Birla House of New Delhi. Since then it is observed as the Martyrs' Day.

1949   Night Airmail service was introduced.

1971   Indian Airline's Fokker Friendship plane was hijacked to Lahore which was subsequently destroyed.

1985   The Constitution 52nd Amendment Bill on automatic disqualification of political defectors was passed by Lok Sabha.

January 31

1561   Bairam Khan was assassinated at Patan in Gujarat.

1963   Peacock was declared as the National Bird of India.

1983   The first floating dry dock was launched in Calcutta.

1985   The Rajya Sabha also unanimously passed the bill for automatic disqualification of political defectors from the membership of either parliament or state legislatures.

FEBRUARY

February 1

1785   Warren Hastings attended the meeting of the Council for the last time and then he resigned from his position of Governor-General of Bengal.

1797   Lord Cornwallis was sworn in as the Governor-General of Bengal.

1827   Bengal Club of Calcutta was established.

1831   The first Fine Arts Exhibition was held in Calcutta.

1835   Darjeeling territory was taken on lease from Sikkim by the East India Company.

1855   East India Railway was formally inaugurated and the inaugural expenses were met from the freight earned in its first coal train from Raniganj to Calcutta during that year.

1881   St. Stephen's College, the oldest college in Delhi with a continuous history, was established.

1884   Postal Insurance Scheme was launched.

1922   Mahatma Gandhi wrote to then vicerory of India that he was intensifying his action and the non-cooperation was to be escalated to civil disobedience.

1949   Press Trust of India took over Associated Press of India.

1964   Unit Trust of India was founded.

1969   The two-man rowing expedition to the Andamans set out from Calcutta.

1972   International Airport Authorities of India was set up.

1976   India's integrated national news agency 'Samachar' was launched. But it disintegrated in 1978.

1977   India's Naval Coast Guard Force was set up.

1985   Muhammad Azharuddin created a world record at Kanpur by slamming three successive centuries in Test cricket since debut.

February 2

1788   Pitt's Regulatory Act was introduced to improve administration in India.

1814   Calcutta Museum was established as a part of Asiatic Society.

1835   T. B. Macaulay threw open the floodgate of western education in India by linking higher education with English language.

1862   Sambhunath Pandit became the first Indian High Court Judge.

1952   India had its first ever cricket Test victory at Madras.

1953   All India Khadi and Village Industries Board was constituted.

February 3

1760   Maratha army led by Sadashiv Rao Bhau completely defeated the Nizam in the battle of Udgir.

1916   Banaras Hindu University was opened.

1925   India's first electric train service started between Bombay and Kurla.

1954   Allahabad Kumbh Mela tragedy caused a loss of more than 500 lives.

1969   C. N. Annadurai expired.

1970   The foundation-stone of India's first and the world's largest coal-based fertilizer plant was laid at Talcher.

1978   Mahakavi Sankara Kurup died.

1983   The foundation-stone of Pragjyotishpur, the capital of Assam, was laid by the Prime Minister.

1988   Indian Navy inducted the first nuclear-powered submarine *INS Chakra*.

February 4

1628   Shajahan was enthroned at Agra.

1757   Clive sent two envoys to Siraj-ud-daula who was advancing towards Calcutta with 40,000 troops. The envoys returned without any settlement.

1973   India's largest merchant ship 88,000 DWT super-tanker *Jawaharlal Nehru* was inaugurated.

1974   The great physicist Satyendra Nath Bose died.

1990   Ernakulam was declared the first totally literate district in the country.

February 5

1630   Sikh Guru Har Rai was born.

1922   In Chauri Chaura 22 police personnel were killed in a mob violence. It upset Gandhiji's non-violent movement for a while.

February 6

1931   Motilal Nehru breathed his last.

1959   Smt. Anna Chandy was appointed as the first woman Judge of Kerala High Court.

February 7

1856   Nawab Wajid Ali Shah of Oudh was forced to abdicate by the East India Company and entire Oudh was annexed by the Company.

1983   Eastern News Agency was established in Calcutta.

1992   The first indigenously built submarine *INS Shalki* joined the navy.

February 8

1705   Aurangzeb had his last military campaign.

1785   Warren Hastings left India.

1872   Lord Mayo, Viceroy of India, was assassinated by a prisoner named Sher Ali in the Andaman Islands.

1897   Zakir Hussain was born at Hyderabad in Andhra Pradesh.

1921   Chamber of Princes was inaugurated by a Royal Proclamation.

1943   Netaji Subhas Chandra Bose left Kiel in Germany in a German U-boat for Japan.

1971   K. M. Munshi, the constitutional authority and a great author, died.

1986   For the first time a prepaid taxi service scheme was introduced at Delhi airport.

1994   Kapil Dev broke Richard Hadlee's world record by taking the 432nd Test wicket in cricket.

February 9

1757   A treaty was signed between Clive and Siraj-ud-daula, conceding the former to fortify Calcutta, and to establish a mint there. Siraj also agreed to pay the reparation for British losses.

1824   Michael Madhusudan Dutta embraced Christianity.

1931   India's first commemorative as well as pictorial stamps were issued on inauguration of New Delhi.

1951   Enumeration work of the first census of free India started.

February 10

1691   In Calcutta the first English factory was established.

1921   Kashi Vidyapith was inaugurated by Gandhiji.
       Foundation stone of India Gate was laid by Duke of Connaught.

1929   J. R. D. Tata was the first Indian to get a pilot's licence.

1931   New Delhi was officially inaugurated.

1979   Itanagar was made the capital of Arunachal Pradesh.

February 11

1861   Brahma Bandhab Upadhyay was born.

1933   The first issue of Gandhiji's *Harijan Weekly* came out from Pune.

1942   Jamnalal Bajaj passed away.

1977   President Fakhruddin Ali Ahmed passed away.

1980   Romesh Chandra Majumdar, a noted historian, died.

February 12

1742   Nana Phadnavis, the great Maratha diplomat, was born.

1871   Charles Freer Andrews was born in Newcastle-on-Tyne in U.K.

1922   Gandhiji persuaded the Congress Working Committee to end the Civil Disobedience Movement.

1928   Gandhiji gave the signal for Satyagraha at Bardoli.

1975   India was declared as a country free of smallpox.

February 13

1713   Jahandar Shah was strangled to death.

1788   Trial of Warren Hastings began in House of Commons for his excesses in India, but ultimately ended in his acquittal.

1856   Oudh, including Lucknow, was annexed by the East India Company.

1879   Nationalist leader Sarojini Naidu was born.

1984   Indira Gandhi inaugurated the construction of submarines in Mazagaon Dock of Bombay.

February 14

1537   Bahadur Shah of Gujarat was drowned in his escape bid when the Portuguese treacherously tried to detain him in Diu.

1556   Akbar was enthroned at Kalanaur in Gurdaspur district of Punjab.

1658   In the family struggle for Delhi throne, Suja was defeated by Dara in the battle of Bahadurpur near Varanasi.

1881   Calcutta Homeopathic Medical College, the first one in India, was established.

1989   Supreme Court brought down the curtain on Bhopal gas disaster litigation.

February 15

1869   Mirza Ghalib died.

1967   The fourth Lok Sabha general election was held.

February 16

1759   French siege of Madras ended.

1943   Dada Saheb Phalke passed away.

1982   Jawaharlal Nehru Invitation International Gold Cup Football Tournament was staged for the first time.

1987   Submarine-to-submarine killer (SSK) missile was inducted in the Indian Navy.

February 17

1618   Thomas Roe, the British ambassador to Emperor Jahangir, left India on his way back to England.

1670   Shivaji captured Singhagarh fort from the Mughals.

1698   Jinjee fort fell to Aurangzeb.

1883   Basudev Balwant Phadke died in Aden prison.

1915   Gandhiji visited Santiniketan for the first time.

1931   Lord Irwin received Gandhiji in the Viceregal Lodge of Delhi for the first time as the leader of the masses.

February 18

3102 B.C.: 'Kali Yuga' (Kali era) started.

1266 Nasiruddin Muhammed Shah died.

1486 Chaitanya Dev was born.

1614 Jahangir captured Mewar.

1836 Ramakrishna Paramahansa Dev (alias Gadadhar Chatterjee) was born.

1905 India Home Rule Society was formed in London by Shyamji Krishnavarma.

1911 H. Picquet carried the world's first official airmail from Allahabad to Naini Junction six miles away, in a Humber Sommer biplane.

1945 'Kali Yuga' (Kali era) ended.

1946 A revolt broke out in the Royal Indian Navy in Bombay.

1971 India established the first satellite communication link via Arvi Satellite Station with Goonbilly in Great Britain.

1979 The world's largest ever cheque of Rs16,640 million was handed over to India by U.S.A.

February 19

1389 Sultan Ghiasuddin Tughlak II of Delhi was killed.

1630 Shivaji, the Maratha ruler, was born at Junner.

1719 Mughal Emperor Farrukhsiyar was assassinated.

1891 The *Amrita Bazaar Patrika* became a daily paper.

1895 Munshi Newal Kishore died.

1915 Gopal Krishna Gokhale expired.

1978 The renowned Bengali singer Pankaj Kumar Mullick, who greatly popularised Rabindra sangeet, died.

1986 Computerised railway ticket reservation was introduced for the first time.

February 20

1707 Aurangzeb expired at Ahmadnagar.

1835 Calcutta Medical College was officially opened.

1846 Lahore was captured by the British.

1847 Royal Calcutta Turf Club was established.

1868   The *Amrita Bazaar Patrika* had its first weekly issue in Bengali.

1947   British Prime Minister Clement Attlee announced that Britain would leave India by a date not later than June 1948.

1950   Sarat Chandra Bose, a leading nationalist and elder brother of Netaji Subhas Chandra Bose, died.

1968   Dr P. K. Sen performed the first heart transplantation in K. E. M. Hospital of Bombay.

1976   Bombay High went into commercial production of crude oil.

1987   Mizoram and Arunachal Pradesh became the 23rd and 24th full-fledged states of the Indian Union.

February 21

1878   Miss Mira Alfassa, mother of Pondicherry Aurobindo Ashram, was born in Paris.

1948   Draft constitution of independent India was presented to the President.

1959   Press Club of India was founded in New Delhi.

1999   Atal Behari Vajpayee and Pakistan's Nawaz Sharif signed Lahore Declaration.

February 22

1845   Serampore and Balasore were bought by the East India Company from the Dutch East India Company.

1885   Jatindra Mohan Sen Gupta, the nationalist leader, was born.

1944   Kasturba Gandhi, Mahatma Gandhi's wife, expired as a prisoner of the British government.

1958   Abul Kalam Azad died.

2000   For the first time photo identity card was declared essential for identification when Assembly election was held in Haryana.

February 23

1768   Col. Smith signed peace treaty with Nizam of Hyderabad who accepted British supremacy.

1952   Employees' Provident Fund and Miscellaneous Provisions Act was passed.

February 24

1483   Babar, the first Mughal Emperor of India, was born.

1961 The government of Madras decided to rename the state as Tamil Nadu.

February 25

1586 Raja Birbal, poet laureate of Akbar's court, was killed in a battle with the rebellious Yusufzai tribe.

1760 Clive left India for the first time and came back again in 1765.

1788 Pitt's Regulatory Act was passed.

1894 Religious leader Meher Baba was born.

1988 India's first tactical surface-to-surface missile Prithvi was successfully test-fired.

February 26

320 Chandragupta I became the ruler of Pataliputra.

1857 First sign of Sepoy Mutiny broke out at Berhampore of West Bengal.

1858 Diwan Maniram Dutta and Piali Barua were hanged for their efforts to reinstate Assam royal family on the throne.

1966 V. D. Savarkar expired.

1972 Vikram Earth Satellite Station at Arvi near Wardha was dedicated to the nation by President V.V. Giri.

1975 The first kite museum 'Shankar Kendra' was established in Ahmedabad.

1983 India's first 'Effluent Disposal Channel' was inaugurated at Vadodara.

February 27

1854 Jhansi was annexed by the East India Company.

1931 Famous revolutionary Chandrasekhar Azad shot himself to avoid arrest in an encounter with British police in Allahabad.

February 28

1568 Chittorgarh of Rana Uday Singh II fell to Akbar after a siege since October 20 of the previous year.

1580 The first Jesuit mission arrived in Akbar's court at Fatehpur Sikri from Goa.

1712 Bahadur Shah I died at Lahore.

1928   C.V. Raman discovered 'Raman Effect' of scattered light, which won him the Nobel Prize.

1936   Kamala Nehru, wife of Jawaharlal Nehru, died in a sanatorium near Lausanne in Switzerland.

1943   The cantilever Howrah Bridge (Rabindra Setu) was opened.

1948   The last batch of British soldiers left India.

1963   Rajendra Prasad, the first president of India, expired.

1968   Auroville, the international township of Sri Aurobindo Ashram, was inaugurated.

February 29

1896   Morarji Ranchhodji Desai, the fourth prime minister, was born.

MARCH

March 1

1640   British got the permission for a business centre in Madras.

1775   Treaty of Purandhar was signed between Nana Phadnavis and the British.

1908   Tata Iron & Steel Co. was established.

1919   Mahatma Gandhi expressed his desire to start Satyagraha against Rowlatt Act.

1969   The first superfast train Rajdhani Express was introduced between New Delhi and Calcutta.

1985   Estate Duty was withdrawn.

1998   The draft of the ninth Five Year Plan was released.

March 2

1700   Raja Ram died at Singhagarh.

1949   Sarojini Naidu died.

1952   Sindri Fertilizer factory was inaugurated.

1982   Mahatma Gandhi Road Bridge was opened at Patna.

March 3

1707   Prince Muazzam succeeded Aurangzeb as Bahadur Shah 1.

1839   Jamshedji N. Tata was born.

1919   Hari Narayan Apte, the well-known Marathi writer, died.

1983   The seventh Non-Aligned Summit met in New Delhi.

March 4

1788   *Calcutta Gazette,* now known as Gazette of *Government of West Bengal,* was first published.

1858   J. P. Walker sailed from Calcutta with 200 convicts, mostly of Sepoy Mutiny, to start a new settlement in the Andaman Islands.

1879   Bethune College was established to impart higher education to women. It was the first women's college in the British empire outside Great Britain.

1951   The first Asian Games were held in New Delhi.

1961   India's first aircraft carrier *INS Vikrant* was commissioned.

March 5

1699   Maharaja Jai Singh II sat on Amber throne.

1783   Fox's India Bill was presented and it was defeated in the British Parliament in the following year.

1851   Geological Survey of India was established.

1928   Lord S. P. Sinha expired.

1931   Gandhiji ended Civil Disobedience Movement as a sequel to Gandhi-Irwin Pact.

March 6

1508   Humayun was born in Kabul.

1775   Treaty of Surat was signed between Raghunath Rao and the British.

1915   Gandhiji and Rabindranath Tagore met for the first time at Santiniketan during the former's second visit there.

1961   India's first financial daily *The Economic Times* was launched in Bombay by the Times of India group.

1991   Prime Minister Chandra Sekhar resigned.

March 7

1835   Resolution was taken to promote European literature and science in India.

1911   S. H. Vatsyayan, an outstanding Hindi writer, was born.

1961   Govind Ballabh Pant died.

March 8

1534   Bahadur Shah of Gujarat sacked Chittorgarh.

1864   Hari Narayan Apte, a well-known Marathi writer, was born.

1948   Air India International was established.

March 9

1285   Balban's favourite son Muhammad was killed by the Mongol raiders.

1986   The first satellite based telephone communication network ITINET was formally commissioned.

March 10

1922   Gandhiji was arrested for the first time near Sabarmati Ashram.

1985   India won Benson & Hedges World Cricket Championship.

March 11

1399   Timur on his way back recrossed the Indus after ransacking northern India including Delhi.

1689   Shivaji's son Sambhaji was tortured to death by Aurangzeb.

1881   The first statue of an Indian, that of Ramnath Tagore, was publicly installed in Calcutta Town Hall.

1948   The first modern ship *Jala Usha* was launched from Visakhapatnam.

1963   The first passenger locomotive of Chittaranjan Locomotive Works was commissioned.

March 12

1612   Usman Khan Lohani, son of Isa Khan, and the last independent Afghan ruler of Bengal, died of wounds after his defeat in the battle of Nekujyal.

1872   Sher Ali, murderer of Lord Mayo, was hanged.

1930   Gandhiji started his Dandi march from Sabarmati Ashram of Ahmedabad for Salt Satyagraha. He also launched Civil Disobedience Movement asking the people to withhold payment of taxes to the British.

1954   Sahitya Akademi was inaugurated by the Government of India.

1967   Indira Gandhi became the Prime Minister of India for the second time.

1993   Bombay reeled under a series of sixteen RDX bomb blasts.

March 13

1800   Nana Phadnavis died.

1878   Vernacular Press Act was passed and the *Amrita Bazaar Patrika* became an English newspaper the following day.

1892   Bombay-Tansa Water Works was opened.

1940   Michael O'Dwyer, ex-Governor of Punjab, indirectly responsible for Punjab atrocities in 1919, was shot dead in London by Udham Singh alias Muhammad Singh Azad.

1963   Arjuna Award was announced for outstanding performance in various sports.

1989   The foundation stone of the first straw-fired thermal power plant was laid at Jakhari village.

March 14

1931   India's first talkie film 'Alam Ara' was released in Bombay.

March 15

1564   Akbar removed Jeziya tax.

1919   Osmania University of Hyderabad was inaugurated.

1969   Indian Navy's first helicopter squadron was commissioned in Goa.

1988   The first Bharat Bandh after independence was called by eight political parties.

March 16

1846   By the Treaty of Amritsar, Kashmir was granted in subordinate sovereignty to Raja Gulab Singh, the Hindu ruler of Jammu.

1860   Dr W. M. Haffkine was born.

March 17

1527   Rana Sangram Singh I of Mewar attacked Babar at Khanua near Agra and lost. Rana promised not to return to Chittorgarh without a victory.

1769   The East India Company imposed crippling restrictions on weavers of Bengal to destroy textile and 'muslin' industries.

1782   Treaty of Salby was signed between the East India Company represented by Anderson and Scindia on behalf of the Maratha chiefs.

1955   I.S.I. (Certification Marks) Regulation 1955 came into force. Sevagram Ashram of Wardha was closed.

1959   Dalai Lama reached India after fleeing from Tibet.

1988   First remote-sensing satellite IRS IA was successfully launched from Baikanur.

March 18   **ORDNANCE DAY**

1801   The first ordnance factory was established in India.

1915   Defence of India Act was passed.

1919   Rowlatt Act was passed replacing Defence of India Act of 1915 and thereby suppressing civil and political liberties of Indians.

1944   Indian National Army (Azad Hind Fauj) under Netaji Subhas Chandra Bose crossed Burma border into India to liberate our country.

1972   World Book Fair was inaugurated in New Delhi.

March 19

1944   Azad Hind Fauj hoisted the national flag on the Indian mainland in north-eastern India.

1970   First off-shore oil well was inaugurated.

1972   India and Bangladesh signed 25-year Peace and Friendship Pact.

1998   A. B. Vajpayee became the Prime Minister for the second time.

       Veteran CPM leader E.M.S. Namboodiripad expired.

March 20

1351   Muhammad Tughlak Shah II died in Sind.

1602   United East Indies Co. of the Netherlands was formed.

1904   C. F. Andrews arrived in India.

March 21

1791   British Army captured Bangalore from Tipu Sultan.

1836   The first public library was opened in Calcutta by J. H. Stoequeler which ultimately became the National Library.

1858   Sepoy mutineers of Lucknow surrendered.

1867   Bombay's Prarthana Samaj was established.

1887   Manabendra Nath Roy alias Narendra Nath Bhattacharya was born.

1977   Internal Emergency declared on June 25, 1975 was withdrawn.

March 22

1739   Nadir Shah gave the signal of general massacre of Delhi people from Sunheri mosque which continued for 58 days.

1793   Permanent Settlement in Bengal and Bihar was proclaimed by Lord Cornwallis.

1890   Ram Chandra Chatterjee was the first person to make a parachute descent.

1893   Masterda (Surya Sen) of Chittagong Armoury Raid Case was born.

1942   Cripps Mission, under the leadership of Sir Stafford Cripps, arrived. Japanese navy and air force touched Port Blair during the Second World War.

1947   Lord Louis Mountbatten, the last viceroy designate, arrived in India.

1957   National Calendar based on Shaka era was adopted. On this date it was Chaitra 1, 1879 Shaka.

1964   The first Vintage Car Rally was organised at Calcutta.

1969   Indian Petrochemicals Corporation Ltd. was inaugurated as the first government sponsored petrochemicals industry.

2000   INSAT 3B was launched from Kourou.

March 23

1351   Muhammad Tughlak's nephew Feroz Shah Tughlak III was enthroned.

1757   Clive captured Chandernagar from the French.

1910   Ram Manohar Lohia was born.

1931   Bhagat Singh along with Sukhdev and Sivaram Rajguru were hanged for Saunder's murder.

1940   Pakistan resolution was adopted by the Muslim League.

1986   The first Women's Company of Central Reserve Police Force was raised in Durgapur Camp.

March 24

1307   The invincible Devagiri (Daulatabad) fort was for the first time captured by Malik Kafur under Alauddin Khilji.

1855   The first long distance telegraphic message was transmitted from Calcutta to Agra.

1863   Lord Satyendra Prasanna Sinha of Raipur (Birbhum) was born.

1902   Anusilan Samity, a dedicated terrorist organisation, was established in Bengal.

1946   British Cabinet Mission headed by Lord Pethick Lawrence arrived in India.

1947   Lord Mountbatten, the Viceroy of India, was installed.

1977   Morarji Desai became the fourth Prime Minister of India and formed the first non-Congress government at the Centre.

March 25

1788   The first advertisement in an Indian language (Bengali) was published in Calcutta Gazette.

1898   Sister Nivedita was initiated to Brahmacharya by Swami Vivekananda.

1983   The most modern oceanographic research ship of the world *Sagar Kanya* was launched.

1986   Country's first milk special train from Anand arrived at Calcutta.

1989   India's first super-computer US made X-MP-14 was dedicated to the nation.

March 26

1972   The first International Sanskrit Conference was inaugurated by President V. V. Giri.

March 27

1117   Channa Kesava temple of Halebid was consecrated.

1552   Sikh Guru Angad expired.

1977   National Emergency declared on December 3, 1971 was revoked.

March 28

1645   Sikh Guru Har Govind expired.

1914   *S. S. Komagata Maru* sailed from Hong Kong to Vancouver of Canada with 372 youths, mostly Sikhs under Gurjeet Singh's leadership.

1941   Netaji Subhas Chandra Bose reached Berlin after his escape from Calcutta.

March 29

1849   Maharaja Duleep Singh stepped down from his deceased father Ranjit Singh's throne and Punjab was annexed by the East India Co.

1857   The first shot of Sepoy Mutiny was fired by Mangal Pandey in Barrackpore near Calcutta.

1859   Emperor Bahadur Shah II Zafar was found guilty of complicity in Sepoy Mutiny and was exiled to Rangoon.

1914   Mother of Sri Aurobindo Ashram came to India for the first time.

1954   National Gallery of Modern Art was opened in Delhi.

March 30

1949   Rajasthan state was established with Jaipur as its capital.

1992   Satyajit Ray was conferred Honorary Oscar award.

March 31

1774   The first office for postal service was opened.

1867   Prarthana Samaj of Bombay was established.

1921   Indian National Congress flag was adopted.

1959   Dalai Lama was given political asylum.

1964   The electric tram ran for the last time in Bombay.

1980   The last I.C.S officer Nirmal Mukherji retired from service.

APRIL

April 1

1839   Calcutta Medical College Hospital started with 20 beds.

1855   The first Bengali primer *Varnaparichaya* was published by Iswar Chandra Vidyasagar.

1869   Income tax was first introduced.

A new Divorce Act came into operation.

1878   Calcutta Museum was opened to public in its present building.

1882   Postal Savings Bank system was introduced.

1889   Madras Weekly *Hindu* which first appeared on September 20, 1888 was converted into a daily newspaper.

1912   The capital of India was officially shifted from Calcutta to Delhi.

1930   Minimum marriageable age of a girl was fixed at 14 and that of a boy at 18 years.

1933   Indian Air Force took to wings.

1935   Reserve Bank of India came into existence.

Indian Postal Order was introduced.

1936   Orissa was made a new state, separate from Bihar.

1937   Administration of India's provinces under Government of India Act 1935 was enforced.

1949   Institute of Chartered Accountants of India was constituted as a statutory body under a special Act of Parliament.

1954   Subroto Mukherji became the first Indian Air Chief.

       South Point School of Calcutta was founded which in 1988 became the largest school in the world.

1956   Companies Act of 1956 came into force.

1957   Naya Paisa was introduced as the beginning of decimal coinage.

       Postage stamps and sale of postal stationery on decimal coinage were introduced.

1962   Metric weights were fully adopted.

1969   India's first atomic power station at Tarapur became operational.

1976   A separate corporation named Doordarshan was set up for television.

1978   India's sixth Five Year Plan commenced.

1987   The name of Indian Standards Institution was changed to Bureau of Indian Standards.

1990   Gold Control Act was withdrawn.

1992   The eighth Five-Year Plan was launched.

April 2

1679   Jeziya tax, abolished by Akbar, was reimposed on the Hindus by Emperor Aurangzeb.

1720   Peshwa Balaji Viswanath died.

1870   Poona Sarvajanik Sabha was founded with the Chief of Aundh as its first President.

1933   Prince Ranjit Singhji of cricket fame died.

1942   Cripps Proposal was rejected by the Congress.

1970   Meghalaya was inaugurated as an autonomous hill state within the state of Assam.

1997   Sumita Sinha established a record when she allowed a 3,200 kg truck to pass over her.

April 3

1680   Shivaji died at Raigarh fort.

1903   Kamaladevi Chattopadhyay was born.

1914   The first Field-Marshal of India S. H. F. J. Manekshaw was born.

1984   Squadron Leader Rakesh Sharma was the first Indian cosmonaut to go on a space flight in Soviet spacecraft Soyuz T 11.

1987   S. H. Vatsyayan expired.

1999   India launched its first global telecom satellite INSAT 1E.

April 4

1769   Hyder Ali dictated peace term in the first Anglo-Mysore war.

1786   Burke brought forward eleven charges of corruption against Warren Hastings in the British Parliament, to which another eleven were added subsequently.

1858   After a bitter battle with the British troops under Hugh Rose, Rani Lakshmi Bai of Jhansi slipped away from Jhansi to Kalpi and then towards Gwalior.

1904   The famous singer Kundan Lal Saigal was born.

1910   Sri Aurobindo reached Pondicherry which ultimately became his seat of meditation and spiritual centre.

April 5 NATIONAL MARITIME DAY FOR MERCHANT NAVY

1659   Suja was defeated in the battle of Muksudabad.

1919   Modern Indian merchant shipping started with the maiden voyage of 5,940 tonne *Liberty* of Scindia Steam Navigation Co.

1930   Gandhiji with his followers reached Dandi to break the salt law.

1940   C. F. Andrews expired.

1949   Bharat Scouts & Guides was established.

1957   The first communist ministry in a state was installed in Kerala.

1961   The first government sponsored pharmaceutical industry, namely Indian Drugs and Pharmaceutical Ltd., was established.

1964   National Maritime Day for the merchant navy was observed for the first time.

1976   Antiquities and Art Treasures Act of 1972 came into effect.

1979   India's first naval museum was formally opened in Bombay.

1986   Sivanandajhula, the longest suspension bridge at Muni-ki-Reti, was completed.

April 6

1606   Prince Khusru rebelled against his father Jahangir.

1664   Sikh Guru Har Kishan breathed his last.

1919   The first all India Hartal (strike) was called by Gandhiji as a part of Civil Disobedience Movement against Rowlatt Act.

1930   Gandhiji was arrested at 1.10 A.M. for breaking the salt law on the previous day.

1942   Japanese planes bombed India for the first time.

1966   Mihir Sen swam across the Palk Strait.

April 7

1818   Bengal State Prisoners Regulation III of 1818 was introduced by the British for detention and deportation of prisoners without trial. This regulation continued till India's independence in 1947.

1920   The great sitarist Ravi Shankar (Bhattacharya) was born.

1929   The first commercial aviation reached India when London-Cairo service of Imperial Airways of U.K. was extended to Karachi.

April 8

1774   Madhav Rao II was born.

1775   Ordnance Board (parent body of Ordnance Services Corps) was constituted.

1831   Ram Mohan Roy landed in England.

1857   Mangal Pandey, who fired the first shot of Sepoy Mutiny, was hanged.

1894   Bankim Chandra Chattopadhyay died.

April 9

1669   Aurangzeb ordered destruction of all Hindu schools and temples.

1756   Ali Bardi Khan, the Tartar Nawab of Bengal, expired in Murshidabad at the age of 80 and his youngest daughter's son Siraj-ud-daula sat on the throne of Bengal at the age of 20 years.

1965   Fighting broke out between Indian and Pakistani forces in Rann of Kutch.

1984   Capt. H. J. Singh of the Indian Army created a world record by crossing 3,340 mt high Banihal Pass in Kashmir on a hang-glider.

1989   Asia's first fully underground Sanjay Hydel Project was commissioned.

April 10

1875   Arya Samaj was founded by Swami Dayanand Saraswati.

1880   Philanthropist Chirravuri Yagneswara Chintamani was born.

1889   Ram Chandra Chatterjee was the first Indian to ascend in a balloon.

1919   Brig. Gen. R. E. H. Dyer issued the infamous crawling and flogging order in Amritsar.

1982   India's multipurpose satellite INSAT IA was launched.

1995   Morarji Desai expired.

April 11

1290   Emperor Muizuddin Kaikobad was killed in his bed.

1887   Artist Jamini Roy was born.

1930   The new 124-metre span steel-rope bridge of Lachhmanjhula (Rishikesh) was opened to public.

1964   Communist Party of India was split into Communist Party of India and Communist Party of India (Marxist).

1999   Agni II missile was test-fired.

April 12

1621   Sikh Guru Tegh Bahadur was born.

1801   William Carey was appointed professor of Bengali language in Fort William College of Calcutta.

1978   India's first double-decker train Singhagarh Express had her maiden run from Victoria Terminus of Bombay to Pune to coincide with the 125th anniversary of Indian Railways.

April 13   JALLIANWALA BAGH DAY

1699   Foundation of Khalsa sect meaning 'the pure', was made by the tenth Sikh Guru Govind Singh.

1772   Warren Hastings was appointed President of East of India Co's Council in Bengal.

1919   Brig. Gen R. E. H. Dyer with 50 soldiers indiscriminately fired on the political congregation at Jallianwala Bagh killing 379 and injuring 1,208 persons.

April 14   FIRE SERVICES DAY

1563   Sikh Guru Arjun Dev was born.

1659   Dara was finally defeated at Deorai by Aurangzeb in the struggle for Delhi throne.

1891   Great lawyer and Harijan leader B. R. Ambedkar was born.

1944   The ammunition ship *S. S. Fort Stikine* blew up in Victoria Dock of Bombay killing over 1,200 people.

1950   Saint Maharshi Ramana breathed his last.

1962   M. Visveswarayya died.

1989   Capt. Ranjan Roy and his wife Lt. Cdr. Rupali Roy commenced their record-breaking round the world in Maruti car.

April 15

1378   Daud Shah was killed.

1469   Sikh Guru Nanak was born.

1658   In the battle of Dharmat, Raja Jaswant Singh, sent by Dara Sukoh and Shahjahan, was defeated by Aurangzeb.

1895   Shivaji Festival was inaugurated by B.G. Tilak at Raigarh fort.

1948   Himachal Pradesh was formed.

1966   Artist Nandlal Bose died.

1994   India along with 124 other nations signed the General Agreement of Trade and Tariff (GATT).

April 16

1608   William Hawkins met Jahangir.

1853   Indian Railways was inaugurated when the first train left Victoria Terminus station of Bombay for Thane.

1910   Malayala Manorama started a children's page.

April 17

1799   Siege of Srirangapatnam began. It ended with Tipu's death on May 4.

1899   Calcutta got thermal electricity.

1975   India's second president Sarvepalli Radhakrishnan expired.

1977   Swatantra Party merged with Janata Party.

1983   The second Rohini satellite was placed in the near earth orbit by SLV-3 rocket.

April 18

1612   Shahjahan married Mumtaz.

1774   Narayan Rao's 10-day old posthumous son Madhav Rao II was installed as Peshwa as a challenge to Raghoba.

1859   Ramachandra Raghunath Tope alias Tantia Tope of Sepoy Mutiny fame, was hanged.

1898   Damodar Hari Chapekar, the first terrorist of India, went to the gallows for murdering Rand and Ayerest in Pune.

1917   Champaran of Bihar was selected by Gandhiji as his first testing ground of Satyagraha.

1930   Surya Sen alias Masterda and his 62 men of the Indian Republican Army raided Chittagong armoury.

1950   Vinoba Bhave started Bhoodan Movement with 80 acres of land in Pachampalli village of Telengana in Andhra Pradesh.

1971   India's first Jumbo jet Boeing 747 namely Emperor Ashok landed in Bombay.

1978   Sobha Singh, builder of modern New Delhi, died at the age of 90.

1991   Kerala was declared the first fully literate state.

1999   Prime Minister A. B.Vajpayee lost by one vote in Lok Sabha.

April 19

1451   Buhlul Khan Lodi captured Delhi.

1882   Eden (Maternity) Hospital was opened in Calcutta.

1950   Shyama Prasad Mukherji was the first cabinet minister to resign.

1975   India's first satellite Aryabhatta was launched.

April 20

1712   Jahandar Shah sat on Delhi throne.

1960   Air India entered jet age with its first Boeing 707 flight to London.

1971   India won the first ever cricket Test 'Rubber'.

1997   Inder Kumar Gujral became the twelfth Prime Minister.

April 21

1451   Buhlul Khan Lodi sat on Delhi throne.

1526   The first battle of Panipat took place between Ibrahim Lodi and Babar. Ibrahim Lodi was slain on the battlefield.

1720   Baji Rao I succeeded Balaji Viswanath.

1938   Urdu poet Muhammad Iqbal died.

1996   Sanjay Thapar of Indian air force parachuted down to geometric North Pole.

April 22

1921   Netaji Subhas Chandra Bose submitted his resignation from Indian Civil Service for service to the nation instead.

1946   The colour of army uniform was changed from khaki to olive green.

1958   Admiral R. D. Katari became the first Indian Chief of the naval staff.

April 23

1504   Sikh Guru Angad was born.

1774   British Commander Col. Chapman destroyed Rohila forces and captured Rohilakhand.

1795   Warren Hastings was honourably acquitted from all impeachments against him.

1992   Satyajit Ray expired.

April 24

525   B. C. : Jain Saint Mahavira expired.

1858   Kunwar Singh breathed his last.

1921   Mother of Pondicherry Aurobindo Ashram finally settled down in Pondicherry.

1972   Jamini Roy, a noted artist, died.

1974   Ramdhari Singh alias 'Dinkar', the leading Hindi poet, died.

1975   2,500th anniversary of Jain Saint Mahavir's Nirvana was observed.

April 25

1982   The first regular colour telecast started in Delhi.

April 26

1903   Gandhiji started legal practice in Transvaal High Court in South Africa and established British Indian Association there.

1920   The mathematician Srinivas Ramanujam expired.

1975   Parliament passed the bill to make Sikkim a state of India, which was effected on May 16.

1980 Positional Astronomy Centre was established in Calcutta.

1990 V. R. P. Menon established a world record in continuous Disco dancing for 463 hours.

The first indigenously built missile boat 'Vibhuti' was launched.

April 27

1526 Babar was proclaimed Badshah of Delhi.

1606 Prince Khusru, who rebelled on April 6, was captured by Emperor Jahangir.

1705 Wagingera fort fell to Aurangzeb.

1748 Mughal Emperor Muhammad Shah died.

1878 Calcutta University gave the first approval for eligibility of women to university education.

1960 National Defence College was inaugurated in New Delhi.

April 28

1701 John Norris of Britain had an audience with Aurangzeb.

1740 Peshwa Baji Rao I expired on the bank of the Narmada.

1786 Additional charges were put up against Warren Hastings.

1943 Netaji Subhas Chandra Bose changed over from a German submarine to a Japanese submarine near Madagascar on his trip from Germany to Japan.

April 29

1236 Iltutmish died in Delhi.

1639 Foundation of Red Fort of Delhi was laid.

1848 Raja Ravi Verma was born.

1939 Subhas Chandra Bose resigned from Congress.

1954 India recognised Tibet as a region of China.

1979 The respected revolutionary Raja Mahendra Pratap died.

April 30

1030 Sultan Mahmud of Ghazni, who repeatedly plundered India, died in his capital.

1863 The Indian Navy of the East India Company was transferred to the British Admiralty.

1870 Dada Saheb Phalke, the pioneer of Indian cinema, was born.

1896   Anandamoyee Ma was born.

1908   Khudiram Bose and Prafulla Chaki threw bombs in Muzaffurpur with a view to kill magistrate Kingsford. But two innocent ladies Mrs and Miss Kennedy were the victims.

1936   Mahatma Gandhi decided to shift his residence to Sevagram Ashram in Wardha.

1991   A volcano in an uninhabited island Barren of Andaman Group erupted for the first time in this century.

MAY

May 1

Observed as May Day in certain states of India.

1897   Ramakrishna Mission was established by Swami Vivekananda.

1908   Prafulla Kumar Chaki, accomplice of Khudiram Bose of Muzaffurpur Bomb case, committed suicide by his own pistol.

1923   Singaravelu Chettiar first observed May Day in India, in commemoration of May Day in Chicago in 1886.

1926   Jim Corbett killed the man-eating leopard of Rudraprayag which took a toll of 125 lives.

1960   Bombay state was bifurcated into Maharashtra and Gujarat.

1972   All coking coal mines were nationalised.

1973   All non-coking coal mines were nationalised.

May 2

1921   Satyajit Ray was born.

1950   Chandernagar was transferred to Government of India.

1959   The first thermoplastic (polyethylene) plant of Alkali & Chemicals Corporation of India was opened at Rishra.

1968   Public Provident Fund Bill was passed by the Lok Sabha.

May 3

1764   Mir Kasim, the deposed Nawab of Bengal, supported by the Emperor of Delhi attacked Patna. But he lost to the British.

1965   Clive landed in Calcutta for the second time.

1913   The first fully Indian feature film 'Raja Harishchandra' was exhibited in Bombay.

1969 President Zakir Hussain died.

1989 The first 50 kilowatt solar power plant was switched on at Gwal Pahari in Haryana.

May 4   **COAL MINERS' DAY**

1799 Tipu Sultan of Mysore was killed in the battle of Srirangapatnam.

1854 India's first postage stamp was officially issued.

1980 It was declared as the Coal Miners' May.

May 5

1479 The third Sikh Guru Amar Das was born.

1786 Additional charges were put up against Warren Hastings.

1883 Surendra Nath Banerji was the first person to go to prison as a journalist.

1888 The great revolutionary Trailokyanath Chakraborty was born.

1916 Gyani Zail Singh was born.

1984 Phu Dorji was the first Indian to climb Mt. Everest without oxygen.

May 6

1529 Nasrat Shah, the Afghan ruler of Bengal, lost to Babar in a battle on the banks of the Gogra river.

1589 The great singer Mian Tansen expired.

1775 Maharaja Nanda Kumar was arrested.

1861 Motilal Nehru was born.

1944 Gandhiji was released from Aga Khan Palace in Pune, which was his last prison term.

May 7

1834 Kingdom of Coorg was annexed by the East India Company on the plea that Raja Veer Rajendra was a cruel tyrant.

1849 Calcutta Female School (presently Bethune School) was established in Calcutta by Elliot Drinkwater Bethune and Ram Gopal Ghose.

1861 Poet Rabindranath Tagore was born.

1907 The first electric tram car of Bombay came into operation.

1973 Foundation-stone of the new capital of Arunachal Pradesh was laid at Itanagar.

May 8   **WORLD RED CROSS DAY**

Observed as the World Red Cross Day in India, being the birthday of the organisation's founder Jean Henri Durant.

1954   The Government of India decided to integrate Chandernagar (earlier under French possession) with West Bengal.

1963   Centenary of the Indian Red Cross was celebrated.

May 9

1540   Rana Pratap Singh of Mewar was born.

1753   Maharaja Surajmal started plundering Delhi.

1866   The nationalist leader Gopal Krishna Gokhale was born.

1874   The first horse-drawn tramcar started running in Bombay.

1975   First electric typewriter was produced.

1986   Tenzing Norgay expired.

May 10

1526   Babar entered Agra, the then capital of India, after his victory in the first battle of Panipat.

1857   Real outbreak of Sepoy Mutiny occurred in Meerut.

1981   The first night cricket match was played in Bombay.

1993   Santoshi Yadav was the first woman in the world to reach Everest summit twice.

May 11

1857   The Sepoy Mutiny broke out in Delhi.

1951   The new and the ninth Somnath temple of Gujarat was opened by President Rajendra Prasad.

1995   The holy shrine of Nooruddin Noorani of Charar-e-Sharif in Kashmir was burnt down by the terrorists,

1998   India conducted three nuclear explosions including one hydrogen bomb.

2000   India's population reached one billion mark as per the population clock.

May 12

1459   Jodhpur was founded by Rao Jodha.

1660   Suja left Bengal for Arakan.

1666 Shivaji arrived at Agra to present himself to Aurangzeb as a part of Purandhar Treaty signed on September 9, 1665.

1827 The government notification on palanquin bearers led to the first large-scale strike on record in Calcutta.

1915 Revolutionary Rash Behari Bose left India for good on the Japanese steamer *Sanuki Maru,* under the assumed name P. N. Tagore.

May 13

1646 Red Fort of Delhi of Emperor Shahjahan was completed.

1791 Battle of Arikera took place and Lord Cornwallis had to retreat back to Madras.

1905 President Fakhruddin Ali Ahmed was born.

1914 *S. S. Komagata Maru* reached Vancouver.

1952 Free India's first Parliament began.

1962 S. Radhakrishnan became the second President of India.

1967 Zakir Hussain became the third President of India.

1978 India's first flagship *INS Delhi* was formally decommissioned.

2000 Miss Lara Dutta was crowned Miss Universe.

May 14

1960 Air India crossed the Atlantic to New York.

May 15

1242 Delhi Sultan Muizuddin Behram Shah's army revolted and put the Sultan to death.

1817 Devendranath Tagore was born.

1873 The resolution was taken in England to dissolve the East India Company on and from June 1,1874.

1878 Young rebels of Brahmo Samaj came out and started Sadharan Brahmo Samaj.

1958 The Gift Tax Act came into force.

1993 Field Marshal K. M. Cariappa expired.

May 16

1911 Tallah water tank of Calcutta, the world's largest overhead water tank, was commissioned.

1960 International Telex Service was inaugurated between India and U.K.

1975   Sikkim lost its independent statehood when it integrated with India as its 22nd state.

1996   Atal Behari Vajpayee took oath as the tenth Prime Minister.

May 17

1498   Vasco da Gama anchored for the first time near Calicut.

1540   Sher Shah defeated Humayun at Hardoi which is known as battle of Kanauj.

1697   The worst desecration of Jagannath temple of Puri took place.

1775   The battle of Arras took place between the British under Col. Keating and the Marathas.

1857   Bahadur Shah II was declared as the independent Mughal Emperor.

1949   India decided to remain within the Commonwealth of Nations.

1976   Four Indians successfully skied down the slopes of Trishul peak and put India on top of the ski map of the world.

May 18

1775   Warren Hastings predicted Nanda Kumar's death sentence.

1912   R.G. Torney's short feature film 'Pundalik' was released at Coronation Cinematograph in Bombay.

1934   Charan Kabi Mukunda Das died.

1974   India's first nuclear detonation was effected undergound in Pokhran in Rajasthan desert.

May 19

1904   Jamshedji N. Tata died.

1913   President Neelam Sanjiva Reddy was born.

1971   The first submarine base of the Indian Navy named Vir Bahu was commissioned at Visakhapatnam.

May 20

1378   Bahmani Sultan Daud Shah was murdered.

1421   Khizr Khan, the first Sayyid ruler of Delhi, expired.

1740   Ali Bardi Khan ousted his brother Sarfaraj in the battle of Giria.

1932   Freedom fighter Bipin Chandra Pal died.

1965   The first Indian team under Commander M. S. Kohli reached Mt. Everest summit.

1972 The foundation-stone of the second Howrah bridge was laid by Indira Gandhi.

1998 Multibarrel rocket system Pinaka was test-fired.

May 21

1855 Bhabatarini Kali temple of Dakshineswar was consecrated by Rani Rasmoni.

1929 India's first air cargo service started between Calcutta and Bagdogra.

1935 Quetta was devastated by an earthquake.

1975 Farakka feeder canal (41.6 km long) connecting the Bhagirathi was formally opened.

1991 Rajiv Gandhi was killed in a bomb explosion.

1994 Sushmita Sen was crowned as Miss Universe at Manila.

May 22

1498 Vasco da Gama met Zamorin of Calicut for the first time.

1545 Sher Shah died of an explosion.

1772 Ram Mohan Roy was born.

1936 Lord Brabourne laid the foundation of the famous Brabourne Stadium of Bombay, the first real stadium in India.

1963 India's first glider Rohini was airborne.

1988 India successfully test-fired Agni, an intermediate range ballistic missile.

May 23

1805 By an order of the Governor General Lord Wellesley a permanent provision was made for the Mughal emperor of Delhi.

1984 Bachendri Pal was the first Indian woman to reach the summit of Mt. Everest.

May 24

1875 Syed Ahmed Khan established Muhammedan Anglo-Oriental School in Aligarh—later known as Aligarh Muslim University in 1920.

1956 2,500th birth anniversary of Lord Buddha was observed.

1960 Dr Miss I. S. Schrudder, the founder of Vellore hospital, expired.

1975 The last smallpox case was detected.

May 25

1611 Jahangir married Meherunissa, who was later named Noor Jahan.

1877 In a great sea tragedy, a passenger steamer *Sir John Lawrence* perished off Orissa coast in a cyclone with 732 passengers.

1886 Revolutionary Rash Behari Bose was born.

1899 Rebel Bengali poet Kazi Nazrul Islam was born.

1924 Asutosh Mukherji expired.

May 26

1739 Afghanistan was severed from India as a result of the treaty between the Mughal Emperor Muhammad Shah and Nadir Shah of Iran.

1957 Janta Insurance Policy was launched in Bombay.

1984 The first Grand Himalayan World Hang-gliding Rally was inaugurated.

1999 ISRO successfully put three satellites into orbit – Indian, German and South Korean.

Sourav Ganguly and Rahul Dravid created a world record of 318 run partnership in one day cricket.

May 27

1951 Taraporewala Aquarium of Bombay was inaugurated.

1957 Copyright Bill was passed; effective from January 21, 1958.

1964 Jawaharlal Nehru, the first Prime Minister of India, expired.

May 28

1414 Khizr Khan captured the throne of Delhi and started Sayyid dynasty.

1572 Rana Pratap Singh ascended the throne of Mewar.

1883 V. D. Savarkar was born.

1970 All India Trade Union Congress formally split.

1989 Marathakavalli David was ordained the first woman Christian priest in India and the second in the world.

1996 Prime Minister A. B. Vajpayee resigned.

May 29

1658 In the battle of Samugarh Aurangzeb defeated Dara Shikoh in the struggle for Delhi throne.

1947   Indian Standards Institution was established.

1953   Sherpa Tenzing Norgay and Edmund Hillary of New Zealand reached the summit of Mt. Everest for the first time in history.

1968   Dara Singh won the world championship title in wrestling.

1977   National Professor Suniti Kumar Chatterji passed away.

May 30

1606   Sikh Guru Arjun Dev died of torture under order from Mughal Emperor Jahangir.

1867   Maulana Muhammad Qasim Nanantawi established Dar-ul-Uloom (House of Learning) at Deoband in U.P.

1919   Poet Rabindranath Tagore renunciated his Knighthood (title Sir) as a protest against Jallianwala Bagh massacre by the British.

1955   N. M. Joshi expired.

1987   Goa became the 25th full-fledged state of the Indian Union.

May 31

1756   Jose Custodio Faria, alias Abbe Faria, the Goan scientist revolutionary, was born.

1818   The first vernacular newspaper *Samachar Darpan* was published.

1977   The first Indian Army team climbed the Kanchenjunga.

JUNE

June 1

1819   Serampore College was established in Bengal.

1835   Calcutta Medical College started functioning fully.

1874   The East India Company was dissolved.

1930   India's first deluxe train Deccan Queen was introduced between Bombay V.T. and Pune.

1944   M.V. Dhurandhar, master painter of Maharashtra, died.

1955   Untouchability (Offence) Act came into force.

1964   Naya Paisa became Paisa.

1970   Monopolies and Restrictive Trade Practices Act passed in 1969 came into force.

1996   H. D. Devegowda became the eleventh Prime Minister of India. President Sanjive Reddy expired.

June 2

1908   Sri Aurobindo was arrested in connection with Manicktola Bomb Case.

1947   Lord Louis Mountbatten announced partition of India.

June 3

1901   Mahakavi G. Sankara Kurup, the first winner of Jnanpith award, was born.

1915   Rabindranath Tagore was conferred Knighthood (title Sir) by the British government.

1947   Indian political leaders accepted partition of India as suggested by the British.

1972   The first modern warship *Nilgiri,* built in Mazagaon Dock of Bombay, was commissioned by Prime Minister Indira Gandhi.

1985   Government of India switched over to 5-day working week.

June 4

1958   Three-men mountaineering team climbed 7,011 mt high Mt. Trishul peak in Garhwal range.

1959   C. Rajagopalachari announced formation of Swatantra Party.

1997   Telecom satellite 2D went into orbit.

June 5

1659   Formal enthronement of Aurangzeb took place in Delhi.

1877   The Malayalam poet Ulloor S. Parameswara Iyer was born.

1879   Narayan Malhar Joshi, the father of Indian Trade Union movement, was born.

1984   Under Operation Blue Star the Indian Army entered into the precinct of the Golden Temple of Amritsar.

June 6

1596   Sikh Guru Har Gobind was born.

1674   Shivaji was crowned in Raigarh fort and took the title Chhatrapati.

1966   The rupee was devalued.

1981   In a railway accident nearly 500 passengers had a watery grave.

1999   Leander Paes and Mahesh Bhupathi was the first Indian pair to win a tennis Grand Slam.

June 7

1539 Humayun was defeated by Sher Shah in the battle of Chausa near Buxar.

1631 Mumtaz Begum of Taj Mahal fame died at Burhanpur at the age of 39 years during her fourteenth childbirth.

1975 National Film Award was converted into National Film Festival with lotus i.e. Kamal as its symbol.

1979 India's second satellite Bhaskara I was launched from Bears Lake in U.S.S.R.

1989 Five-year old Sheetal Pandya covered a distance of 1,600 km on roller skating, starting on April 18.

1997 Mahesh Bhupati was the first Indian to win a tennis Grand Slam title as an individual.

June 8

1658 Agra fort surrendered to Aurangzeb and Emperor Shahjahan was imprisoned for the rest of his life.

1707 Prince Muazzam (Shah Alam) won the battle of succession against Prince Azam at Jajau near Agra.

1936 India's civil radio network took the name All India Radio, i.e., AIR.

1948 India-U.K. air service was inaugurated by Air-India which was India's first international air service.

June 9

1659 Baluchi chief of Dadar, Jiwan Khan, treacherously handed over Dara Shikoh to Aurangzeb.

1964 Lal Bahadur Shastri became the Prime Minister of India.

June 10

1246 Sultan Alauddin Masud Shah of Delhi was deposed.

1246 Nasiruddin Muhammad Shah I sat on Delhi throne.

1966 Production of MIG (Russian) air force plane started at Nasik.

1972 The first fully air-conditioned luxury-cum-cargo boat *Harshavardhana* was launched at Mazagaon Dock, Bombay.

1999 Nedunbassery, a private international airport, became operational.

June 11

1964   Nehru's ashes, as per his own wish, were strewn all over the country.

June 12

1972   D.G. Tendulkar died. He was the author of monumental eight volume biography of Mahatma Gandhi.

June 13

1290   Khilji chief Jalal-ud-din Feroz Shah ascended the throne of Delhi and that was the end of Slave dynasty.

1731   Swedish East India Co. was formed.

1757   Robert Clive started his march for Murshidabad with 1,000 Europeans, 2,000 Indian troops and 8 pieces of cannon to fight Siraj-ud-daula.

1940   Udham Singh was hanged in London for the murder of Michael O'Dwyer, who happened to be the Governor of Punjab during the dark days of Jallianwala Bagh tragedy.

1943   Netaji Subhas Chandra Bose arrived at Tokyo from Germany.

June 14

1905   The famous classical musician Hirabai Barodekar was born.

1909   E. M. S. Namboodiripad was born in Palghat in Kerala.

1945   Viceroy Lord Wavell broadcast the desire to meet India's top political leaders in Shimla on June 25 by releasing all political leaders in the meantime.

June 15

1908   Calcutta Stock Exchange was opened.

June 16

1925   Nationalist leader Chitta Ranjan Das died.

June 17

1756   Nawab Siraj-ud-daula attacked Calcutta with 50,000 soldiers.

1757   Clive reached Katwa and captured the fort on his way to attack Murshidabad.

1917   Mahatma Gandhi made Hriday Kunj his home in Sabarmati Ashram.

1928   Pandit Gopa Bandhu Das of Orissa died.

June 18

1576   The great battle of Haldighati took place between Rana Pratap and Akbar.

1758   French General Bussy took leave of Nizam Salabat Jung which marked the end of French prosperity in India.

1858   Rani Lakshmibai of Jhansi died in the battlefield near Gwalior while fighting the British.

1946   The first Satyagraha Movement of Goa was launched for its liberation from the Portuguese.

1956   Hindu Succession Act was passed.

1987   M. S. Swaminathan got the first World Food Prize.

June 19

1716   Banda Bahadur was tortured to death by Farrukhisyar.

1949   People of Chandernagar, the French Indian settlement, decided by plebiscite in favour of settlement's merger with the Indian Union.

1981   India successfully launched its geo-stationary satellite APPLE.

1987   Orthinologist Salim Ali died.

June 20

712   Muhammad Bin Quasim of Arabia attacked Rawar in Sind and killed its Hindu King Dahir.

1858   Gwalior fell to the British and thereby Sepoy Mutiny virtually ended.

1873   Y. M. C. A. was established in India.

1916   S. N. D. T. Women's University was established at Pune.

June 21

1756   Holwell, in command of British troops in Calcutta, surrendered to Siraj-ud-daula. The controversial Black-hole Tragedy that night took a toll of 123 British prisoners.

1862   Gnanendra Mohan Tagore was the first Indian to pass Barrister-at-Law from Lincoln's Inn.

1948   C. Rajagopalachari was appointed as the last Governor General of India.

1991   P. V. Narasimha Rao took oath as the ninth Prime Minister.

June 22

1555   Humayun declared Akbar as his heir-apparent after Humayun's victory at Sirhind against Sikandar Suri.

1897   Damodar Hari Chapekar shot at Rand and Ayerest at Pune, when both died. This was the first terrorist act in India.

1939   Subhas Chandras Bose formed Forward Bloc after separating from the Indian National Congress.

1948   The British king relinquished his title 'Emperor of India.'

June 23

1661   On the occasion of King Charles II's marriage to the Princess of Portugal, the British got Bombay from Portugal as a dowry.

1757   Battle of Plassey took place. Siraj-ud-daula attacked the British under Clive, lost the battle and fled on a camel's back.

1761   Peshwa Balaji Baji Rao, the Maratha ruler, died a broken-hearted man after losing the third battle of Panipat.

1810   Bombay's Duncan Dock was completed.

1953   Shyama Prasad Mukherji died as a prisoner in Kashmir.

1980   Sanjay Gandhi, Indira Gandhi's second son, died in a plane crash.

1985   Air-India's Jumbo jet Kanishka exploded over the Atlantic Ocean when 329 people on board perished.

June 24

1206   Qutub-ud-din Aibek was crowned at Lahore.

1763   Murshidabad was captured by the British for the second time and Mir Zafar was put on the throne again.

1869   Damodar Hari Chapekar, virtually the first terrorist of India, was born.

1961   The first India-made supersonic fighter HF 24 took to air.

1963   National Telex Service was introduced by the Post & Telegraph Department.

1980   President V. V. Giri expired.

1986   Government of India approved maternity benefits for unwed mothers as well.

June 25

1529   Babar returned to his capital Agra after his victory in Bengal.

1931   Prime Minister V.P. Singh was born.

1932   India played first official cricket Test match at Lords in U.K.

1945   Lord Wavell, Viceroy of India, met India's top political leaders to find out a solution to political uneasiness.

1975   Internal Emergency was signed by President Fakhruddin Ali Ahmed and it was proclaimed in the early hours of the next day by Prime Minister Indira Gandhi.

1983   India became Prudential World Cup Champion in cricket.

June 26

1980   Oil was struck in the Bay of Bengal.

1982   Air India's first Boeing 'Gaurishankar' crashed at Bombay.

June 27

1839   Maharaja Ranjit Singh of Punjab died.

1964   Teen Murti House became Nehru Memorial Museum.

1967   The first India-made passenger plane Avro HS 748 was handed over to Indian Airlines.

June 28

1838   Bankim Chandra Chattopadhyay was born.

1921   Prime Minister Narasimha Rao was born.

1972   Prof. P. C. Mahalanobis, the eminent statistician, died.

1981   China opened the land route to Kailash and Mansarovar.

June 29

1757   Clive entered Murshidabad and put Mir Zafar on the throne as Nawab of Bengal, Bihar and Assam.

1864   Ashutosh Mukherji of Calcutta University fame was born.

1873   Poet Michael Madhusudan Dutta died.

1893   Prof. Prasanta Chandra Mahalanobis was born.

June 30

1799   Krishna Raja Udiyar was reinstated in Mysore.

1855   Armed Santhals of Bhognadighi in Bengal revolted.

1917   Dadabhai Naoroji breathed his last.

1978   Independent India's first flagship *INS Delhi*, decommissioned on May 13, lowered her ensign and commissioning pennant.

JULY

July 1

1781 Battle of Porto Novo took place between Hyder Ali and the British.

1852 First postage stamp was introduced in Sind and was known as Scinde Dawk.

1862 Calcutta High Court was inaugurated.

1879 Postcard was introduced in India.

1882 Bidhan Chandra Roy was born.

1909 William Hurt Curzon Wyllie, Political A.D.C in India Office of London, and Dr Lalkala were shot dead at the Imperial Institute of London by an Indian revolutionary Madan Lal Dhingra.

1941 C.Y. Chintamani died.

1955 Imperial Bank of India was nationalised and renamed State Bank of India.

1962 Bidhan Chandra Roy expired.

1964 Industrial Development Bank of India was established.

1975 Prime Minister Indira Gandhi announced 20-point Programme for national emancipation.

1997 India's first Science City was opened in Calcutta.

July 2

1757 Siraj-ud-daula was stabbed to death by Muhammad Beg.

1916 Zoological Survey of India was established.

1972 Prime Minister Indira Gandhi and President Zulfikar Ali Bhutto of Pakistan signed the Shimla Agreement.

1983 The first unit of the indigenously built nuclear power station was commissioned at Kalpakkam near Madras.

July 3

1760 Maratha army captured Delhi.

1879 Basudev Balwant Phadke was arrested.

1979 The actual work of the second Howrah bridge, cable-stayed type, the first of its kind in India and of the longest span in the world, started.

July 4

1760   Mir Zafar's son Miran, despised as a monster, was killed by a thunderbolt on the bank of the Gandak near Patna.

1789   The East India Company signed a treaty with the Nizam and Peshwa against Tipu.

1881   The so-called Toy Train between Siliguri and Darjeeling started operating.

1902   Swami Vivekananda expired.

1986   Sunil Gavaskar made the record-breaking 115th Test appearance in cricket.

1999   Leander Paes and Mahesh Bhupathi won Wimbledon Doubles tennis title.

July 5

1658   Murad was imprisoned by Aurangzeb.

1947   India Independence Act 1947 was introduced in the British Parliament and received Royal assent on July 18.

1948   *HMS Achilles* was acquired by the Indian Navy and was recommissioned as India's flagship *HMIS Delhi*.

1968   The first submarine of India arrived from Soviet Russia.

1981   Rajan Mahadevan made a world record by reciting 31,811 digits of value of 'pi' from memory.

1998   Anti-tank missile Nag was test-fired.

Dolphin City was inaugurated in Mahabalipuram.

July 6

1787   Indian Botanic Garden was established in Sibpur.

1837   R. G. Bhandarkar was born.

1901   Shyama Prasad Mukherji was born.

1944   For the first time Gandhiji was addressed as 'Father of the Nation' by Netaji.

1959   The first successful open-heart surgery was performed in Vellore hospital.

July 7

1763   Mir Zafar was reinstated as the Nawab of Bengal.

1799   Ranjit Singh captured Lahore.

1896   Cinema first came to India when a team of Lumiere agents of France showed cinematographic films in Watson Hotel in Bombay.

1943   Azad Hind Fauj was handed over to Netaji Subhas Chandra Bose by Rash Behari Bose.

1948   Damodar Valley Corporation was formed.

1998   In one-day cricket Sourav Ganguly and Sachin Tendulkar created a world record of opening partnership of 252 runs.

July 8

1858   After the fall of Gwalior fort on June 20, Sepoy Mutiny virtually ended and Lord Canning declared peace.

1918   Montague-Chelmsford Report on reforms of the Indian constitution was published.

1954   Prime Minister Jawaharlal Nehru opened the world's largest canal of Bhakra-Nangal Hydroelectric Project in Punjab.

July 9

1533   Chaitanya Dev breathed his last.

1875   Bombay Stock Exchange was established.

1951   The first Five-Year Plan (1951-56) was published.

1969   Lion was chosen National Animal of India by the Board of Wildlife.

July 10

1965   The first N.C.C. College for women was inaugurated at Gwalior.

July 11

1630   The first foreign lady to come to Calcutta namely Begum Rezabeebeh Sookeas expired.

1832   British Parliament rejected the appeal of the puritan Hindus against the abolition of Sati.

1889   Sova Bazar Club was the first Indian football team to play a tournament. It was against St. Xaviers in Trades Cup.

July 12

1489   Buhlul Khan Lodi of Delhi died.

1674   Shivaji signed a treaty of friendship with the East India Co.

1823   The first India built steamship *Diana* was launched at Calcutta.

July 13

1830   The embryo of the legendary institution Scottish Church College was implanted by Alexander Duff and Ram Mohan Roy. It started with only five pupils.

1905   The suggestion of boycott of British goods was first advocated by *Sanjibani*, a Bengali weekly of Calcutta.

1929   Jatindra Nath Das commenced his historic hunger-strike.

1977   Civil honours like Bharat Ratna, Padma Vibhushan, etc. introduced in 1954 by the Government of India were withdrawn.

July 14

1636   Aurangzeb was appointed the Viceroy of Deccan by Shahjahan.

1656   Sikh Guru Har Kishan was born.

July 15

1788   Ghulam Kadir, the infamous son of Zabita Khan, captured Delhi.

1926   The first motorbus service started in Bombay.

1955   President Rajendra Prasad announced the conferment of highest national honour 'Bharat Ratna' on Prime Minister Jawaharlal Nehru.

1986   Sandhya Agarwal created a world record by scoring 190 runs in women's cricket Test match.

July 16

1856   Remarriage of Hindu widows was legalised.

1905   Resolution on boycott of British Goods was first taken in a public meeting at Bagerhat, now in Bangladesh.

1981   India's first geo-stationary satellite APPLE was put into the parking slot of 102^0 East longitude.

July 17

1489   Nizam Khan was proclaimed Sultan of Delhi under the title Sikandar Shah II Lodi.

1682   By virtue of an order of the East India Co. issued on November 14, 1681 Bengal was made into a separate Presidency, independent of Madras.

1948   Women were made eligible for any public service including Indian Administrative Service and Indian Police Service.

1950 Country's first air-crash of a passenger plane took place in Pathankot.

July 18

1857 Bombay University was established.

1947 India Independence Act 1947 got the Royal assent and came into force.

1980 Wholly India-built Satellite Launch Vehicle SLV-3 put ROHINI RH 75, a 35 kg satellite, in a near earth orbit.

The first colour telecast was made from Madras TV Centre and was watched simultaneously in Madras and Delhi.

July 19

1763 Mir Kasim was badly defeated by the British troops at Katwa.

1918 Sidney Rowlatt submitted a report on Indian administration advocating rigorous steps to curb political activities.

1969 The Government of India nationalised fourteen major Indian banks.

1974 Udham Singh's ashes were brought from London to New Delhi.

July 20

1296 Alauddin Khilji proclaimed himself as the Sultan of Delhi after assassinating Jalaluddin Khilji.

1761 Madhav Rao I became the Peshwa.

1905 First partition of Bengal was approved in London by the Secretary of State of India.

July 21

1658 Aurangzeb celebrated his informal enthronement.

1883 Star Theatre, India's first public theatre hall, opened in Calcutta.

1906 W. C. Bonerjee died.

1920 Sarada Ma, consort of Shri Ramakrishna Paramahansa Dev, expired.

1947 National Flag was adopted by the Constituent Assembly.

1963 Kashi Vidyapith was raised to the status of a university.

July 22

1702 The two rival East India Companies, old and new, amalgamated as United Company of Merchants Trading to the East Indies, and got the Royal seal in Britain.

1918 India's first ace pilot Indra Lal Roy was killed in an air-battle with German planes over London.

1933 Nationalist leader Jatindra Mohan Sen Gupta died.

1981 India's first geo-stationary satellite APPLE started functioning.

July 23

1555 Humayun entered Delhi after his victory over Sikandar Suri at Sirhind.

1856 Bal Gangadhar Tilak was born.

1906 Chandrasekhar Azad, the famous revolutionary of Hindustan Republican Army, was born.

1927 Regular broadcasting first started in Bombay.

July 24

1890 Sova Bazar Club was the first Indian team to beat an English football team East Surrey.

1932 Ramakrishna Mission Seva Pratisthan was established.

1989 Most of the opposition members of the Lok Sabha resigned, which was accepted.

2000 S. Vijaylakshmi became the first woman Grand Master in chess.

July 25

1813 The first boat race took place in Calcutta.

1955 It was announced in the Lok Sabha that the Government of India has asked the Portuguese Government to close its legation in New Delhi.

1977 Neelam Sanjiva Reddy became the sixth President of India.

1982 Zail Singh was sworn in as the seventh President of India.

1987 Rangaswamy Venkataraman was sworn in as the eighth President.

1992 S. D. Sharma became the ninth President of India.

1997 K. R. Narayanan became the tenth President of India.

July 26

1614 Jahangir received the Rana of Mewar with exceptional courtesies.

1844 Gooroodas Banerjee was born.

1876 Indian Association, based on a more democratic principles, was inaugurated in Calcutta.

July 27

1889 British India Committee, Branch of Indian National Congress, was opened in London under Dadabhai Naoroji, William Wedderburn, W. S. Caine and William Digby.

1897 Bal Gangadhar Tilak was arrested for the first time.

1972 Charu Majumdar, who masterminded Naxalite Movement, died in prison.

1994 Jaspal Rana won World Shooting Championship.

July 28

1914 *S.S. Komagata Maru* was forced to leave Vancouver and sailed for India.

1979 Charan Singh became the fifth Prime Minister of India.

July 29

1748 The first troops of British army landed in India to assist the East India Company, in fighting the French.

1785 Wintle ascended in a balloon for the first time in this country.

1876 Science Association was established.

1891 Ishwar Chandra Vidyasagar died.

1911 Mohan Bagan won the IFA shield for the first time.

1980 India regained the gold medal in hockey in Moscow Olympic.

1982 Dilip Bose was elected in the management of Davis Cup Nations.

1983 The first pilotless plane MINI was successfully tested.

2000 Seema Bhadoria pulled a plane weighing 3,390 kg by her teeth.

July 30

1886 S. Muthulakshmi Reddi was born.

1957 Export Risk Insurance Corporation of India (Private) Ltd. was formed.

July 31

1924 Madras Presidency Club pioneered radio broadcasting.

1933 Gandhiji left Sabarmati Ashram for good.

1948 Calcutta State Transport Corporation was established and was the first road transport system of any state government.

1980 The superstar playback singer of Hindi films Md. Rafi died.

1993 The first floating maritime museum was inaugurated in Calcutta.

AUGUST

August 1

1672 English laws were introduced and Court of Judicature was set up as directed by the Company.

1846 Dwarkanath Tagore died in London.

1899 Kamala Nehru was born.

1916 Annie Besant started the Home Rule League.

1920 Bal Gangadhar Tilak expired early in the morning.

Mahatma Gandhi renounced the Kaiser-e-Hind medal vested upon him by the Viceroy in 1915.

Gandhiji's Non-Cooperation Movement formally started.

1953 All airlines in India were nationalised by an act of Parliament known as the Air Corporation Act.

1957 National Book Trust was set up.

1975 Durba Banerjee was the first professional lady pilot in the world to command a commercial passenger flight.

1999 Nirad C. Chaudhuri expired.

August 2

1763 After the capture of Murshidabad, the British troops fought with Mir Kasim at Giria. Mir Kasim was defeated again.

1858 Parliament passed the bill to take over the administration of India from the East India Company by the British crown. The title Viceroy was introduced for the supreme representative of British Government in India.

1970 India's first woman career-diplomat Muthamma Chothivia Beliappa was appointed as the Ambassador to Hungary.

1999 Brahmaputra Mail train collided head-on with Awadh-Assam Express at full speed at Ghaisal while running on the same line in opposite directions.

August 3

1780 Gwalior was captured by Captain Bruce under Major Popham.

1886 Maithili Sharan Gupta, the Hindi scholar, was born.

August 4

1845   Pherozshah Merwanji Mehta, a great Indian lawyer and social worker, was born.

1935   Govt. of India Act of 1935 got the Royal assent.

1956   India's first nuclear research reactor Apsara was commissioned.

1967   Nagarjunasagar Dam, the world's longest masonry dam, was commissioned.

August 5

1775   Maharaja Nandakumar was hanged in Calcutta. It happened to be the last hanging for forgery by the British in India.

1991   Justice Leila Seth became the first woman Chief Justice of a High Court.

August 6

1862   Madras High Court was inaugurated.

1906   Chitta Ranjan Das and some other Congress leaders published the newspaper *Vande Mataram*.

1925   Surendra Nath Banerji died.

1986   India's first scientifically documented test-tube baby was born.

August 7

1871   Abanindranath Tagore was born.

1905   Indian National Congress declared boycott of British goods.

1941   Rabindranath Tagore breathed his last.

1985   Geet Sethi became the third Indian to be the World Amateur Billiards Champion.

August 8

1942   Quit India resolution was passed by the Indian National Congress in its Bombay session.

1967   Central Government, for the first time since independence, suffered a token defeat in the Lok Sabha.

August 9

1683   By a charter, the British Crown gave the power to the East India Company to declare and make war and peace in Asia.

1788   Ghulam Kadir blinded Delhi Emperor Shah Alam II with his own dagger.

1925   Members of Hindustan Socialist Republican Association looted the government treasury from the mail train near Kakori, about 22 km from Lucknow.

1942   Quit India Movement started on Gandhiji's Do or Die call on August 8 in Bombay.

1969   The name of Ochterlony Monument of Calcutta was changed to Shahid Minar.

1970   Trailokyanath Chakraborty, a freedom fighter died. He spent 30 years of his life in prison – probably the longest prison term suffered by any freedom fighter.

1971   India and U.S.S.R signed a 20-year Treaty of Peace, Friendship and Cooperation.

August 10

1860   Vishnu Narayan Bhatkhande was born.

1894   President V.V. Giri was born.

1979   Satellite Launching Vehicle SLV-3 was launched.

August 11

1347   Alauddin Hasan Gangu assumed royalty and founded Bahmani dynasty.

1908   Khudiram Bose was hanged at the age of 19 years.

August 12

1602   Abul Fazl, Akbar's minister, was murdered at the instigation of Salim Mirza, later Emperor Jahangir.

1765   Mughal emperor conferred Diwani of Bengal, Bihar and Orissa on the East India Company. This action was an important event in the political and constitutional history of British India.

1919   Nuclear scientist Vikram Ambalal Sarabhai was born.

August 13

1784   Pitt's India Bill was introduced in the British Parliament for improvement of the administration in India.

1891   The three great defenders of Manipur, Senapati Tikendrajit Singh, his brother Agnesh Sena and General Thangal were hanged on their own soil by the British.

1951   The first aircraft designed and manufactured in India namely Hindustan Trainer 2 or HT2 had its maiden flight.

1956   Lok Sabha passed the National Highways Bill.

August 14

1862   Bombay High Court was inaugurated.

1947   India was partitioned into India and Pakistan.

1988   Morarji Desai was conferred Nishan-e-Pakistan, the highest civil honour of Pakistan.

August 15   INDEPENDENCE DAY

1772   The East India Company took the decision for separate civil and criminal courts in districts.

1854   East India Railway ran its first passenger train from Calcutta to Hooghly, a distance of 37 km. But it was officially inaugurated in 1855.

1872   Sri Aurobindo was born.

1947   India after partition was declared independent of the British rule.

Defence gallantry awards – Param Vir Chakra, Mahavir Chakra and Vir Chakra were instituted.

Jawaharlal Nehru was sworn in as the first Prime Minister of free India after partition.

1972   Postal Index Number, i.e. PIN code, was introduced.

1982   Nationwide colour telecasting and National Programme of TV was inaugurated at Delhi.

1990   The medium range land-to-air missile *Akash* was successfully launched.

August 16

1886   Ramakrishna Paramahansa Dev expired in the early hours of the morning.

1946   Muslim League observed Direct Action Day which turned into a communal riot resulting in Great Calcutta Killing with official figures about 5,000 killed and 15,000 injured.

August 17

1780   Philip Francis and Warren Hastings fought a gun duel. Francis was shot but survived. Hastings escaped unhurt.

1909   Madan Lal Dhingra was hanged in Pentonville prison for Wyllie and Lalkaka murders.

1947   After independence of India the first contingent of British troops sailed for home.

August 18

1800 Fort William College was established at Calcutta by Lord Wellesley.

1872 Pandit Vishnu Digambar, a blind musician revolutionary of Maharashtra, was born.

1900 Vijayalakshmi Pandit was born.

1945 Netaji Subhas Chandra Bose was reported to be seriously injured and badly burnt in a plane crash in Taihoku airport in Taiwan and probably expired between 8 and 9 P.M. in the nearby Japanese military hospital.

1951 Indian Institute of Technology was opened in Kharagpur.

August 19

1600 Ahmadnagar was captured by Akbar.

1666 Shivaji escaped in a fruit basket from Aurangzeb's internment in Agra.

1757 The first rupee coin of the East India Company was minted in Calcutta.

1918 President Shankar Dayal Sharma was born.

1939 Foundation-stone of Mahajati Sadan of Subhas Chandra Bose's conception was laid in Calcutta by Rabindranath Tagore.

1949 Bhubaneswar became the capital of Orissa.

August 20

1828 The first session of Ram Mohan Roy's Brahmo Samaj was held in Calcutta.

1897 Ronald Ross discovered malaria parasites in anopheles mosquito while working in Presidency General Hospital, now SSKM Hospital, in Calcutta.

1917 British Parliament declared the policy of gradual realisation of responsible government of India.

1921 Mopla uprising started in Malabar region of Kerala.

1944 Prime Minister Rajiv Gandhi was born.

1979 Prime Minister Charan Singh resigned only after 23 days of assumption of office of prime minister.

1995 In a major railway accident Purusattam Express and Kalindi Express collided.

August 21

1790　Dindigul was captured by the British troops under General Meadows.

1931　Pandit Vishnu Digambar died.

1972　Wildlife Preservation Act was passed.

August 22

1320　Nasiruddin Khusru was defeated by Gazi Malik.

1921　Mahatma Gandhi made a bonfire of foreign clothes.

1979　President Sanjiva Reddy dissolved the Lok Sabha and general election was ordered at the end of the year to ensure political stability in the Central government administration.

August 23

1947　Vallabhbhai Patel was appointed Deputy Prime Minister of India.

1986　Shambhoo Anbhawane of Bombay broke the world record of longest duration typing Marathon.

1995　Country's first cellular phone was commercially introduced in Calcutta.

August 24

1600　The first ship of the East India Company *Hector* (500 tonnes) touched Surat.

1690　Job Charnock landed and settled at Calcutta and this date is considered as the foundation day of the city.

1925　R.G. Bhandarkar died.

1969　V.V. Giri became the fourth president of India.

1974　Fakhruddin Ali Ahmed became the fifth President of India.

August 25

1351　Sultan Feroz Tughlak Shah III entered Delhi after enthronement.

1888　Allama Mashriqi was born.

1957　Indian Polo Team won the World Cup.

1963　Allama Mashriqi died.

1977　Edmund Hillary's jet-boats left Haldia port on its Ocean to Sky Expedition to the Himalayas up the Ganga.

August 26

1303 Alauddin Khilji captured Chittorgarh of Padmini fame.

1910 Mother Teresa was born in Skopje of Yugoslavia.

1914 Bengali revolutionaries waylaid a cartload of 50 Mauser pistols and 46,000 rounds of ammunition while being unloaded at Calcutta port.

1989 Sumita Laha of Bengal set a new world record in squat by lifting 227.5 kg in the seventh National Power-lifting Championship.

August 27

1604 *Adi Granth Sahib* was installed in the Golden Temple of Amritsar.

1781 Hyder Ali fought the battle of Pallilore with the British.

1870 Sashipada Banerji of Calcutta established the first labour organisation namely Shramajivi Sangha.

1976 Major General Gertrude Ali Ram, the first woman General of the Indian Army, became the first Director of Military Nursing Services.

1982 Anandamoyee Ma expired.

1999 Sonali Banerji of Allahabad became the first marine engineer.

August 28

1904 The first car rally was held from Calcutta to Barrackpore.

1972 General Insurance Business Nationalisation Bill was passed.

1986 Bhagyashree Sathe was the first woman to earn a Grand Master norm in chess.

August 29   NATIONAL SPORTS DAY

1905 Hockey wizard Dhyan Chand was born.

1947 A drafting committee was set up with B. R. Ambedkar as the Chairman to draft constitution of India.

1976 Rebel poet Kazi Nazrul Islam died while visiting Dhaka of Bangladesh.

1994 Tushar Kanti Ghose expired.

August 30

1569 Akbar's eldest son Sultan Salim Mirza (Jahangir) was born.

1659 Dara Shikoh was put to death by Aurangzeb.

1751   The British, under Clive, captured Arcot from Chanda Saheb.

1773   Peshwa Narayan Rao was murdered by his uncle Raghunath Rao.

1936   Madame Bhikaji Cama died.

August 31

1956   The President gave his assent to the States Reorganisation Bill.

1968   The first two-stage rounding rocket ROHINI MSV 1 was successfully launched.

1983   India's unique three-in-one satellite INSAT-1B was deployed from the American space shuttle Challenger.

SEPTEMBER

September 1

1858   Court of Directors of East India Co. held its last meeting in East India House in London.

1942   Indian National Army was formed by Rash Behari Bose.

1947   Indian Standard Time was introduced.

1956   Life insurance business was nationalised and Life Insurance Corporation was formed.

1965   Pakistani forces crossed the ceasefire line in Kashmir.

September 2

1573   Akbar won a decisive battle near Ahmedabad and captured Gujarat.

1946   Jawaharlal Nehru became the Prime Minister of undivided India.

1970   Vivekananda Rock Memorial at Kanyakumari was inaugurated by President V.V. Giri.

1998   Pilotless training aircraft Nishant was successfully flown.

September 3

1767   Col. Smith routed the combined forces of Nizam and Hyder Ali in the battle of Changama.

September 4

1665   Treaty of Purandhar was signed between the Mughals and the Maratha ruler Shivaji.

1825   Dadabhai Naoroji was born.

1887   Gandhiji sailed for U.K. for his Bar-at Law.

September 5   **TEACHERS' DAY**

1612   The East India Company's marine under the British government, was founded with 4 small fighting ships.

1698   A rival East India Company was formed in England.

1763   Mir Kasim fought the British at Udaynala near Rajmahal and lost the battle.

1888   President Sarvepalli Radhakrishanan was born in 1962. This day was declared as Teachers' Day of India.

1957   Wealth Tax Bill was passed.

1997   Mother Teresa expired in Calcutta.

September 6

1657   Shahjahan suddenly fell ill which caused domestic struggle for succession.

1889   Sarat Chandra Bose was born.

September 7

1931   Second session of Round Table Conference started in London.

September 8

1320   Gazi Malik was hailed as Sultan.

1952   The first World Convention on Copyrights was signed at Geneva by 35 nations including India.

1960   Feroz Gandhi, husband of Indira Gandhi, died.

1962   The Chinese made first incursion into the Indian territory in the eastern sector.

1988   Vijaypat Singhania reached Ahmedabad from London in his micro-light single engine aircraft.

September 9

1850   Bhartendu Harish Chander, a poet and dramatist, was born.

1915   Jatindra Nath Mukherji, alias Bangha Jatin and his companions fought a battle with the British police at Kaptipada on the bank of the Buri Balang river in Orissa.

1920   Anglo-Oriental College of Aligarh was converted into Aligarh Muslim University.

1943   Four youths were hanged for spreading the seed of revolt amongst the Indian Army in Madras area.

1949 Hindi was accepted as the National Language.

1982 Sheikh Abdullah of Kashmir expired.

1990 Salauddin and his wife Neena Chowdhury started to establish the world's fastest car driving record across the world.

September 10

1872 Prince Ranjit Singhji, the renowned cricketer, was born.

1887 Freedom fighter Govind Ballabh Pant was born.

1915 Jatindra Nath Mukherji, alias Bagha Jatin, expired in Balasore Hospital.

1966 The Indian Parliament approved the creation of Punjab and Haryana states.

1976 Indian Airline's Boeing 737 was hijacked to Lahore.

September 11

1893 Swami Vivekananda delivered his first speech in the World Parliament of Religions in Chicago.

1895 Acharya Vinoba Bhave was born.

1948 Md. Ali Jinnah, the founder of Pakistan, died.

September 12

1398 Timur reached the banks of the Indus with 92 squadrons of horses and crossed the river at Attock, where Alexander the Great had crossed it nearly seventeen hundred years earlier.

1786 Lord Cornwallis took office of Governor General and Commander-in-Chief.

1966 Mihir Sen swam the Dardanelles.

September 13

1500 Pedro Alvarez Cabral reached Calicut and established the first European (Portuguese) factory in India.

1929 Jatindra Nath Das died on the 63rd day of hunger-strike at 1:05 A.M. in Lahore Central Jail.

1948 Police action was taken against recalcitrant Hyderabad state by the Government of India and peace was declared on September 17.

September 14

1803 Delhi was captured by Lord Lake.

1820 In a meeting in Calcutta it was decided to start the Agri-Horticultural Garden.

1868   Swami Virjanand expired.

September 15

1860   M. Viseswarayya was born.

1909   C. N. Annadurai, one of the founders of Dravida Munnetra Kazhagam, was born.

1948   Independent India's first flagship *INS Delhi* (alias R.N. Achilles) arrived at Bombay port.

1959   First television programme started in Delhi.

1978   Ararat Erevan of Armenia was the first foreign team to win I.F.A Shield, jointly with Mohan Bagan.

September 16

1931   Political prisoners in Hijli detention camp (near Kharagpur) were fired upon by the prison authorities. Two died and many were injured.

1977   Kesarbai Kerkar expired at Bombay.

September 17

1867   Artist Gaganendranath Tagore was born.

1876   Bengali novelist Sarat Chandra Chattopadhyay was born.

1879   E. V. Ramaswami Naicker was born.

1948   Hyderabad was annexed by India after the Police Action of Indian troops that entered into the state on September 13.

1949   Dravida Munnetra Kazhagam was founded.

1956   Oil and Natural Gas Commission was set up.

1982   India and Ceylon played the first cricket Test match.

September 18

1615   British Ambassador Thomas Roe landed at Surat for representing King James I of England to Emperor Jahangir.

1803   The British captured Puri.

1967   Nagaland adopted English as the medium of instruction.

1986   The first all women crew flew the jet plane from Bombay to Goa.

September 19

1581   Sikh Guru Ram Das expired.

1893   Swami Vivekananda delivered the famous speech in the World Parliament of Religions held in Chicago.

1936 Vishnu Narayan Bhatkhande died.

2000 Karnam Malleswari won the Olympic bronze medal in weight-lifting.

September 20

1388 Sultan Feroz Tughlak Shah III of Delhi expired.

1819 The Goan scientist-revolutionary Jose Custodio Faria died.

1856 Sri Narayana Guru was born.

1857 British troops recaptured Delhi from the mutineers.

1871 John Paxton Norman, the officiating Chief Justice of Bengal, was stabbed to death by a Wahabi fanatic.

1878 Madras newspaper *The Hindu* was first published as a weekly issue with G. S. Aiyer as the editor.

1983 APPLE satellite stopped functioning.

September 21

1790 Palghat with 60 guns surrendered to British troops under Gen. Meadows.

1857 Delhi Emperor Bahadur Shah II surrendered to the British after the fall of Delhi on the previous day.

1933 Annie Besant died.

1966 Mihir Sen swam across Bosphorus Channel.

September 22

1539 Guru Nanak expired at Kartarpur, now known as Dera Baba Nanak.

1599 Twenty-four merchants gathered in London Founder's Hall to start a new company for business in India, which ultimately was known as East India Company.

1914 Madras port was bombarded by the German light cruiser Emden.

1977 Cosmos soccer team of U.S.A., led by world famous Pele, arrived at Calcutta for two exhibition matches.

1979 Maulana Abdul Ali Moudoodi, the founder leader of Jamait-e-Islam, died.

1997 Urdu farce *Adrak-ka-Panja* was staged 9,000th time.

September 23

1862 Sriniwas Shastri, a great patriot and politician, was born.

1863 Rao Tula Ram expired.

1929 Child Marriage Restraint Bill (Sarda Act) was passed.

1965 Ceasefire was ordered in Indo-Pak conflict.

September 24

1726 The East India Company was authorised to set up municipal corporations and mayor's courts in Bombay, Calcutta and Madras.

1859 Dhundu Pant alias Nana Saheb of Sepoy Mutiny fame breathed his last in Nepal.

1861 Madame Bhikaji Cama was born.

1932 Pritilata Waddedar was the first woman terrorist to sacrifice her life for the country's freedom.

September 25

1524 Vasco da Gama came to India for the last time as a Viceroy of Portuguese India and died soon thereafter at Cochin on December 24.

1974 The fifth Five-year Plan was finalised.

September 26

1820 Ishwar Chandra Vidyasagar was born in Birsingha village of Bengal.

1919 The first meeting of the Rotary Club of India was held in Calcutta.

1975 Equal Remunerations Ordinance for both male as well as the female employees was promulgated.

1998 Sachin Tendulkar notched up a world record of 18th century in one-day cricket.

September 27

1760 Mir Kasim became the Nawab of Bengal replacing Mir Zafar.

1781 Hyder Ali and the British fought the battle of Salangarh.

1833 Ram Mohan Roy died in Stapleton Grove of Bristol in England.

1907 Bhagat Singh, the great revolutionary, was born.

1958 Mihir Sen was the first Indian to swim across the English Channel.

1977 The famous dancer Uday Shankar expired.

1981 Rent-a-Car system came to India.

1995 Calcutta Metro Railway ran its full length between Tollygunj and Dum Dum

September 28

1837   Bahadur Shah II, the last Mughal Emperor, ascended the throne of Delhi.

1929   Lata Mangeshkar, the greatest movie playback singer, was born.

1977   Edmund Hillary abandoned his Ocean to Sky Expedition at Nandaprayag.

September 29

1836   Madras Chamber of Commerce and Industry was established.

1914   *S. S. Komagata Maru* arrived at Budge Budge from Vancouver.

1942   Matangini Hazra was shot dead at Tamluk in Bengal at the age of 72, while leading a Congress procession as the standard bearer in August Movement.

1959   Smt. Arati Saha successfully swam the English Channel.

1962   Birla Planetarium was opened in Calcutta.

1970   First sewage water reclamation plant for its industrial usage was commissioned by Union Carbide in their Chemicals & Plastics Plant in Bombay.

1977   India and Bangladesh signed an agreement of sharing the Ganga water.

September 30

1687   Aurangzeb annexed Golconda of Hyderabad.

1908   Ram Dhari Singh alias Dinkar, the great Hindi poet, was born.

1993   A devastating earthquake took a heavy toll of life and property in Maharashtra region.

OCTOBER

October 1

1574   Sikh Guru Amar Das expired.

1847   Annie Besant was born in London.

1953   Andhra Pradesh became a separate state of India.

1958   India began changing over to metric system of weight.

1967   India Tourism Development Corporation was set up.

1978   The minimum marriageable age of a girl was raised from 14 years to 18 years and that of a boy from 18 to 21 years.

1980 First Division Football League and I.F.A. Shield Tournament of Calcutta were abandoned as a result of soccer violence causing several deaths.

October 2

1869 Mahatma Gandhi was born.

1904 Lal Bahadur Shastri was born.

1906 Raja Ravi Verma died.

1929 Gandhiji made the Navajiban Karyalaya a public trust.

1951 Bharatiya Jana Sangh was formed by Shyama Prasad Mukherji.

1952 Community Development Programme was launched.

1955 Integral Coach Factory at Perambur in Madras turned out its first railway coach.

1961 Shipping Corporation of India was formed in Bombay.

1971 Gandhi Sadan, formerly Birla House of Delhi, where Mahatma Gandhi was assassinated, was dedicated to the nation by the President of India.

1985 The Dowry Prohibition Amendment Act came into force.

1988 The longest road bridge above the sea joining Mandapam and Pamban was opened.

October 3

1670 Shivaji plundered Surat for the second time.

1831 Mysore was taken over by the British.

1880 First Marathi musical play 'Sangeet Sakuntal' was staged in Pune by Annasaheb Kirloskar.

1977 Indira Gandhi was arrested on corruption charges. This was the first instance of an ex-prime minister being arrested.

1978 India's first test-tube baby and the second in the world was born at Calcutta. It was officially recognised much later.

1984 India's longest distance train Himsagar Express was flagged off from Kanyakumari for Jammu Tawi.

1992 Geet Sethi won the World Professional Billiards Championship.

October 4

1752 As per the Gregorian calendar, October 4 was called October 15 and every fourth year a leap-year.

1977   External Affairs Minister A. B. Vajpayee addressed U.N. General Assembly in Hindi, the first ever address in this language.

October 5

1676   The British Crown gave the power to the East India Company of minting two types of coins in Bombay, which were to be called rupee and pice.

1805   Lord Cornwallis died at Ghazipur.

1868   Renowned Assamese writer Lakshminath Bezbaruah was born.

1989   Meera Sahib Beevi became the first woman Judge of the Supreme Court.

October 6

1860   Indian Penal Code was passed into law. It came into force on and from January 1,1862.

1949   Jawaharlal Nehru laid the foundation-stone of National Defence Academy at Kharakvasla.

October 7

1586   The Mughal army entered Srinagar in Kashmir.

1708   Sikh Guru Govind Singh expired resulting from a stab-wound.

1860   Dr W. M. Haffkine arrived in Bombay.

1919   Gandhiji's *Navajivan* magazine was published.

1950   Mother Teresa founded the Missionaries of Charity in Calcutta.

1992   Rapid Action Force was raised.

October 8

1919   Gandhiji's *Young India* magazine started.

1932   Royal Indian Air Force was commissioned.

1979   National leader Jayaprakash Narayan expired.

October 9

1877   Pandit Gopa Bandhu Das of Orissa was born.

1931   Indian Air Force came into existence.

1949   Territorial Army was formed.

1970   Bhaba Atomic Research Centre in Bombay produced Uranium 233.

1976   International direct dialling was introduced between Bombay and London.

1990 The first oil tanker *Motilal Nehru* was delivered.

October 10

1756 Clive sailed from Madras with 5 ships-of-war and five other vessels, with 900 European and 1,500 Indian sepoys, to recapture Calcutta.

1978 Rohini Khadilkar was the first woman to become the National Chess Champion.

1991 India won the team title in World Carrom Championship.

1992 The second Hooghly bridge (Vidyasagar Setu) was opened.

October 11

1737 Worst cyclone on record in India hit Calcutta.

1902 Jayaprakash Narayan was born in Sitabdiara village in Bihar.

October 12

1967 The Socialist leader and a great parliamentarian Ram Manohar Lohia died.

The Working Committee of Jammu and Kashmir National Conference unanimously voted in favour of permanent accession of the state to India.

October 13

1542 Emperor Akbar was born at Amarkot in Sind.

1911 Sister Nivedita expired.

1999 Atal Behari Vajpayee became the Prime Minister for the third time.

October 14

1240 Sultan Raziya was put to death.

1825 The Grenadier Company in Assam refused to march in pretext of bad weather resulting in its court-martial.

1953 Estate Duty Act came into force.

1956 B. R. Ambedkar embraced Buddhism.

October 15

1686 Aurangzeb signed a peace treaty with Bijapur.

1918 Sai Baba of Shirdi expired.

1932 The first airline namely Tata Sons Ltd. was started by the Tatas.

1988 Ujwala Patil was the first Asian woman to sail round the world.

1994   Polar Satellite Launch Vehicle put Satellite IRS P2 into orbit.

October 16

1905   First partition of Bengal was effected by Lord Curzon.

1959   National Council of Women's Education was inaugurated.

1968   Hargovind Khorana got the Nobel Prize for medicine and physiology.

October 17

1605   Emperor Akbar died.

1870   Calcutta port came under the management of a statutory body.

1906   Swami Rama Tirtha expired.

1920   Communist Party of India was formed in Tashkent.

1940   Gandhiji launched Individual Satyagraha.

1979   Mother Teresa got the Nobel Prize for peace.

October 18

1972   The first multi-role helicopter SA 315 was test flown in Bangalore.

1980   The first Himalayan Car Rally was flagged off from Brabourne Stadium of Bombay.

October 19

1689   Raigarh fort surrendered to Aurangzeb with Sambhaji's widow and her child.

1774   Supreme Court judges and new council members from England landed at Calcutta to purify the administration run by the East India Company earlier.

1889   First successful oil well was sunk in Digboi.

1952   Sriramula Potti commenced his fast unto death for separate Andhra state.

1970   Indian Air Force got the first Indian made Russian supersonic combat aircraft MIG 21.

1983   S. Chandrasekhar shared Nobel Prize in physics.

1988   In a tragic coincidence, in the worst ever air disasters of both Indian Airlines and Vayudoot, a total of 164 people lost their lives.

October 20

1568   Chittorgarh was attacked by Akbar.

1774 Calcutta was made the capital of India.

1960 The first All India Mountaineering Expedition conquered Nanda Ghunti peak.

1962 China attacked India and tried to penetrate deep inside India through Arunachal Pradesh.

October 21

1296 Alauddin Khilji ascended the throne of Delhi after declaring himself 'Sultan' on July 20.

1934 Jayaprakash Narayan established Congress Socialist Party.

1943 Azad Hind Government was formed in Singapore with Netaji Subhas Chandra Bose as the Head of the State.

October 22

1680 Rana Raj Singh of Mewar died.

1796 Peshwa Madhav Rao II committed suicide.

1873 Swami Rama Tirtha was born.

1879 The first treason case against British rule was filed against Basudev Balwant Phadke.

1962 Bhakra Nangal Multipurpose River Valley Project, India's biggest, was dedicated to the nation by Prime Minister Jawaharlal Nehru.

October 23

1623 Famous Hindi poet Tulsidas of Hindi Ramayana fame died.

1764 Mir Kasim was defeated in the battle of Buxar.

1943 Rani of Jhansi Brigade of the Indian National Army (Azad Hind Fauj) was formed by Netaji Subhash Chandra Bose in Singapore. Azad Hind Government (I.N.A) declared war on the United Kingdom and the United States of America at 00.15 A.M.

October 24   UNITED NATIONS DAY

1505 Don Francis de Almedia of Portugal arrived at Cochin with the title Viceroy of India.

1577 Amritsar city was founded by the fourth Sikh Guru Ram Das. The name of the city came from the pond Amrit Sarovar dug by him.

1579 Jesuit Father S. J. Thomas Stephens was the first Englishman to come to India. He arrived at Goa in a Portuguese ship.

1605 Emperor Jahangir (Prince Salim) ascended the throne.

1618 Emperor Aurangzeb was born at Dohad in Gujarat.

1851 First telegraph line was opened between Calcutta and Diamond Harbour.

1947 Kashmir was invaded by Pakistani tribesmen.

1975 Bonded labour system was abolished by an ordinance and came into effect from the next day.

1982 Sudha Madhavan was the first lady to run a Marathon race.

1984 Metro Rail of Calcutta had its first commercial run between Esplanade and Bhowanipore stations, a distance of 4 km.

October 25

1964 The military tank produced at Avadi was named Vijayanta.

1971 National Committee on Science and Technology was set up.

October 26

1930 Dr. W. F. M. Haffkine died.

1934 All India Village Industries Association was formed with Gandhiji as its patron.

1962 Consequent to Chinese invasion the President made a Proclamation of Emergency for the first time.

1969 Apollo 11 astronauts Armstrong and Aldrin, the first men to land on the moon, arrived at Bombay.

1999 Supreme Court ruled that life imprisonment meant actual imprisonment of 14 years, exclusive of any remission.

October 27

1904 Jatindra Nath Das was born.

1907 Brahma Bandhab Upadhyay died.

1921 President K. R. Narayanan was born.

1947 Maharaja Hari Singh of Kashmir signed the Instrument of Accession to India.

1969 Darshan Singh Pheruman died of fasting on Chandigarh issue.

October 28

1627 Emperor Jahangir expired.

1867 Sister Nivedita was born in Ireland.

October 29

1851   British Indian Association of Bengal was established.

1920   Jamia Millia Islamia was established through the efforts of Zakir Hussain.

1999   A supercyclone devastated Orissa's coastal area.

October 30

1883   Swami Dayanand Saraswati died.

1909   The renowned nuclear scientist Homi Bhabha was born.

1945   India joined the United Nations as one of the original nations, though then under the British rule.

1956   Ashok Hotel was opened in Delhi, which was the first 5-star deluxe hotel of India.

October 31

1875   Vallabhbhai Patel was born.

1920   The inaugural session of All India Trade Union Congress was held in Bombay.

1966   Mihir Sen swam across the Panama Canal.

1984   Prime Minister Indira Gandhi was shot dead by her own security guards. Her son Rajiv Gandhi was sworn in as the sixth Prime Minister.

NOVEMBER

November 1

1858   Administration of India was taken over by the British Crown from the East India Company. The then Governor General took the title 'Viceroy' which followed thereafter till independence.

1881   Calcutta Tramways Company ran their first horse-drawn tram on Sealdah-Armenian Ghat track.

1913   Ghadar Movement was initiated at San Francisco by Tarak Nath Das.

1950   The first steam locomotive came out of Chittaranjan Locomotive Works assembly line.

1954   French territories Pondicherry, Karikol, Mahe and Yanon were transferred to Government of India.

1956   Delhi became a Union Territory. Likewise Andaman and Nicobar Islands as well as Laccadive, Minicoy and Amindivi Islands became Union Territories.

Madhya Pradesh, India's biggest state, was created mainly on linguistic basis.

1961   Passenger plane AVRO HS748 built by Hindustan Aeronautics had its maiden flight.

1967   The old Punjab state was broken into two separate states Punjab and Haryana with Chandigarh as the capital of both. Chandigarh itself was made a Union Territory.

All India Radio started commercial advertisements from Bombay, Nagpur and Pune.

1973   Laccadive, Minicoy and Amindivi Islands were renamed as Lakshadweep.

The name of Mysore state was changed to Karnataka.

1985   Helicopter Corporation of India, later renamed Pawan Hans, started functioning.

2000   Chattishgarh state was newly formed.

November 2

1534   Sikh Guru Ram Das was born.

1774   Robert Clive probably committed suicide in England.

November 3

1948   Prime Minister Jawaharlal Nehru delivered his maiden speech in the U.N. General Assembly.

1962   Gold Bond Scheme was announced keeping in view the Chinese attack.

2000   Direct-to-Home (DTH) telecom services was opened to all by the Government of India.

November 4

1509   Alfonso de Albuquerque succeeded Almeida as the Viceroy of Portuguese India.

1822   Delhi's water supply scheme was formally opened.

1889   Jamnalal Bajaj, a freedom fighter, was born.

1915   Pherozeshah Mehta died.

1936 Shakuntala Devi, the human calculating machine, was born.

1947 The great heroism of Major Somnath Sharma in Badgaon of Kashmir earned him the first-ever Param Vir Chakra, unfortunately posthumously.

1954 Himalayan Mountaineering Institute was established in Darjeeling.

1970 Pandit Sambhu Maharaj, the Kathak King of India, died.

1984 O. B. Agarwal became world champion in amateur snooker.

November 5

1556 The second battle of Panipat took place between Akbar and Hemu, when Hemu was defeated and beheaded in the battlefield.

1870 Chitta Ranjan Das was born.

1920 Indian Red Cross Society was founded.

1927 Viceroy Lord Irwin met Gandhiji and other Congress leaders and announced the impending visit of Simon Commission.

1945 Trial of INA prisoners began in the Red Fort of Delhi.

November 6

1763 Patna was captured by the British from Mir Kasim.

1888 Gandhiji took admission in Inner Temple to be a Barrister.

1925 Meera Behn landed at Bombay for service to India.

1943 The Andaman and Nicobar Islands were handed over to Netaji Subash Chandra Bose by Japan during the Second World War. The names of the islands were changed to Shahid and Swaraj Dweeps.

1962 The National Defence Council was set up.

1988 Gandhiji was readmitted as a Bar-at-Law.

2000 Jyoti Basu retired as the Chief Minister of West Bengal after 23 years of uninterrupted rule.

November 7

1858 Bipin Chandra Pal was born.

1862 Bahadur Shah II, the last Mughal Emperor, breathed his last in British captivity in Rangoon.

1888 C.V. Raman was born.

1925 Miss Madelein Slade (Meera Behn) came to Sabarmati Ashram.

1990 The National Front Government at the Centre was voted out of power.

November 8

1661   Sikh Guru Har Rai expired.

1999   Rahul Dravid and Sachin Tendulkar scored a world record partnership of 331 runs in one-day cricket.

November 9

1236   Ruknuddin Feroz Shah was executed.

1270   The great Saint Namdeo was born.

1877   Urdu poet Md. Iqbal was born.

1947   Junagarh was annexed to the Indian Union.

1960   First Indian Air Chief Subroto Mukherji died.

2000   Uttaranchal was carved out of Uttar Pradesh as a new state.

November 10

1659   Shivaji killed Afzal Khan near Pratapgarh fort.

1698   Calcutta was sold to the East India Company.

1848   Surendra Nath Banerji was born.

1922   Inner Temple debarred Gandhiji as a Barrister.

1990   Chandra Shekhar became the eighth Prime Minister of India.

November 11

1888   Maulana Abul Kalam Azad was born.

1958   Indian Explosive factory was inaugurated at Gomia.

1973   The first International Philatelic Exhibition was opened in New Delhi.

November 12

1781   Nagapatnam was captured by the British.

1930   The first Round Table Conference started in London with 16 Indian princes, 56 Indian and 23 British representatives, but none from the Indian National Congress.

1936   Kerala temples were thrown open to all Hindus.

1946   Pandit Madan Mohan Malaviya expired.

1996   Saudi Arabia's Jumbo jet aircraft and a Kazakhistan plane collided in mid-air in Haryana sky.

November 13

1780   Maharaja Ranjit Singh of Punjab was born.

November 14   CHILDREN'S DAY

1681   The East India Company ordered Bengal to be a separate Presidency.

1889   Jawaharlal Nehru was born.

1955   Employees' State Insurance Corporation was inaugurated.

1957   Children's Day of India was officially announced to synchronise with Jawaharlal Nehru's birthday.

1977   Srila Prabhupada of ISKCON passed away at Brindavan.

November 15

1621   The strong Kangra fort, which resisted even Akbar's army, surrendered to Jahangir's forces.

1830   Ram Mohan Roy sailed for England.

1913   The news of the receipt of Nobel Prize for literature reached Rabindranath Tagore.

1949   Nathuram Vinayak Godse and Narayan Dattatreya Apte were hanged for Mahatma Gandhi's murder.

1982   Vinoba Bhave expired in his Paunar Ashram.

2000   Jharkhand, the 28th state of India, was born.

November 16

1713   Balaji Vishwanath was appointed as Peshwa by Shahu.

1835   Rani Lakshmi Bai of Jhansi was born.

1860   The first batch of Indian contract workers landed in Natal of South Africa.

1893   Annie Besant landed at Tuticorin.

November 17

1525   Babar entered India for the fifth time by way of Sind to conquer India, which he did.

1915   Vishnu Gopal Pingle was hanged in Talegaon prison near Pune.

1928   Lala Lajpat Rai died from the injuries sustained from the lathi charge on him on October 30.

1932   The third Round Table Conference began.

1966   Reita Faria was elected Miss World in a beauty contest in London.

November 18   **TERRITORIAL ARMY DAY**

1727   Jaipur city was founded by Maharaja Jai Singh II. The architect was Vidyadhar Chakraborty of Bengal.

1772   Peshwa Madhav Rao I died and was succeeded by his younger brother Narayan Rao.

1948   500 people got drowned when the ferry steamer *Narayani* capsized and sank near Patna.

1955   For the first time the topmost Soviet leaders President Nicolai Bulganin and Nikita Krushchev landed at Delhi for a visit to India.

1972   Tiger was chosen as the National Animal.

1973   Holy Mother of Sri Aurobindo Ashram of Pondicherry breathed her last.

November 19

1838   Keshab Chanda Sen was born.

1917   Indira Gandhi was born.

1982   The ninth Asian Games started in Delhi.

1994   Aiswarya Rai won Miss World title.

1995   Karnam Malleswari set a world record in weight-lifting.

1997   Kalpana Chawla became the first Indian woman to go into space in space-shuttle Columbia

November 20

1750   Tipu Sultan was born.

1917   Bose Research Institute was founded at Calcutta.

November 21

1517   Sikandar II Lodi of Delhi expired.

1921   Prince of Wales (later King Edward VIII) landed at Bombay and Indian National Congress observed All India Hartal.

1947   Post-independence postage stamp was issued for the first time.

1962   Ceasefire was declared by China in Indo-China border conflict.

1963   India's space programme began with the launching of an equatorial rocket from Thumba.

1970   C.V. Raman expired.

1973   Govind Das was felicitated on completing 50 years as a parliamentarian, an unprecedented record.

November 22

1968   Lok Sabha approved renaming of Madras state as Tamil Nadu.

1997   Diana Hayden was crowned Miss World.

November 23

1857   Lucknow was relieved from sepoy mutineers by Colin Campbell.

1926   Shri Satya Sai Baba was born.

1937   Jagdish Chandra Bose expired.

1983   Commonwealth Summit was held in New Delhi, its first meet in India.

1997   Nirad C. Chaudhuri completed hundred years of his life.

November 24

1824   Calcutta merchants voted a lakh of rupees to the first person who would navigate a steamship to India.

1926   Sri Aurobindo attained Purna Siddhi, i.e., full enlightenment.

1961   Grand Lodge of India was instituted.

1986   In the first ever ruling of its kind in the country by any speaker, seven sitting MLAs of Tamil Nadu were expelled.

1988   Lalduhoma was the first member of the Lok Sabha to be disqualified under the anti-defection law.

November 25

1538   The Turkish naval expeditionary force which arrived in India retreated with the arrival of a Portuguese fleet.

1866   Allahabad High Court was inaugurated.

1879   The saint poet T. L. Vaswani was born.

November 26

1890   National Professor Suniti Kumar Chatterjee was born.

1949   Constitution of Independent India was signed by the President of the Constituent Assembly and declared passed with immediate effect.

1960   Subscriber Trunk Dialling (STD) was introduced for the first time between Kanpur and Lucknow.

November 27

1001   Jaipal lost the battle with Sultan Mahmud of Ghazni.

1795   The first public performance of a Bengali play took place on a stage on Ezra Street in Calcutta, owned by G.S. Lebedev.

1948   National Cadet Corps was established.

November 28

1956   Chou En-lai, Prime Minister of communist China, arrived in India.

1962   K. C. Dey, the well-known blind singer of Bengal, died.

1996   Capt. Indrani Singh became the first woman to command Airbus A300 aircraft.

1997   Prime Minister I. K. Gujral resigned.

November 29

1961   The world's first cosmonaut Yuri Gagarin of Russia arrived at New Delhi.

1970   Haryana was the first state to achieve hundred per cent village electrification.

November 30

1759   Emperor Alamgir II of Delhi was murdered by his minister.

1858   Jagdish Chandra Bose was born.

1889   The foundation-stone of the Glass House in Lal Bagh Garden of Bangalore was laid.

1909   The great scholar Romesh Chandra died.

1999   World's largest Metrewave Radio Telescope was opened at Narayangaon.

2000   Priyanka Chopra was crowned Miss World.

DECEMBER

December 1

1886   Raja Mahendra Pratap was born.

1933   India's first daily passenger air service started between Calcutta and Dhaka.

1963   Nagaland became the sixteenth state of India.

1990   Vijayalakshmi Pandit expired in Dehradun.

December 2

1552   St. Francisco Xavier died in China.

1911   King George V and Queen Mary were the first British King and Queen to land in India at Bombay. Gateway of India of Bombay was erected at that spot.

1918 Gooroodas Banerjee died.

1942 Sri Aurobindo Ashram School was established at Pondicherry. Later it was known as Sri Aurobindo International Centre of Education.

1965 Border Security Force came into being.

1989 V. P. Singh was sworn in as the seventh Prime Minister.

1999 Insurance business was opened to private sector.

December 3

1790 Lord Cornwallis took away the power of administering criminal justice from the Nawab of Murshidabad and removed the Sadar Nizamat Adalat to Calcutta.

1882 Artist Nandalal Bose was born.

1884 India's first president Rajendra Prasad was born.

1889 Khudiram Bose of Muzaffarpur Bomb Case was born.

1971 Indo-Pak war broke out and the President declared National Emergency.

1979 Hockey wizard Dhyan Chand expired.

1984 In the world's worst industrial pollution disaster more than 3,000 people died and more than 50,000 people needed medical treatment in Bhopal due to leakage of a toxic gas from Union Carbide's insecticide plant.

December 4

1661 Murad was executed.

1796 Baji Rao II was made the Peshwa.

1829 Burning of the Hindu widows on husband's funeral pyre, known as Sati was abolished by Viceroy Lord William Bentinck.

1860 Agostino Lourenco from Margao got his Doctorate in chemistry in Paris. Probably that was the first Doctorate Degree for an Indian from a foreign university.

1888 Historian Ramesh Chandra Majumdar was born.

1910 Ramaswamy Venkataraman, the eighth president, was born.

1959 India and Nepal signed an agreement on Gandak Irrigation and Power Project.

1967 The first rocket ROHINI RH 75 was launched from Thumba.

December 5

1657   Murad proclaimed himself Emperor.

1905   Sheikh Md. Abdullah of Kashmir was born at Soura of Kashmir.

1943   Japanese aircraft bombed Calcutta during the day time, the only daylight raid on Calcutta.

1950   Sri Aurobindo passed away at Pondicherry.

1951   Artist Abanindranath Tagore expired.

1999   Yukta Mookhey was crowned Miss World.

December 6

1732   Warren Hastings, the first Governor of the East India Company, was born in Churchill village of Oxfordshire in U.K.

1907   The first terrorist dacoity related to freedom struggle took place in Chingripota railway station (now in Bangladesh).

1946   Home Guard Organisation was set up.

1956   B. R. Ambedkar breathed his last.

1992   Babri Masjid was destroyed.

December 7

1782   Hyder Ali of Mysore died.

1825   *Enterprise* reached Calcutta, the first steamship to India.

1856   The first official Hindu widow marriage was arranged by the Hindus.

1995   Communication satellite INSAT 2C was launched.

December 8

1875   The great liberal leader Tej Bahadur Sapru was born at Aligarh.

1879   The great revolutionary Jatindra Nath Mukherji, alias Bagha Jatin, was born.

1900   The renowned dancer Uday Shankar was born.

1967   *INS Kalvari,* the first submarine, was commissioned.

December 9

1484   Blind poet and saint Surdas was born.

1761   Tara Bai of Pune died.

1825   Rao Tula Ram, a distinctive hero of 1857 Sepoy Mutiny, was born.

1870   Dr I. S. Schrudder of Vellore Hospital was born.

1898   Belur Math was consecrated.

1946   The Constituent Assembly's first meeting was held in the Constitution Hall of New Delhi.

December 10

1878   Muhammad Ali Jauhar, one of the founders of Jamia Millia Islamia, was born at Rampur.

1879   Chakravarty Rajagopalachari was born.

1942   Dr Dwarkanath Kotnis died in China.

1992   Country's first hovercraft service started in Gujarat.

December 11

1687   The East India Company was authorised to grant the first Municipal charter to Madras.

1780   General Goddard captured Bassein fort of Bombay.

1845   First Anglo-Sikh war broke out.

1858   Bankim Chandra Chattopadhyay and Jadu Nath Bose became the first Graduates in Arts from Calcutta University.

1946   Rajendra Prasad was elected Chairman of the Constituent Assembly.

1958   Wilson Jones became the World Champion in Amateur Billiards.

December 12

1758   French General Lally sieged Madras fort held by the British. The siege ended with Lally's retreat on February 16, 1759.

1882   Bankim Chandra Chattopadhyay's Bengali novel *Ananda Math* was published.

1901   Rabindranath Tagore started his Brahmacharya Ashram at Santiniketan.

1911   King George V and Queen Mary held Delhi Durbar. The King annulled the first partition of Bengal.

1959   President D. D. Eisenhower of U.S.A. arrived in New Delhi.

1964   Maithili Saran Gupta, the famous Hindi poet, expired.
        Jet trainer HJT-16 made its inaugural flight.

1965   The first military tank Vijayanta rolled out of assembly line at Avadi.

1971   Parliament approved abolition of privy purses and privileges of the rulers of princely states.

1976   Remains of martyr Madan Lal Dhingra arrived in New Delhi from U.K.

1992   Lord Buddha's huge statue was installed in Hussain Sagar lake in Hyderabad city.

December 13

1232   Gwalior was captured by Iltutmish.

1675   Sikh Guru Tegh Bahadur was beheaded in Delhi.

1772   Narayan Rao became the Peshwa at Satara.

1972   The first agricultural aeroplane Basant was produced.

1977   Michel Ferreira scored highest break of 1,149 under the new rules in the National Billiards Championship.

December 14

1931   For the first time two school girls Shanti Ghose and Suniti Ghose used revolvers to kill C. G. B. Stevens, magistrate and collector of Comilla, now in Bangladesh.

December 15

1749   Shahu, grandson of Shivaji, died.

1803   Under the Treaty of Deogaon between Bhonsle and the East India Company, Orissa with Cuttack came under company rule.

1950   Vallabhbhai Patel expired.
        Planning Commission was established.

December 16   NAVY DAY

1515   Portuguese Governor Alfonso de Albuquerque died near Goa.

1929   Calcutta Electric Supply Corporation started digging a tunnel under the Hooghly river.

1951   Salar Jung Museum was established at Hyderabad.

1952   Sriramalu Potti laid down his life fasting for a separate Andhra state.

1966   Precision Instrument Factory at Kota, the first major instrument factory, was formally opened.

1971   Indo-Pakistan ceasefire was agreed upon. East Pakistan emerged as an independent sovereign country Bangladesh.

1985   The first Fast Breeder Test Reactor (FBTR) was commissioned at Kalpakkam.

December 17

1645 Noor Jahan Begum, widow of Jahangir, died.

1715 Sikh Chief Banda Bahadur Bairagi surrendered to the Mughals at Gurdaspur.

1929 Bhagat Singh and Rajguru fired at and killed Assistant Police Superintendent Saunders, whom they mistook to be Scott, Superintendent of Police of Lahore.

1940 Gandhiji suspended Individual Satyagraha Movement.

1996 National Football League was introduced.

December 18

1398 Amir Timur captured Delhi from Sultan Nasrat Shah.

1960 National Museum was inaugurated in New Delhi.

1995 An unidentified aircraft air-dropped arms and ammunitions in Purulia of West Bengal

December 19

1927 Uttar Pradesh (then United Provinces) Automobile Association was formed.

1961 The Indian Army marched into Portuguese possessions Goa, Daman, Diu, Nagar Haveli, etc. and liberated them after four and a half centuries of Portuguese occupation.

December 20

1686 Job Charnock abandoned Hooghly after some skirmishes with the Mughal troops and settled in Sutanuti.

1757 Clive became the Governor of Bengal.

1876 Bankim Chandra Chattopadhyay wrote the national song Vande Mataram.

1942 First Japanese air-raid on Calcutta took place.

1955 Indian Golf Union was formed.

1985 A diamond-studded crown worth Rs 52 million was installed on Venkateswara idol at Tirupati.

December 21

1788 Ghulam Kadir was captured by Scindia and put to death.

1952 Saifuddin Kitchlu was the first Indian to get the Lenin Peace Prize of U.S.S.R.

1974   INS Satavahana, the first establishment to give submarine training, was commissioned at Visakhapatnam.

December 22

1241   Lieutenant Bahadur Tair of Mongol Chief Hulagu Khan captured Lahore.

1843   Debendranath Tagore, father of Rabindranath Tagore, became a Brahmo.

1853   Sarada Ma, consort of Ramkrishna Paramhansa Dev, was born.

1887   Srinivasa Ramanujam was born.

1940   Manabendra Nath Roy announced foundation of Radical Democratic Party.

December 23

1465   Virupaksha II of Vijayanagar was defeated in the battle of Tellikota by the combined Muslim forces of Ahmednagar, Bidar, Bijapur and Golconda.

1894   'Pous Mela' was inaugurated in Santiniketan by Rabindranath Tagore.

1901   Brahmacharya Ashram at Santiniketan was formally opened.

1912   Viceroy Lord Hardinge II entered New Delhi on an elephant to initiate the new imperial capital, but was injured in a bomb incident.

1926   Swami Shraddhanand was murdered.

1929   Gandhiji was received by Lord Irwin only a few hours after an attempt on Irwin's life.

1968   India's first meteorological rocket *Menaka* was successfully launched.

1969   Moon-rock was kept on exhibition in New Delhi.

1995   360 people perished on the spot in a disastrous fire in a school function as Mandi Dabwali in Haryana.

2000   Calcutta was officially renamed Kolkata.

December 24

1524   Vasco da Gama died at Cochin while he was the Viceroy of Portuguese India.

1894   First Medical Conference was held at Calcutta.

1921   Visva Bharati was established by Rabindranath Tagore.

1973 E.V. Ramaswamy Naicker expired at Vellore.

1989 Esselworld, the country's first amusement park, was opened in Bombay.

2000 Viswanathan Anand was crowned World Chess Champion.

December 25 CHRISTMAS DAY

1763 Surajmal of Bharatpur was killed.

1771 Mughal Emperor Shah Alam II was installed on Delhi throne under the protection of Maratha power.

1861 Philanthropist and national leader Madan Mohan Malaviya was born.

1876 Md. Ali Jinnah, the founder of Pakistan, was born.

1892 Swami Vivekananda sojourned on the mid-sea rock for three days at Kanyakumari.

1924 The first All India Communist Conference was held in Kanpur.
      Atal Behari Vajpayee was born.

1972 Chakravarty Rajagopalachari expired.

1974 Air India's Boeing 747 was hijacked on its flight to Rome.

1994 President Zail Singh expired.

December 26

1530 Babar died at Dholpur near Agra.

1666 Sikh Guru Gobind Singh was born.

1801 Bengal and Madras had Supreme Courts.

1831 Henry Louis Vivian Derozio died.

1904 The first cross-country motor-car rally between Delhi and Bombay was inaugurated.

December 27

1797 Urdu poet Mirza Ghalib was born.

1861 The first public auctions of tea were held in Calcutta.

1911 'Jana gana mana ....' was first sung in Calcutta session of the Indian National Congress.

1975 Chasnala coal mine disaster took a toll of 372 lives.

1987 The first hot-air Cross India Balloon Expedition started.

December 28

1688 Shivaji's son Sambhaji was captured by Aurangzeb and was tortured to death.

1883 Surendra Nath Banerji convened a National Conference under Bharat Sabha which continued till December 30.

1885 Indian National Congress had its first session in Bombay with 72 representatives from all over India, with W. C. Bonerjee as its President.

1896 'Vande Mataram' was first sung in Calcutta session of the Indian National Congress.

1921 Prince of Wales (later King Edward VIII) opened Victoria Memorial Hall at Calcutta.

1928 First talkie film 'Melody of Love' was screened in Calcutta.

December 29

1530 Humayun succeeded Babar.

1788 Lt. A. Blair and Lt. R. H. Colbrook left India's mainland for survey of Andaman and Nicobar Islands.

1844 W. C. Bonerjee, the first President of Indian National Congress, was born in Kidderpore of Calcutta.

1972 The work on Calcutta Metro Railway started.

1977 The world's largest open-air-theatre 'Drive In' was opened in Bombay.

December 30

1706 Francois Martin, founder and Governor General of Pondicherry, died.

1803 The East India Company acquired control of Delhi, Agra and Broach along with other territories by the Treaty of Surji Arjangaon with Scindia.

1879 Ramana Maharshi was born in Tiruchuzhi near Madurai.

1887 K. M. Munshi, the founder of Bhartiya Vidya Bhavan, was born.

1906 All India Muslim League was founded with Salimullah Khan, Nawab of Dhaka, as its president.

1971 Scientist Vikram Sarabhai died in Trivandrum.

December 31

1599 Queen's consent was given to East India Company.

1802 Peshwa Baji Rao II came under British protection.

1929 At the stroke of midnight at Lahore, Gandhiji led congressmen in a vow for Swaraj – nothing less than full independence.

1984 Rajiv Gandhi became the Prime Minister for the second time.

2001 ONWARDS

January 4

2001 Indigenously built Light Combat Aircraft completed maiden test flight.

January 17

2001 Agni II, the 16 tonne missile with a range of 2,000 km was test-fired with 'solid motor'.

January 25

2002 Arjan Singh was made the first Air Marshal of IAF.

January 26

2001 A devastating earthquake of 7.9 intensity of Richter scale completely devastated Bhuj area.

March 3

2005 Golden Temple of Amritsar to be referred to as Harmandir Sahib.

March 11

2001 Pulella Gopichand became virtually the world champion in badminton.

Harbhajan Singh was the first Indian bowler to achieve a hat-trick in Test cricket.

March 16

2005 Pankaj Advani is the second cueist in the world to have won both billiards and snooker amateur world titles.

March 18

2001 It was declared Ordnance Factory Day of India on the beginning of 200th anniversary celebration of the first ordnance factory.

March 26

2001 P. N. Bhagawati, the former Chief Justice of India, was appointed the Chairman of world's Human Rights Commission.

March 31

2001 Sachin Tendulkar was the first cricketer to score 10,000 runs in one-day international.

April 7

2005 Amiya Thakur won the World Ladies Billiards Championship.

April 18

2001 Geosynchronous Satellite Launch Vehicle (GSLV-D1), weighing 401 tonnes took off from Shrihorikota.

April 29

2005 Bula Chowdhury became the first woman swimmer to swim in five continents and seven seas.

May 3

2005 Arjun Mondal (92 cm) and Manashi Ghose (79 cm) got married and was thus the shortest couple in the country, if not of the world.

May 5

2005 Polar Satellite Launch Vehicle PSLV C6 placed two satellites CARTOSAT and HAMSAT in a high polar orbit.

May 6

2005 Dola Banerjee won the first international gold medal in archery.

June 12

2005 BRAHMOS a supersonic cruise missile, was tested at Chandipore.

June 23

2003 Chandan Thakur and Dipti Pradhan tied their nuptial knot 4 mt under water – the first Indian couple to do so.

July 6

2003 Sania Mirza was the first Indian girl to win Grand Slam in tennis.

July 18

2002 A. P. J. Abdul Kalam was elected eleventh President of India.

July 21

2003 Ajoy and Monisha of Chandigarh got married following rituals of four different religions.

July 26

2003 East Bengal Club became the first club to win an international football tournament on a foreign soil.

August 29

2005 In a Hindu family a daughter got the same rights as a son in inheritance of property.

August 31

2003 Chaitali Dhenki was the first woman to win the world's 81 km swimming competition of Murshidabad.

September 28

2003 India's most advanced satellite INSAT 3E was successfully launched.

October 24

2001 Sachin Tendulkar and Sourav Ganguly excelled their own world record by scoring 256 runs in opening wicket in one-day international.

December 13

2001 Five terrorists fired indiscriminately inside the Parliament complex killing nine person.

December 24

2002 Delhi Metro-rail, the second in the country, was inaugurated.

PART C
LIST OF DYNASTIES

PART C

LIST OF DYNASTIES

Accession Year		**ADIL SHAHI OF BIJAPUR**
	AD	
1.	1490	Yusuf Adil Shah
2.	1510	Ismail
3.	1534	Mallu
4.	1535	Ibrahim I
5.	1557	Ali I
6.	1580	Ibrahim II
7.	1626	Muhammad Adil Shah
8.	1659	Ali II Dilir Khan (Ended in 1687 to Mughals.)
		AHOM (ASSAM) RAJA
1.	1230	Chu-Kapha
2.	1268	Chu-Toupha, son of I
3.	1281	Chu-Benpha
4.	1293	Chu-Kangpha
5.	1332	Chu-Khampha
	1364-1368	Interregnum
6.	1369	Chu-Taopha
7.	1372	Chu-Khamethepa
	1405-1414	Interregnum
8.	1414	Chu-Dangpha
9.	1425	Chu-Jangpha, son of 8
10.	1440	Chu-Phukpha, son of 9
11.	1458	Chu-Singpha, son of 10
12.	1485	Chu-Hangpha, son of 11
13.	1491	Chu-Simpha
	1497-1506	Interregnum
14.	1506	Chu-Humpha
15.	1549	Chu-Klunpha, son of 14
16.	1563	Chu-Khrunpha
17.	1615	Chu-Chanipha
18.	1640	Chu-Rumpha
19.	1643	Chu-Chinpha
20.	1647	Kuku Raikhoya Gohani

21.	1655	Jayadeva Simha (Chukum)
22.	1665	Kodayaditya Simha
23.	1677	Parbatiya Kunria
24.	1681	Lora Raja
25.	1683	Gadadhara Simha
26.	1689-1713	Rudra Simha
27.	1715-1721	Siva Simha
28.	1723-1726	Phuleswari, wife of 27
29.	1729-1730	Pramatheswari Devi
30.	1732-1736	Sarveswari Devi
31.	1738-1743	Sarveswari Devi
32.	1744	Pramatha Simha
33.	1751	Rajeswara Simha
34.	1771	Lakshmi Simha Narendra, son of 33
35.	1779	Gaurinatha Simha, son of 34
36.	1792	Bharata Simha Maharana
37.	1793	Sarvananda Simha
38.	1796	Bharata Simha
	1796	Gauriratha Simha, restored by British
39.	1808	Kamaleswara Simha, not crowned
40.		Raja Chandra Kanta Simha, fled
41.		Purandara Simha, great grandson of 33
		— expelled by the Burmese.
42.		Yogeswara Simha, under Burmese control
	1824	Burmese expelled by the British
	1833	British forced Purandara Simha to surrender his territories

ARAVIDU OF VIJAYANAGAR

(See Saluva, Sangama and Taluva Dynasties)

1.	1542	Rama Raya (de facto ruler)
2.	1570	Tirumala, brother of 1
3.	1572	Sriranga I, son of 2
4.	1586	Venkata II, brother of 3

5.	1614	Sriranga II, son of 2nd brother of 2
6.	1618	Ramadevaraya, son of 5
7.	1630	Venkata III, grandson of 1
8.	1642	Sriranga III (Adopted-ended in 1649)

BAHMANI OF GULBARGA

1.	1347	Alauddin Hasan Gangu (Abdul Muzaffar Alauddin Bahman Shah)
2.	1358	Muhammad Shah I, son of I
3.	1377	Mujahid Shah, son of 2
4.	1378	Daud Shah, 2nd son of I
5.	1378	Muhammad Shah II, grandson of 1
6.	1397	Ghiasuddin, son of 5
7.	1397	Samsuddin, second son of 5
8.	1397	Tajuddin Feroz Shah, third son of 4
9.	1422	Ahmad Shah I, brother of 8
10.	1435	Alauddin Ahmad Shah II, son of 9
11.	1457	Alauddin Humayun Shah, son of 10
12.	1461	Nizam Shah, son of 11
13.	1463	Muhammad Shah III, son of 11
14.	1482	Mahmud Shah II, son of 13
15.	1518	Ahmad Shah III, son of 14
16.	1521	Alauddin Shah, son of 14
17.	1521	Waliullah Shah, son of 14
18.	1524	Kalimullah Shah, son of 15 (Fled in 1528)

BARID SHAHI OF BIDAR

1.	1492	Qasim I Barid Shah
2.	1504	Amir I
3.	1538	Ali
4.	1582	Ibrahim
5.	1589	Quasim II
6.	1592	Mirza Ali
7.	1609	Amir II (Ended in 1619)

BIKANER RAJ (RAJA)

1.	1488	Bikaji, son of Jodha of Jodhpur
2.	1504	Naroji, nephew of 1
3.	1505	Laukaranji, brother of 2
4.	1526	Jayatsiji, son of 3
5.	1542	Kalyana Singh, son of 4
6.	1571	Raya Singh, son of 5
7.	1612	Dalpat Singh, son of 6
8.	1614	Sura Singh, brother of 7
9.	1631	Karan Singh, son of 8
10.	1669	Anup Singh, son of 9
11.	1698	Sarup Singh, son of 10
12.	1700	Sajjan Singh, brother of 11
13.	1736	Jorawar Singh, son of 12
14.	1745	Gaja Singh, cousin of 13
15.	1787	Raja Singh, son of 13
16.	1787	Surat Singh, regent
17.	1828	Ratna Singh, son of 16
18.	1851	Sardar Singh, son of 17
19.	1872	Dungar Singh, descendant of 13
20.	1887	Ganga Singh, brother of 19

BRITISH CHIEF (NO DYNASTY)

A. Governor of the Presidency of Fort William

	1758	Robert Clive (Later Lord)
	1760	John Holwell
	1760	Henry Vansittart
	1764	John Spencer
	1765	Lord Clive
	1767	Henry Verelest
	1769	John Cartier
	B.	**Governor of Bengal**
April 13,	1772	Warren Hastings

		C.	**Governor General of Bengal**
			(By Regulating Act)
October	1774		Warren Hastings
February	1785		Sir John Macpherson (Temporary)
September	1786		Lord Cornwallis
October	1793		Sir John Shore
March	1798		Lt. Gen. Sir Alured Clarke (Temporary)
May	1798		Lord Richard Wellesley
July 30,	1805		Lord Cornwallis (For the second time)
October	1805		Sir George Barlow (Temporary)
July	1807		Lord Gilbert Illiot Minto I
October 4,	1813		Lord Hastings, earlier Earl of Moira
January	1823		John Adams (Temporary)
August 1,	1823		Lord Amherst
March	1828		William B. Bayley (Temporary)
July 4,	1828		Lord William Cavendish Bentinck
		D.	**Governor General of India**
			(Charter Act of 1833)
	1833		Lord William Cavendish Bentinck
March 20,	1835		Sir Charles Metcalfe (Temporary)
March 5,	1836		Lord Auckland
February 28,	1842		Lord Edward Ellenborough
June	1844		William Willbarforce Bird (Temporary)
July	1844		Lord Henry Hardinge
January 12,	1848		Lord Dalhousie
February	1856		Lord Charles Canning (till 31.10.1858)
		E.	**Governor General and Viceroy**
			(Under British Crown)
November 1,	1858		Lord Charles Canning
March	1862		Lord Elgin 1
November	1863		Maj. Gen. Sir Robert Napier (Temporary)
			Col. Sir William Denison (Temporary)
January	1864		Sir John Lawrence
January 12,	1869		Lord Richard Bourke Mayo

January	1872	Sir John Strachey (Temporary)
	1872	Lord Napier (Temporary)
May	1872	Lord Northbrook
April	1876	Lord Robert Lytton I
June	1880	Lord Ripon I
December	1884	Lord Dufferin
December	1888	Lord Lansdowne
January	1894	Lord Elgin II
January	1899	Lord George Nathaniel Curzon
April-Dec.	1904	Lord Ampthlin (Officiated for Lord Curzon on leave)
November 19,	1905	Lord Minto II
November 23,	1910	Lord Hardinge II
April 5,	1916	Lord Chelmsford
April 2,	1921	Lord Rufus Isaacs Reading
	1925	Lord Lytton II (Officiated during Lord Reading's leave)
April 3,	1926	Lord Irwin (Later Lord Halifax)
	1929	Lord Goschen (Officiated during Lord Irwin's leave)
April 17,	1931	Lord Freeman Freeman-Thomas Willingdon
May-August	1934	Sir George Stanley (Officiating)
April 18,	1936	Lord Linlithgow
June-Oct.	1938	Lord Brabourne (Officiating)
October 20,	1943	Lord Wavell
December	1946	Sir John Colville (Officiating)
March 24,	1947	Lord Louis Mountbatten (Up to August 14, 1947)
May	1947	Sir John Colville (Officiating)
	F.	**After Independence**
August 15,	1947	Lord Louis Mountbatten only as Governor General (not as Viceroy)
June 21,	1948	C. Rajagopalachari (The only Indian Governor General)

January 26,	1950	Under the Constitution India became a Republic with a President.

CHALUKYA-EASTERN (VENGI OF ANDHRA)

1.	624	Kubja Vishnuvardhan I, brother of Pulakesin II (Chalukya of Maharashtra)
2.	641	Jayasimha, son of 1
3.	673	Indra-Bhattaraka, brother of 2 (for 7 days)
4.	673	Vishnuvardhana II, son of 3
5.	682	Mangi Yuvaraja, son of 4
6.	706	Jayasimha II, son of 5
7.	719	Kokkili Vikramaditya, brother of 6
8.	719	Vishnuvardhana III, elder brother of 7
9.	755	Vijayaditya I, Bhattaraka, son of 8
10.	772	Vishnuvardhana IV, son of 9
11.	808	Vijayaditya II, son of 10
12.	847	Kali Vishnuvardhana V, son of 11
13.	849	Vijayaditya III, son of 12
14.	892	Chalukya Bhima I, brother's son of 13
15.	921	Vijayaditya IV, son of 14
16.	921	Amma I, son of 15
17.	927	Vijayaditya V, son of 16 (15 days)
18.	927	Tadapa (Taila I), brother of 13
19.	927	Vikramaditya, brother of 15 (11 months)
20.	928	Bhima III, brother of 17
21.	928	Yuddhamalla II, son of 18
22.	935	Chalukya Bhima II, brother of 16
23.	945	Amma II, son of 21
		Taila II, son of 21
24.	970	Danarnava, brother of 23 (died in 973). Unexplained interval of about 27 years thereafter without any ruler.
25.	1000	Saktivarman, son of 24
26.	1011	Vimaladitya, brother of 25

| 27. | 1019 | Rajaraja Narendra, son of 26 |
| 28. | 1031 | Vijayaditya VI, half brother of 27 |

CHALUKYA-KALYANI (SOUTH INDIA)

1.	973	Nurmadi Taila II or Tailapa
2.	997	Satyashraya, son of 1
3.	1008	Vikramaditya V, brother's son of 2
4.	1015	Ayyana, brother of 3 (abdicated)
5.	1015	Jayasimha II, brother of 3
6.	1042	Somesvara I, brother of 5
7.	1068	Somesvara II, son of 6
8.	1076	Vikramaditya VI, son of 6
9.	1127	Somesvara III, son of 8
10.	1138	Prema Jagadekamalla II, son of 9
11.	1149	Nurmadi Taila III, brother of 10
12.	1163	Jagadekamalla III, brother of 10
13.	1184	Somesvara IV, son of 11 (up to 1200)

CHALUKYA-MAHARASHTRA (BADAMAI)

1.		Jayasimha
2.	525	Ramaraja, son of 1
3.	550	Pulakesin I, son of 2
4.	566	Kirtivarman I, son of 3
5.	597	Mangalesa, son of 3 (regent for 6 from 597 to 609)
6.	609	Pulakesin II, son of 4
7.	655	Vikramaditya I, son of 6
8.	681	Vinayaditya, son of 7
9.	696	Vijayaditya, son of 8
10.	733	Vikramaditya II, son of 9
11.	747	Kirtivarman II, son of 10 up to 753. Ended to Rashtrakutas.)

CHAND OF KUMAON

| 1. | 1261 | Thohar Chand |
| 2. | 1276 | Kalyan Chand |

3.	1297	Triloki Chand
4.	1304	Damara Chand
5.	1322	Dharma Chand
6.	1345	Abhaya Chand
7.	1367	Garur Gyan Chand
8.	1420	Harihar Chand
9.	1421	Udhyan Chand
10.	1422	Atma Chand
11.	1423	Hari Chand
12.	1424	Vikrama Chand
13.	1438	Bharati Chand
14.	1462	Ratna Chand
15.	1488	Kirti Chand
16.	1504	Partap Chand
17.	1518	Tara Chand
18.	1534	Manik Chand
19.	1543	Kali Kalyan Chand
20.	1552	Puran Chand
21.	1556	Bhisma Chand
22.	1561	Bala Kalyan Chand
23.	1569	Rudra Chand
24.	1597	Lakshmi Chand
25.	1621	Dhalip Chand
26.	1624	Bijaya Chand
27.	1625	Trimal Chand
28.	1638	Baz Bahadur Chand
29.	1678	Udyot Chand
30.	1698	Gyan Chand
31.	1708	Jagat Chand
32.	1720	Debi Chand
33.	1726	Ajit Chand
34.	1730	Kalyan Chand
35.	1748	Dip Chand
36.	1777	Mohan Chand

37.	1779	Pradhaman Chand
38.	1786	Mohan Chand (restored)
39.	1788	Sib Singh Chand
40.	1788	Mohan Chand (again)
41.	1790	Kumaon was conquered by the Gorkhalis.

CHANDELLA OF KHAJURAHO

1.	831	Nanika
2.		Vakpati
2.(a)		Jeja (?)
3.		Vijaya
4.		Rahila
5.	900	Harsha, son of 4
6.	925	Yasovarman, son of 5
7.	955	Dhanga, son of 6
8.	999	Nanda, son of 7
9.	1035	Vidyadharadeva, son of 8
10.		Vijayapaladeva
11.		Devadharmadeva, son of 10
12.	1049	Kirtivarmadeva, brother of 11
13.	1100	Sulakshanavarmadeva, brother of 12
14.	1117	Jayavarmadeva or Kirtivarman II, son of 13
15.		Prithvivarmadeva
16.	1129	Madanavarmadeva, son of 15
17.	1167	Paramardideva, son of 16
18.	1213	Trailakyavermadeva, son of 17
19.	1261	Viravarman, son of 18
20.	1289	Bhojavarman, son of 19

CHANDRA (LUNAR) RACE OF MAHABHARATA IN HASTINAPUR AND INDRAPRASTHA

(Of doubtful historical base)

| 1. | Brahma | 3. | Samudra |
| 2. | Arti | 4. | Chandra |

5.	Vrihaspati	35.	Vrateshetra
	Boodh		Sahotra
	Pururava		Hasti (founded Hastinapur
	Ayu (Jadu)		near Meerut)
	Nahus		Ajmira
10.	Yayati		Riksha
	Puru	40.	Sambaran
	Jammejaya		Kuru (The place of his
	Prachinwat		meditation is known as
	Pravidhana		Kurukshetra)
15.	Pravira		Parikshit (adopted)
	Henasua		Jahnu
	Charupada		Suratha
	Soodvata	45.	Brihadratha
	Bahoogva		Sarvabhauma
20.	Sanjati		Jaysena
	Hungvati		Radhika
	Rudrasu		Ajutayu
	Gritachi	50.	Gradhna
	Ratinava		Devatithi
25.	Tansu		Riksha
	Sumita		Bhimsena
	Ribya		Dilip
	—	55.	Pratip
	—		Santanu son of 55
30.	—		Vichitavirya, son of 56
	Dushyanta (husband		Pandu (of Mahabharata)
	of Sakuntala)		Yudhisthir (in
	Bharat (son of 31)		Indraprastha), son of 58
	Bharadwaja	60.	Abhimanyu
	Manyu		(never ruled)

Parikshit
(posthumous
son of 60)
Janmejaya, son of 61
Asamanja
(Satanik)
Adhuna
(Aswamedhdutta)
65. Mahajana
Jessrita
Debasena
Ugrasena
Suresena
70. Sutashma
Resmaraja
Bachil
Satpala
Naraharideva

75. Jessrita
Bhupata
Seobhana
Medhavi
Sravana
80. Keekan
Budharut
Dusunuma
Adelika
Huntavarna
85. Dundpala
Dunsala
Senpala
Khevanraj (Killed by his
rebel chief for mal-
administration.
Chandra race
ends)

CHANDRA RACE OF RAJAGRIHA (MAGADHA)

(Of doubtful historical base)

1. Jarasandha (Contemporary of Yudhisthir of
   Mahabharata)
   Jayatsen (Sahadev), son of 1
   Meghasandhi (Marjari), grandson of 1
   Sompai
5. Shrutsava
   Ayutava
   Niramitra
   Sonikhrita
   Vrihatsena
10. Senjita
   Srutanjaya
   Veerha

		Suchi
		Samya
15.		Subrata
		Dharma
		Sushrama
		Drutasena
		Sumati
20.		Subali
		Sumita
		Satyajita
		Viswajita
		Ripunjaya (Slain by Pritadhana. Chandra Race ends.)
25.		Pritadhana
		Paluka
		Viswakupa
		Rajaka
		Nandivardhana (Resigned in 642 B.C. in favour of Sisunaga, probably a prince of Takshaka race from the Himalayas. See Sisunaga dynasty.)

CHAUHAN OF AJMER

1.		Samantaraj
2.		Jayaraj, son of 1
3.		Vigraharaj I, son of 2
4.		Chandraraj I, son of 3
5.		Gopendraraj, son of 3
6.		Durlabha I, son of 4
7.		Chandraraj II, son of 6
8.		Guhaka, son of 7
9.		Chandana, son of 8
10.		Vakpati I, son of 9
11.	950	Simharaj, son of 10
12.	974	Vigraharaj II, son of 11

13.		Durlabha II, son of 11
14.		Govinda, son of 13
15.		Vakpati II, son of 14
16.	1030	Viryarama, son of 15
17.	1085	Durlabha III, son of 16
18.		Vigraharaj III, son of 16
19.		Prithviraj I, son of 18
20.	1130	Ajaraj or Salhana, son of 19
21.	1150	Arnoraj, son of 20
22.		Vigraharaj IV, son of 21
23.	1166	Prithivibhata, grandson of 21
24.	1170	Somesvara, son of 21
25.	1177	Prithviraj II, son of 24 (of Sanyukta fame)

CHOLA OF TANJORE

1.	846	Vijayalaya
2.	871	Aditya I
3.	907	Parantaka I, son of 2
4.	947	Rajaditya I, son of 3
5.	949	Gandaraditya, son of 2
6.	956	Arinjaya, son of 2
7.	956	Aditya II, son of 6
8.	957	Parantaka II, son of 7
9.	970	Mudurantaka Uttama, son of 5
10.	985	Rajaraja I, son of 7
11.	1012	Parakesharivarman Rajendra I, son of 10
12.	1044	Rajakesharivarman Rajadhiraja I, son of 11
13.	1059	Rajendra II
14.	1063	Virarajendra
15.	1067	Adhirajendra
16.	1070	Koluttunga I Choladeva
17.	1118	Vikrama Chola
18.	1133	Kulottunga II
19.	1146	Rajaraja II (Ended in 1173)

DOGRA OF KASHMIR

(Under the British)

1.	1846	Gulab Singh
2.	1857	Ranbir Singh, son of 1
3.	1885	Pratap Singh, son of 2
4.	1925	Hari Singh, brother's son of 3 (Ended in 1947)

GAHADAVALA OF KANAUJ

1.		Chandradeva
2.	1080	Madanachandra, son of 1
3.	1114	Govindachandra, son of 2
4.	1154	Vijayachandra, son of 3
5.	1170	Jayachandra, son of 4 (Ended in 1193 by Md. Ghori)

GANGA OF KALINGA (ORISSA)

1.		Mita Varma I
2.	515	Indradhiraja or Indra Varma I
3.	539	Ananta Varma Deva I
4.	548	Devendra Varma Deva I
5.	548	Satya Varma Deva
6.	560	Maha Maha Samanta Varma
7.	565	Rajasimha Hasti Varma
8.	580	Rajasimha Indra Varma II
9.	595	Dhanarnava
10.	620	Indra Varma III
11.	660	Gunarnava
12.	675	Devendra Varma II
13.	680	Jaya Varma
14.	695	Ananta Varma II
15.	715	Nanda Varma
16.	753	Rajendra Varma
17.	770	Ananta Varma III
18.	801	Devendra Varma III
19.	810	Rajendra Varma II

20.		Vajra or Vajrahasta I
21.		Narasimha Bhupendra Varma
22.	894	Devendra Varma IV
23.		Gunarnava
24.	895	Vajrahasta II
25.	938	Gundama
26.	941	Kamarnava I
27.	976	Vijayaditya
28.	979	Ananta Varma IV
29.	1014	Kamarnava II
30.	1015	Gundama
31.	1018	Madhu Kamarnava III
32.	1037	Ananta Varma V
33.	1070	Devendra Varma Raja V
34.	1077	Ananta Varma Chodaganga VI
35.		Premadi Deva
36.	1131	Chodagangadeva or Rajendra Chodaganga
37.	1147	Kamarnava IV
38.	1156	Raghava
39.	1170	Raja Raja I
40.	1194	Ananga Bhimadeva I
41.	1198	Raja Raja II
42.	1211	Ananga Bhimadeva II
43.	1238	Narasimhadeva I
44.	1264	Bhanudeva I
45.	1278	Narasimhadeva II
46.	1306	Bhimadeva III
47.	1328	Narasimhadeva III
48.	1352	Bhanudeva II
49.	1378	Narasimhadeva IV
50.	1414	Bhanudeva III
		(See Suryavamshi Gajapati dynasty)

GANGA OF SOUTHERN MYSORE

1.		Konganivarman
2.		Madhava I
3.		Ayavarman
4.		Madhava II (Simhavarman)
5.		Avinita

GHORI OF MALWA

1.	1401	Dilwar Khan Ghori (Sahabuddin)
2.	1406	Husang Shah (Alp Khan)
3.	1435	Mahmud Shah (Ended in 1436)

GUHILA/SISODIA OF MEWAR/UDAIPUR

(Continued from Surya Race)

1.	568	Guhil (Grahaditya or Goho)
2.	586	Bhoja, son of I
3.	606	Mahendra
4.	626	Nagaditya
5.	646	Siladitya
6.	661	Aparajita
7.	688	Mahendra II
8.	734	Kalabhoja (Bappa)
9.	764	Khuman I
10.	773	Mattat
11.	793	Bhartibhata I
12.	813	Aghasimha, son of 11
13.	828	Khuman II
14.	853	Mahayaka
15.	878	Khuman III
16.	942	Bhartibhata II
17.	951	Allata
18.	972	Naravahana
19.	973	Shalibahana
20.	977	Saktikumara
21.	993	Ambaprasad

22.	1007	Suchivarman
23.	1021	Naravarman
24.	1035	Kirtivarman
25.	1051	Yograj
26.	1068	Vairata
27.	1088	Hanspal
28.	1103	Vairisimha
29.	1107	Vijayasimha
30.	1127	Arisimha
31.	1138	Chaudasimha
32.	1148	Vikramsimha
33.	1158	Ranasimha
34.	1168	Kshemasimha
35.	1172	Samantasimha
36.	1179	Kumarasimha
37.	1191	Mathanasimha
38.	1211	Padmasimha
39.	1213	Jaitrasimha
40.	1261	Tejasimha
41.	1273	Samarasimha, son of 40
42.		Ratnasimha
43.	1301	Hamir
44.		Ksherasimha
45.	1382	Lakshmasimha
46.	1421	Mokala
47.	1433	Kumbha, son of 46
48.	1468	Udaya, son of 47
49.	1473	Raimal
50.	1509	Sangram Singh I, son of 49
51.	1530	Ratna Singh, son of 50
52.	1532	Vikramaditya, son of 50
	1535	Banbir, usurper
53.	1537	Udaya Singh II, son of 50 (founder of Udaipur)

54.	1572	Pratap Singh II, son of 53
55.	1597	Amar Singh I, son of 54
56.	1620	Karna Singh, son of 55
57.	1628	Jagat Singh, son of 56
58.	1652	Raj Singh, son of 57
59.	1680	Jai Singh, son of 58
60.	1698	Amar Singh II, son of 59
61.	1716	Sangram Singh II, son of 60
62.	1734	Jagat Singh, son of 61
63.	1751	Pratap Singh II, son of 62
64.	1754	Raj Singh II, son of 63
65.	1761	Ari Singh, son of 64
66.	1773	Hamir, son of 65
67.	1778	Bhim Singh, brother of 66
68.	1828	Jawan Singh, son of 67
69.	1838	Sardar Singh, adopted son of 68
70.	1842	Sarup Singh, adopted brother of 69
71.	1861	Sambhu Singh, adopted grand nephew of 70
72.	1874	Sajjan Singh, first cousin of 71
73.	1884	Fateh Singh, a descendant of 61
74.	1930	Bhopal Singh, son of 73
75.	1955	Bhagwat Singh, adopted great nephew of 73

GUPTA OF MAGADHA

1.		Krishnagupta
2.		Harshagupta, son of 2
3.		Jibitagupta 1, son of 2
4.		Kumaragupta, son of 3
5.		Damodaragupta, son of 4
6.		Mahasenagupta, son of 5
7.		Mahadevagupta, son of 6
8.	672	Adityasena, son of 7
9.		Devagupta, son of 8
10.		Vishnugupta, son of 9

11.		Jibitagupta, son of 10

GUPTA OF PATALIPUTRA

		Sir Gupta
1.	305	Ghatotkacha
2.	320	Chandragupta I
3.		Kacha, son of 2
4.	350	Samudragupta, son of 2
5.	380	Chandragupta II, Vikramaditya, son of 4
6.	414	Kumaragupta I, Mahendraditya, son of 5
7.	455	Skandagupta Vikramaditya, son of 6
8.	480	Puragupta, son of 6
9.		Budhagupta, son of 8
10.	485	Narasimhagupta Baladitya, son of 8
11.	507	Vainyagupta
12.	510	Bhanugupta
13.	530	Kumaragupta II, son of 10
14.		Vishnugupta, son of 11

GURJARA-PRATIHARA OF MALWA

1.		
2.	725	Nagabhata I
3.		
4.		Devaraja
5.	783	Vatsaraja, grand nephew of 2
6.	805	Nagabhata II, son of 5
7.		Rambhadra
8.	840	Bhoj (Mihira Pratihara), grandson of 5
9.	885	Mahendrapala I, son of 8
10.	912	Mahipala I, son of 9
11.		Mahendrapala II, son of 10 (Ended in 1017.)

HOYSALA OF DORASAMUDRA (KARNATAKA)

1.	1027	Nripakama
2.	1047	Vinayaditya, son of 1
3.	1063	Ereyagna, son of 2

4.	1103	Ballala I, son of 3
5.	1110	Tribhuvanamalla Vishnuvardhana, brother of 4
6.	1152	Tribhuvanamalla Narasimha I, son of 5
7.	1173	Tribhuvanamalla Vira-Ballala II, son of 6
8.	1220	Narasimha II, son of 7
9.	1233	Vira Someswara, son of 8
10.	1254	Vira Narasimha III, son of 9
11.	1292	Vira Ballala III, son of 10
12.	1342	Ballala IV
13.	1343	Vira Virupaksha (absorbed by Vijayanagar in 1346)

IMAD SHAHI OF BIDAR

1.	1485	Fateh Ullah Imad-ul-Mulk
2.	1504	Alauddin
3.	1529	Darya
4.	1560	Burhan
5.	1568	Tufal (Ended in 1574, absorbed by Ahmadnagar.)

JAT OF BHARATPUR

1.		Badan Singh
2.	1756	Surajmal, adopted son of 1
3.	1763	Jawahir Singh, son of 2
4.	1768	Ratan Singh
5.		Nawab Singh
6.	1773	Naval Singh, brother of 5
7.	1773	Ranjit Singh, brother of 5

KACHHWA OF AMBER/JAIPUR

1.	967	Dhola Rai (of Dausa)
2.	1036	Kakil Deo, son of 1, founder of dynasty in Amber.
	1129	Usurped by Parihars
		....
22.		Prithvirai

23.		Biharimal, son of 22
24.		Bhagwan Das, adopted son of 23
25.	1589	Man Singh, son of 24
26.	1614	Bhau Singh, son of 25
27.	1621	Jai Singh, great grandson of 25
28.	1667	Ram Singh I, son of 27
29.	1688	Bishan Singh, grandson of 28
30.	1699	Jai Singh II, son of 29
31.	1743	Ishwari Singh, son of 30
32.	1750	Madho Singh I, brother of 31
33.	1768	Prithvi Singh, son of 32
34.	1778	Pratap Singh, brother of 33
35.	1803	Jagat Singh, son of 34
36.	1820	Jai Singh III, posthumous son of 35
37.	1835	Ram Singh II, son of 36
38.	1880	Madho Singh II, adopted
39.	1922	Man Singh II, adopted

KADAMBA OF SOUTH-WEST DECCAN

1.	345	Mayurasarman
2.		Kangavarman, son of 1
3.		Bhagiratha, son of 2
4.		Raghu, son of 3
5.		Kakusthavarman, brother of 4
6.		Santivarman, son of 5
7.		Mrigesavarman, son of 6
8.		Mandhatrivarman, grandson of 5
9.		Ravivarman, son of 7
10.		Harivarman, son of 8
11.		Krishnavarman
12.		Ajayavarman, son of 11

KAKATIYA OF WARANGAL (ANDHRA PRADESH)

1.		Beta I
2.		Prola I, son of 1

3.		Tribuhuvabanamalla Beta II, son of 2
4.		Prola II, son of 3
5.	1158	Prataparudra I, son of 4
6.	1196	Mahadeva
7.	1199	Ganapati, son of 6
8.	1262	Rudramba
9.	1295	Prataparudra II, (Ended 1323 to Tughlaks)

KALCHURI OF SOUTH MAHARASHTRA

	1015	Gangeyadeva
	1040	Lakshmi Karna, son of Gangeyadeva
		Bijjala II
	1167	Rudramurari Sovideva, son of Bijjala II
	1175	Mallikarjuna
	1176	Saukama
		Ahavamalla Singhana (Ended in 1184 by Someswara IV of Chalukya of Kalyani)

KANYA OF MAGADHA

B.C.

1.	72	Vasudeva
2.	63	Bhumimitra, son of 1
3.	49	Narayana, son of 2
4.	37	Susarman, son of 3 (End of dynasty in 27 B.C.)

KHILJI OF DELHI

A.D.

		Yagnish Khan
1.	1290	Jalaluddin Feroz Shah
2.	1296	Ruknuddin Ibrahim Shah I, son of I
3.	1296	Aluddin Feroz Muhammad Shah I, newphew of 1
4.	1316	Sahib-ud-din Umar Shah, son of 3
5.	1316	Qutubuddin Mubarak Shah, son of 3
6.	1320	Nasir-ud-din Khusru Shah, slave of 5 (Dynasty ended in September 1320.)

KHILJI OF MALWA

1.	1436	Mahmud Khan Khilji
2.	1469	Muhammad Shah (Ghiasuddin)
3.	1500	Nasiruddin Shah
4.	1510	Mahmud II Shah, son of 2
		(Ended in 1531. Bahadur Shah of Gujarat killed him and his seven sons)

KSHATRAPA (SHAKA) OF GUJARAT AND WESTERN RAJPUTANA

1.	119	Nahapana
2.	126	Chastana
3.		Jayadaman, son of 2
4.		Rudradaman, son of 3
5.	150	Damajadan, son of 4
6.	178	Jivadaman, son of 5
7.	180	Rudrasimha I, son of 4
8.	200	Rudrasena I, son of 7
9.	222	Sanghadaman, son of 7
10.	222	Prithvisena, son of 8
11.	226	Damasena, son of 8
12.	232	Damajadasri I, son of 8
13.	236	Viradaman, son of 11
14.	238	Yasodaman I, son of 11
15.	238	Vijayasena, son of 11
16.	250	Isvaradatta
17.	254	Damjadasri II, son of 11
18.	258	Rudrasena II, son of 13
19.	276	Viswasimha, son of 18
20.	278	Bhatridaman, son of 18
21.		Simhasena, son of 18
22.	294	Viswasena, son of 20
23.	309	Rudrasimha II
24.	318	Yasodaman II, son of 23
25.		Simhasena, sister's son of 23

| 26. | 348 | Swami Rudrasena |
| 27. | 388 | Rudrashimha |

KUSHANA OF NORTH-WESTERN INDIA

1.	10	Huemo Kadphises I
2.	45	Kadphises II or (Wima Kadphises)
3.	78	Kaniska
4.	111	Hubiska
5.	180	Vasudeva (Ended in 226)

LODI OF DELHI

1.	1451	Buhlul Khan Lodi
2.	1489	Sikandar Shah II Lodi, son of 1
3.	1517	Ibrahim II Lodi, son of 2 (Ended in 1526 to Mughals)

MANIKYA OF TRIPURA

1.		Maha Manikya
2.	1431	Dharma Manikya, son of 2
3.		Ratna Manikya, son of 2
4.		Mukut Manikya, son of 3
5.		Pratap Manikya, brother of 4
6.	1490	Dhanya Manikya
7.	1515	Dhwaja Manikya, brother of 6
8.	1520	Deva Manikya, brother of 6
9.		Indra Manikya, brother of 8
10.		Vijay Manikya, brother of 9
11.	1563	Ananta Manikya, son of 10
12.	1567	Udai Manikya (Gopi Prasad), father-in-law of 11
13.	1572	Jay Manikya, son of 12
14.	1577	Amar Manikya, brother of 10
15.	1586	Rajdhar Manikya, son of 14
16.		Ishwar Manikya, son of 15
17.		Yashodhar Manikya, son of 16
18.		Kalyan Manikya, antecedents unknown

19.	1660	Govinda Manikya, son of 18
20.	1661	Chhatra Manikya (Nakshtra Roy), brother of 19
	1667	Second reign of 19
21.	1676	Ramdev Manikya, son of 19
22.	1685	Ratna Manikya II, son of 21
23.	1712	Mahendra Manikya (Ghanashyam Barthakur), step-brother of 22
24.	1713	Dharma Manikya II, (Durjay Singh), son of 23
25.		Jagat Manikya, a descendant of 20
		Second reign of 24
26.	1729	Mukunda Manikya (Chandramoni), brother of 24
27.	1739	Jaya Manikya (Rudramoni)
28.	1744	Indra Manikya, son of 26
29.		Vijay Manikya, brother of 27
30.	1760	Krishna Manikya, brother of 28
31.	1781	Jahnavi Devi, widow of 30
32.	1785	Rajdhar Manikya, nephew of 30
33.	1809	Durgamoni Manikya
34.	1813	Ramgaya Manikya
35.	1826	Kashi Manikya
36.	1829	Krishna Manikya, son of 34
37.	1849	Ishwar Chandra Manikya, son of 36
38.	1862	Bir Chandra Manikya, brother of 37
39.		Radha Kishore Manikya, son of 38
40.	1909	Birendra Kishore Manikya, son of 39
41.	1923	Bir Bikram Manikya, son of 40 (Manikya rule virtually ended with the death of No. 41 on May 17, 1947.)

MARATHA OF THANJAVUR

1.	1673	Ekoji or Vyankoji
2.	1684	Shahaji, son of 1
3.	1711	Serfoji, son of 1

4.	1729	Tukoji or Tulajaji I, son of 1
5.	1736	Baba Sahab, son of 4
6.	1737	Sujan Bai
7.	1740	Pratap Singh
8.	1765	Tulajaji II, son of 7
9.	1788	Amara Singh, son of 7
10.	1798	Serfoji II, son of 8
11.	1833	Sivaji II
		(Ended in 1855 to the British)

MAUKHARI OF GAYA

		Yagna-Varman
		Sardula-Varman, son of 1
		Ananta-Varman, son of 2
		....
		Hari-Varman
		Aditya-Varman
		Isvara-Varman
	550	Isana-Varman
	576	Sarva-Varman
	580	Avanti-Varman

MAURYA OF MAGADHA

B.C.

1.	321	Chandragupta Maurya
2.	297	Bindusara Amitraghata
3.	273	Ashoka Priyadarshin, son of 2
4.	232	Kunala, son of 3
5.	232	Dasaratha
6.	224	Sangata (Samprati)
7.	216	Salisuka
8.	206	Samasarman
9.	199	Satadhanwan
10.	191	Brihadratha (End of dynasty in 184 B.C., see Sunga dynasty)

	A.D.	MUGHAL OF DELHI
1.	1526	Babar
2.	1530-39	
	1555-56	Humayun, son of 1
3.	1556	Akbar, son of 2
4.	1605	Jahangir (Salim), son of 3
5.	1628	Shahjahan, I, son of 4
6.	1659	Aurangzeb (Alamgir I), son of 5
7.	1707	Shah Alam I or Bahadur Shah I, son of 6
8.	1712	Jahandar Shah, son of 7
9.	1713	Farrukhsiyar, nephew of 8
10.	1719	Raif-ud-durajat, grandson of 7
11.	1719	Raif-ud-daula, or Shahjahan II, grandson of 7
12.	1719	Nekusiyar, grandson of 6
13.	1719	Muhammad Shah, grandson of 7
14.	1748	Ahmad Shah, son of 13
15.	1754	Alamgir II, son of 8
16.	1759	Shah Alam II, grandson of 6
17.	1806	Akbar Shah II, son of 16 (Titular emperor)
18.	1837	Bahadur Shah II Zafar, son of 17
		(Ended in 1857 to the British)

MUSLIM KING OF KASHMIR

(Shah Mirza and Chakk dynasties)

1.	1338	Samsuddin Shah Mirza
2.	1342	Jamshid
3.	1343	Alauddin Ali Sher
4.	1354	Shiabuddin
5.	1373	Qutubuddin
6.	1389	Sikandar Shah
7.	1413	Amir Khan Ali Shah
8.	1420	Zainul Abedin
9.	1470	Hyder Shah Haji Khan
10.	1472	Hasan Shah

11.	1481	Muhammad Shah
12.	1483	Fath Shah
	1492	Second reign of 11
	1513	Second reign of 12
	1514	Third reign of 11
	1517	Third reign of 12
	1520	Fourth reign of 11
13.	1527	Nazak Shah
	1530	Fifth reign of 11
	1537	Second reign of 13
14.	1540	Hydar Mirza Doghlat (Humayun's governor)
15.	1552	Ibrahim
16.	1555	Ismail
17.	1556	Habib Shah (End of Shah Mirza dynasty in 1562 to the Chakks)

CHAKK OF KASHMIR

| 18. | 1562 | Hussain Ghazi Shah Chakk |
| 19. | 1578 | Yusuf Shah Chakk (Akbar annexed Kashmir in 1586) |

NAGA OR KARATAKA (KARKATA) OF KASHMIR

1.	627	Durlabhavardhana
2.	661	Durlabhaka Pratapaditya, son of 1
3.	713	Chandrapida, grandson of 1
4.		Tarapida, brother of 3
5.	724	Lalitaditya I Muktapida, brother of 3
6.	760	Kuvalayapida
7.		Lalitaditya II
8.		Prithivyapida
9.		Sangramapida I
10.	779	Jayapida Vinayaditya, grandson of 5
11.	813	Ajitapida
12.	850	Anangapida
13.	853	Utpalapida (See Utpala dynasty)

NANDA OF MAGADHA

B.C.

1.	361	Mahapadmananda
2.		Sukalpa

Probably eight other rulers thereafter.

(Ended in 321 B.C. See Maurya dynasty.)

A.D.   **NAWAB OF BENGAL**

1.	1717	Murshid Quli Khan
2.	1725	Suja-ud-daula, son-in-law of 1
3.	1739	Sarfaraj Khan, son of 2
4.	1740	Ali Bardi Khan, brother of 3
5.	1756	Siraj-ud-daula, grandson of 4
		(Under East India Company.)
6.	1757	Mir Zafar
7.	1760	Mir Kasim, son-in-law of 6
	1763	Mir Zafar (again)
8.	1765	Nizam-ud-daula, son of 6
		(The British became *de facto* rulers.)
9.	1766	Saif-ud-daula, brother of 8

NAWAB OF OUDH

1.	1722	Sadat Ali Khan I
2.	1739	Safdar Jang, sister's son of 1
3.	1754	Suja-ud-daula, son of 2
4.	1775	Asaf-ud-daula, son of 3
5.	1797	Wazir Ali, son of 4, deposed by 6
6.	1798	Sadat Ali Khan II, son of 3
7.	1814	Ghazi-ud-din Haidar, son of 6
8.	1827	Nasiruddin Haidar, son of 7
9.	1837	Ali Shah, brother of 7
10.	1842	Amjad Ali Shah, son of 9
11.	1847	Wajid Ali Shah, son of 10
		(Removed by the British in 1856.)
12.	1856	Birjis Qudir, son of 11

NAYAK OF THANJAVUR

1.	1535	Cherappa
2.	1580	Achutappa, son of 1
3.	1600	Raghunatha, son of 2
4.	1633	Vijaya Raghava, son of 3
		(Ended in 1673 to the Marathas)

NIZAM (ASAF JAHI) OF HYDERABAD

1.	1724	Mir Qamar-ud-din Asaf Jah
2.	1748	Mir Ahmad Nasir, son of 1
3.	1750	Hidayat Mohi-ud-daula Muzaffar, nephew of 2
4.	1751	Mir Asaf-ud-daula (Salabat Jung), brother of 2
5.	1761	Mir Nizam Ali Khan, brother of 2
6.	1803	Mir Akbar Ali Khan, brother of 2
7.	1829	Nasir-ud-daula, son of 6
8.	1857	Afzal-ud-daula, son of 7
9.	1869	Mir Mahbub Ali Khan, son of 8
10.	1911	Mir Osman Ali Khan, brother's grandson of 9

NIZAM SHAHI OF AHMADNAGAR

1.	1490	Ahmad Ibn Nizam Shah
2.	1508	Burhan I
3.	1554	Hussain
4.	1565	Murtaza
5.	1588	Miran Hussain
6.	1589	Ismail
7.	1590	Burhan II
8.	1594	Ibrahim
9.	1595	Ahmad II
10.	1595	Bahadur (Ended in 1600 to the Mughals, but limped till 1636.)

PALA OF BENGAL

		Shri Vapyata
		Dayitavishnu
1.	750	Gopala
2.	770	Dharampala, son of 1
3.	810	Devapala, newhew of 2
4.	850	Vigrahapala I (Surapala I), nephew of 3
5.	854	Narayanapala, son of 4
6.	908	Rajyapala, son of 4
7.	940	Gopala II, son of 6
8.	960	Vigrahapala II, son of 7
9.	988	Mahipala I, son of 8
10.	1038	Nayapala, son of 9
11.	1055	Vigrahapala III, son of 10
12.	1070	Mahipala II
13.	1075	Surapala II
14.	1077	Rampala, son of 11
15.	1120	Kumarapala, son of 13
16.	1125	Mahendrapala (Gopala III), son of 14
17.	1149	Madanapala, uncle of 15
18.	1161	Govindapala (doubtful if Gopala's descendant)
19.		Indradyumna

PALLABHI (VALLABHI) OF GUJARAT

1.	495	Senapati Bhatarka
2.		Dharmasena I, son of 1
3.	520	Dronasimha, son of 1
4.	526	Dhruvasena I, son of 1
5.	540	Dharapatta, son of 1
6.	559	Guhasena, son of 5
7.	571	Dharmasena II, son of 6
8.	605	Siladitya I, son of 7
9.	615	Kharagraha I, son of 7
10.	620	Dharmasena III, son of 9

11.	629	Dhruvasena II, son of 9
12.	641	Dharmasena IV, son of 11
13.	651	Dhruvasena III, grandson of 8
14.	656	Kharagraha II, nephew of 8
15.	667	Siladitya II, nephew of 14
16.	691	Siladitya III, son of 15
17.	722	Siladitya V, son of 16
18.	760	Siladitya V, son of 17
19.	766	Siladitya VI, son of 18

PALLAVA OF KANCHIPURAM

1.	275	Simhavarman I
2.		Skandavarman I (Siva)
3.		Buddhavarman I
4.		Buddyankura
5.		Kumaravishnu I
6.		Skandavarman II
7.		Viravarman
8.		Skandavarman III
9.	436	Simhavarman II
10.		Skandavarman IV
11.		Kumaravishnu II
12.		Buddhavarman II
13.		Kumaravishnu III
14.		Simhavishnu
15.	600	Mahendravarman I
16.	630	Narasimhavarman I
17.		Mahendravarman II
18.	670	Parameshwaravarman I
19.	680	Narasimhavarman II (Rajasimha)
20.	720	Mahendravarman III
21.	728	Parameshwaravarman II
22.	731	Nandivarman II
23.	796	Dantivarman
24.	846	Nandivarman III

		Nripatungavarman
25.	885	Aparajitavarman
26.		Kampavarman (Ended in 903)

PANDYA OF KERALA/MADURAI (FIRST)

1.		Kadungon
2.		Maravarman Avanisulamani
3.		Seliyan Sendan
4.		Arikesari Paransuka Maravarman
5.		Koccadaiyan (Ranadhira)
6.		Maravarman Rajasimha
7.	765	Jatila Parantaka Nedanjadaiyan
8.	815	Srimana Srivallabha
9.	862	Vargunavarman
10.	880	Parantaka Viranarayana
11.	905	Maravarman Rajasimha II (Ended in 920.)

PANDYA OF KERALA (SECOND)

1.	1166	Vikram Pandya
2.	1190	Jatavarman Rajagambhiradeva
3.	1216	Mahavarman Sundara Pandya I
4.	1238	Mahavarman Sundara Pandya II
5.	1251	Jitavarman Sundara Pandya
6.	1268	Mahavarman Kulashekhara (Annexed by Cholas in 1309.)

PARAMAR OF MALWA

1.	825	Krishna Upendra
2.		Vairisimha I, son of 1
3.		Siyaka, son of 2
4.		Vakpati I, son of 3
5.		Vairisimha II, son of 4
6.	950	Harshadeva Siyaka II, son of 5
7.	974	Vakpati II, son of 4
8.	995	Sindhuraja, son of 6
9.	1018	Bhoj, son of 8

10.	1055	Jayasimha
11.	1071	Udayaditya
12.	1085	Lakshmideva, son of 11
13.	1104	Naravarman, son of 11
14.	1133	Yasovarman, son of 13
15.	1138	Jayavarman, son of 14
16.		Ajayvarman, son of 14
17.	1160	Vindhyavarman, son of 16
18.		Subhatavarman
19.	1211	Arjunavarman, son of 18

PESHWA OF MAHARASHTRA

Vishwanath

1.	1713	Balaji Viswanath
2.	1721	Baji Rao I, son of I
3.	1740	Balaji Baji Rao, son of 2
4.	1761	Madhav Rao I, son of 3
5.	1772	Narayan Rao, brother of 4
6.	1773	Raghunath Rao, or Raghoba, uncle of 5
7.	1774	Madhav Rao II, son of 4
8.	1796	Baji Rao II, son of 6
		(Ended in 1818 to the British)

PRAVAGUPTA OF KASHMIR

1.	949	Pravagupta
2.	950	Kshemagupta, son of 1
3.	958	Abhimanyu, son of 2
4.	972	Nandigupta son of 3
5.	972	Tribhuvana, grandson of 9 ⎱Utpala⎰
6.	975	Bhimagupta, grandson of 9 ⎰Dynasty⎱
7.	981	Didda, wife of 4
8.	1003	Sangramaraja, brother's son of 7
9.	1028	Hariraja, son of 8
10.	1028	Anandadeva, son of 8 (abdicated)
11.	1063	Kalasadeva, son of 10

| 12. | 1089 | Utkarsa, son of 11 |
| 13. | 1089 | Harsadeva, son of 12 (Ended in 1111) |

PUSHYABHUTI OF THANESWAR

1.		Naravardhana
2.		Rajyavardhana, I, son of 1
3.		Adityavardhana, son of 2
4.	585	Prabhakarvardhana, son of 3
5.	605	Rajyavardhana II, son of 4
6.	606	Harshavardhana Siladitya, son of 4

RAJA OF MYSORE

1.	1399	Vijaya Raja (and Krishna Raja)
2.	1423	Hira Bettada Chama Raja, son of 1
3.	1458	Thimma Raja, son of 2
4.	1478	Arberal Chama Raja, son of 3
5.	1513	Bettada Chama Raja, son of 4
6.	1552	Appana Timma, son of 5
7.	1571	Hire Chama Raja, son of 5
8.	1576	Bettada Udaiyar, cousin of 7
9.	1578	Raja Udaiyar, brother of 8
10.	1617	Chama Raja I, grandson of 9
11.	1637	Immadi Raja, son of 9
12.	1638	Kanthirava Narasa Raja, son of 8
13.	1659	Kempa Deva Raja, grandson of 7
14.	1672	Chikka Deva, grandson of 7
15.	1704	Kanthirava Raja, son of 14
16.	1714	Dodda Krishna Raja, son of 15
17.	1731	Chama Raja II
18.	1736	Chikka Krishna Raja (adopted)
19.	1766	Nan Raja, son of 18 (strangled)
20.	1771	Chama Raja III, brother of 19
21.	1776	Chama Raja IV, of Karuhalli (adopted and chosen by Hyder Ali)
	1795	Tipu Sultan, son of Hyder Ali

| 22. | 1799 | Mummadi Krishna Raja, son of 21 |

RAJA OF TRIGARTA (KANGRA)

1.	1315	Jayasimha
2.	1330	Prithvi
3.	1345	Purva
4.		Rupa
5.		Sringara
6.		Megha
7.		Hari
8.		Karma
9.		Samara
10.		Devanga
11.		Narendra
12.		Suvira
13.		Prayaga
14.		Rama
15.	1528	Dharma
16.	1563	Manikya
17.	1570	Jaya
18.	1585	Vriddhi
19.	1610	Triloka
20.	1630	Hari
21.		Chandrabhan
22.		Vijaya Rama
23.	1687	Bhima
24.	1697	Alama
25.	1700	Hamira
26.	1747	Abhaya
27.	1761	Ghamanda
28.	1773	Tega
29.	1776	Sansara
30.	1823	Aniruddha
31.	1829	Ranavira

RASHTRAKUTA OF SOUTH INDIA

1.		Dantivarman
2.		Indra I, son of 1
3.		Govindaraja I, son of 2
4.		Karka I, son of 3
5.		Indra II, son of 4
6.	752	Dantidurga, son of 5
7.	760	Krishna I, son of 4
8.	775	Govinda II, son of 7
9.	780	Dhruva Nirupama, son of 8
10.	794	Govinda III, son of 9
11.	814	Amoghavarsha I, son of 10
12.	878	Krishna II, son of 11
		Jagattunga
13.	915	Indra III, grandson of 12
14.	927	Amoghavarsha II, son of 13
15.	930	Govinda IV, son of 13
16.	935	Amoghavarsha III, son of 12
17.	939	Krishna III, son of 16
18.	967	Khottiga, son of 16
19.	972	Amoghavarsha IV, son of 16
20.	982	Indra IV, grandson of 17

RATHORE (RAO) OF JODHPUR/MARWAR

1.	1212	Sheoji
2.	1273	Asthan
3.	1292	Doohad
4.	1309	Raipal
5.	1313	Kanhapal
6.	1323	Jalansi
7.	1328	Chada
8.	1344	Thida
9.	1357	Kanhadev and Salkha
10.	1374	Viramdev

11.	1383	Chunda
12.	1424	Kanha
13.	1427	Ranmal
14.	1438	Jodha
15.	1488	Satpal
16.	1491	Suja
17.	1515	Ganga
18.	1532	Maldev
19.	1562	Chandrasen
20.	1581	Udaya Singh
21.	1595	Sur Singh
22.	1619	Gaj Singh I
23.	1638	Jaswant Singh I
24.	1678	Ajit Singh, posthumous son of 19
25.	1724	Abhaya Singh
26.	1749	Ram Singh, son of 21
27.	1751	Bhakta Singh
28.	1752	Vijay Singh
29.	1793	Bhim Singh
30.	1803	Maan Singh
31.	1843	Takht Singh
32.	1873	Jaswant Singh II
33.	1895	Sardar Singh
34.	1911	Sumer Singh
35.	1918	Umaid Singh
36.	1947	Hanuwant Singh

SALUVA AND TALUVA OF VIJAYANAGAR

1.		Gunda
2.	1485	Saluva Narasimha
3.	1490	Timma, son of 2
4.	1490	Immadi Narasimha, brother of 2, assassinated in 1503 (See Taluva dynasty)

SANGAMA OF VIJAYANAGAR

1.	1336	Sangama Bukka
2.	1339	Harihara I, brother of 1
3.	1344	Bukka I, brother of 1
4.	1377	Harihara II, son of 1
5.	1404	Virupaksha I, son of 3
6.	1405	Bukka II, brother of 5
7.	1406	Devaraya I, brother of 5
8.	1422	Ramchandraraya, son of 7
9.	1422	Vira Vijayaraya, son of 8
10.	1422	Devaraya II, son of 9
11.	1446	Vijayaraya II, son of 9
12.	1447	Malikarjuna, son of 10
13.	1465	Virupaksha II, brother's son of 10
14.	1466	Rajasekhara, son of 12
15.	1485	Virupakasha III, son of 13, killed by one of his own sons.

(See Taluva dynasty)

SATAVAHANA (SATAKARNI) OF ANDHRA

B.C.

1.	202	Simuka
2.	197	Krishna
3.	179	Sri Mallakarni
4.	169	Purnat Sanga
5.	151	Satakarni
6.	111	Lambodara
7.	93	Apilaka
8.	81	Sangha
9.	63	Sataswati Satakarni
10.	45	Skanda Satakarni
11.	38	Mrigendra Satakarni
12.	35	Kuntala Satakarni
13.	27	Sata Satakarni
14.	26	Pulumayi I

A.D.

15.	6	Megha Satakarni
16.	44	Arishta Satakarni
17.	69	Hala
18.	74	Mandalaka
19.	79	Purindrasena
20.	84	Sundara Satakarni
21.	85	Vilivayakura I
22.	85	Sivalakura
23.	113	Vilivayakura II Gautamiputra
24.	138	Pulumayi II Vashisthiputra
25.	170	Sivashri Vashisthiputra
26.	177	Sivaskanda Satakarni
27.	184	Yajnashri Gautamiputra
28.	213	Vijaya
29.	219	Vadashri Vashisthiputra
30.	229	Pulumyi III (Ended 236)

SAYYID (SYED) OF DELHI

1.	1414	Khizr Khan
2.	1421	Muizuddin Mubarak Shah II, son of 1
3.	1433	Muhammad Shah IV, grandson of 1
4.	1445	Alauddin Alam Shah, son of 3
		(Ended in 1451. See Lodi dynasty)

SENA OF BENGAL

Vira Sena

....

1.	1060	Samanta Sena
2.	1080	Hemanta Sena
3.	1097	Vijaya Sena
4.	1159	Ballala Sena, son of 3
5.	1178	Lakshmana Sena I, son of 4
6.	1205	Madhava Sena (or Biswarup Sena)
7.	1206	Keshava Sena

8.	1230	Surya Sena
9.		Narayana Sena
10.		Lakshmana Sena II

SIKH GURU

1.		Nanak (born 1469)
2.	1539	Angad, disciple of 1
3.	1552	Amar Das, disciple of 2
4.	1574	Ram Das, son-in-law of 3
5.	1581	Arjun Dev, son of 4
6.	1606	Har Govind, son of 5
7.	1645	Har Rai, grandson of 6
8.	1661	Har Kishan, son of 7
9.	1664	Tegh Bahadur, second son of 6
10.	1675	Govind Singh, son of 9 (Murdered in 1708.)

SISUNAGA OF MAGADHA

(The earliest dynasty with a historical base.
See Chandra Race of Rajagriha.)

B.C.

1.	642	Sisunaga
2.		Kakavarna
3.		Kshemadharman
4.		Kshattranjas
5.	519	Bimbisara
6.	491	Ajatasatru, son of 5
7.	459	Darsaka
8.	434	Udaya
9.	401	Nandivardhana
10.		Mahanandin (Ended in 361 B.C. See Nanda Dynasty.)

SLAVE DYNASTY OF DELHI (Ilbari Turk as Sultan)

A.D.

1.	1193	Muizuddin Muhammad Ghori
2.	1206	Qutub-ud-din Aibek, slave of 1

3.	1210	Aram Shah, son of 2
4.	1211	Samsuddin Altamas (lltutmis), slave and son-in-law of 2
5.	1236	Rukn-ud-din Feroz Shah I, son of 4
6.	1236	Raziya, daughter of 4
7.	1240	Muizuddin Behram Shah, son of 4
8.	1242	Alauddin Masud Shah, son of 5
9.	1246	Nasiruddin Muhammad Shah I, son of 4
10.	1266	Ghiasuddin Balban, son-in-law of 9
11.	1286	Kai Khusru, grandson of 10
12.	1287	Muizuddin Kaikobad, grandson of 10
13.	1290	Kayumars, son of 12 (Ended in 1290 to Khilji)

SULTAN OF BENGAL

(Early Ilyas Shahi)

1338	Fakhruddin Mubarak Shah (East Bengal)
1349	Ikhtiyaruddin Gazi Shah (East Bengal)
1339	Alauddin Ali Shah (West Bengal)
1345	Samsuddin Elias Shah (West Bengal)
1352	Samsuddin Elias Shah (Whole of Bengal)
1358	Sikandar Shah I
1389	Ghiasuddin Azam Shah
1396	Saifuddin Azam Shah
1406	Samsuddin
1414	Alauddin Feroz Shah

(Hindu-Muslim)

1415	Ganesh (Danujabarmandev)
1417	Jalaluddin (Jadunarayan), son of Ganesh
1418	Mahendradev, son of Ganesh

(Later Ilyas Shahi)

1442	Nasiruddin Muhammad Shah I
1460	Ruknuddin Barbak Shah
1474	Samsuddin Yusuf Shah
1481	Sikandar Shah II

1481	Jalaluddin Fath Shah
	(Abyssinian)
1486	Barbak, the eunuch, Sultan Shahzada
1486	Malik Indil, Feroz Shah
1489	Nasiruddin Muhammad Shah II
1490	Sidi Badr, Samsuddin Muzaffar Shah
	(Husain Sahi)
1493	Alauddin Husain Shah (of Arab descent)
1518	Nasiruddin Nasrat Shah
1533	Alauddin Feroz Shah
1533	Ghiasuddin Mahmud Shah
1538	Humayun (Emperor of Delhi)
	(Sur/Suri)
1539	Sher Shah Suri (Emperor of Delhi)
1540	Khizr Khan
1545	Muhammad Khan Suri
1555	Khizr Khan, Bahadur Shah
1561	Ghiasuddin Jalal Shah
1564	Son of Ghiasuddin Jalal Shah
	(Afghan)
1564	Taj Khan Karrani
1572	Sulaiman Karrani
1572	Bayazid Khan Karrani
1572	Daud Khan Karrani
	(Ended in 1576 to Mughals)

SUNGA OF MAGADHA

B.C.

1.	184	Pushyamitra Sunga
2.	148	Agnimitra, son of 1
3.	140	Basujestha
4.	133	Basumitra, son of 3
5.	125	Andhraka, son of 4

B.C.

6.	123	Pulindaka
7.	120	Ghoshavesu, son of 6
8.	117	Vajramitra
9.	108	Bhagavata
10.	82	Devabhuti, son of 9 (Murdered in 72 B.C. See Kanya dynasty)

SUR (SURI) OF DELHI (AFGHAN)

A.D.

1.		Ibrahim Khan
2.		Hassan Khan
3.	1539	Fari-ud-din Sher Shah
4.	1545	Islam Shah, son of 3
5.	1552	Md. Adil Shah, nephew of 3
6.	1553	Ibrahim Suri, nephew of 3
7.	1554	Firuz Shah
8.	1554	Mubarik Khan (Muhammad Adil Shah)
9.	1555	Sikandar Suri (an usurpur), brother of 3 (Ended in 1555 to the Mughals)

SURYA (SOLAR) RACE OF RAMAYANA

(Of doubtful historical base)

1.	Brahma		Sravas
	Mareecha		Vrihadaswa
	Kashyapa	15.	Dhundumar
	SURYA		Dridhaswa
5.	Manu Vaivasawata		Hariaswa
	Ikshwaku		Nikumbha
	Vikukshi		Varunaswa
	Kakutastha	20.	Senajita
	An-Prithu		Yavansawa
10.	Visgundhi		Mandhata
	Ardhaka		Purkutchu
	Yavan		Aroona

25. Trividhoona
    Atraruna
    Sutvrita
    Trisanku
    Harishchandra
30. Rohitaswa
    Harita
    Champa
    Vijaya
    Baruka
35. Briksha
    Bahuka or Usita
    Kesi
    Asamanja
40. Ansuman
    Dilip
    Bhagiratha (of Gangasaga)
    Srutasena
    Navaga
45. Ambarish
    Sindhudipa
    Ajutayu
    Rituparna
    Nala
50 Siruha
    Sevadasa
    Ashmaka
    Maluka
    Dasaratha
55. Aidvira
    Viswasaha
    Kharbhanga
    Dirghabahu
    Dilip
60. Raghu
    Aja

Dasaratha Ramachandra of
Ramayana Lava (founder
of Lahore, his brother
Kusha founder of
Kushinara)
65. Atitha
    Nisida
    Nala
    Poondrika
    Meghandhanya
70. Bala
    Sula
    Bajrannava
    Sojunsa
    Visitaswa
75. Vidrita
    Hiranya
    Puspaka
    Sudarsana
    Agnivarna
80. Sigra
    Murroo
    Prisisuta
    Satsunda
    Amarsunda
85. Avasana
    Viswasava
    Prasenjita
    Takshka
    Maga
    Brihatbala
90. Brihatvira
    Urukriya
    Buchvrida
    Prithvibhauma
    Bhanu

95. Sahadena Brihadasma	120. X
Pritikusa	X
Supritika	Mahartia
100. Marudeva	Antarita
Sonikestra	Akilsena
Puskara	125. Kanakasena
Rekha	Maha Muddan Sena
Sumitra I	Sudanta
105. Amitrajita	Ajay Sena
Brihatraja	Padmaditya
Bariketu	130. Sivaditya
Kirtanjaya	Haraditya
Rananjaya	Suryaditya
110. Sanjaya	Somaditya
Sakya	Siladitya
Sudipa	135. Grahaditya (Goho)
Sangala	Nagaditya
Prasenjit	Bhagaditya
115. Romika	Devaditya
Suratha	Aswaditya
Sumitra II	140. Kalbhoj
X	Grahaditya (Goho/Guhil)
X	(See Guhila of Mewar)

SURYAVAMSHI GAJAPATI OF KALINGA (ORISSA)

(From Ganga Dynasty)

1.	1435	Kapilendra Gajapati (adopted son of Bhanudeva III)
2.	1466	Purusattam, son of 1
3.	1497	Prataprudra Deva, son of 2 (Ended in 1514)

TALUVA OF VIJAYANAGAR

(See Saluva and Sangama Dynasties)

1.	1503	Taluva Vira Narasimha
2.	1509	Krishnadevaraya, half brother of 1
3.	1529	Achutaraya, half brother of 2

PART D
INDEX

PART D

INDEX

4.	1542	Venkataraya, son of 3
5.	1542	Sadasivaraya, nephew of 3 (Deposed in 1570. See Aravidu dynasty)

TUGHLAK OF DELHI

1.	1320	Giasuddin Tughlak Shah I
2.	1325	Muhammad Tughlak Shah II, son of 1
3.	1351	Feroz Tughlak Shah III, nephew of 1
4.	1388	Ghiasuddin Tughlak Shah II, grandson of 3
5.	1389	Abu Bakr Shah, grandson of 3
6.	1389	Muhammad Tughlak Shah III, son of 3
7.	1394	Sikandar Shah I, son of 6
8.	1394	Nasiruddin Mahmud Shah II, son of 6
9.	1395	Nasrat Shah, grandson of 3
	1399	Nasiruddin Mahmud Shah II, restored
10.	1413	Daulat Khan Lodi (did not assume royalty) (Beginning of Sayyid dynasty in 1414)

UTPALA OF KASHMIR

(See Naga/Karataka Dynasty)

		Utpalapida
		Sukhavarman, son of Utpala
1.	855	Avantivarman, son of Sukhavarman
2.	883	Sankaravarman, son of 1
3.	902	Gopalavarman, son of 2, probably murdered
4.	904	Sankata, brother of 3 (died within 10 days of accession)
5.	904	Sugandha, mother of 3
6.	906	Partha
7.	921	Nirjitavarman, father of 6
8.	923	Chakravarman
9.	933	Suryavarman
	934	Suryavarman dethroned. No. 6 restored
	935	Partha dethroned. No. 8 restored

10.	936	Sambhuvardhana usurped the throne.
		No. 8 regained the throne by killing him.
11.	937	Unmattavanti, son of 6
	939	Suravarman II, deposed and Utpala dynasty ends.
		(a) Viradeva
		(b) Kamadeva son of (a)
		(c) Prabhakaradeva, son of (b) and minister of Kashmir
	939	(d) Yasakaradeva, son of (c)
	948	(e) Varnata, uncle of (d) for one day only
	948	(f) Sangramadeva, son of (d) (murdered by minister Pravagupta of Pravagupta dynasty.)

VAKATAKA OF MADHYA PRADESH

1.		Vindhyasakti
2.		Pravarasena I, son of 1
3.		Rudrasena I, grandson of 2
4.		Prithvisena, I son of 3
5.		Prabhavati Gupta, widow of son of 4
6.		Pravarasena II, son of 4
7.		Narendrasena, son of 6
8.		Prithvisena II

VISHNUKUNDIN OF VENGI (ANDHRA)

1.		Madhavavarman
2.		Vikramendravarman I
3.		Indrabhattaraka
4.		Vikramendravarman II
5.		Govindavarman
6.	556	Mahadevavarman
7.	616	Manchana

QUTUB SHAHI OF GOLCONDA

1.	1518	Quli Qutub-ul-Mulk
2.	1543	Jamsheed
3.	1550	Subhan (dethroned)
4.	1550	Ibrahim
5.	1580	Muhammad
6.	1612	Sultan Muhammad
7.	1626	Abdullah
8.	1672	Abul Hasan Tana Shah (Annexed by Aurangzeb in 1687)

PRESIDENT (RASHTRAPATI) OF INDIA (NO DYNASTY)

1.	26.01.1950	Rajendra Prasad
2.	13.05.1962	S. Radhakrishnan
3.	13.05.1967	Zakir Hussain (Died 03.05.1969)
	03.05.1969	V. V. Giri (Acting)
	July 1969	Chief Justice Md. Hidayatullah (Officiating)
4.	24.08.1969	V. V. Giri
5.	24.08.1974	Fakhruddin Ali Ahmed (Died 03.02.1977)
	03.02.1977	B.D. Jatti (Acting)
6.	25.07.1977	Neelam Sanjeeva Reddy
7.	25.07.1982	Zail Singh
8.	25.07.1987	R. Venkataraman
9.	25.07.1992	Shankar Dayal Sharma
10.	25.07.1997	K. R. Narayanan
11.	25.07.2002	A. P. J. Abdul Kalam

PRIME MINISTER OF INDIA (NO DYNASTY)

	Date	Prime Minister
	20.09.1946	Jawaharlal Nehru (Undivided India) till 14.08.1947
1.	15.08.1947	Jawaharlal Nehru (After partition)
	27.05.1964	Guljarilal Nanda (Officiating)
2.	09.06.1964	Lal Bahadur Shastri
	11.01.1966	Guljarilal Nanda (Officiating)
3.	24.01.1966	Indira Gandhi
4.	24.03.1977	Morarji Desai
5.	28.07.1979	Charan Singh
	14.01.1980	Indira Gandhi (Again)
6.	31.10.1984	Rajiv Gandhi
7.	02.12.1989	Viswanath Pratap Singh
8.	10.11.1990	Chandra Sekhar
9.	21.06.1991	P.V. Narasimha Rao
10.	15.05.1996	Atal Behari Vajpayee
11.	01.06.1996	H.D. Deve Gowda
12.	21.04.1997	Inder Kumar Gujral
	19.03.1998	Atal Behari Vajpayee (Again)
	30.12.1999	Atal Behari Vajpayee (Again)
13.	22.05.2004	Manmohan Singh

PART D
INDEX

PART D

INDEX

Calcutta Gazette, A106, B21, B26
Calcutta Polo Club, A140
Calicut,
   – Chinese Naval Expedition,
     A41
   – Embassy to China, A41
   – Vasco da Gama, A47
   – P.A. Cabral, A47
   – factory, A48
   – defeat of Portuguese navy,
     A47
   – attack on Goa, A58
   – Dutch alliance, A64
   – all women police station,
     A244
California, A180
Caliph-al-Monsoor, A19
Cama, Madame Bhikaji K.R.,
   – b. A139
   – in Europe, A169
   – d. A202
Cambay, A87
Cambridge, A199
Cambridge Missionaries, A153
Cambridge University, A146
Camera, A127
Camerson, A107
Campbell, Collin, B83
Campbell, Dr., A126
Cana, T., A13
Canada,
   – Sikh migrant, A170
   – Ghadar Movement, A178
Candolim, A92
Cannanore, A46
Canning, Lady Charlotte, A134
Canning, Lord
   – widow marriage, A134

   – Sepoy Mutiny, A136
   – Gov. Gen. & Viceroy, A137
Cape Canaveral, A256
Cape Comorin, A33, A36
Cape of Good Hope,
   – S.S. Enterprise, A119
   – S.S. Hindustan, A127
Car – See Motor Car
Cardinal, first, A21
Carey, Mrs. Mary, A92
Carey, W.,
   – arrival, A108
   – Professor of Bengali, A111,
   – Bengali grammar, A111
   – Marathi grammer, A112
   – Marathi–English dictionary,
     A112
   – Samachar Darpan, A115
   – Serampore College, A116
   – paper making machine, 122
Cariappa, General,
   – b. A167
   – King's Commission, A182
   – Commander-in-Chief, A214
   – Field Marshal, A263
   – d. 274
Carnatic Wars, A90, A91
Caron, Francois, A75
Carpet, (World's finest), A265
Carr Tagore & Co., A123, A128
Carr, W., A123
Carsetji, A, A127
Cartwright, A68
Castro, Joa de, A54
Catechism of Xavier, A55
Catharine de Braganza, Princess,
   A73
Cavilhao, J.P. de, A46

H

Hindu Succession Act, A224, B47

Hindu University, Banaras, A168, B13

Hindu Widows' Remarriage Act, A134

Hinduja, Dr. Indira, A264

Hindustan, S.S., A127

Hindustan 10, Car, A214

Hindustan Aircrafts Ltd., A204

Hindustan Aeronautics Ltd., A243, A276

Hindustan Lever, A203

Hindustan Motors Ltd., A206, A214

Hindustan Photo Films Mfg. Co., A229

Hindustan Republic Army, A196, B55

Hindustan Shipyard, A205

Hindustan Socialist Republican Assn., A189

Hindustan Teleprinters Ltd., A246

Hindustan Trainer Aircraft HT2, A218, B59

Hira, Ustad, A70

Hiraki, Rita, A278

Hirjee, C., A227

Hirwani, N., A266

His Majesty's Indian Navy–*See* Indian Navy

History of India, Mill's A115

Hita Harivamsa, A47, A54

Hitler, A127

HIV, A264

Hiuen Tsang, A16

HJT 16, Jet Trainer, A234, B87

H.M.T. Watch Factory, A230, B11

Hockey,

– Amsterdam Olympic, A192
– Rangaswamy Cup, A192
– Lady Ratan Tata Cup, A203
– Hazrat Mahal Trophy, A248
– Moscow Olympic, A253, A254
– Hazrat Mahal Trophy, A248
– Aswini Kumar, A254

Hodson, Lt. W.S.R., A135

Hogg Market, Sir Stewart, A147

Holland, A202, A261

Hollebeke, A179

Holwell, J.Z,

– Calcutta Police Force, A87
– Blackhole tragedy, A92
– Clive's successor, A92

Home Guard Organisation, A209

Homoeopathic Treatment, A124

Homoeopathic Medical College and Hospital, A130, B16

Home Rule League–*See* All India H.R. League

Home Rule Movement, A180, A199

Hong Kong, A178, A273, B26

Hooghly,

– Portuguese, A59, A68
– English & Dutch Settlements, A69, A70
– Bengal Pilot Service, A75
– Job Charnock, A79
– Maharaja Nanda Kumar, A96
– Ram Mohan Roy, A99
– Charles Wilkins, A102
– Shri Ramkrishna Dev, A132
– Saradamoni Devi, A132
– E.I. Rly., A132
– Jute Spinning Mill, A134
– Sarat Ch. Chattopadhyay, A148

Hooghly Docking & Engineering Co, A257

INDEX
2001 A. D. ONWARDS

FIRST TIME IN INDIA
(GENERAL)
First Time in the World •
World Champion / Record••

Ace Pilot, A181
Advertisement, A106
Advertising Film, A203
Agricultural Plane, A243
Agricultural University, A230
AIDS Victim, A264
Air Cargo Service, A193
Air Chief, A221
Air-conditioned Railway Coaches, A202
Air-conditioned Ship, A243
Air-conditioned Train (full) A271
Aircraft, A218, A288
Aircraft, Supersonic, A230
Aircraft Carrier, A230
Airline, A198
Airmail, A175•
Airmail Stamp, A194•
Airman Killed in War, A181
Air Marshal, A286
Air Raid, A205
Air Rifle Champion, A285
Air Service, Daily, A199
Air Service to U.K., A212
Alcohol-fuelled Car, A240
All India Athletic Competition, A188
All India Kite Flying Contest, A246
All India Motor Race, A221
All India Photographic Exhibition, A135
All India Strike, A182
Alloy Steel Plant, A234

Amusement Park, A270
Antarctic Visit, A229
Antarctic Expedition, A255
Anti-defection Law, A267
Anti-smoking campaign in State, A266
Anti-tank Missile, A279
Apple Tree, A180
Arab (Muslim) Invasion, A18
Archbishop, A55
Arjuna Award, A232
Art School, A131
Ascent of Mt. Everest, A220•
Asian Games, A218
Atomic Power Station, A238
Atomic Reactor, A226
Automobile Association, A170
Automobile Tyre Plant, A202
Badminton, A252••
Bahai House of Worship, A265
Balloon Ascent, A105
Bank, European, A98
Bank, Indian, A163
Bank, Joint Stock, A105
Bar Association, A135
Barrister, A140
Battery-operated Bus, A266
Bharat Ratna, A222
Bicycle Industry, A203
Billiards (Amateur and Open) A212, A227••
Bishop, A52
Blind School, A158

FIRST WOMAN
First Time In the World•
World Champion / Record••

Advocate, A188
Airbus Command, A277
Air Flight, A194
Air Force-Active Service, A281
Air Vice-Marshal, A287
Alderman, A156
Antarctica, A249
Archery, Gold Medal, A289
Army Brigade, A207
Army Lt. General, A247
Around the World in Car, A269•
Astronaut, A279

Bachelor of Arts, A155
Bachelor of Medicine, A160
Bank, A232
Bharat Ratna, A243
Billiards, World Champion, A289••
Bishop, A277
Boarding School, A116
Bus Driver, A274

Cabinet Minister, A202
Chess, Grand Master, A283
Chess, National Champion, A251
Chief Justice, A272
Chief Minister, State, A233
Christian Priest, A229
Civil Engineer, A203
Command of Aircraft, A246
Commercial Pilot, A217
Congress President, A181
Cosmonaut, A279
Cricket Score, Highest, A264••

Doctor, A131
Diplomat, (Career), A240
Diplomat (Politician), A212

English Channel Swimmer, A228
Entrance Examinee, A150

Female Hospital A153
Film Artist, A178
Film Producer and Director, A190
Fine Arts, A151
Football Coach, A277

Governor, State, A150
Govt. Employee, A152
Gurudwara Siromoni Prabandhak
    Committee, President, A280

High Court Judge, A228

Indian Administrative Service,
    A219
Indian Foreign Service, A240
Indian Police Service, A243

Jnanpith Award, A249

Lawyer, A188
Legislator, A156

Marathon Runner, A257
Marine Engineer, A282
Master of Arts, A155
Master of Science, A200